THE CULTURAL GEOGRAPHY OF
COLONIAL AMERICAN LITERATURES

Ralph Bauer presents a comparative investigation of colonial prose narratives in Spanish and British America from 1542 to 1800. He discusses narratives of shipwreck, captivity, and travel, as well as imperial and natural histories of the New World, in the context of transformative early modern scientific ideologies and investigates the inter-connectedness of literary evolutions in various places of the early modern Atlantic world. Bauer positions the narrative models promoted by the "New Sciences" during the sixteenth and seventeenth centuries within the context of the geo-political question of how knowledge can be centrally controlled in outwardly expanding empires. He brings into conversation with one another writers from various parts of the early modern Atlantic world including Álvar Núñez Cabeza de Vaca, Gonzalo Fernández de Oviedo y Valdes, Samuel Purchas, William Strachey, Mary Rowlandson, Carlos de Sigüenza y Góngora, William Byrd, and Hector St. John de Crèvecoeur.

RALPH BAUER is Assistant Professor at the University of Maryland, College Park. His articles have appeared in numerous collections and journals.

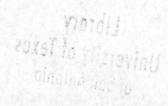

CAMBRIDGE STUDIES IN AMERICAN LITERATURE AND CULTURE

Editor
Ross Posnock, *New York University*

Founding Editor
Albert Gelpi, *Stanford University*

Advisory Board
Sacvan Bercovitch, *Harvard University*
Ronald Bush, *St. John's College, Oxford University*
Wai Chee Dimock, *Yale University*
Albert Gelpi, *Stanford University*
Gordon Hunter, *University of Kentucky*
Walter Benn Michaels, *University of Illinois, Chicago*
Kenneth Warren, *University of Chicago*

THE CULTURAL GEOGRAPHY OF COLONIAL AMERICAN LITERATURES

Empire, Travel, Modernity

RALPH BAUER

CAMBRIDGE
UNIVERSITY PRESS

PUBLISHED BY THE PRESS SYNDICATE OF THE UNIVERSITY OF CAMBRIDGE
The Pitt Building, Trumpington Street, Cambridge CB2 1RP, United Kingdom

CAMBRIDGE UNIVERSITY PRESS
The Edinburgh Building, Cambridge, CB2 2RU, UK
40 West 20th Street, New York, NY 10011–4211, USA
477 Williamstown Road, Port Melbourne, VIC 3207, Australia
Ruiz de Alarcón 13, 28014 Madrid, Spain
Dock House, The Waterfront, Cape Town 8001, South Africa

http://www.cambridge.org

First published 2003

Printed in the United Kingdom at the University Press, Cambridge

Typeface Adobe Garamond 11/12.5 pt.   *System* LATEX 2ε [TB]

A catalogue record for this book is available from the British Library

ISBN 0 521 82202 5 hardback

Meinen Eltern

Contents

Illustrations

Acknowledgments

As it would be impossible to thank here all the people who have helped shape this book in one way or another during the years it's taken, I want to mention specifically only those to whom I've been most indebted in every stage of its development. In its inspiration, the book owes primarily to the vision and nurture of Wolfgang Binder and Helmbrecht Breinig; in its conception, to the generosity, mentorship, and advice of Stephen Carl Arch, Aníbal González Pérez, Earl Fitz, Christine Daniels, Ned Watts, Clint Goodson, and Stephen Rachman; in its gestation, to the rich intellectual community headed by Norman Fiering at the John Carter Brown Library, to the good conversation of Len Tennenhouse, Joe Bizup, Joe Roach, David Waldstreicher, and the Yale English junior faculty, as well as to the constructive comments of Michelle Burnham, Jim Egan, James Levernier, and Dana Nelson; in its birth, to the friendships, mentorships, and collegiality of John Auchard, George Allen Cate, Robert Levine, Gary Hamilton, Bill Sherman, Orrin Wang, Marshall Grossman, David Norbrook, Jonathan Auerbach, Kent Cartwright, Vincent Carretta, Andy Rennick, Eyda Merediz, and Mariselle Meléndez; in its growth, to the support, comments, and criticism of Gordon Sayre, Nancy Ruttenburg, Fred Luciani, Julie Solomon, Cynthia J. Van Zandt, Fredrika Teute, Nancy Siraisi, and Jorge Cañizares-Esguerra, as well as to the free spirit, encouragement, and erudition of David Shields, Raquel Chang-Rodríguez, and Rolena Adorno; finally, in its completion, to the interest, support, and patience of Ross Posnock, Ray Ryan, and Leigh Mueller, as well as to the helpful comments of the anonymous readers of Cambridge University Press.

Along the way, its development was furthered by various financial grants, including dissertation fellowships at Michigan State University, an in-residence fellowship at the John Carter Brown Library, and a summer faculty grant at the University of Maryland. Thanks also to Susan Danforth and Richard Hurley of the John Carter Brown Library, Teresa Vargas Marugán of the Museo Nacional del Prado, Christine Woollett of the Royal Society of London, Beth Green of the Huntington Library, Catherine H. Grosfils of the Colonial Williamsburg Foundation, and the staff of the Beinecke Rare Book Library at Yale University for their help with the illustrations. Two early versions of Chapter 4 have appeared in the journals *American Literature* and *Colonial Latin American Review*. Thanks to the editors for permitting me to reproduce my ideas here and to the anonymous readers who have helped shape them with their insightful comments. Thanks also to Leon Jackson, Ximena Gallardo, Jason Smith, Rich Wisneski, Erik Hofstee, Jane Chung, and Shiara Ortiz Pujols for their long-standing friendships. Most of all, I thank my wife, Grace Crussiah, to whose love and support this book owes its sustenance. Its errors and immaturities are entirely my own.

CHAPTER I

Prospero's progeny

> But this rough magic
> I here abjure; and when I have required
> Some heavenly music (which even now I do)
> To work mine end upon their senses that
> This airy charm is for, I'll break my staff,
> Bury it certain fathoms in the earth,
> And deeper than did ever plummet sound
> I'll drown my book.
>
> (Prospero in Shakespeare's *The Tempest*)

In the last scene of Shakespeare's *The Tempest*, Prospero, the exiled duke of Milan about to return to Italy, vows to abjure the magic that has empowered him to conquer his New World island, command its creatures, and even wreck the Neapolitan ship of state. Combining the ancient knowledge of his books, the savage sensualism of his slave Caliban, and the powerful eloquence of his servant Ariel, who translates his will into forces of nature, Prospero's magic becomes firmly aligned with witchcraft and the black arts. But in a final charm he "discovers" to the shipwrecked court a new future in the relationship between his aristocratic power and the Neapolitan monarchy: his daughter Miranda and the royal heir Ferdinand, soon to be married, playing "at chess." Once back in Italy, Prospero's dukedom will no longer be secured by his Renaissance magic but rather by his progeny Miranda – who, innocently, knows nothing of the dangerous worlds of Medeas and Thessalian witches – whose name (from "mirar," to see or look) signals new ways of knowing, and whose marriage to the royal heir promises peace and stability after "this late tempest" for generations to come.[1]

I invoke *The Tempest* at the outset of this book because it aptly sets the stage for the questions I want to ask about the European encounter with the Americas. Since the Renaissance battles between the Ancients and the Moderns, the "fact" of America has invariably been among the first to be invoked in arguments for scientific progress.[2] Even today, there persists a hardy tradition in the historiography of modernity that would see the so-called "Scientific Revolution" of the seventeenth century as the more-or-less direct result of an inherent inadequacy of Renaissance natural philosophy to absorb the new empirical data accumulating with the early modern voyages of discovery.[3] The defenders of Humanism, by contrast, have continued to challenge this Whiggish narrative of scientific progress. Renaissance natural philosophy never formed a "single grid" that rigidly imposed a uniform order on all new information, they objected, but presented the curious with an eclectic amalgam of Aristotelian, Plinean, Neoplatonic, Hermetic, and Arabic textual traditions that was, in many ways, "perfectly suited" to handle the early modern explosion of empirical knowledge without cataclysmic cognitive dissonance.[4] No longer taking for granted the inherent inadequacy of Renaissance learning in the face of new experience, recent cultural historians of science have explained the transformations in early modern knowledge mainly in terms of changing social, political, and economic infrastructures during the early modern period.[5] But while the Whiggish narratives of scientific progress had oversimplified the transformative impact of the early modern discoveries upon Europe's consciousness, the recent cultural and social histories of early modern science have often been too limited in their geographic scope, accounting for changes in scientific epistemologies and infrastructures predominantly in a domestic or national context. As a result, the question of what the historian John H. Elliott once called the "uncertain impact" of the New World upon the Old has largely been left in abeyance.[6]

Prospero's incantations and renunciations of his Renaissance magic as he moves to and fro his New World island reinforce the urgency of this question; but they also remind us that the early modern changes in Western knowledge cannot be understood in terms of a one-directional "impact" of the New World upon the history of the Old, let alone upon particular national histories; rather, they suggest that modernity is the product of the complex and inextricable *connectedness* of various places and histories, of the way in which these places *acted upon each other*. On the one hand, in its trans-oceanic movements between Old World settings and New World subtexts,[7] *The Tempest* reaffirms recent trends in both early American and early modern European studies to abandon proto-nationalist historical narratives and to see the cultural developments on either side of the ocean within the context of transatlantic imperial systems.[8] On the other hand, the Mediterranean setting of this Anglo American play in the Habsburg cultural sphere of influence urges us to adopt not only an imperial and trans-atlantic but also a hemispheric and trans-national perspective on the early modern world.[9] It reminds us that, from the point of view of the early seventeenth century, the question of the "impact" of the New World upon the Old was primarily a "Spanish" question, some minor English forays notwithstanding. It is for this reason that *The Tempest* has long been regarded not only as Shakespeare's "American play" by Anglo American critics but also as Shakespeare's "Latin American play" by Latin American critics who saw there a recognition of Spanish America's important role in the making of the very culture of modernity by which it has subsequently been marginalized.[10]

This book explores how various places and histories are connected and act upon each other in new cultural formations. Specifically, it places the transformations in Western knowledge occurring during the early modern period in the geo-political context of European settler colonialism in Spanish and British America from 1500 to 1800. As early as the legal battles between the Spanish crown on the one hand and Columbus and his heirs on the other over the "Rights of Discovery," European settler colonialism in the New World had raised unprecedented questions about the political constitution of modern overseas empires that were never entirely resolved until their final breakup during the late eighteenth and early nineteenth centuries. Whereas the first conquests and colonizations of the New World had largely depended on private initiative, with the European monarchies ready to grant individuals quasi-feudal contractual relationships as incentives, the monarchies, in a "second conquest," subsequently attempted to centralize the political administration over the newly conquered territories in order to channel the economic profits to be reaped from the exploitation of the New World in ways most profitable to the imperial metropole.[11] But the attempts at political and economic centralization frequently met with the resistance of the colonial Creole elites, who jealously guarded their neo-feudal dominions that had arisen in the New World simultaneously and co-dependently with the centralizing states of Europe as the products of transatlantic mercantilist economies.[12]

Of paramount importance in this geo-political conflict over imperial centralization was the question of how knowledge could be centrally produced and controlled in the centrifugal cultural dynamics of outwardly expanding geo-political systems. It is one of the arguments of this book that the transformations in the organization of early modern knowledge must in part be understood as a response to the distinct geo-political questions raised by European settler colonialism in the Americas. The European encounters with the New World had unleashed an unprecedented inflation in the value of empirical forms of knowledge, as explorers such as Amérigo

Vespucci returned with "news" that held the claim that with "this voyage of mine" the ancient authorities stand "confuted," thus proving that "practice is of greater worth than theory."[13] This inflation of empirical knowledge, accelerated by mechanical reproduction through print, exerted formidable stress upon what Stephen Shapin has called the traditional "trusting systems" of the Old World. New ways of trusting had to be found that would uphold the existing social orders. One particularly "modern" attribute of these newly emerging trusting systems was, Shapin observes, their inscription in social space: "Those who cannot directly witness a phenomenon must either reject its existence or take it on trust from those who have, or from testimony still more indirect."[14] This book investigates how these early modern "trusting systems" were ordered not only in social space in Europe but also in geographic space in early modern settler empires. In particular, it understands the trans-atlantic networks of relations engaged in the making of the early modern scientific paradigm of "natural history" ("historia natural") in terms of territorialized economies of knowledge production, "empires of truth" that were structured by a geo-political order that might be characterized as forms of "epistemic mercantilism." The poetics of this mercantilist production of knowledge demanded a division of intellectual labor between imperial peripheries and centers, the effacement of colonial subjects, and the transparency of colonial texts as the providers of raw "facts." In the early modern scientific paradigm of natural history, the basic theorem postulating the environmental determination of all living forms generally, and of human faculties in scientific debates over "creolization" particularly, hereby rationalized its own modes of production in terms of geographic hierarchies. In theory, these imperial economies of knowledge production thus resembled the mercantilist economies of material production, based as they were on a regulated and protected balance of exchange in the eastward flow of raw materials – wood, sugar, gold, silver, furs, cotton, and tobacco – and the westward flow of refined consumer products and manufactured goods. In practice, however, these imperial epistemic economies, like their material counterparts, existed but as logocentric utopias that engendered their own modes of geo-political resistance and were frequently undermined by colonial subjects.

We are reminded of the geo-political dimension in the history of Western knowledge by the more recent epistemological crisis in the Human Sciences and Humanities precipitated largely by the de-colonization of the so-called "Third World" during the second half of the twentieth century, when ex- and post-colonial "friends" turned theorists in order to expose the imperialist politics of modern Western scientific and literary discourses, particularly that of modern anthropology.[15] At a time when trans-national migration and de-colonization, multinational capitalism and neocolonialism are eroding the ethnic, demographic, political, economic, and epistemic bases of the modern nation states,[16] it is an appropriate moment also for a comparative reflection upon the geopolitics of scientific and literary discourses in the early modern period, which brought about the forms of knowledge now in crisis. While this book is in part inspired by the recent post-colonial critique of modern anthropology, it also insists on the important historical *differences* between early modern European settler empires in the Americas and nineteenth- and twentieth-century empires in Africa and Asia. As Anthony Pagden has reminded us, in many respects the nineteenth- and twentieth-century European empires, from which the recent "post-colonial" critique has emerged, were antithetical to the earlier European empires in the Americas:

[The] real intellectual significance for Europeans of their several experiences in America was that these had demonstrated what successful empires should *not* attempt to be. By 1800 most of enlightened Europe had been persuaded that large-scale overseas settlement of the kind pursued, in their different ways, by Spain, Britain and France in the Americas could ultimately be only destructive to the metropolis itself. They had shown that every immigrant community, no matter what its cultural origins or the degree of self-rule it is able to exercise, will one day come to demand economic self-sufficiency and political autonomy.[17]

In the geo-political constellations of the European settler empires in America before the nineteenth century, the Creole descendants of the European conquerors often occupied an "ambiguous" social and legal space, neither colonized nor colonizers but rather *colonials*, who often (though not always) stood apart from the geo-political interests of the imperial metropolis and from what post-colonial criticism has come to conceptualize as the colonized "subaltern" – the Native Americans and Africans whose land or labor was being exploited in the imperial economies.[18]

The twentieth-century Caribbean writer and critic Aimé Césaire has recognized this triangular geo-political constellation of early modern settler colonialism in the Americas in his own reading of Shakespeare's *The Tempest*, entitled *Une tempête; d'après "La tempête" de Shakespeare. Adaptation pour un théâtre nègre* (1967). There, Césaire reads Prospero as a new type of social being as well as a new type of knower who had emerged in the Americas during the sixteenth century but remained utterly alien to European social theory. In the age of centralizing monarchies, the American conqueror re-incarnated the power of the old European aristocracy in his colonial neo-feudal dominion in the New World; but his power was based on the exploitation of un-free labor and natural resources at the periphery of globalizing mercantilist systems rather than on inalienable land and local estate economies. Moreover, he was a new type of knower who had access to the persuasive power of empirical forms of knowledge in a new world of experience without being guaranteed to share the metropolitan geo-political interests of the European monarchies. In Césaire's *Une tempête*, Prospero's magic therefore stands somewhere between Caliban's "black magic," incarnate in the Yoruba trickster-god of truth and deception Eshu-Elegbara, and the scientific rationalism of the early modern imperial state, represented by the Inquisition.[19] His power is vested in the control he exerts over the New World's material and epistemological resources, upon which the mercantilist arrangement between nobility and bourgeoisie had come to depend. "I WANT them to eat," he exclaims after Ariel has made the tantalizing banquet vanish before the eyes of the royal court:

ARIEL: That's despotism. A while ago you made me snatch it away just when they were about to gobble it up, and now that they don't want it you are ready to force-feed them.
PROSPERO: Enough hairsplitting! My mood has changed! They wrong me by not eating. They must be made to eat out of my hand like chicks. That is a sign of submission I insist they give me.
ARIEL: It's evil to play with their hunger as you do with their anxieties and their hopes.
PROSPERO: That is how power is measured. I am Power.

The profits to be reaped from the economic exploitation of the New World's natural resources depend on Prospero's collaboration in the mercantilist arrangement; in turn, it is his proximity to these resources that empowers his struggle against the imperial state in its efforts to assert its territorial claim over the New World island first discovered and conquered by Prospero's magic. Yet, for precisely that reason, his power is suspect and must be policed by the imperial metropolis.

[W]hen they learned that through my studies and experiments I had managed to discover the exact location of these lands many had sought for centuries, and that I was making preparations to set forth to take possession of them, they hatched a scheme to steal my as-yet-unborn empire from me. They suborned my people, they stole my charts and documents and, to get rid of me, they denounced me to the Inquisition as a magician and sorcerer.[20]

As Césaire is aware, the control and ownership of knowledge was of utmost importance in the geo-political conflict between the Creole elites and the imperial administrators in early modern transoceanic settler empires. This book explores the ways in which the imperial states attempted to secure Prospero's "charts and documents" as well as the ways in which he resisted the theft of his knowledge.

TOWARD A CULTURAL GEOGRAPHY OF COLONIAL AMERICAN LITERATURES

In exploring the consequences of European settler colonialism in the Americas for the making of early modern Western knowledge, this book seeks to make an intervention in the historiography not primarily of science but rather of "Literature," particularly of "early American Literature." A field that has long inhabited a marginal place in the modern Humanistic disciplines (where it was invented as a handmaiden to American national literary histories),[21] early American literature in English has only recently been re-theorized broadly from an "Atlantic" perspective, hereby following suit with currents in the social, political, and economic historiography of the early Americas.[22] William Spengeman has hereby been most vocal in re-defining "early American literature" broadly as a "New World of Words," as all writing that attempts to "make room in the language for the New World [and has] helped to create the stylistic circumstances in which that writing is now received." As defined by Spengeman, early American literature would henceforth include also the "literarily important" English writings of the Renaissance and the Enlightenment such as Thomas More's *Utopia*, William Shakespeare's *The Tempest*, John Milton's *Paradise Lost*, and Daniel Defoe's *Robinson Crusoe* – in short, all those texts that "discover to modern readers the origins of their modernity."[23] This book adopts the basic premise underlying much of the recent revisionary literary historiography undertaken by Spengeman and others – that early American literature cannot be understood in isolation from early modern European literature and from the larger "Atlantic" context from which both emerged; but it also departs particularly from Spengeman's approach in some of its major premises. First, it proposes not only a transatlantic but also a comparative, hemispheric, and trans-national perspective by juxtaposing texts from various places of the colonial Americas, such as New Spain, Virginia, Chile, New England, Peru, and New York.[24] For all of Spengeman's (well-founded) critique of the anachronism of proto-nationalist paradigms in early American literary studies, his own New Critical theorization of the field in terms of (mono)linguistic "competence" (i.e. English) is equally problematic for an understanding of the early modern world, which was

still pervasively polyglot.[25] The discovery and conquest of America, in particular, was a thoroughly trans- (or, more accurately, "pre-") national and
trans-linguistic process, often involving Italian explorers who seemed remarkably unconcerned about their tenuous command of Spanish and, even
more remarkably, about the inadequacy of Latin as a linguistic base for communicating with Native Americans;[26] "second-son" conquerors from the
petty nobility of Castile whose culture and language had been infused with
Arabic influences by centuries of co-existence in southern Spain;[27] multiple
African and Native American cultures and languages that participated in
these historical processes and the making of their literary record;[28] German
financiers and printers, many of them – like the Crombergs – living in
Spain;[29] courtly aristocrats and dynasts, such as the Holy Roman Emperor
Charles V, who allegedly once claimed that "I speak Spanish to God, Italian
to women, French to men, and German to my horse";[30] English pirates,
such as Sir Francis Drake, who was described by a contemporary Spaniard
as being "very Spanish in his ways and well acquainted with Castile and
its affairs";[31] and poets such as Sir Philip Sidney, who was a cousin not
only of the Spanish poets Diego Hurtado de Mendoza and Garcilaso de
la Vega but also of the Peruvian mestizo historian Garcilaso de la Vega, el
Inca. The early modern literary world was, as Roland Greene has put it, a
"transatlantic family."[32]

If this book therefore proposes to take not only an east–west but also a
north–south perspective on "early American literature," its second premise
is that *history mattered* in this Atlantic world and that the *differences* in literary and generic evolutions in various places must be understood in terms
of their distinct socio-historical developments. If I here place primary emphasis on the *colonial* literatures in the Spanish and British empires, it
is due to my sense that our appreciation of the distinct poetics of colonial texts has hitherto benefited little from the recent expansion of the
field of early American literature to include also the "literarily important"
European writings of the Renaissance and the Enlightenment – an expansion which has left Euro-centric epistemological assumptions about literary
value unchallenged. Rather than reiterating the conventional New Critical
lamentations about the aesthetic "lacks" and "lags" of colonial American
writing vis-à-vis European literary history,[33] this book aims to historicize
the "uneven" evolution of literary forms in order to take seriously the challenge that colonial forms of prose – "accounts," "relations," "reports," "true
histories," "notes," "guides," and "letters" – present to modern Western
categories of knowledge, such as "Literature." As Raymond Williams has
reminded us, in early modern times, "literature" still corresponded mainly

to "the modern meanings of literacy"; it meant both "an ability to read and a condition of being well-read." If "Literature" (with a capital "L") has in modern times come to privilege the discursive and generic evolutions of Europe – what Williams calls the "modern complex of *literature, art, aesthetic, creative,* and *imaginative*" – it is due to issues not of linguistic competence but rather of "social and cultural history."[34] In adopting such a broader understanding of "literature," this book focuses on three central motifs recurring in early modern prose narratives about the Americas – shipwreck, captivity, and travel. Following Fredric Jameson, it approaches these narratives as "socially symbolic acts" within the specific historical context of imperial politics and suggests that these recurring tropes are the "ideologemes" of early modern imperialism that not only "narrate" real or imagined events but also "narrativize" transforming ideologies by proposing "imagined resolutions to... social contradiction[s]." Jameson's multi-layered approach to textual analysis is particular useful for my purposes here, for his call to "Always historicize!" moves significantly beyond the conventional Marxist practice of reading texts as representations of non-discursive infrastructures; instead, Jameson presses for an understanding of the *forms* of representation in terms of political history, social context, and the modes of its own production; in short, for an "ideology of form" by which "symbolic messages [are] transmitted to us by the coexistence of various sign-systems which are themselves traces or anticipations of modes of production."[35] The early American accounts of shipwreck, captivity, and travel, I argue, narrativize the new forms of knowledge production in an age when the aristocratic model of "conquest" was being displaced not only as a political foundation – for regulating the relationship between the monarch and his subjects – but also as a way of knowing and representing the world in the globalizing economies of transoceanic empires.

Finally, while recent New Historicist scholarship has alerted us to the socio-political underpinnings of early modern European literary genres,[36] this book inquires into the geo-political dimensions of the evolution of early modern prose forms from the point of view of the colonial Americas. For example, while some New Historicist critics have called our attention to the crucial role that Renaissance Humanism, translation, and metaphor played as "colonial discourse" in the European discovery and conquest of America,[37] this book asks why colonial American writers, like Prospero in the last scene of Shakespeare's last play, frequently renounced Humanist rhetoric and wrote – as the eminent Cuban writer José Lezama Lima observed in his seminal essay *La expresión americana* (1959) – "in the prose of a primitive who receives the dictate of the landscape."[38] While other critics have made arguments for the "American" or "colonial" origins of the European novel,[39] this book asks why the novel remained conspicuously absent as a genre from colonial American literary production at a time when Europeans wrote a *Utopia*, a *New Atlantis*, a *Don Quixote*, or a *Robinson Crusoe*.

In exploring the cultural geography of early modern literary developments, this book must complicate some of the epistemological assumptions of modern historicism. As Hayden White has explained, Western historical discourse since the nineteenth century has invariably been ordered by what he calls an "archetypal plot of discursive formations," which renders familiar new domains of experience. Building on Kenneth Burke's taxonomy of the four "master tropes" of human cognition and rhetoric – metaphor, metonymy, synecdoche, and irony – White argues that this archetypal plot in modern historical discourse has ordered these four master tropes in a chronological dialectic:

[The] narrative "I" of the discourse moves from an original metaphorical characterization of a domain of experience, through metonymic deconstructions of its elements, to synecdochic representations of the relations between its superficial attributes and its presumed essence, to, finally, a representation of whatever contrasts or oppositions can legitimately be discerned in the totalities identified in the third phase of discursive representation.[40]

Metaphor, as Burke had defined it, brings out the similarities between dissimilar things, the "thisness of a that, or the thatness of a this." The operative code of metonymy, by contrast, is "to convey some incorporeal or intangible state in terms of the corporeal or tangible." Synecdoche operates in the opposite direction, apprehending the concrete part as "representative" of the abstract invisible principle. Finally, "irony" emerges when "all the sub-certainties [are] considered as neither true nor false, but contributory."[41]

From this point of view, the history of early modern prose genres may be seen in terms of White's tropological plot as the apprehension of the New World in the languages of the Old. For example, in his "dialectical theory" of the (English) novel in Europe, Michael McKeon has argued that the origin of the novel during the eighteenth century was only the final product of a long process of ideological, epistemic, and generic destabilizations and transformations beginning in the sixteenth and seventeenth centuries. His thesis can be schematically summarized as a three-pronged dialectical argument: the "novel" emerged (in England) at the beginning of the eighteenth century in the context of an epistemological "extreme skepticism" antithetical to the earlier "naïve empiricism" that had produced the genre of the "true history" during the seventeenth century, which was itself antithetical to the "romance idealism" that had produced the genre of the "romance" during the sixteenth century.[42] McKeon's narrative of such a dialectical literary history of modern prose genres can thus be seen as corresponding to White's archetypal plot of tropological transformation in the apprehension of new domains of experience: the "romance idealism" prevailing in the early sixteenth-century Renaissance chronicles of the discovery and conquest of the New World seeks to assimilate the new to the known, thus pointing to the dominance of a metaphorical code of cognition; this metaphorical code then undergoes a process of "metonymic deconstruction" (White's term) in the antithetical "scientific" discourses of the "true history," which apprehends truth in terms of its empirically verifiable particulars, places emphasis on collecting and observing, and represents the New World in terms of identity and difference. The eighteenth century, by contrast, privileged the invention of abstract taxonomies and laws formulated on the basis of the collected particulars, thus operating in the opposite direction to the metonymical code: the concrete part is now seen as "representative" of the abstract invisible principle, in the way of synecdoche.[43] The fictional discourses parodying these various tropological strategies arising during the early seventeenth century in Spain and during the early eighteenth century in England evidence the predominantly ironic code of "the novel."[44]

When considering the historical evolution of prose discourses in the colonial Americas within the theoretical framework of such an "archetypal plot," however, it is apparent that their evolution did not follow the same pattern of tropological transformation as it did in Europe. Instead, discourses of one tropological variety predominated in the colonies at times when discourses of another variety predominated in the metropole. For example, while the early Americas did not produce any grand taxonomies and theories of nature such as those of a Bacon, a Newton, or a Linnaeus, they produced a great amount of what has been called "nature reportage," emphasizing the collection of particulars.[45] Nor did the colonies produce any prose fictions parodying the metonymic codes of "true history" as did the early modern novels of Europe;[46] and when prose fictions did arise in the Americas – during the last decades of the eighteenth century – they parodied (as we shall see) not the metonymic codes of seventeenth-century "true histories," but rather the synecdochic codes dominating in speculative natural philosophy in the metropole during the eighteenth century.

In order to historicize the uneven and *co-dependent* literary evolutions of metropolis and colony in early modern imperial systems, we must investigate how these tropological codes are ordered not only in historical time but also in geographical space; in other words, we must place literary history in the context not only of the historical but also of the spatial dialectics that were foundational in the making of modernity. World-system theorists such as Immanuel Wallerstein and cultural geographers such as Henri Lefebvre and Edward Soja have alerted us to the shortcomings of modern Western philosophies of history since the nineteenth century in unduly privileging history and time over geography and space. This "overdeveloped historical contextualization," Soja argues, has resulted in the practice of treating space as "fixed, dead, undialectical; [and] time as richness, life, dialectical." He therefore calls for a "reassertion of space" in our historical accounts that would illuminate the "triple dialectic of space, time, and social being, a transformative re-theorization of the relations between history, geography, and modernity."[47] While Soja has hereby in mind Hegelian and Marxian theories of history, his critique was especially inspired by what he calls the "ambivalent spatiality" of Michel Foucault.[48] As the reader may recall, Foucault had notoriously postulated four great "epochs" in the history of the Western organization of knowledge, each of which produced internally coherent epistemic systems ("epistemes") structuring and sanctioning the distribution of historically discrete discursive formations. Thus, the emergence of the early modern scientific discourse of natural history was, according to Foucault, only the surface manifestation of a more profound shift in the structure of the Western knowledge regulating the relationship between words and things that occurred around the end of the sixteenth century. Natural history, he wrote at that time, "finds its locus in the gap that is now opened up between things and words."

This event is the sudden separation, in the realm of Historia, of two orders of knowledge henceforward to be considered different... [Previously] History was the inextricable and completely unitary fabric of all that was visible of things and of the signs that had been discovered or lodged in them... But, from the seventeenth century on, there can no longer be any signs except in the analysis of representations according to identities and differences. That is, all designation must be accomplished by means of a certain relation to all other possible designations... Identity and what marks it are defined by the differences that remain. An animal or a plant is not what is indicated – or betrayed – by the stigma that is to be found imprinted upon it; it is what the others are not; it exists in itself only in so far as it is bounded by what is distinguishable from it. Method and system are simply two ways of defining identities by means of the general grid of difference.[49]

While, in his early works, Foucault had remained somewhat vague as to the causes of the epistemic transformations he postulated, in his later works he increasingly sought to bring them into connection with the changing modalities of exercising power in the modern state.[50]

Of course, Foucault's totalizing scheme of "sudden" cataclysmic ruptures occurring at certain times in the structure of Western knowledge has long been subject to critiques from various quarters. Thus, critics have pointed out not only important threads of continuity between the medieval past and modern forms of knowledge but also significant geographic variations.[51] Indeed, Foucault's archive was suspiciously confined to Francophone sources; and even within this limited archive he had only cursorily considered non-European spaces in his account of modernity – when pondering the role that colonial outposts, such as the Jesuit missions of Paraguay, played as "heterotopias" ("other spaces") in the formation of the modern structures of power/knowledge.[52] While recent "postcolonial" critics have therefore been strongly indebted to Foucault's poststructuralist accounts of the Human Sciences, they have also critiqued them for remaining "assertively European." As Edward Said has suggested, much of what Foucault had written "makes greatest sense not as an ethnocentric model of how power is exercised in modern society, but between Europe and the rest of the world": of the way in which Europe produced, occupied, ruled, and exploited the non-European world.[53]

This book places the evolution of prose discourse about the New World in the context of two spatial dialectics of early modern imperialism. On the one hand, it investigates literary history in terms of the north–south dialectic underlying the making of modern Western culture on the example of the inter-connectedness of Spanish (Catholic) and British (Protestant) imperial discourses about the Americas. Thus, a "British" American discourse evolved in large part in a dialectical process of translating, editing, and commentating "Spanish" American discourses. On the other hand, it places the evolution of prose discourse in the colonial Americas in the context of an east–west dialectic with metropolitan discourses about the New World. Thus, while the narrative models of early modern natural history evolved in part as a response to the geo-political questions raised by settler colonialism in the Americas, colonial American writers in turn creatively appropriated and hybridized the rhetorical strategies of early modern science for their own political ends. In an intra-imperial struggle for power between peripheries and centers, colonial and metropolitan prose discourses evolved by parodying each other – as European narratives of shipwreck, for example, turn into colonial narratives of captivity in historical moments of intra-imperial geo-political conflict; metropolitan prose fictions parody New World "true histories" in moments of imperial consolidation; and (post-)colonial travel satires parody European natural histories in moments of imperial dissolution.

When setting out to explore the "triple dialectic" of space, time, and social being in the making of modern knowledge, the early seventeenth-century reform of natural philosophy proposed by Francis Bacon, long an icon of modernity,[54] provides an illustrative test case and strategic point of departure. In *The Advancement of Learning* (1605), Bacon addressed himself to the question of how to "joyn Rationall and Experimental Philosophy in a regular correspondence." No longer would the natural philosopher be confined to the study of the ancient texts of Aristotle and Pliny – which are but the "volumes of men"; from now on, he would also consult "the volumne of the world." Knowledge of these "volumne[s] of the world" would be attained by means of "observation" and a mechanical routine of eliminative "induction," making a gradual ascent from the level of the observably particular to the ever more general level of theory. For this purpose, Bacon's manifesto for a New Science established a strict grid of "rules" circumscribing the production of natural knowledge. "We must march," he wrote, "by line and level, and all the way, even from the first perception of senses,... by a certain rule, and constant method of proceeding." The objective of this method was to "circumvent" man's (probably erroneous) "[j]udgements" and to penetrate to the "things themselves."[55]

A central aspect of Bacon's "rules" for the New Sciences concerned the role of language. "[F]or all that concerns ornaments of speech, similitudes, treasury of eloquence, and such like emptiness," he wrote, "let it be utterly dismissed." No longer would the natural historian indulge in making reference to "antiquities, and citations or testimonies of authors... everything in short which is philological."[56] Henceforth the language of Natural History was to be purely referential of "things," stripped of all "Varnish of fine Metaphors and glittering Allusions," as the prominent Baconian Samuel Parker put it.[57] This injunction on language became the proclaimed policy of the Royal Society of London, founded in 1660 for the promotion of the New Sciences. By the second half of the seventeenth century, Thomas Sprat, the first historian of the Royal Society, could celebrate the Society's achievements in correcting the previous "excesses" of Natural Philosophy: "They [the Fellows] have... reject[ed] all the amplifications, digressions, and swellings of style... return[ed] back to the primitive purity, and shortness, when men deliver'd so many things, almost in an equal number of words... [and] exacted from all their members, a close, naked, natural way of speaking... [as in] the language of Artizans, Countrymen, and Merchants, before that, of Wits, or Scholars."[58]

Traditionally, the Baconian injunction to strip the "Varnish" of metaphor from language in the Natural Sciences was seen as an indication of Baconianism's "antipathy" to language and rhetoric in general.[59] More recently, however, historians have shown that Bacon, as well as the Fellows of the Royal Society, never wrote themselves in the style of "Artizans, Countrymen, [or] Merchants" for which they called. As for their own style, they never disclaimed, Brian Vickers observes, "all use of rhetoric or of appeal to the imaginations, but merely specified the situations in which the exercise of these faculties was permissible."[60] There was one area, in particular, where metaphor was no longer welcome – in scientific observation, which required a "close, naked, natural way of speaking." For the problem with observation was, as Bacon knew, that the observer's mind could not be trusted. The mind of man, he wrote, is "far from being a smooth, clear, and equal glass, (wherein the beams of things reflect according to their true incidents)" but rather "like an enchanted glass, full of superstition and imposture."[61] The language of the observer had to be "reduced" to transparency and made like "clear" glass, stripped of all the "enchantments" of metaphor that might be clouding his delivery of "things." Fundamental to the Baconian reform of Natural Philosophy was therefore a strict division of the disciplines as well as a division of intellectual labor within the "new" sciences. We must "divide," he wrote, "Natural Philosophy into two parts; the mine and the furnace; and make two professions, or occupations of natural philosophers; some to be miners and some to be smiths." Whereas the "miner" was to confine him/herself to "the Production of Effects," by digging "the bowels of Nature," the "smith" would conduct an "Inquisition of Causes." These "two parts, Speculative and Operative," as Bacon called them, must "be considered separately, both in the intention of the writer, and the body of the Treatise." The secrets of nature would thus be unlocked in a prescribed order in which the eyewitness would surrender his first-hand observations to the detached "speculator" to be refined into the "true axioms" of modern knowledge.[62]

Who were these "refiners" of natural knowledge and who the "diggers," working nature's "bowels"? In their classical sociologies of knowledge, Emile Durkheim and Karl Mannheim argued that the Baconian division of intellectual labor, by aiming to include the rising middling classes in the modern production of knowledge, represented a progressive response to the increasing complexities of modern life developing on the heels of scientific discovery and progress.[63] Since Theodor Adorno's and Max Horkheimer's studies in the essentially hegemonic aspects of Enlightenment rationalism in general and the scientific division of intellectual labor in particular,[64] however, some historians have cast a more critical light on the rise of the Baconian reforms. Especially in recent post-structuralist critiques of modern knowledge, Bacon himself has come to be regarded primarily as an English statesman whose "detached" philosophical treatises had an "interest" – not so much in the welfare of humanity at large but rather in the advancement of the English monarchical state in its quest to expand its power. As one critic has suggested, Bacon's proposals for the reform of the law and government were of a piece with his reforms of Natural Philosophy in their devotion to the interests of the Jacobean "centralizing monarchy" in making the production, ownership, and organization of knowledge the "department of the state."[65] As Julie Solomon explains, the state's growing interest in the production of knowledge responded to the potential challenges that the new ways of knowing on the part of the increasingly mobile commercial classes presented to an immobile king's claim to absolute power and knowledge. Thus, Bacon's programmatic work in the advancement of learning aimed to confront the rising dangers of empiricism by finding strategies for "containing, while advocating, the experimental, exploratory, and technological activities of scientific subordinates." For this purpose, Bacon organized science "hierarchically," dividing those who "analyze data and forge axioms . . . at the top of the ladder" from those who "collect raw data and organize experiments . . . in the trenches." The promotion of an early modern ideology of "objectivity" arose in this context out of the politically charged conversation among dominant and subordinate groups in their competing claims to the material world and resulted in the imposition upon experiential testimony of an authorial ideal that Solomon calls "epistemic self-distancing" – the effacement of the eye-witness's subjectivity in the delivery of facts.[66]

In light of the socio-political aspects of Baconianism pointed out in the recent post-structuralist debate about modern knowledge and the state, however, two considerations are noteworthy: first, that England was not an absolute monarchy at the time when Bacon articulated his program in the New Sciences (despite James' occasional pretensions);[67] and, second, that Baconianism was absorbed in England not only by the political language of absolutism but also by the antithetical language of Republicanism.[68] Bacon himself, though doubtlessly obliged to the Jacobean court, seems remarkably vague on the question of how to reconcile absolutist with representative forms of government – especially next to contemporaries such as Hobbes. Whereas it is unclear whether Bacon favored absolute monarchical power or a more balanced, Republican model, there can be little doubt as to where his primary concern lay as an English statesman: in the building of a cohesive national infrastructure supporting an overseas empire that would allow England to compete in the geo-political contest against her European neighbors. This could only be achieved, he believed, by reconciling the interests of many and most variable groups and individuals at a time of rapid socio-economic change.

The promotion of overseas colonialism hereby came to play an integral part in Bacon's political philosophy. A colonial empire would channel diverse individual interests in ways most productive for the nation's wealth and power at large by deflating the social pressures at home, expanding England's sphere of influence abroad, and by increasing revenue from colonial trade: "So shall your majesty in this work have a double commodity, in the avoidance of people here, and in making use of them there."[69] Bacon therefore continuously pointed out the virtues inherent in the colonial project. "Plantations are," he wrote, amongst man's "ancient, primitive, and heroical works" in their dual mission to convert heathens and civilize barbarians.[70] Thus, if in "Of Plantations," Bacon outlined a general plan for colonization by suggesting that "The People wherewith you Plant, ought to be Gardners, Plough-men, Labourers, Smiths, Carpenters, Joyners, Fishermen, Fowlers," his treatises on the advancement of learning followed the same geo-political program – the colonials in the "bowels" of nature would provide the epistemic raw material, and the metropolitan natural philosopher would refine it into "truth."[71] Bacon, a royal counselor as well as a stockholder and member of the council for the newly formed Virginia Company, articulated his reforms of natural knowledge in a historical context in which the onslaught of empirical forms of knowing was raising questions not only about the socio-political order at home but also about a newly emerging geo-political order in which overseas colonies must be kept in a position subordinate and peripheral to, as well as dependent upon, the imperial metropolis. The geo-political aspect of Bacon's program for modern knowledge calls our attention to a cultural dialectic in the making of modernity that Immanuel Wallerstein has called the "geoculture" which was being produced on "the periphery of and in response to and in relation to a 'center' culture" and which was at once the "manifestation of, and the undergirding for, global capitalism."[72] If the Baconian reform of Natural Philosophy came to stand as the most foundational model in the modern organization of knowledge, it was in part because it provided a rationale for dividing intellectual labor not only as experiential testimonies traveled through social space, between dominant and subordinate sectors in the early modern social orders of Europe, but also as they traveled across geographic space, in the territorialized hierarchies connecting colonial peripheries to metropolitan centers in early modern settler empires.

POWER AND KNOWLEDGE IN THE CULTURE OF THE BAROQUE

It may appear anachronistic to assert the importance of geo-political questions of empire at stake in Baconian science. After all, while England had had a colony in Ireland – which Bacon would later call an enterprise as different from that in Virginia "as Amadis de Gaul differs from Caesar's Commentaries" – it did not establish its first New World colony until 1607 – two years *after* the first publication of *The Advancement of Learning* – and overall appeared rather sluggish in getting on the early modern imperialist train when compared to some of its continental neighbors, such as Spain and Portugal.[73] When taken out of the isolation of its national context and put into a wider trans-national perspective, however, the importance of the geo-political interests at stake in early seventeenth-century British reforms of knowledge become quite readily apparent.

We may again take *The Tempest* as a guide through the complex geography of modernity in the making and remember that Prospero was not an English merchant but rather an Italian aristocrat in exile whose power had quickened on his colonial island. Prospero herein resembles not so much the bourgeois English merchant but rather the Iberian discoverers and conquerors of America who had established their neo-feudal dominions in the New World at the same time as feudalism was being supplanted by Habsburg absolutism in continental Europe. In what we might call a "Nietzschean moment" in *The Tempest*, the social conflict of the play is resolved not by the subjugation of the representatives of the commercial middling classes but by Prospero's sacrifice of his aristocratic will to power, honor, and revenge to the moral, political, and epistemic orders of enlightened modernity.[74] The New World subtext and the continental southern European setting in *The Tempest* thus call our attention to the wider trans-national context in which the formation of modern forms of power/knowledge emerged. It is largely as a historical reflection on the imperial New World origins of Habsburg absolutism in continental Europe, I would submit, that *The Tempest* inquires into the potential fallout of England's budding colonial project in Virginia on the English political landscape at home, on the growing conflict between a long English tradition of limited monarchy and Jacobean absolutist aspirations.[75] It is in light of the sixteenth-century geo-political connection between Spanish imperialism in the Americas and Habsburg absolutism in Europe that Prospero's progeny – Miranda, her great catch Ferdinand, and her enslaved step-brother Caliban – are all manifestly related as a (more-or-less happy) early modern family.

As quiet as it's kept, the so-called "father of modern science" Francis Bacon conceived his program for the reform of Natural Philosophy with a keen awareness of, and engagement with, sixteenth-century Spanish science and empire in the New World.[76] This awareness is attested to when we compare the famous title page of the 1620 edition of Bacon's *Instauratio Magna* (The Great Instauration), which shows a ship passing through the pillars of Hercules signifying the limits of ancient knowledge, with that of Andres García de Céspedes' earlier *Regimiento de Navegación* (Madrid, 1606), from which the design for Bacon's plate was quite obviously lifted (see Illustrations 1.1 and 1.2).[77] From the vantage point of early seventeenth-century Englishmen such as Shakespeare or Bacon, the Iberian experience with overseas colonialism in the Americas during the sixteenth century had some important lessons to teach about the symbiotic relationship between the consolidation of national state power at home and imperial expansion abroad. As Bacon put it, "Their greatness consisteth in their treasure, their treasure in their Indies, and their Indies, if it be well weighed, are indeed but an accession to such as are masters...So as this axle-tree, whereupon their greatness turneth, is soon cut in two by any that shall be stronger than they at sea."[78] In the development of this symbiotic relationship between overseas imperialism and absolutism in Europe, the case of imperial Spain had provided what Perry Anderson has called the "system-setting" prototype.[79] Although Spain, or more accurately "the Spains," had lacked in national governmental cohesiveness, with the various kingdoms retaining their own distinct cultural and economic identities even after being united under the imperial crown,[80] dynastic political consolidation of power had continually been aided by an aggressive expansionism, beginning with the marriage of Ferdinand of Aragon and Isabella of Castile in the context of the re-conquest of Granada; the marriage of their daughter Juana and the Habsburg Philip the Fair; the marriage of the Spanish monarchy and the imperial crown with the election of their son Charles V as Holy Roman Emperor after the first conquests in the New World; and especially with the marriage of Philip II and Queen Mary I at a time when Spain commanded an empire larger than the world had seen to date. "[T]he multiple effects of its American Empire on Spanish Absolutism became

1.1 Frontispiece of Andres García de Céspedes' *Regimiento de Navegación*
(Madrid, 1606).

1.2 Frontispiece of Francis Bacon's *Instauratio Magna* (1620).

increasingly determinant for its future," Anderson writes, for "The supply of huge quantities of silver from the Americas henceforward became a decisive 'facility' of the Spanish State" by allowing the Habsburg state to hire the huge conscript armies that facilitated its aggressively expansionist dynastic politics in Europe and to crush domestic opposition to political centralization by the cities and the local aristocracies.[81] Spain's American empire had advanced the establishment of an absolute monarchy by providing the fiscal base necessary for administrative centralization and military enforcement of economic protectionism, which, in turn, profited the rising bourgeoisie as well as the nobility who, though losing some of their former autonomies, were granted lucrative offices in imperial service.

Yet, Spanish expansionism in the Americas had not naturally translated into a bigger treasury at the disposal of the monarchy but had to be made profitable to the "common" wealth by decisive state intervention in the imperial economy and political administration.[82] Indeed, the enormous influx of bullion from the New World had brought the most powerful empire the world had seen to the brink of economic disaster. "España son las Indias del extranjero" ("Spain is the America of foreigners"), sixteenth-century Spanish officials cried. The American gold had increased the cost of production in Castile to such a degree that foreign manufacturers were able to gain entry into the colonial markets and even to Castile itself. Europe's source for gold and silver, Spain was increasingly becoming the dumping ground for foreign manufactured goods.[83] The increasing chasm between the intrinsic value of gold and the nominal value of money in sixteenth-century Spain resulted not only in an unprecedented economic but also in an epistemological debate over the nature of "wealth" from which emerged – a hundred years before Colbert – the economic theories of Luiz Ortiz, the crown's comptroller of public finance during the 1580s, who has been called the "first European Mercantilist."[84] In this context of economic and epistemological crisis, precipitated in large part by the economic exploitation of the New World, the Habsburg state centralized control over economic production, regulating imports and exports, as well as protecting its colonial raw materials and markets through the supervision of the Casa de Contratación (House of Trade), established in Seville already in 1503 under Ferdinand and Isabella, in order "to exercise total control over trade with the New World."[85]

The Latin American critic Angel Rama has described the literary consequences of these administrative changes as the formation of what he called the "lettered city" of the New World, the imperial bureaucracies established in the process of the "second conquest" of America by the imperial state. Presented with the formidable task of sustaining an administrative apparatus over the world's first trans-oceanic empire, the Habsburg monarchy dispatched to the New World an army of *letrados*, or imperial bureaucrats, who were directly connected and subordinated to royal power lodged in the vice-regal courts. Due to their ability to manipulate writing in largely illiterate societies, the *letrados* were able to attain a degree of social importance in the New World that they lacked in the Old: "Amid the grammatological tendencies of European culture in the early modern period, writing took on an almost sacred aura, and doubly so in American territories where it remained so rare and so closely linked to royal authority." The utopian architectural design of these logocentric cities made of letters, Rama suggests, mirrored that of the Baroque cities built of stone, laid out in the ubiquitous checkerboard grid that has endured until the present day. The first material realization of the modern dream of order, the American continent became the "experimental field" for absolutist monarchies in their quests for "abstractions, rationalizations, and systematizations," a dream of order that seemed possible only in a "New World" imagined as a *tabula rasa*.[86]

There were, of course, important repercussions of this new dream of order for Peninsular Spain, too. John H. Elliott chronicles an increasing conviction that various brands of Protestant, Erasmian, and Illuminist heresies were on the advance even within Spanish cities and that internal unrests such as the *Comunero* revolt of 1529 had in part been instigated by a conspiracy between converted Jews (*conversos*) within the homeland and foreign powers abroad. All of this resulted in the increase of the Inquisition's power and in a growing obsession with the purity of "Spanish" lineage (*limpieza de sangre*). This ideology of pure Spanish ancestry, rather than aristocratic standing, became increasingly the prerequisite for the holding of government offices. While this cultural paranoia did much to lend Spain's national culture the cohesiveness it had formerly lacked, it was at the expense not only of dissidents but also of some sectors of the traditional aristocracy (whose well-documented family trees were rarely spotless in this regard). "[B]y the end of the 1560s," Elliott writes, "the 'open' Spain of the Renaissance had been transformed into the partially 'closed' Spain of the Counter-Reformation."[87]

This general perception of crisis had profound impacts not only on structures of government and the economy but also on the culture at large. In his magisterial analysis of an emerging "culture of the Baroque," José Antonio Maravall has described Spain during the second part of the sixteenth century as an "authoritarian court culture," where all venues of cultural production, such as science, the arts, and literature, gradually "came under the influence or even under the mandate of the rulers, who granted subsidies, guided appeal toward a certain taste, or (should the case arise) prohibited certain works." The Habsburg state was hereby the first in Europe to employ mass communication in an attempt to ideologize the masses with full programmatic rigor. The quest to channel human productivity toward the benefit of the state resulted, Maravall argues, in a new need for knowledge also of the human being, "in the sense of an empirical knowing based on observation and directed toward [the] practical, operative end" of domination and manipulation of human conduct. The scientific discovery of "differential psychology" in this context promoted a belief in the diversity of individuals and peoples, reducing them to "types."[88] It is in this historical context that a "new science" arose in sixteenth-century Spain, as Baroque men of learning such as Juan Huarte de San Juan, Francisco Hernández, and Juan Luis Vives first theorized the diversity of human faculties in terms of environmental determinisms.[89]

One of the most influential examples of this new science during the early modern period was the treatise in differential psychology entitled *Examen de ingenios para las ciencias*, written by the Spanish physician Dr. Juan Huarte de San Juan (1529–88).[90] Richard Carew's 1594 English translation (itself based on an Italian translation) alone was published six times in four editions by 1616. The basic premise of *Examen* was that every mind was endowed by nature with its own type and level of "genius" and must function conjunctively with its attending physical faculties.[91] In particular, Huarte was interested in the natural causes of the diversity of human talents or "wits" ("ingenio"): "none has clearly and distinctly delivered what that nature is which makes a man able for one science, and incapable of another, nor how many differences in wits there are found in mankind, nor what Arts or Sciences do answer each in particular, nor by what tokens this may be known, which the thing that most importest." He therefore deduced the diversity of human psychological traits from the diversity in physiological characteristics, in particular the four basic bodily "temperatures" (heat, cold, moisture, dryness) – from which "issues all the abilities of man," he wrote, and "all his virtues and vices, and this great variety of wits which we behold." "Temperature" determines not only individual external features but also the varying talents and intellectual maxima in every man. The reason for this diversity of bodily "humours" among men, Huarte argued, is to be found in the specific properties of the natural environment in which each resides. For ethnic differences in individuals and nations derive, as Huarte saw it, not from racial differences but rather from climate, environment, and diet:

[T]he manners of the soul, follow the temperature of the body, in which it keeps residence, and that by reason of the heat, the coldness, the moisture, and the drought, of the territory where men inhabit, of the meats which they feed on, of the waters which they drink, and of the air which they breath; some are blockish, and some wise, some of woorth, and some base, some cruel, and some merciful. That the difference of nations, as well in composition of the body as in conditions of the soul, springeth from the variety of this temperature: and experience itself evidently shows this, how far are different Greeks from Tartarians: Frenchmen from Spaniards: Indians from Dutch: and Ethiopians from English.[92]

While much of Huarte's theory was derived from the Classical model of Galen's *Natural Faculties*, what was original to his *Examen* was that it applied this Natural History of man to social theory, thereby providing a rationale for the division of labor in the modern society and knowledge. It should be forbidden, he argued, that man be allowed "to study that science which is agreeable for him [according to] his own choice"; rather, he proposed to the monarch that a

law should be enacted, that no carpenter should exercise himself in any work which appertained to the occupation of an husbandman, nor a tailor to that of an architect, and that the Advocate should not minister Phisicke, nor the Phisistion play the Advocate, but each one exercise only that art to which he beareth a natural inclination and let passe the residue.[93]

It would therefore be the responsibility, as well as the prerogative, of the state to "discover" the particular wits of individuals and to assign them a suitable profession in a way that renders them most profitable to the commonwealth. For this purpose, Huarte provided an elaborate scheme that assigned to each natural climate a certain constellation of bodily humors, the corresponding talents and wits, and the appropriate professions. For example, he argued that humid climates were conducive to the faculty of memory but only dry climates to the faculty of understanding, thus making the two mutually exclusive but the former conducive to the study of Latin, Grammar, Divinity positive, Cosmography, and Arithmeticke, and the latter to School Divinity, Theory of Physick, logic, and natural and moral philosophy.[94]

It was in the context of this intellectual debate about the environmental determination of human faculties that theories of creolization and degeneration emerged in sixteenth-century Spanish historiography about America.[95] First used to distinguish slaves of African descent born in the Americas from those born in Africa, during the course of the sixteenth century the term "Creole" increasingly referred, mainly in a pejorative sense, also to American-born Spaniards in distinction to those born on the Iberian Peninsula. By the mid seventeenth century, it gained currency also among English natural philosophers, thus making the "debate over creole culture," as Karen Ordahl Kupperman observes, a theme of "powerful continuity in European responses [to America]."[96] The early modern debate about the determining influences of the American environment rationalized geographic centralization not only of the political, legal, and administrative but also of the epistemic apparatuses in early modern settler empires: by bringing American nature in connection with the moral and intellectual constitution of its inhabitants, European natural historians constituted themselves at the center and American Creoles at the semi-periphery of scientific authorship in the production of knowledge about the New World's natural and human "resources." Colonial Creoles throughout the Americas, in turn, frequently upheld (or withheld) empirical knowledge in their relations with the metropolis in a discourse of racial difference in which they sought to define the "White" identity of their settler communities in counter-distinction to Native Americans and Africans. While this discourse of inherent racial difference would finally prevail as a Western ideology in the aftermath of the breakup of the European settler empires in America during the late eighteenth century, throughout the colonial periods this discourse was continually in competition with the dominant European discourse about creolization in rationalizing colonial difference.[97]

THE CULTURAL GEOGRAPHY OF COLONIAL AMERICAN LITERATURES

This book explores the geo-political underpinnings of this "new" science emerging in sixteenth-century Spain and seventeenth-century England and compares its consequences for the formal evolution of colonial prose narrative in Spanish and English. To be sure, when comparing the Spanish to the British ideologies and infrastructures in transatlantic knowledge production, Rama's metaphor of the Baroque "lettered city" has only limited conceptual value. In Spain and Spanish America, this "lettered city" was underwritten by a patrimonialist ideology that Roberto González Echevarría has characterized as a "cluster of connections" between "secrecy (or privacy of knowledge), origin and power" that became "encrypted in the concept of the Archive." It is no accident, as he notes, that Spain's first archive, erected by Charles V at Simancas (though only finished by Philip II), was established with the emergence of the "new" state propagated by the Catholic Monarchs in a building that had formerly housed a prison: "Power, secrecy and law stand at the origin of the Archive... [I]t was the building that encrypted the power to command... The mystery of the object, its prestige, is made a functional part in the foundation of the modern state."[98] Early modern Protestant theorists of knowledge, by contrast, preferred the metaphor of a "republic" (rather than a "city") of letters when characterizing their forms of literary and scientific exchange. In British America the imperial economy of knowledge was underwritten not by a patrimonialist but rather by a "liberal" ideology that emerged in part in a dialectic with Catholic Spanish imperialism and became codified in the concept of "the public."[99] Despite the important differences between the "patrimonialist"

Catholic and the "liberal" Protestant empires, both were similarly based on transatlantic economies that were stratified in geographic space not only in their material infrastructures but also in their scientific ideologies. The following chapters explore the implications of these similarities and differences for the ways in which prose narrative evolved in each realm.

The next two chapters discuss the role that sixteenth- and seventeenth-century New World narratives of shipwreck played in the formation of the geo-political order that I have called "epistemic mercantilism." In the context of centralizing empires, New World tales of shipwreck narrativize the demise of the aristocratic ideal of "conquest" not only as a way of life but also as a way of knowing, thereby announcing a "new" science in which the colonial subject is effaced and historiographic authorship concentrated in the imperial metropolis. Thus, Chapter 2 places the textual evolution of Álvar Núñez Cabeza de Vaca's *Relación* (1537–55) about his odyssey through North America in dialogue with the court historian Gonzalo Fernández de Oviedo y Valdés' *Historia general y natural de las indias* (1535). I argue that both the transformation in Spanish imperial discourse from "conquest" to "pacification" and the emergence of a proto-ethnographic "realism" in Cabeza de Vaca's account must be seen in the context of the Habsburg monarchy's geo-political and legal struggle to centralize imperial administration over the newly conquered territories. Cabeza de Vaca's "epic" hereby presents a meta-historical allegory that replaces "magic" for "miracle" as the preferred model of knowing in the Catholic empire and that rationalizes the imperial economy of knowledge production that constructs the scientific authority of imperial historians such as Oviedo.

Chapter 3 investigates the translation of this new scientific historiography about the New World into an emerging British imperial context during the early seventeenth century by tracing the incorporation and subordination of empiricist shipwreck narratives, such as Cabeza de Vaca's *Relación* and William Strachey's "True Reportory," in Samuel Purchas' *Hakluytus Posthumus* (1625). Whereas in the graduated spiritual order of Catholic New World historiography, "magical" ways of knowing had been displaced as Native American "devil worship" only if they could not be subsumed within Counter-Reformation orthodoxy, the Protestant New World historians promoted a disenchanted sense of reality in dialectical antithesis to Catholic "superstition." In editing and contextualizing his eyewitness sources, Purchas became one of the first British New World historians to articulate what we might call an early modern "historicist" epistemology by self-consciously implementing the Baconian method. In their mercantilist poetics and politics, Purchas' works distinguish themselves from both the aristocratic model of history promoted by his predecessor Richard Hakluyt and the bourgeois model promoted by writers such as John Smith.

The remaining chapters investigate the implications of these imperial epistemic economies for the development of prose discourse in the colonial Americas. Chapters 4 and 5 explore the geopolitics of colonial captivity narratives, as they comply with, exploit, parody, and transgress against the mercantilist production of knowledge in order to advance an emerging Creole patriotism in the historical context of intra-imperial conflict. Thus, Chapter 4 offers a comparison of two seventeenth-century captivity narratives written by American Creoles – the Chilean Francisco Núñez de Pineda y Bascuñán and the New Englander Mary Rowlandson – in such moments of intra-imperial crisis – the so-called "rebelión de 1655" in Chile and King Philip's War in New England (1675). I argue that both colonial captivity accounts exploit their claim to eyewitness experience by subordinating historiographic rhetoric to first-person narrative in order to authorize political arguments against imperial centralization. While Chapter 4 asks how colonial captivity narratives appropriate the rhetorical model of the "true history" in the context of a seventeenth-century "naïve empiricism," Chapters 5 and 6 investigate how two elite Creole men of science from New Spain and Virginia – Carlos de Sigüenza y Góngora and William Byrd respectively – appropriate and parody the authority of the natural philosopher in the context of the "extreme skepticism" emerging with Baroque and post-Newtonian science in the age of circum-global empires. Thus, Chapter 5 explores the metonymical relationship between form and content in Sigüenza y Góngora's *Infortunios de Alonso Ramírez* (1690) and argues that the plain language and plot of pirate captivity allegorize the theft of colonial knowledge not only by Protestant piracy but also by the mercantilist epistemic order of the Baroque Lettered City in which the elite Creole historian Sigüenza y Góngora inhabits an ambivalent cultural location. Similarly, Chapter 6 reads William Byrd's *History of the Dividing Line betwixt Virginia and North Carolina* (1738) as a meta-historical satire of post-Newtonian natural philosophy in the age of "circum-Atlantic" empire, in particular in its dialogue with Peter Kolb's *Present State of the Cape of Good Hope* (1731). It argues that Byrd's "creolean humours" in his textual construction of the borderline between the two colonies clash two anti-thetical conceptions of space – one in terms of Newtonian rationalism and another in terms of the empirical knowledge of settlers "building and dwelling" on the colonial frontier.

Finally, Chapter 7 compares two (post-)colonial texts written during the Revolutionary eras, when the political ties holding the old European settler empires in the Americas began to rupture – *El lazarillo de ciegos caminantes* (1776) by Alonso Carrió de la Vandera (alias Concolorcorvo) and *Letters from an American Farmer* (1782) by Hector St. John de Crèvecoeur (alias Farmer James). Both texts participate in a more general disruption of the mercantilist transatlantic division of intellectual labor by exposing and parodying the utopian fiction of "authenticity" in eyewitness experience upon which the cultural authority of the Enlightenment historiographer had rested. The result of this disruption is a breakup of what has been called the "lost paradigm" of natural history at the end of the eighteenth century, a breakup that would issue into the modern disciplines that underwrote the new empires based on "invaded" colonies emerging during the nineteenth century.

Traversing as it does some 300 years and a vast geographical space circumscribed by Madrid, Buenos Aires, Lima, Mexico City, Boston, and London, this book can make no claim to offering an exhaustive or comprehensive historical narrative about the evolution of prose in the early modern world. It can offer only exemplary case studies intended to illustrate the importance of cultural geography to literary history. I confine my discussion here primarily to the evolution of prose discourse because of its unique and privileged status in Western ideologies of truth. I focus on Creole subjects not because the early Americas did not have a multitude of other social groups involved in the production of early American literatures, but because their comparative study would require different methodological tools from the ones applied here.[100] Finally, I focus on Spanish and British American materials not only because they have not hitherto been sufficiently compared, or because I would discount the importance of Portuguese, Dutch, or French contributions to the literary history of the New World, but rather because I would argue that it was in the Spanish and the British empires where the early modern geo-political dialectic between imperial consolidation and Creole resistance was most manifest, resulting, in the late eighteenth and early nineteenth centuries, in a breakdown of the old imperial order.

CHAPTER 2

Mythos and epos: Cabeza de Vaca's empire of peace

Here is a better life in place of Darës, Eryx; here I lay down my
gauntlets and my art.

(Entellus in Virgil's *Aeneid*)

Now you will be thoroughly convinced, son Sancho, of what I have
often told you before, that all things in this castle are done by way of
enchantment.

(Don Quixote in Cervantes' *Don Quixote*)

[T]here are two journeys in every odyssey, one on worried water, / the
other crouched and motionless, without noise. / For both, the "I" is
a mast; a desk is a raft for one, foaming with paper, and dipping the
break / of a pen in its foam, while an actual craft carries the other to
cities where people speak a different language.

(Omeros in Derek Walcott's *Omeros*)[1]

On 27 June 1527, 600 men under the leadership of Pánfilo de Narváez
set out from Sanlúcar de Barrameda, Spain, to "conquer and govern" La
Florida, a land known to hold fabulous riches, the mythic Fountain of
Youth, and the legendary Seven Cities of Cíbola. What had so auspiciously
begun, however, took disastrous turns once the conquerors landed near
Tampa Bay on 14 April 1528. After their inland advance on horse had been
repelled by hostile terrain and Indians, they hastily constructed rafts in the
hope of re-joining their ships but were wrecked in a storm on the North
American Gulf Coast. The survivors were captured by local Indians, and
only four of them would live to reach Mexico City, after an eight-year
odyssey that took them all across the North American continent to the
Pacific and finally back to New Spain, naked and on foot. One of them,
the treasurer of the wrecked expedition by the name of Álvar Núñez Cabeza
de Vaca, later returned to Spain, where he appealed to the emperor Charles
V for recognition of his long years of loyalty, suffering, and toil. Having
brought no spoils of conquest, the luckless conqueror offered a different
commodity in the hope that it would be equally acceptable to his monarch: a

"relación" ("account"), "brief rather than lengthy," of his North American odyssey:

Mas como ni mi consejo, ni diligencia aprovecharon para que aquello a que éramos idos fuesse ganado conforme al servicio de Vuestra Magestad, y por nuestros peccados permittiesse Dios que de quantas armadas a aquellas tierras an ido, ninguna se viesse en tan grandes peligros, ni tuviesse tan miserable y desastrado fin, no me quedó lugar para hazer más servicio deste, que es traer a Vuestra Magestad relación de lo que en nueve años por muchas y muy estrañas tierras que anduve perdido y en cueros, pudiesse saber y ver, ansí en el sitio de las tierras y provincias y distancias dellas, como en los mantenimientos y animales que en ellas se crían, y las diversas costumbres de muchas y muy bárbaras naçiones con quien conversé y viví, y todas las otras particularidades que pude alcançar y conoscer, que dello en alguna manera Vuestra Magestad será servido.

[S]ince neither my counsel nor diligence prevailed in order that the endeavor upon which we were embarked be completed as service to Your Majesty, and since no expedition of as many as have gone to those lands ever saw itself in such grave dangers or had such a wretched and disastrous end as that which God permitted us to suffer on account of our sins, I had no opportunity to perform greater service than this, which is to bring to Your Majesty an account of all that I was able to observe and learn in the nine years that I walked lost and naked through many and very strange lands, as much regarding the locations of the lands and provinces and the distances among them, as with respect to the foodstuffs and animals that are produced in them, and the diverse customs of many and very barbarous peoples with whom I conversed and lived, plus all the other particularities that I could come to know and understand, so that in some manner Your Majesty may be served.

It was empirical "information" and particular detail ("all that I was able to observe and learn"), instead of gold and silver, he had to offer, "because this alone is what a man who came away naked could carry out with him."[2]

A narrative of shipwreck and captivity, Cabeza de Vaca's *Relación* presents a stark contrast to most of the Spanish Renaissance chronicles of the discovery and conquest both in content and in form. Because of the apparent "realism" of his descriptions of Native American cultures and the North American landscapes, modern historians have long regarded him as America's "first ethnographer" and his text as documentary source material more factual than the chronicles written by most of his contemporaries.[3] Because of its conspicuous lack of the rhetorical figures of verisimilitude, his narrative has often puzzled literary critics who have regarded it as something of an anomaly in the discursive landscape of Spanish Renaissance historiography. Thus, critics have noted a tension between various rhetorical molds at work in this text – between "story" and "discourse," "history" and "novel," "journalism" and "history," "history and fiction," between "the chronologic," "objective," and the "episodic."⁴ Recently, Cabeza de Vaca's account has become a favorite among New Historicist literary critics, who have been intrigued by its representation of new alterities and identities produced in the Euro-American colonial encounter, by "the discovery of the Self with respect to the Other," and the permanent "replantation of a subject before a changeable alterity."⁵ Because of Cabeza de Vaca's sympathetic representation of Native Americans and his plea for a peaceful approach to Spain's mission in America, Beatriz Pastor, for example, has argued that his account represents a "discourse of failure" which "demythified" an ideology of conquest and evidenced the author's "radical" attempt to "subvert the established order" of Spanish imperialism. The origin of the pacificism evidenced by this text lay in its author's experience of shipwreck and captivity among the Indians, which caused in him a fundamental "metamorphosis" leading to a "more objective" approach to reality as revealed by "actual experience," and to a "new identity" that underscores the importance of this narrative in the "development of Spanish American consciousness and thinking."⁶ Other critics have followed in the tracks of Pastor's seminal reading. What raises Cabeza de Vaca to a position of "singular importance in American history," one reader argued, was the "drastic change" he underwent in the "wilderness of North America"; for, whereas "the humanity of the Indians and their way of life did not interest him very much" before his American odyssey, "[t]he shipwreck led to a ... life-changing religious awakening."⁷ In the words of another recent critic, Cabeza de Vaca's narrative "*reveals* his *evolving attitude* toward and relationship to the North American natives," which had "*enlightened* this explorer" in an "*illuminating, redemptive experience*."⁸ In short, Cabeza de Vaca's account appears, in these readings, as more "enlightened," "realistic," and "American" than the Renaissance chronicles of the discovery and conquest. The "American" qualities of his narrative are seen as evidence of a breakdown of European ideology, or false consciousness, during the author's encounter with the "hard fact" of an American "Other," thus pointing forward to an emancipatory "reversal of the project of domination" and the triumph of enlightenment over medieval Manichean fantasy mechanisms in the face of redemptive New World experience.⁹

But while such readings seem plausible enough with respect to the historical person of Cabeza de Vaca himself – whose eight-year stay among Native Americans must surely have had a profound impact on him – they have tended to mystify his text's own ideological inscription and rhetorical sophistication. As Enrique Pupo-Walker has reminded us, all of the published versions of his account were written only *after* his return to Castile and took shape in a "careful series of rewritings."[10] The version most commonly read today, for example, was not published until eighteen years after his return to Spain – in 1555 (in Valladolid); and even the earlier Zamora edition of 1542 was not a "private" journal or memoir, as it is often read,[11] but rather Cabeza de Vaca's highly official report to the emperor, in correspondence with his formal obligations as royal treasurer of the Pánfilo de Narváez expedition. Thus, in their encyclopedic study of the history of Cabeza de Vaca's life, the Narváez expedition, and its literary record, Rolena Adorno and Patrick Pautz have left no doubt as to the thoroughly "retrospective nature" of Cabeza de Vaca's writings by showing how his texts were mediated by the author's various objectives when writing them back in Spain.[12] Particularly, Cabeza de Vaca's proposal for a peaceful approach to Spain's imperial expansion in the Americas was hardly "radical" or "subversive" at the time when Cabeza de Vaca was writing but, on the contrary, complicit with and foundational in a gradual transformation of Spanish imperialist policy from violent to "peaceful conquest."[13] José Rabasa has therefore questioned the "purported originality of Cabeza de Vaca's advocacy of peaceful colonization"; instead he suggests that the "language of love and pacification" in the *Relación* may be seen as but yet another ideology – what he calls the "flip side" of "a menacing regime of terror" dressed in law and reason. Against the grain of a long critical tradition that has separated "story" from "discourse" in this narrative and privileged the former over the latter, Rabasa argues that the discourse of pacification takes priority over the story of shipwreck and captivity in Cabeza de Vaca's narrative, not vice versa.[14]

If the first-hand experience of eyewitnesses such as Cabeza de Vaca in the New World cannot be seen as the cause for this discursive transformation in Spanish imperial policy from conquest to pacification, however, what did cause such a change?[15] After having recognized the "demythification" of an ideology of conquest at work in Cabeza de Vaca's *Relación*, we must go on to investigate the ideology underlying the (early) modern project of "demythification" that Cabeza de Vaca's epic narrative promotes, an "enlightenment" ideology that has made the representation of reality in this text appear to be more "natural," "authentic," and "realistic" to its modern readers than that prevailing in the Renaissance chronicles of discovery and conquest. What's at stake in Cabeza de Vaca's *Relación*, I want to argue, is not so much a conflict between European and (Native) American cultures and ways of knowing – between a European self and an American other – but rather a conflict between two ideas of empire and an epistemic conflict between two ideas of knowledge as they arose in the geo-political dialectic between European expansionism and centralizing monarchy. Cabeza de Vaca's sixteenth-century narrative about the New World may thereby be seen at the forefront of a larger historical process in which the Renaissance Humanism that had underwritten the seignorial system of rights and obligations underpinning the workings of the Holy Roman Empire since the Middle Ages would gradually be supplanted by the new "mercantilist" order of knowledge that would divide intellectual labor in the socio- and geo-political hierarchies of the Baroque state. In other words, the discourse of "demythification" operates in this narrative to the end of displacing "conquest" not only as a way of life but also as a way of knowing and representing: a knowing no longer conceived of as the impressing of the individual subject's will upon the world through the creative power of language but rather as a "learning" and "understanding," by privileging objects over subject and finding over making in the territorialized economies of knowledge production of trans-oceanic empires. The narrative that begins, like Cortés' *Cartas de Relación*, as a "magical" story of conquest, fame, and fortune, is aborted by shipwreck but transforms into a "miraculous" story of pilgrimage that finally leads to the *nostos* of the effaced proto-scientific observer in submission to the supreme volition of the Christian monarch and the royal court historian. The tropes of shipwreck and pilgrimage in Cabeza de Vaca's *Relación* hereby bring to bear powerfully on the reader a long rhetorical tradition in Western culture that narrativizes not only the historical "stripping" of the conquistador by depriving him of his horse, sword, and cape but also a meta-historical "stripping" of his most powerful weapon – his Classical metaphor, which translates and creates New World realities through rhetorical eloquence.

CABEZA DE VACA'S *RELACIÓN*, 1537–1555

As Rolena Adorno and Patrick Pautz have established, there are no fewer than eight different versions of the story of the Narváez expedition in the writing of which Cabeza de Vaca was directly or indirectly involved.[16] Five of these are relevant for my purposes here: (1) the so-called "Joint Report" that three of the four survivors of the Narváez expedition (not including the African slave Estebanico) gave to Viceroy Antonio de Mendoza after their return to New Spain in 1536;[17] (2) the royal chronicler Gonzalo Fernández de Oviedo y Valdés' account in his *Historia general y natural*, which was based on the "Joint Report" and prepared in 1540; (3) the first edition of Cabeza de Vaca's *Relación*, published in Zamora in 1542; (4) Oviedo's addition of a seventh chapter to his earlier six-chapter account of the Pánfilo de Narváez expedition in 1548, after reading Cabeza de Vaca's 1542 *Relación* (in which he commented on the differences between Cabeza de Vaca's account and his own version based on the "Joint Report"); and (5) the second edition of Cabeza de Vaca's account, published in Valladolid in 1555 together with an account of his South American ventures, entitled *Relación y comentarios*. Although the "Joint Report" has been lost, Adorno and Pautz have roughly reconstructed its contents through an analysis of Oviedo's working method and diction.[18] Their analysis shows that between the "Joint Report" (as far as is reconstructable from Oviedo) and the 1542 text, there are major changes, the latter being a substantial expansion of the former. Between the two primary texts – of 1542 and 1555 – there are also minor though significant differences.[19]

Since Andrés González Barcia's eighteenth-century edition, Cabeza de Vaca's narrative has been commonly known as "Naufragios" ("Shipwrecks").[20] Although this designation already appeared in the running heads and table of contents of the 1555 edition, both original sixteenth-century editions of Cabeza de Vaca's account about the Pánfilo de Narváez expedition were entitled not *Naufragios* but rather *Relación*.[21] Generally, this designation identified a text as belonging to a genre that originated, as Roberto González Echevarría has shown, in legal discourse, especially notarial rhetoric, denoting an eyewitness account in a legal dispute. A defining characteristic of the genre of the *relación*, as it originated in the Old World context, was its humble, plain, though highly official character, as well as its appeal to the authority of first-hand experience.[22] Semiotically, the *relación* was characterized by a distinct positionality and directionality in early modern social space, traveling from the private person relating it "upward" to the government official at the receiving end. In the New World context of overseas expansionism during the sixteenth century, however, the term *relación* took on a new meaning, now becoming, as Walter Mignolo has shown, largely synonymous with the terms *historia* (history) and *crónica* (chronicle), "in order to refer to a historiographic text."[23] The reasons for this infiltration of the genre of the "historia" by the legal discourse of the "relación" must be seen in the context not only of an increasing importance of empirical knowledge during the New World discoveries but also of important socio- and geo-political changes in historiographic authorship accompanying Spanish imperial expansionism. Whereas the authority of the historian in the Old World rested mainly on his noble social standing, few of the chroniclers of the New World, typically of humble social origins, could shore up their trustworthiness with names and titles. While the *relación* retains, in its New World context, the conventions of an appeal to eyewitness experience, it becomes defined by its positionality and directionality not only in social space but also in geographic space: it moves "upward" in social space at the same time as it moves "inward" in geographic space from imperial periphery to center in an increasingly territorialized imperial chain of command. Thus, the New World *relación* might travel from colonial provinces to the viceregal capitals, from the viceregal capitals to Seville, and, ultimately, from Seville to Madrid, which first becomes the fixed imperial capital in 1561 under Philip II, who broke with the long tradition of his ancestors, still observed by his father, of moving the court about the empire.[24] This new geography of historiographic authorship in the New World context is particularly manifest in one of the most common sub-genres of the *relación* – the *relación de méritos y servicios* (the account of merits). As González Echevarría points out, "many of the adventures and misadventures, by people who were marginal to society, found their way to legal or quasi-legal documents in which lives large and small were told in search of acquittal or social advancement."[25] During the colonial period, (mostly male) Spanish Americans produced thousands of these *relaciones de méritos*, often paying for the printing out of their own pocket, thus making this type of writing "one of the major genres of publishing in colonial Spanish America."[26]

In several regards, Cabeza de Vaca's first account of his North American odyssey can be seen as serving purposes not unlike that of a conventional *relación de méritos* – to gain royal favors based on the merit of the author's conduct while in service of the Crown.[27] Indeed, his return to Spain seems to have been primarily motivated by his intention to seek an appointment as governor of the still unconquered La Florida, based on his service during the Pánfilo de Narváez expedition. Although he had to learn upon arrival in Spain that the office had already been assigned to the newly rich conqueror of Peru, Hernando de Soto, Cabeza de Vaca was offered a "consolation prize" by being granted a conditional appointment as governor of the La Plata region in December of 1540.[28] By the time that his narrative about Florida was published in Zamora in 1542, Cabeza de Vaca had already embarked for La Plata in order to replace the governor Juan de Ayolas (who was presumed to have died in a conquering expedition) and to bring in line the settlers, who had arrived there under the leadership of Pedro de Mendoza in 1535 but then refused to pay the taxes required by the Crown. Although Cabeza de Vaca would eventually fare better than his counter-part de Soto in North America (who died during the expedition), his South American venture was fraught with difficulties from the start. When he arrived on the scene after a long and arduous inland journey across Brazil, he found himself in a fierce power struggle with the lieutenant governor Domingo de Irala, who had been left in charge after Ayolas' disappearance. Irala and his allies, who considered the arrival of Cabeza de Vaca in La Plata as a threat to the status quo,[29] rose up against his authority under Irala's leadership and, in 1545, shipped him back to Spain in chains in order to indict him before the Council of the Indies for alleged abuse of power.[30] Cabeza de Vaca's *Comentarios* – the report written by his scribe Pero Hernández about his South American venture and published together with the second edition of his *Relación* about La Florida in Valladolid in 1555 – was written mainly to vindicate him from these charges.[31] Thus, while both the 1542 and the 1555 editions of his account about North America were composed in order to gain royal favors, the varying biographical circumstances in which Cabeza de Vaca prepared each edition warrant recognition of, as Adorno and Pautz have argued, "not only . . . two editions of Cabeza de Vaca's narrative but also . . . two conceptions of his work."[32] The 1542 edition was primarily addressed to the emperor; it was written in part to support Cabeza de Vaca's application for another imperial office and in part as his belated fulfillment of a formal requirement incumbent on his previous duties as the royal treasurer of the Narváez expedition, as explicitly stipulated in the instructions he had received from the Crown in his letter of appointment in 1527 – "to make a particular account . . . so that we may be informed of everything."[33] The 1555 publication, by contrast, which included both Hernández' account of the La Plata venture and Cabeza de Vaca's *Relación* about La Florida, was mainly an "exercise in the recovery of political and social prestige and the last public action Cabeza de Vaca took to defend his past governorship and his good name."[34]

But while the 1555 edition of Cabeza de Vaca's narrative seems indeed more clearly conceived as a public text than had been the 1542 edition, it is important to bear in mind what a "public" text was in sixteenth-century Habsburg Spain. Neither the legal stipulations of Cabeza de Vaca's official appointment in 1527 nor his own personal interest in an apologia can fully account for why his accounts were printed. On the one hand, a printed version went beyond what was required by the specific terms of his appointment – presumably already satisfied by either one of the previous two (and now lost) manuscript accounts filed by two or three of the survivors about the Indies – which was to make an official (though not public) record for the archive. On the other hand, it is also noteworthy that, unlike many of the *relaciones de méritos y servicios* of other conquerors, Cabeza de Vaca's 1542 publication was not financed by himself but rather by a book trader from Medina del Campo, Juan Pablo Musetti, and printed while Cabeza de Vaca was in South America by the two Zamora printers Augustín de Paz and Juan Picardo.[35] While Adorno and Pautz have persuasively discredited earlier arguments that Cabeza de Vaca's 1542 text had been pirated and published by others without his consent, it seems clear enough that the moving forces behind this first publication were not his own. If this can be seen as a testimony to the close inter-relationship between the history of printing and European imperialism in the New World, it is significant that the frontispiece of Cabeza de Vaca's 1542 account was adorned not by his own family crest but rather by the Habsburg imperial eagle (see Illustration 2.1). As Adorno and Pautz show, the printers had used the same woodcut of the Habsburg coat of arms in their earlier publication of the works of the imperial chronicler Florian de Ocampo, all of which were published "with royal endorsement" and "at the emperor's command."[36] While the interests of the book-seller Musetti, as well as the printers Paz and Picardo, in these publications must be seen as primarily private and economic in nature, the Zamora and Medina del Campo printing and bookselling establishments not only profited handsomely from their close relations with the court but apparently also aimed to exploit this connection by marketing Cabeza de Vaca's narrative with a similar aura of official approbation and authority.

If the historical circumstances surrounding the 1542 publication of Cabeza de Vaca's narrative still primarily illustrate how early modern printing businesses sought to enhance the authority of their books by availing themselves of their ties to state officialdom,[37] the 1555 edition of Valladolid exemplifies how the expanding printing business was also increasingly co-opted by the early modern state, which had begun to involve itself in the circulation of printed texts as early as the Catholic Kings' royal decree, issued from Toledo in 1502, which stipulated that books of learning published in Spain and imported books of whatever variety henceforth required a royal license.[38] However, of overall greater importance than the actual repression of printed books during this pre-Tridentine era – when many books still circulated that were later condemned by the Inquisition – was the active promotion, through royal patronage and protection, of certain works that the Crown deemed desirable, while leaving others to the vicissitudes of a market-place without copyright protection laws. First, beginning with the publication of Antonio de Nebrija's famous dictionary of the Castilian language, printed at Salamanca in 1492, the Catholic Kings initiated the granting of the so-called "royal privilege" ("privilegio royal"), which prohibited unauthorized re-printing of a work so designated (as well as the

2.1 Frontispiece of Cabeza de Vaca's *Relación* (Zamora, 1542).

importation of other editions of it) for a determined period and stipulated severe penalties for any infractions.[39] Second, the Habsburg crown under Charles V established the office of "His Royal Majesty's Printer," the official organ of the state, endowed with special patronage and protections by the Crown in an increasingly competitive book market. Significantly, it was the first appointee to this office during the court's residence at Valladolid, Francisco Fernández de Córdova, who published Cabeza de Vaca's *Relación y comentarios* in 1555.[40] This fact is helpful for understanding why this edition once again displayed on its frontispiece not the author's own family crest but rather Charles V's coat of arms – despite the fact that this time Cabeza de Vaca himself was surely involved in its preparation, with the author now at court in Valladolid (see Illustration 2.2).[41] In keeping with the tradition of patronizing and protecting certain works favored by the Crown, Cabeza de Vaca's book was also published "con privilegio."[42] The price of the book was thus fixed at 85 maravedis, and Cabeza de Vaca was granted the exclusive right of printing and selling for a period of ten years, stipulating a fine of 10,000 maravedis for any violations of his copyright.[43] Significantly, however, while these terms were still referred to as a "privilegio" on the title page of *Relación y comentarios* (in keeping with the long tradition of this practice), the actual elaboration of specifics in an appended document refers to this agreement not as a "privilegio" but rather as a "licencia y facultad," a "licence and authorization."[44] This "license to print" had apparently been added in light of a new policy, signed into law the following year, requiring that no book "dealing with matters pertaining to these our Indies" be printed without a royal license.[45] Thus, the terminological change in reference to the mutual relationship entered into by Crown and author in Cabeza de Vaca's 1555 re-edition reflects a larger shift in imperial policy, from a predominantly pro-active involvement through patronage and protection to a restrictive involvement through censor and suppression with regard to publications about the Indies.[46] This shift, manifest in the preliminary matter of Cabeza de Vaca's 1555 text, suggests a complex cultural composite of interests in the New World subject matter of the narrative, involving not only privately interested authors, printers, and book-traders, as well as the growing curiosity on the part of the reading public, but also the official interests of the state. Thus, as Jürgen Habermas would remind us, "the public" in Habsburg Spain was synonymous with "state-related" and the authority to police. "To publish" meant in this context not so much to perform "for" as it meant to perform "before" the public.[47] The social positionality and directionality of the published versions of Cabeza de Vaca's *Relación* in sixteenth-century imperial culture must therefore be

2.2 Frontispiece of Cabeza de Vaca's *Relación y comentarios* (Valladolid, 1555).

seen as moving not only "upward" and "inward" from the private individual to the state official or court society, but also as moving "downward" and "outward" from the imperial absolutist monarchical court to the royal subject in imperial Spain and her colonial dependencies.

Given the legalistic connotations of the generic designation "relación" in sixteenth-century Spain on the one hand and the "public" nature of Cabeza de Vaca's accounts on the other, it is necessary to place the textual history of his narrative not only in the biographical context of the author's personal legal troubles and relations with the court, but also in the context of the Crown's own legal troubles – namely, its struggle in a wider debate over the constitution of the Spanish empire. Cabeza de Vaca's narrative was summoned in this public courtroom at a critical moment and was superbly equipped to bear testimony on behalf of Habsburg centralizing geopolitics.

THE GEOPOLITICS OF "PACIFICATION"

The early expeditions of discovery and conquest had been largely private enterprises encouraged by the Crown with grants of political and economic privileges, a tradition that harked back to the seignorial empire of the Middle Ages and especially the *reconquista*, the Christian re-conquest of Spain from the Moors.[48] The practice of awarding the American conquerors an *encomienda* (a grant of native tribute labor) had its legal foundation in the medieval *Libri feudorum,* which had codified the contractual relationship of "obligations and rights" between emperor and feudal lords in which the latter expected royal favors in exchange for loyalty and military service.[49] However, as early as the Catholic Kings' dealings with Columbus, the Crown, while realizing its dependency on private initiative in the overseas conquests, had been suspicious of the conquerors' quasi-feudal privileges and did not miss an opportunity for re-appropriating administrative authority over the American territories. Gradually, the Crown abandoned its earlier, "liberal" policy and "undertook to recover sovereignty in its overseas territories" by revoking many of the privileges conceded earlier in a long series of legislative acts. Consequently, Clarence Henry Haring writes, the descendants of the conquistadors, the Creoles, found themselves "debarred from all high posts of administration by the old aristocracies of the metropolis," thus accentuating the "tendencies to centralization and uniformity."[50] In 1524 – three years before the embarkation of the Pánfilo de Narváez expedition – the Crown had established the Council of the Indies, located in Seville, in order to oversee all government activity in the Americas.[51] A year later, it issued the *Ordenanzas sobre el buen tratamiento de los Indios*

(Ordinances for the good treatment of the Indians), tacitly targeted at the American conquerors in its implication that the Indians were not currently receiving "good treatment." In 1528, the Crown established the Audiencia in Mexico, a council of royally appointed judges, thereby supplanting Cortés as chief magistrate and governor of New Spain.[52] In 1535 – one year before Cabeza de Vaca's return to New Spain – the first viceroy, Antonio de Mendoza, arrived in Mexico and the Crown enacted laws that limited the original grant of *encomiendas* "in perpetuity" to the conquerors and their descendants to a duration of two or three lifetimes. In 1537 – the year of Cabeza de Vaca's return to Spain – Pope Paul III issued the bull *Sublimis Deus*, which asserted the capacities and rights of the American Indians as children of God and direct subjects of the emperor, the implication being that they could not legally be held in personal servitude by the conquerors.[53] In 1542 – the year of the first publication of *Relación* in Zamora – the Crown passed the so-called "New Laws," which overwrote the earlier Laws of Burgos and stipulated that all Indian slaves forced into personal service for individual Spaniards were to be emancipated immediately and that all *encomiendas* were to revert to the Crown upon the death of their present incumbent. This was the most serious blow yet to the aristocratic pretension of the American conquerors. "At one stroke," writes David Brading, the Crown "sought to terminate the institution which had been the foundation of the society established by the conquerors."[54]

Not surprisingly, this shift in imperial policy was greeted with outrage and defiance by the conquerors throughout the Americas and even led to civil war in Peru and the death of viceroy Blasco Núñez de Vela. In New Spain, viceroy Antonio de Mendoza saved himself from a similar fate only by invoking the power inherent in his office to suspend the implementation of the New Laws until the Crown had listened to the protests of the *encomenderos'* agents, immediately dispatched from Mexico to Spain. The Council of the Indies finally compromised in 1545 by allowing the grants to continue after the death of the original grantee for another lifetime and by implementing the *repartimientos de labor* (obligatory drafts of native laborers from each village for work either in agriculture or in the mines), albeit now in return for a modest daily wage. Nevertheless, for the conquerors, these developments signaled that the Crown was "determined to assert its authority, defining the encomienda as a pension charged on royal tribute rather than as a seignorial benefice." While in Peninsular Spain and metropolitan Europe a "growing tendency to absolutism, bureaucracy, and mercantilism was prevailing over lineage and great seignorial houses," the conquistadors and their descendants repeatedly demonstrated that they understood the world "in feudal terms."[55]

In 1550, the legal battle over the future of the Spanish empire between colonial neo-feudalism and Habsburg absolutism came to a head in Valladolid, in the debates between Juan Ginés Sepúlveda and Bartolomé de Las Casas. The former represented the interests of the American conquerors in arguing that the Indians were, in the Aristotelian sense, "natural slaves," while the latter's indictments of colonial abuses and arguments for a peaceful approach to conversions – doubtlessly well-founded and sincere in their noble intention – were readily co-opted by the Habsburg monarchy in order to justify its new course of imperial administration. In short, what was at stake in Valladolid was, according to Brading, "the political constitution of the Spanish empire in America."[56]

Thus, both content and generic designation of Cabeza de Vaca's accounts must be seen in the context of this legal struggle between the Habsburg centralizing geopolitics and the insubordinate conquerors' neo-feudal aspirations. During the 1540s, the "demythification" of an ideology of conquest was hardly a "subversive" ideological enterprise but rather had become an integral strategy in absolutist political propaganda. The Habsburg monarchs thereby fashioned themselves as the harbingers of Christ's millennial reign of peace after a victorious struggle against seignorial discord, tyranny, and confusion. Thus, Charles V – the addressee of the 1542 Proem of Cabeza de Vaca's account – frequently fashioned himself as the new Augustus, the emperor of peace. In the famous portrait commemorating his victory at Mühlberg, commissioned from the Italian painter Titiano, for example, he is seen riding through a landscape at sunset conveying the peaceful calm after the raging battle has ended; similarly, in the sculpture commissioned from the artist Leone y Pampeo Leoni, we find him in his favorite pose of "dominating over fury" (see Illustrations 2.3 and 2.4). On 16 April 1550, he suspended all further conquests until the Valladolid debates were concluded in September later that year, and his successor, Philip II (1554–98), replaced the word "conquest" with "pacification" altogether when defining the new official Spanish policy for the administration of its American territories.[57] In a set of ordinances issued in 1573, the Council of the Indies laid down definitively the terms concerning the Indies: "Discoveries are not to be called conquests," they stipulated:

Since we wish them to be carried out peacefully and charitably, we do not want the use of that term to offer any excuse for the employment of force or the causing of injury to the Indians... They are to gather information about the various tribes, languages and divisions of the Indians in the province and about the lords whom they obey. They are to seek friendship with them through trade and barter, showing them great love and tenderness and giving them objects to which they will take a liking.[58]

2.3 Titiano's portrait of Charles V at Mühlberg.

As Tzvetan Todorov has lucidly pointed out in his commentary on these ordinances, it is not "conquests" that are to be banished but only "the *word conquest*; 'pacification' is nothing but another word to designate the same thing." "Pacification" thus functions "within the colonialist ideology, against the enslavement ideology."[59] Indeed, whereas the word "conquest" had, in its Latin root *conquaerere*, merely meant "to seek out" or "bring together," it now became associated, in the letters of Las Casas and the law, with the "tyrannical, Mohammedan, abusive, improper, and infernal"

2.4 Leone y Pompeo Leoni's sculpture of *Charles V Dominating Fury*.

practices of the conquerors.[60] If the legitimacy of Spanish imperialism in America and the subjugation of the American Indians to Spanish rule were thus never at issue in this substitution of "conquest" by "pacification," what was very much at stake was the question of who would exercise imperial power in the Americas and reap the spoils of conquest/pacification of the New World.

Most crucial in this geo-political tug of war was the ownership of interpretative control and authority over words and signs in the production of knowledge about the empire, especially since the invention of the printing press and the increasing importance of empirical information in overseas enterprises seemed to have quickened the magic power of metaphors "translating" the New World into the Old.[61] Perhaps the most memorable and originary instance in the history of the New World attesting to the geo-political problem of the spatial control of knowledge in colonial settler empires is the circumstance under which the very first permanent European settlement on the American continent was founded: Hernán Cortés' colony at Veracruz in 1519. After having blatantly defied the explicit injunction issued by his imperial superior, the royally appointed governor of Cuba, Diego Velázquez, *not* to found any settlements on *tierra firme*, Cortés, in a sophistic and convoluted rhetorical maneuver in his first letter to Charles V, invoked the medieval code of Spanish Roman Law, the Siete Partidas, in order to explain to the monarch why his famous command "¡Quemad las naves!" ("Burn the ships!") represented not an act of treason but rather of loyalty to the king.[62]

Troubled by the potential implications of such rhetorical ingenuity for royal sovereignty in the New World, the Habsburg crown launched a large-scale campaign in "literary production and suppression" in order to centralize control over the production of knowledge in the imperial metropolis.[63] Thus, the Crown established the office of the *cronista mayor*, the official historian commissioned by the court.[64] Also, it issued various decrees banning the texts that had articulated the neo-feudal ideology of conquest: Cortés' *Cartas de relación*, which had gone through several editions in Spanish, Latin, French, and Italian, were banned in March 1527 throughout the empire; the works of López de Gómara (who had exalted Cortés' achievements), as well all the other histories of the conquest, were banned from exportation to America in 1553[65]; and the romances of chivalry, so cherished by the American conquistadors for supplying the Old World cultural subtext of *reconquista* for the conquerors' New World endeavors,[66] had since 1531 been banned – albeit unsuccessfully – from exportation to the colonies.[67] Finally, when, during the 1550s, there was an upsurge of publications on the Indies – including texts as diverse as those of Gómara, Cieza de León, Zárate and Las Casas – the state became alarmed and, in 1556, issued the restrictions on publications relating to the New World already in evidence on the preliminary matter of Cabeza de Vaca's publication the year before.[68]

Thus, the period between Cabeza de Vaca's shipwreck in North America in 1527 and the second publication of his account of these events in 1555 marked a transformation of imperial policy in the Americas and a cultural "retroping" of Spanish imperial identity in the course of which the Renaissance dream of conquest was exposed as falsehood.[69] This discursive shift from "conquest" to "pacification" in official political discourse, while inspired by some well-intentioned Dominican monks, must primarily be seen in the context of a geo-political dialectic between Habsburg absolutism promoting a discourse of "pacification" and a colonial (*criollo*) neo-feudalism promoting a discourse of "conquest." As we will presently see in a reading of Cabeza de Vaca's *Relación*, the author therefore ascribes the reasons for the Florida expedition's failure to certain participants' "false" chivalric ideology of *caballería* while firmly aligning himself with the absolutist and mercantilist values of the Habsburg state. In order to illustrate the dense rhetorical signification of this text, I trace the elaboration of this theme through several versions of Cabeza de Vaca's account.

THE SHIPWRECK OF CONQUEST

As Adorno and Pautz have shown, it is a mistake to assume (as many scholars had previously done) that the 1555 version of Cabeza de Vaca's account is merely a corrected and polished version of the 1542 edition; rather, they argue, the Valladolid text "reconceptualizes the original account" of 1542 for a different context and audience: "The modifications in the 1555 edition are not linguistic and stylistic but substantive."[70] While I would agree that many of the substantive differences between the two versions must be seen in the context of Cabeza de Vaca's personal biography – and that, from this point of view, both versions served "equally well" in the varying circumstances in which they were written – I would argue, first, that there are also subtle but significant linguistic differences between the various versions of Cabeza de Vaca's account which point to the author's growing responsiveness to the geo-political interests of the imperial state as discussed above; and, second, that from a rhetorical point of view the textual history of Cabeza de Vaca's *Relación*, including the unpublished as well as the two published versions of 1542 and 1555, does manifest a gradual growth in refinement when seen in the larger cultural context of an emerging imperial culture in sixteenth-century Spain.

Most of the events related in the first part of the *Relación* – leading up to the demise of the Narváez expedition – may be said to revolve around the underlying thematic conflict between an individualist and a corporatist idea of the imperial project. Even before the expedition's departure from its Caribbean base in Santo Domingo, this conflict manifests itself for the first time when "nos faltaron de nuestra armada más de ciento y quarenta hombres que se quisieron quedar allí por los partidos y promesas que los de la tierra les hizieron" ("more than a hundred and forty of the men deserted us, for they decided to stay there, influenced by the offers and promises made to them by the folk of the island").[71] The decision not to return to the ship due to individualist ambition jeopardizes the imperial mission, threatening to disrupt the chain of command that links the sovereign at the top and center with the common foot-soldier at the bottom and periphery of the imperial order. The conflict between leaving and returning soon evolves into a disagreement between two ways of proceeding once the North American mainland comes into sight: the governor and leader of the expedition, Pánfilo de Narváez, favors leaving the ships behind and penetrating the interior by horse. Others, such as Cabeza de Vaca himself and the imperial "scribe" along on the expedition, firmly oppose leaving the ships:

> Yo respondia que me parescia que por ninguna manera devia dexar los navios sin que primero quedassen en puerto seguro y poblado . . . El governador siguio su parescer y lo que los otros le consejavan. Yo, vista su determinacion, requerile de parte de Vuestra Magestad que no dexasse los navios sin que quedassen en puerto y seguros, y ansi lo pedi por testimonio al escrivano que alli teniamos. (1555: Favata/Fernández, 18–19)

> I replied that I thought we should by no means leave the ships until they were first settled in a safe harbor where there were people . . . The governor followed his own inclinations and the advice of the others; seeing his determination, I adjured him in Your Majesty's name not to leave the ships unless they were in a harbor and safe, and requested it in writing through the scribe that we had with us. (1555: López Morillas, 14–15)

There is more at stake in this passage than a factual recording of a private disagreement over the best means of transportation in pre-Hispanic Florida. Alejandro González Acosta has argued that there is an allegorical affinity in much of early modern literature, such as Cabeza de Vaca's text, between the

image of the ship and the image of the mother, corresponding to the motific homology of shipwreck and orphanage. The ship, he argues, represents the "mother, the protective breast." In shipwreck, "the (last) umbilical cord ruptures which remains with the 'matria'. The castaway-orphan is born into a hostile world, deprived of his protective uterus and his isolating amniotic liquid."[72] The sixteenth-century Spanish reader, however, would have found a historically more concrete allegorical referent for the ship in Habsburg public culture – the Habsburg monarchy, as emblematized by the Argonautic myth. The Habsburgs fashioned themselves, as Mary Tanner has shown, in direct lineage to Jason, as the redeemers of the Golden Fleece: "the Argo symbolized the ideology of the Hapsburgs, who distilled the imperial myth into its modern crystalline form."[73] The year after the publication of Cabeza de Vaca's *Relación* at Valladolid, in 1556, Philip II had, upon his acceptance of the sovereignty of the Netherlands and Burgundy, even set out on a ship on which was built and painted a copy of the original Argo.

Of course, the appropriation of the ship metaphor by the corporate state was hardly particular to Habsburg culture but had a tradition at least as old as Horace. Similarly, the association of the horse with aristocratic individualism, autonomy, and cunning in Western culture is at least as old as Odysseus' famous feat at Troy. Significantly, in Cabeza de Vaca's *Relación*, the expedition's wreck proceeds in a straight plot line from the governor's decision to proceed by horse. It is not, however, the ship itself that is wrecked – there is no "shipwreck" in Cabeza de Vaca's account – but rather the expeditionaries that chose to abandon it: after the ships have left to meet up with the landed troops in another spot farther west and the penetration of the interior of Florida by horse has failed, the desperate men construct four rafts in order to regain contact with the ships. When Cabeza de Vaca and the men on his boat can no longer keep pace with that of the governor (who had kept the healthiest men to himself), he implored his superior:

que para poderle seguir me diesse un cabo de su varca, y el me respondio que no harian ellos poco si solos aquella noche pudiessen llegar a tierra. Yo le dixe que, pues via la poca possibilidad que en nosotros avia para poder sequirle y hazer lo que avia mandado, que me dixiesse que era lo que mandava que yo hiziesse. El me respondio que ya no era tiempo de mandar unos a otros, que cada uno hiziesse lo que mejor le pareciesse que era para salvar la vida, que el ansi lo entendia de hazer. Y diziendo esto se alargo con su varca. Y como no le pude seguir, arribe sobre la otra varca que yva metida en la mar, la qual me espero. (1555: Favata/Fernández, 44)

to give me a line from his boat to help me follow him, and he answered me that if they themselves reached land that night, it was as much as they could do. I told him that in view of the little chance we had to follow him and do what he had ordered, he had better tell me what his orders to me were. He answered that this was no time for some to give orders to others, that each must do what seemed best to him to save his life, and that that was what he intended to do. And so saying, he drew away his with his boat, and as I could not follow I caught up with the other boat that was well out to sea, which waited for me. (1555: López Morillas, 37)

The subsequent wreck of all the rafts and the death of Pánfilo de Narváez' band (of which the reader learns later in the narrative) are thus attributed to the breakdown of the corporate imperial body in America due to the individualist ambitions of autonomous *hidalgos*.

As Pier Luigi Crovetto has pointed out in his analysis of the formalization of the shipwreck motif in the literatures of the New World as a prefiguration of the novel, the protagonist typically suffers shipwreck following a series of "multiple disobedience against paternal authority (the king)." The loss of institutional contact with paternal authority results "in an immediate and successive mutation characterized as a 'barbarization.'"[74] In *Relación*, this "barbarization" resulting from aristocratic insubordination against the paternal authority of the monarch is realized by the gradual descent into chaos, anarchy, and even cannibalism of Narváez and his faction.

[E]stando desembarcados, el governador avia revocado el poder que el contador tenia de lugarteniente suyo, y dio el cargo a un capitan que traya consigo que se dezia Pantoja...Allende desto, Pantoja, que por teniente avia quedado, les hazia mal tratamiento, y no lo podiendo sufrir, Sotomayor, hermano de Vasco Porcallo, el de la ysla de Cuba, que en la armada avia venido por maestre de campo, se rebolvio con el y le dio un palo de que Pantoja quedo muerto. Y assi se fueron acabando. Y los que morian, los otros los hazian tasajos. (1555: Favata/Fernández, 67–8)

[W]hen they had disembarked, the governor revoked the authority that the auditor had had as his lieutenant and gave the office to a captain whom he had brought with him, whose name was Pantoja...this Pantoja, who had become lieutenant, treated them very badly; and Sotomayor, the brother of Vasco Porcallo, from the island of Cuba, who had come in the fleet as an officer of high rank, was unable to bear it. He rebelled against him and gave him such a blow that Pantoja died of it; and so they gradually died off. And the others dried the flesh of the ones who died. (1555: López Morillas, 57–8)

The first half of Cabeza de Vaca's *Relación* thus articulates an ideological opposition in which an older idea of empire – the empire of "(re-)conquest," held together by the voluntary loyalty of largely autonomous neo-feudal conquerors – is being supplanted by a newer idea of empire – an empire of "peace," based on a corporate, centralized state.

This allegorical signification is especially apparent when we compare the text of the Valladolid edition of 1555 to that of the earlier Zamora edition of 1542 and the "Joint Report" (as far as is evident from Oviedo).[75] In both of Cabeza de Vaca's published versions, the thematic opposition between desertion of and loyalty to the Habsburg state, as emblematized by the ship, is notably accentuated while the author carefully positions himself on the "right" side of this ideological divide. Thus, when arriving at the port of Santo Domingo, the published versions add that the captains of the ships go on land while "I" – mentioned for the first time here – remains "en la mar con los pilotos, . . . porque aquel era un muy mal puerto y se solían perder muchos navios en él" ("at sea with the pilots, . . . for that harbor was a very poor one and many ships were often lost there").[76] The subsequent passages in which we encounter the narrative "I" further elaborate this opposition. For example, after relating the altercation between Cabeza de Vaca and the governor with regard to the latter's plan to proceed by horse, Cabeza de Vaca inserts a digression from the plot which was absent from the "Joint Report" as far as we can tell from Oviedo:[77]

Y despues desto proveydo, en presencia de los que alli estavan me dixo que pues yo tanto estorvava y temia la entrada por tierra, que me quedasse y tomasse cargo de los navios y la gente que en ellos quedava, y poblasse si yo llegasse primero que el. Yo me escuse desto. Y despues de salidos de alli aquella misma tarde, diziendo que no le parescia que de nadie se podia fiar aquello me embio a dezir que me rogava que tomasse cargo dello. Y viendo que importunandome tanto, yo todavia me excusava, me pregunto que era la causa porque huya de aceptallo, a lo qual respondi que yo huya de encargarme de aquello porque tenia por cierto y sabia que el no avia de ver mas los navios ni los navios a el, y que esto entendia viendo que tan sin aparejo se entravan por la tierra adentro, y que yo queria mas aventurarme al peligro que el y los otros se aventuravan, y passar por lo que el y ellos passassen, que no encargarme de los navios y dar ocasion que se dixesse que como avia contradicho la entrada me quedava por temor, y mi honrra anduviesse en disputa, y que yo queria mas aventurar la vida que poner mi honrra en esta condicion. El, viendo que comigo no aprovechava, rogo a otros muchos que me hablassen en ello y me lo rogassen, a los quales respondi lo mismo que a el. Y ansi proveyo por su teniente para que quedasse en los navios un alcalde que traya que se llamava Caravallo. (1555: Favata/Fernández, 19–20)

After all was ready, in the presence of all those who were there, he told me that because I had made so much trouble and feared going inland, I should stay there and take charge of the ships and the crews who remained in them, and set up a settlement if I arrived before him. I refused to do this. After we left there, on that same afternoon, saying that he believed he could not trust anyone else to do it, he sent a message to say that he begged me to undertake the duty. And, seeing that even though he insisted so urgently I continued to refuse, he asked me why I was reluctant to accept? To which I replied that I did not want to accept that duty because I felt certain, and was convinced, that he would never see the ships again, nor the ships him, and that I believed this because I could see how ill equipped they were for starting inland, and that I preferred to run the risk that they were running and endure what he and they were enduring, rather than take charge of the ships and let it be said that, because I had objected to the expedition inland, I had stayed behind out of fear, and that my honor would be impugned; and that I preferred to risk my life rather than place my honor in that position. The governor, seeing that he could not persuade me, asked many others to speak to me about it and beg me to do it, to whom I replied as I had to him; and so he appointed his lieutenant to stay with the ships, an officer named Caravallo who had come with him. (1555: López Morillas, 15–16)

The effect of this added passage is two-fold. On the one hand, as Adorno and Pautz have pointed out, it "presents himself as placing honor above personal safety" and thus as a "loyal, brave, and honor-bound subject of the emperor."[78] On the other hand, it explains how he, despite his alleged protestations against proceeding by horse, ended up as part of the equestrian conquering expedition that abandoned the ships after all. The characterization of the horsemen as a representation of chivalric disloyalty is finally completed by the inclusion of a passage in both of Cabeza de Vaca's versions which relates a plot to desert the governor but which was apparently again absent from the "Joint Report":[79]

[E]ntre la gente de cavallo se començo la mayor parte dellos a yr secretamente, pensando hallar ellos por si remedio y desamparar al governador y a los enfermos, los quales estavan sin algunas fuerças y poder. Mas como entre ellos avia muchos hijosdalgo y hombres de buena suerte, no quisieron que esto passasse sin dar parte al governador y a los officiales de Vuestra Magestad. Y como les afeamos su proposito y les pusimos delante el tiempo, en que desamparavan a su capitan y los que estavan enfermos y sin poder, y apartarse sobre todo del servicio de Vuestra Magestad, acordaron de quedar, y que lo que fuesse de uno fuesse de todos, sin que ninguno desamparasse a otro. (1555: Favata/Fernández, 33)

[M]ost of the horsemen began to steal away, in the belief that they could find some recourse for themselves and abandon the governor and the invalids, who were absolutely weak and powerless. But as there were many nobles and men of good family among them, they refused to allow this to happen without reporting it to the governor and Your Majesty's officers; and as we reproached them for their intentions and reminded them of the plight in which they were leaving their captain and those who were ill and powerless, and, in particular, for leaving Your Majesty's service, they agreed that they would remain and that the fate of one would be that of all, and that none would abandon another. (1555: López Morillas, 27)

While the breakdown of the imperial chain of command risked by "them" (the horsemen) is still averted here by the intervention of "us" ("men of good family"), disaster is inevitable when the governor reveals himself to be one of "them."

Apart from sharpening the allegorical opposition between equestrian conquerors and pedestrian subjects, Cabeza de Vaca's published versions also manifest a keen awareness of sensitive religious matters. Habsburg policy in America had aimed to dismantle the de-centralized authority of the mendicant orders, especially the Franciscans, by disciplining missionaries such as Diego de Landa – one of the most fervent advocates of violent conquest and infamous for the cruelties he had perpetrated in Yucatán – only to reinstate them later as secular bishops subordinated to the church hierarchy and subjected to the watchful eye of the Inquisition.[80] Most important in this project was the appropriation by the state of the authoritative language of Christianity that had been used in order to justify crusades, conquests, and re-conquests during centuries of struggle between Christian knights and Muslim "infidels." In Cabeza de Vaca's *Relación*, the Manichean opposition between Christians and heathens, which had structured the chronicles of the conquest and also his own narrative before the relation of his "shipwreck," yields to a new opposition between *two kinds* of Christians: the nominal, "false" Christians – whom Las Casas would refer to as the "so-called Christians"[81] (here: "Christians") – and the "true" Christians following the "pacific" approach to Indian conversion ostensibly promoted by the Habsburg state (here: Christians). Interestingly, as Adorno and Pautz' comparative analysis of Oviedo and Cabeza de Vaca's 1542 text shows, the latter "goes much further than Oviedo (and therefore the Joint Report) in claiming serious conflict with the Spanish slave hunters whom the men encountered in Sinaloa."[82] This suggests that Cabeza de Vaca's famous antipathy to slave-raids and conquests seems to have crystallized only *after* he had returned to Spain. In any case, it is only there and then that Cabeza de Vaca constructs the strong opposition between himself (and his three compatriots) on the one hand and the "Christians" who want to convert the Indians through conquest and enslavement on the other. The Indians found and Christianized in northern New Spain by Cabeza de Vaca toward the end of his journey are subsequently persuaded only with difficulty to trust the "Christians" and settle down in peace. The 1542 version reads here:

E después que los huvimos embiado, debaxo de cautela los cristianos nos embiaron con un alcalde que se llamava Zebreros y con él otros tres cristianos, donde parece quanto se engañan los pensamientos de los hombres, que nosotros andávamos a

les buscar libertad, y quando pensávamos que la teníamos, succedió tan al contrario. Y por apartarnos de conversación de los indios, nos llevaron por los montes
despoblados, a fin que no viéssemos lo que ellos hazían ni sus tratamientos,
porque tenían acordados de ir a dar en los indios que embíavamos assegurados y de
paz. (1542: Adorno/Pautz, 1: 252)

And after we had sent them away the Christians sent us off under the guard of
an *alcalde* who was named Cebreros and three other Christians with him, from
which it is evident how much men's thoughts deceive them, for we went to them
seeking liberty and when we thought we had it, it turned out to be so much to the
contrary. And in order to remove us from conversation with the Indians, they led
us through areas depopulated and overgrown so that we would not see what they
were doing nor their conduct, because they had conspired to go and attack the
Indians whom we had sent away reassured and in peace. (1542: Adorno/Pautz, 1: 253)

The 1555 version, by contrast, reads in the same place:

Despues que ovimos embiado a los indios en paz, y regraciandoles el trabajo que
con nosotros avian passado, los christianos nos embiaron debaxo de cautela a un
Zebreros alcalde, y con el otros dos, los quales nos llevaron por los montes y
despoblados por apartarnos de la conversacion de los indios y porque no viessemos
ni entendiessemos lo que de hecho hizieron, donde paresce quanto se engañan
los pensamientos de los hombres, que nosotros andavamos a les buscar libertad,
y quando pensavamos que la teniamos, suscedio tan al contrario. (1555: Favata/
Fernández, 131)

After we had sent off the Indians in peace, thanking them for the hardships they
had endured with us, the Christians delivered us under guard to a certain Zebreros,
a justice of the peace, and two other officials who were with him. These led us
through forests and empty lands in order to keep us from conversing with Indians
and from either seeing or hearing what they had in fact done. From this fact appears how often men's thoughts are frustrated, for we wanted only to seek freedom
for the Indians, and when we thought we had done so the exact opposite
occurred. (1555: López Morillas, 114–15)

The later version adds that Cabeza de Vaca had sent away the Indians
"in peace" after "thanking" them and that the "Christians," by contrast,
had accompanied them under guard in order to prevent Cabeza de Vaca
from seeing and "understanding" ("ni entendiessimos") what had been
done to the Indians. Furthermore, the sequence of sentences is altered,
putting the reflection on the futility of human designs *after* relating the
willful deception by the "Christians." The effect of this revision is the
accentuation of the contrast between Cabeza de Vaca and the "Christians"
while linking more clearly the futility of human designs to do good (his
failure to secure the Indians' freedom) to the *active* deceptiveness on the
part of the "Christians," who cunningly led him into a "forest" ("montes")
by creating false truths. What *appears* to be a struggle between Christians

and infidels in the New World *resembling* the Spanish struggle against the Moors in the Old World of signs is "in truth," Cabeza de Vaca suggests, a struggle between "false" and "true" Christianity – between a religion of conquest on the one hand and of pacification on the other.

Thus, the textual history of Cabeza de Vaca's account manifests a growing rhetorical acumen that suggests an elevated sensitivity and obligation to the demands of a transforming Habsburg imperial culture on the part of the author, once again "held in respect as a man of professional competence and experience" after the severest terms of his previous sentence had been lifted by court and king and his record as governor of La Plata had been vindicated.[83] His narrative constructs, in the later versions more persuasively than in the earlier ones, an opposition between two distinct ideas of empire. The chivalric worldview that still pervades the beginning of the narrative – when the expedition set out to "conquer and govern" La Florida – appears, from the point of view of the narrative's end, as a world of madness in false resemblances, a "Baroque" view of the world as a "world turned up-side down."[84] Moreover, the "de-mythification" of an ideology of conquest in Cabeza de Vaca's narrative entails a shift not only in the way that the subject perceives the world but also, as we will presently see, in the way he *knows* the world, as a "magic" New World of individual empowerment yields to a New World of misfortunes, humiliation, and pilgrimage.

FROM MAGIC TO MIRACLE

Following the account of his shipwreck and captivity, Cabeza de Vaca's narrative relates the events of his journey through North America, including a number of miraculous healings and, in one famous instance, even the resuscitation of a dead person. The miraculous incidents related in this part of Cabeza de Vaca's account have been subject to much controversy among historians and theologians since the sixteenth century as well as the focus of great fascination among modern literary critics.[85] José Rabasa, for example, has read this narrative as "a text that brings to light what should have remained secret" and argued, borrowing from Freud, that it manifests a "repression" of a Native American "magical" knowledge that had been experienced by the author during his journey in a world where "magic sense, works" and that is now trying to speak from his text.[86] However, it would be a mistake to identify magic too easily with "Amerindian knowledge" that is "contrary to Western values" in the sixteenth-century context. There would not have been any doubt in the minds of Cabeza de Vaca's early modern readers "that magic makes sense" because magic had a long tradition also in European culture and was still widely practiced in Europe.[87] As recent historians of religion have shown, the forms of Christianity that prevailed in early sixteenth-century Spain were a far cry from the Christianity of the intellectuals and inquisitors that would later prevail during the Counter-Reformation. As such, pre-modern Christianity was not so much an institutionalized religion as it was a culture, closer to other decentralized modern religious cultures, such as Hinduism, rather than to modern Christianity. The Christianity that the Spanish conquerors and missionaries first brought to America was a "local religion" of saints that were regarded as resident patrons of their communities "very much in the same way as the tutelary deities were perceived by Mesoamericans."[88] As Fernando Cervantes has suggested, the "view of the extirpators and of too many subsequent thinkers that Christianity sat, in its purity, like a layer of oil over Mesoamerican magic is a highly misleading one," because the Christian religion was "itself intermingled with a great deal of magic. Necromancers, enpsalmers and conjurers of clouds often competed directly with parish priests in early modern Castile."[89] If fifteenth-century Christianity in Europe had already abounded in magical practices, magic was further reinvigorated in the context of the European discovery and conquest of America, which corresponded with a revival of the Renaissance mysticism of Ficino and Pico della Mirandola, as well as a new scientific hope of controlling nature through magic. The writings of the early conquerors teemed with mystical fantasies such as the philosopher's stone, elixirs of life, the Fountain of Youth, and most of all, of course, the magically redemptive power of gold.[90] The conquest of America was in essence an "alchemical" quest insofar as it was driven not merely by the lust for material gain but by the belief in the magic power of gold to afford salvation and the transformation of the world. "Gold is most excellent," Columbus wrote in a famous passage; "of gold there is formed treasure and with it whoever has it may do what he wishes in this world and come to bring souls into Paradise."[91]

Thus, while magic was not yet primarily identified with Native American knowledge during the sixteenth century, it was in the process of becoming so in the imperial context in which Cabeza de Vaca was writing. If, however, by the middle of the sixteenth century, magic came increasingly under attack in the New World on the part of the church authorities, it was not, Cervantes explains, because post-Tridentine theologians thought that magic was "superstitious or irrational or even 'wrong'" but, on the contrary, because they feared "that it was powerful and efficacious and, therefore, dangerous."[92] The conquerors and settlers frequently relied on

Indians not only for the physical knowledge of the environment but also for the healing powers inherent in "local spiritual forces that they [the Indians] understood much better."[93] Responding to both this fear of uncontrollable magic on the one hand and the attacks of Protestant reformers on the other, Counter-Reformation inquisitors began expending substantial intellectual energies on "domesticating" certain magical practices within official Catholic teaching and worship while sharpening the defining borderline between "orthodox" Catholic ritual and "magical" remedies. In the process, magical practices that were not subsumed within orthodox Catholic ritual increasingly became associated with heathen "idolatry."[94] This colonial process corresponded, Cervantes shows, with a fundamental shift in the way that black magic was perceived in sixteenth-century Spanish theological discourse. Throughout the Middle Ages and the Renaissance, the definitions of black magic had been dominated by Thomist theology (as expounded in Thomas Aquinas' *Malleus maleficarum*), which posited an essential consistency between nature and salvation on the one hand and the ultimate impotence of Satan against God and His Church on the other. From this point of view, black magic was seen as *malefice* and, as such, as primarily a social crime. During the course of the sixteenth century, and especially in the context of the Reformation and the Counter-Reformation, however, the conviction about the impotence of Satan was "badly shaken" and black magic came to be perceived primarily as an offence against the First Commandment and, thus, as a crime against God Himself.[95]

Cervantes' argument about diabolism in the New World and Spain illuminates the colonial dimension of a larger process that the English historian Keith Thomas has called the "decline of magic" during the sixteenth century in Western culture at large. The loss of credibility for magical practices was not the "natural" result of the advent of modern science and technology, Thomas argued, but primarily a consequence of a change in the institutional organization of religion during the Reformation and the Counter-Reformation, which sought to centralize and control human agency in the manipulation of the natural world.[96] Satan came to be seen as an active agent skilled in the knowledge of nature and tempting those seeking worldly success to enter into "semi-feudal contracts with him [by] mortgaging their souls in return for a temporary access of supernatural knowledge or power. Such Faustian legends were in common circulation during the sixteenth and seventeenth centuries. They made excellent cautionary tales, revealing Satan as a trickster and showing how his recruits always came to a bad end."[97] Whereas in the feudal court culture of the

Middle Ages and the Renaissance, locally diverse magical practices had not been perceived as inherently dangerous, during the sixteenth-century re-organization of religion occurring in the context of dynastic state formations and overseas empires, the manipulation of nature by the individual came to be perceived as a threat to ecclesiastic and secular authorities, who aimed to unify not only language but also the cultural perception of reality by driving a wedge between natural phenomena and their spiritual powers. However, as Thomas also points out, while both the Reformation and the Counter-Reformation similarly promoted a rationalized and disenchanted sense of reality, the Protestant emphasis on the single sovereignty of God would eventually dissolve the world of spirits and miracles entirely, while the Catholic concept of a "graded hierarchy of spiritual powers" permitted acts of healing if they were performed in the service of God, if they were presented in the guise of miracles. Indeed, the Catholic ritual of exorcism, Thomas continues, "with the sign of the cross, symbolic breathing (insufflatio), holy water, and the command to the Devil to depart in God's name," was prescribed by the Counter-Reformation Church in numerous manuals of exorcism for humans suffering from supernaturally inflicted torments.[98]

Cabeza de Vaca's *Relación* may in this context not only be seen as an example of such early modern cautionary tales against magic to which Thomas is referring but also provide insights into the inter-relation between European colonialism in the New World and foundational transformations in Western knowledge at large, as suggested by Cervantes. For example, the description of the tempest that afflicts the imperial expedition in the first chapter of the narrative is rendered in a way that not only links it to the neo-feudal aspirations of the conquerors but also creates the impression that it was the product of Indian black magic or witchcraft:

En esta tempestad y peligro anduvimos toda la noche sin hallar parte ni lugar donde media hora pudiessemos estar seguros. Andando en esto oymos toda la noche, especialmente desde el medio della, mucho estruendo y grande ruydo de bozes, y gran sonido de cascaveles y de flautas y tamborinos y otros instrumentos que duraron hasta la mañana que la tormenta cesso. En estas partes nunca otra cosa tan medrosa se vio. (1555: Favata/Fernández, 9–10)

We spent the whole night in the storm and in this danger, without finding a single place or spot where we could be safe for half an hour at a time. And meanwhile we heard all night long, especially after midnight, a mighty crashing and sound of voices, and loud sounds of bells and flutes and tambourines and other instruments, which lasted until morning when the storm abated. Nothing so fearful had ever been seen in these parts. (1555: López Morillas, 8–9)

Similarly, the afflictions of the Indians that Cabeza de Vaca miraculously cures are attributed to the presence of the Devil. Cabeza de Vaca's account of a "mala cosa" ("evil thing") – absent from the "Joint Report"[99] – which, according to some Indians' relations, happened some fifteen years earlier, details the occasional appearance of a being that they called:

mala cosa, y que era pequeño de cuerpo, y que tenia barvas... [y que] davales tres cuchilladas grandes por las hijadas con un pedernal muy agudo, tan ancho como una mano y dos palmos en luengo. Y metia la mano por aquellas cuchilladas y sacavales las tripas... Y quando el queria, tomava el buhio o casa y subiala en alto, y dende a un poco caya con ella y dava muy gran golpe. (1555: Favata/Fernández, 85)

"Bad Thing," and that he was small of stature and had a beard... and [that he] gave them three great slashes in the side with a very sharp flint a handbreadth wide and two long, and that he would put his hand into those slashes and pull out their entrails... and that when he wished he could take a hut or house and lift it into the air and then, a little later, let it fall with a great crash. (1555: López Morillas, 73)

Cabeza de Vaca's description of "mala cosa" resembles here other representations of the Devil that are common in many colonial histories of the early Americas. Unlike many of the later histories, however, his *Relación* does not portray the American natives as Devil worshippers but rather as the Devil's victims, whom a rationalized conversion, predicated on a steadfast faith in God and the Catholic Church, would secure for salvation.

Nosotros les diximos que aquel era un malo, y de la mejor manera que podimos les davamos a entender que si ellos creyessen en Dios nuestro Señor y fuessen christianos como nosotros no ternian miedo de aquel, ni el osaria venir a hazelles aquellas cosas, y que tuviessen por cierto que en tanto que nosotros en la tierra estuviessemos el no osaria parescer en ella. (1555: Favata/Fernández, 86)

We told them that he was a demon and as best we could gave them to understand that if they would believe in God Our Lord and were Christians like ourselves, they would have no fear of him, nor would he dare to come and do those things to them; and that they could be certain that as long as we stayed in the land he would not dare to appear in it. (1555: López Morillas, 73–4)

It is significant, in this context, that Cabeza de Vaca does not portray Native American religious rites as a form of idolatry or Devil worship, as would many of the late sixteenth- and seventeenth-century writers of the Counter-Reformation, such as the Jesuit José de Acosta.[100] If Cabeza de Vaca's text is one of the earliest manifestations of this attempt to define "Catholic" ritual in opposition to "magic" by associating the latter with Native American cultural practices, his descriptions of "mala cosa" are still informed not by this newer idea of black magic as "idolatry" (which would be left to later writers) but rather (following some of his contemporaries such as Las Casas) by the idea of "*malefice*," to be combated with Catholic rituals of exorcism. His miraculous healings follow these prescriptions of the orthodox Catholic ritual of exorcism with remarkable consistency:

La manera con que nosotros curamos era santiguandolos, y soplarlos, y rezar un paternoster y un avemaria, y rogar lo mejor que podiamos a Dios nuestro Señor que les diesse salud y espirasse en ellos, que nos hiziessen algun buen tratamiento. Quiso Dios nuestro Señor y su misericordia que todos aquellos por quien suplicamos, luego que los santiguamos dezian a los otros que estavan sanos y buenos. (1555: Favata/Fernández, 58)

The way in which we cured was by making the sign of the cross over them and blowing on them and reciting a Pater Noster and an Ave Maria; and then we prayed as best we could to God Our Lord to give them health and inspire them to give us good treatment. God, Our Lord, and His mercy, willed that as soon as we made the sign of the cross over them, all those for whom we prayed told the others that they were well and healthy. (1555: López Morillas, 49)

Nevertheless, the *Relación* manifests a first step in the displacement of Western man's magic by God's miracles in the identification of "magic" with Native American knowledge. When describing Native American healing practices Cabeza de Vaca's descriptions are reminiscent of the kind of "magical healing" that was still popularly being practiced by conjurers, sorcerers, and cunning men roaming the countrysides of Europe during the early sixteenth century, but which was increasingly becoming the exclusive prerogative of the king.[101] Their ceremony consisted of "soplando al enfermo" ("blowing on the sick person") and of using a "piedra caliente, trayendola por el estomago" ("hot stone and passing it over the stomach"); for (as one Indian pointed out to him) "las piedras y otras cosas que se crias por los campos tienien virtud" ("the stones and other things that grow in the fields have virtue"). Of course, Cabeza de Vaca refuses to engage in this kind of magic but, when confronted with "tanta necesidad" ("such pressure"), he finally compromises by replacing "stones and other things that grow in the fields" with the cross (1555: Favata/Fernández, 57; 1555: López Morillas, 49). His passive obedience to Catholic orthodoxy works miracles, for when he is near starvation, he is fed by the Indians, and when he is near freezing, he is miraculously warmed by "un árbol ardiendo" ("a tree burning") – never mentioned, as far as we can tell from Oviedo, in the "Joint Report" – as signs of God's mercy for his submission to Catholic morality at the end of his spiritual pilgrimage (1555: Favata/Fernández, 69):

A las vezes me acontescio hazer leña donde despues de averme costado mucha sangre no la podia sacar ni a cuestas ni arrastrando. No tenia, quando en estos trabajos me via, otro remedio ni consuelo sino pensar en la Passion de nuestro Redemptor Jesuchristo y en la sangre que por mi derramo, y considerar quanto mas seria el tormento que de las espinas el padescio que no aquel que yo entonces suffria. (1555: Favata/Fernández, 88)

Sometimes it happened that I went for wood in places where, after gathering it had cost me much blood, I could neither carry nor drag it. When I was in these difficulties, my only solace was to think of the passion of our Redeemer Jesus Christ, and the blood he shed for me, and to consider how much greater was the torment he suffered from the thorns than that I was then experiencing. (1555: López Morillas, 75)

In a characteristically Baroque fashion, the "world turned up-side down" by man's will to power through natural magic, and the afflictions suffered as a result of the aberrations and seductions instigated by the Devil, are remedied by the miracles that God bestowed upon the passive individual as a reward for his or her subordination to a rationalized Christian morality.

It is in this context that the changes in the 1555 text accentuating the miraculous and salutary effects that the four pilgrims had on the natives must be seen. Thus, whereas, in the 1542 text, he had reported that "Y entre todas estas gentes se tenía por muy cierto que veníamos del cielo, porque todas las cosas que ellos no alcancan, ni tienen noticia de donde vienen, dizen que vienen del cielo" (1542: Adorno/Pautz, 1: 232) ("And among all these peoples, it was taken for certain that we came from the sky, because all the things that they do not have or do not know the origin of, they say come from the sky" [1542: Adorno/Pautz, 233]), in the 1555 version the explanatory subclause ("porque...cielo" ["because...sky"]) is absent.[102] Adorno and Pautz have argued that the "general tendency of the editorial hand at work in the 1555 edition to enhance the natives' view of the four men as supernatural suggests that the suppression in the 1555 edition of the mundane explanation...of the 1542 text was deliberate" and explainable in terms of the "self-promoting" intention of the 1555 text.[103] It is not, however, a "self-promotion" in the sense of an assertion of the powers of an autonomous will, but rather an illustration of the miraculous powers of the individual who subordinates his or her will to Catholic morality. Significantly, in the narrative, it is only *after* Cabeza de Vaca has been stripped of his cape and sword and become a naked pilgrim that he is able to perform miracles through the practice of Christian ritual. Like Dante's literary journey to hell, Cabeza de Vaca's New World journey is fashioned by the author as a spiritual and epistemological awakening to the recognition that only reliance on faith in the Catholic cosmic order will lead to truth and redeem from affliction:

Luego el pueblo nos ofrescio muchas tunas, porque ya ellos tenian noticia de nosotros y como curavamos y de las maravillas que Nuestro Señor con nosotros obrava; que aunque no oviera otras, harto grandes eran abrirnos caminos por tierra tan despoblada y darnos gente por donde muchos tiempo no la avia, y librarnos de tantos peligros y no permitir que nos matassen, y substentarnos con tanta hambre, y poner aquellas gentes en coracon que nos tratassen bien, como adelante diremos. (1555: Favarata/Fernández, 78–9)

Then they offered us many prickly pears, for they had heard of us, and how we cured folk, and the marvels that Our Lord did by our hands. Had we done no more works than these, they were great enough to smooth our way through such sparsely settled territory, and to furnish us with people in a place where often there were none, and to deliver us from so many perils and not allow them to kill us, and to keep us alive through so much hunger, and to incline the hearts of those people to treat us well, as I shall recount. (1555: López Morillas, 66–7)

Thus, if "magic" was not yet primarily associated with "Amerindian" knowledge at the time when Cabeza de Vaca was writing his accounts about North America, his narrative participated in a cultural transformation in the course of which magic would gradually be displaced by the active intervention of secular and ecclesiastic authorities – by domesticating it within Catholic ritual or by constituting it as Amerindian idolatry. His narrative illustrates that man's "magic" as a tool of conquest/knowledge must lead him astray to succumb to the tricks of the Devil. "Truth" will be revealed to him only by "miracle" when relying on faith in God and king. Interestingly, while the episodes dealing with miracles were frequently discredited (as we will see in the next chapter) by the foreign translators of Cabeza de Vaca's *Relación*, such as Ramusio and Purchas, they were emphasized and amplified by Spanish historians of the New World.[104] Both the Reformation and Counter-Reformation historians of the New World aimed at a subordination of the individual's will to an absolute and universal "objectivity" by demonizing magic as Native American idolatry; but while the Catholic historians allowed for the truth of supernatural healing as long as the power ultimately belonged to God (as "miracles"), their Protestant counterparts defined a rationalized objectivity in dialectical antithesis to Catholic "superstition."

STRIPPING THE METAPHOR: CABEZA DE VACA'S
NEW WORLD EPIC

In order to discern how Cabeza de Vaca is able to persuade his early modern (and even some of his modern) readers of this new, disenchanted, idea of truth, it is necessary to elucidate the dense rhetorical signification of some of the central motifs – such as "shipwrecks" in "tempests" and "wanderings" through "forests" – that his text brings to bear on the reader. On the one hand, *Relación* makes use, as Kun John Lee has argued, of the Biblical source of the shipwreck motif, specifically of Pauline typology. Cabeza de Vaca "portray[s] himself as the Spanish Paul among American Gentiles," she argues, who recognizes in his shipwreck among them God's providential plan to permit the Gentiles to be among "God's chosen people through the sacrificial death of Jesus and to have part with the Jews in God's blessing and promises."[105] On the other hand, as many critics have also noted, the motifs of shipwreck and wandering in this text connect with the Classical tradition, particularly the *Odyssey*, its "scientific" and "ethnographic" qualities notwithstanding. While some have therefore seen this New World narrative as a modern epic of sorts,[106] others have spoken about an anti-epic, arguing that in its "cancellation of riches, glory, and power as fundamental motors of action," this text rejects "the previous model of epic action."[107]

In light of my argument about the politics of form in Cabeza de Vaca's *Relación*, it is salient to re-visit this critical debate about the precise relationship between this text and the epic tradition in more detail here. In doing so, however, it must be observed at the outset that, despite many readers' strong sense of the epic qualities of this narrative, we find no explicit references to the *Odyssey* or the epic tradition anywhere in Cabeza de Vaca's text. What we do find is a number of most curious discrepancies between the 1555 revision and the earlier edition of 1542. In the account of his first Indian captivity among the Mariames following the wreck of the rafts, for example, Cabeza de Vaca makes the following amendment:

Con este concierto yo quede alli y me dieron por esclavo a un indio con quien Dorantes estava, *el qual era tuerto, y su muger y un hijo que tenia y otro que estava en su compañia, de manera que todos eran tuertos.* (1555: Favarata/Fernández, 65; emphasized phrase absent from 1542: Adorno/Pautz, 1: 128)

I stayed there, and they gave me as a slave to an Indian who was with Dorantes, *who was one-eyed, as were his wife and son and another Indian who was with him: so that all of them had only one eye each.* (1555: López Morillas, 56; emphasized phrase absent from 1542: Adorno/Pautz, 1: 129)

Before inquiring into the significance of this addition, it should be pointed out to the English reader that the meaning of the word "tuerto" can be slightly ambiguous in this context: in the *Diccionario de autoridades*, "tuerto" is defined as "que le falta un ojo" ("lacking an eye"), while the *Diccionario de la lengua española* defines it as "[f]alto de la vista en un ojo" ("lacking sight in one eye"). Thus, while Frances López Morillas has translated *tuerto* as "one-eyed" in the full translation of the 1555 edition cited here, Adorno and Pautz, in the marginal annotations to their edition of the 1542 text, have translated "tuerto" as "blind in one eye," not "lacking an eye."[108] If I retain López Morillas' version here for consistency's sake, I also note Adorno and Pautz' translation at this point because I will momentarily argue that the question of translation – the translation from Spanish into English ("blind in one eye" rather than "one-eyed") as well as Cabeza de Vaca's translation of his New World "experience" – real or imagined – when writing back in Spain ("era tuerto" rather than, say, "faltaba de ojo") is significant.

Putting aside the question of translation for the moment, we do have to wonder why Cabeza de Vaca added this curious reference in his 1555 revision in the first place – thirteen years after he had omitted it in the first publication in 1542 and perhaps as much as twenty years after allegedly having witnessed this scene in America. This addition is complemented by another alteration in the 1555 version in reference to the Mariames: "Matan sus hijos y mercan los agenos. No dura el casamiento mas de quanto estan contentos, y con una higa deshazen el casamiento" (1555: Favata/Fernández, 70) ("[T]hey kill their own children and trade in those of others; their marriages last only as long as they are happy together, and they dissolve marriages by the use of an amulet" [1555: López Morillas, 60; compare 1542: Adorno/Pautz, 139]). Even if these additions could possibly be explained in terms of a belated recollection of additional facts, we would still have to ask why, among a potentially infinite number of minor details experienced during an eight-year journey necessarily omitted from a short narrative account thereof, these were deemed by the author as significant enough to warrant amendment. We must therefore conclude that Cabeza de Vaca made these changes in the 1555 edition in order not only to provide more factual accuracy but also to enhance the rhetorical effect of his narrative as a reliable eyewitness source of particular bits of information about the Mariames. If this inclusion of additional ethnographic facts enhances the "scientific" appeal of his narrative, this effect is also furthered by the division of the account into distinct chapters with titles, which Cabeza de Vaca first supplied only in his 1555 edition.

At least with regard to the former addition, which evokes Odysseus' epic captivity in Polyphemus' cave, it is possible that Cabeza de Vaca was partially inspired by Oviedo's summary of the "Joint Report"; for Cabeza de Vaca's revision of the 1542 version when preparing the 1555 edition seems to have been influenced by Oviedo's *Historia general y natural*, which Cabeza de Vaca had presumably read after his return from La Plata.[109] Significantly, it was the royal chronicler Oviedo, not Cabeza de Vaca or one of his later editors, who first referred to the failed Narváez expedition as "naufragios."[110] However, as Adorno and Pautz note, the sense in which Oviedo applied this term was "not with the literal meaning of 'shipwrecks' but rather the figurative one of 'disasters' or 'calamities,'" thus evidencing the "moralizing purpose" to which Oviedo lent his account of the Narváez expedition.[111] A similar case could be made for Oviedo's use of the word "peregrinaciones" ("pilgrimages") in reference to the expeditionaries' experiences (IV: 309), which Cabeza de Vaca then adopts for the first time only in his 1555 revision – in the "Proem" addressed to the emperor (1555: Favata/Fernández, 3). Significantly, Oviedo, in his account of the Pánfilo de Narváez expedition, had repeatedly invoked the "peregrinación de Ulixes" as a metaphor for Narváez' fate and commented upon his loss of an eye ("perdió un ojo") during his earlier confrontation with Cortés in order to elaborate the moral significance of his story (IV: 299):

Si Pánfilo de Narváez no perdiera la memoria de cómo fué tractado en la Nueva España, e mirara cuán al revés le salieron sus pensamientos, no buscara otros torbellinos e fatigas, e contentárase con que, seyendo un hidalgo que pasó a estas partes con una espada e una capa a buscar la vida, alcanzó honra e mujer virtuosa hijadalgo, e le dió Dios hijos e hacienda con que bastantemente pudiera pasar, segund el ser de su persona... e aun después que salió de la prisión e uñas de Cortés, halló a su mujer, María de Valenzuela, que había algunos años que le atendía en tan buena fama e reputación, como pudo estar Penélope; puesto que no tejía e destejía, como aquélla, por la dubda que tenía o esperanza de la venida de su marido Ulixes... e aconsejándole yo, como amigo, que se sosegase ya en su casa e compañía de su mujer e hjios, e diese gracias a Dios, pues tenía en qué vivir e con qué pasar este vado mundano e tan lleno de inconvinientes, como sus deseos guiaban a este mandar hijos ajenos, debiérale de parescer que lo que yo decía no era tan a su propósito como lo que él negociaba. E así acabó como negocios mal fundados, e para su muerte e otros muchos solicitados. (IV: 285)

If Pánfilo de Narváez had not forgotten how he was treated in New Spain and could have seen how his intentions came out backward, he would not have looked for other reckless and fatiguing adventures, and would have been satisfied with being an hidalgo who came to these parts with a sword and cape in search of a living and found honor and a virtuous wife, daughter of an hidalgo, and

God gave him children and enough wealth to get by on, according to his life-style... Even after he got out of prison and out of Cortés' claws, he found his wife, Maria de Valenzuela, who had for some years been blessed with as good fame and reputation as Penelope may have had, but she did not weave or unravel as Penelope did because of the doubt she had or the hope for the return of her husband Ulysses... I advised him as a friend to remain peacefully at home in the company of his wife and children and to give thanks to God since he had a place to live and the wherewithal to pass through this worldly vale so full of woes. However, since his desires moved him to order others about, it must have seemed to him that what I was saying was not so fitting as what he was doing. And that's the end of it – like any bad business – owing to his death and many previous demands made on him.[112]

What is the larger moral connection that Oviedo aimed to draw here for his sixteenth-century reader between one-eyed Pánfilo de Narváez' demise and Ulysses' pilgrimage? After all, Pánfilo de Narváez' one-eyedness would seem to associate him not with Ulysses but with his epic antagonist, Polyphemus. However, already in the *Odyssey* the figure of one-eyed Polyphemus may be read, as Max Horkheimer and Theodor Adorno (among others) have pointed out, as Odysseus' older sense of identity as an Iliadic raider of cities who knew the world through conquest and whose behavior had "not yet become objectified in the form of 'character.' "[113] Polyphemus' single eye, they argue, recalls the "nose and the mouth, more primitive than the symmetry of eyes and ears, which, with the security guaranteed by two unified perceptions, is the virtual prerequisite of identification, depth, and objectivity."[114] Thus, Odysseus' epic encounters with the monsters in general, and one-eyed Polyphemus in particular, de-mythify the mythos of man as demigod and the aristocratic value of a warrior's glory (*kleos*). According to Horkheimer and Adorno, the *Odyssey* had hereby initiated a long process in Western culture – what they called the "Dialectic of Enlightenment" – in which the individual asserts his/her self through self-denial: "Man's domination over himself, which grounds his selfhood, is almost always the destruction of the subject in whose service it is undertaken."[115] Odysseus "kills" his Iliadic self by re-incarnating it as monsters in the first-person narrative that he relates to the Phaiakians, but only after he emerges naked and destitute on their island from traumatic shipwreck and ritual cleansing – after spiritual death and rebirth – as a "better" man.[116]

But when noting Oviedo's fusion of the Homeric antithesis between Odysseus and Polyphemus in the character of Pánfilo de Narváez, we must also bear in mind that neither Oviedo nor most of his contemporary readers in Spain would have been directly familiar with the Homeric originals of the epic hero but only with their medieval mediations – in a long manuscript tradition based on a first-century Latin version of the *Iliad* ("Ilias latina"), through Virgil's rewriting of the two Homeric poems in the *Aeneid*, and, of course, by way of a medieval hagiographic appropriation of the Greek hero that had culminated in Dante's *Divine Comedy*.[117] Thus, when inquiring into the relationship between the *Odyssey* and sixteenth-century accounts of the Pánfilo de Narváez expedition, it is necessary to place this investigation not in the context of the Homeric original ("Odysseus"), but rather in the context of its Latin and medieval commentaries, mainly by way of Virgil and Dante respectively, where "Ulysses" is a deeply problematic figure who comes to a notoriously bad end.

In the *Aeneid*, for example, it was precisely Homer's Odyssean "cunning" that became the object of Virgil's moral and meta-fictional critique when rewriting the Homeric epics for imperial Rome. As in the *Odyssey*, in the *Aeneid*, too, the motif of shipwreck was crucial in the elaboration of this new epic enterprise. As the reader will recall, however, it was here not the epic hero himself, Aeneas, who suffered shipwreck but rather his helmsman, Palinurus, who suffered and died vicariously after the Trojan party left Dido's Carthage. David Quint has argued that the substitution of Palinurus for the hero Aeneas as the sufferer of shipwreck represents Virgil's critique of the Homeric hero in a series of "repetitions with a difference" in which Virgil redefined the epic hero for a new age that demanded the individual's self-sacrifice for the community – the *pietas* and *clementia* that Aeneas must acquire in the course of his own epic pilgrimage. The reason for this ethical transformation in the *Aeneid*, Quint argues, has to do with the different political structure of Roman (and especially Augustan) imperialism: whereas the Greek empire had been a colonial settler empire, a loose confederation of city states spread through the Mediterranean, the Roman empire was based on a centralized absolutist model. It is in its articulation of an ethos demanding the sacrifice of the individual's independent will that Quint sees the profound influence of the *Aeneid* on the subsequent history of Western literature:

Virgil's politicization of epic for the ends of empire demanded a curbing of the Homeric heroic will, and the flatness and passivity of Aeneas became the virtuous traits of the other hero-leaders of the imperial epic . . . As opposed to the wandering Odysseus and the rebellious Achilles, the hero of empire became an executive type who places duty over individual desire, the goals of history over the present moment. The reaches of political power would thus extend not merely over space and time, but over the inner man.[118]

The articulation of an ethical discourse of *pietas* and *clementia* in the *Aeneid* is accompanied by a meta-fictional commentary on the new epic poem's form. As Quint goes on to show, the poet's use of *letras*, like its hero's use of *armas*, is self-consciously restrained in the *Aeneid* – plain, disciplined, passive, and, thus, subordinated to the higher "truth" of the imperial order. While Virgil had generally upheld the value of rhetoric as the protector of virtue, he was also wary of the potential dangers that the aristocratic values espoused by the Homeric hero presented to imperial claims of universal truth. Rome had prospered precisely, as Cicero put it, because of "our scrupulous attention to religion and our wise grasp of a single truth."[119]

If the Homeric epic hero had been re-interpreted thus negatively in subsequent post-Hellenic epics, Ulysses was further demoted from pagan Hades to Christian Hell during the Middle Ages, in Dante's Augustinian re-reading in *Inferno*, where we find the Greek hero eternally encased in ice in the Seventh Circle. It is in the context of this late medieval "hagiographic substratum" that Enrique Pupo-Walker has seen the significance of the shipwreck motif also in Cabeza de Vaca's *Relación*. According to Pupo-Walker, Cabeza de Vaca follows a hagiographic tradition of narrators who, after their experience of shipwreck, reflect back upon the "via non vera," their lives before the path-breaking disaster, and the subsequent pilgrimage of introspection, confession, conversion, and salvation. Like these literary predecessors, the narrator of *Relación* portrays the shipwreck as an eye-cleansing experience with providential significance. As God's hand effecting a change of the pilgrim's "animo" (the rational apparatus of the mind), shipwreck confronts the individual with a new beginning and the opportunity for moral re-evaluation. The literary motif of "naufragios" thus signals a general progression from loss to recovery, from perdition to salvation, from a state of sin to an awareness and rejection of the sin of Odyssean pride.[120]

Moreover, there is another significance in the shipwreck motif, as well as in the oblique reference to the *Odyssey* in Cabeza de Vaca's *Relación* and the explicit reference in Oviedo. For, as Pupo-Walker notes, the transformation of the protagonist from conqueror to pilgrim in Cabeza de Vaca's *Relación* is accompanied by a series of "subtle rhetorical inversions" which gradually transform the narrative from a *historia* to a spiritual autobiography following the relation of Cabeza de Vaca's shipwreck.[121] Although Pupo-Walker does not push this point, it is again instructive to see this rhetorical inversion in the context of Dante's *Divine Comedy* and its own meta-fictional dialogue with the epic tradition. In other words, we must see this rhetorical inversion not only as the "natural" form following from the humble circumstances of Cabeza de Vaca's existence in the colonial frontier but also as a deliberate authorial device that betrays a consciousness of the traditional connection between *armas* and *letras* and of the "dual journey" – fictional and meta-fictional – that has been an integral part of the epic genre from Homer's *Odyssey* to Derek Walcott's *Omeros*. Thus, in the *Inferno*'s famous "Prologue" scene, the poet had compared himself, the imminent pilgrim before his return to "the path that does not stray," to a man who, having been shipwrecked but now safely ashore, turns back to regard his former "passo" in the "selva oscura" which almost led him to perdition. He "cannot clearly say how I had entered the wood" because he was "so full of sleep just at the point where I abandoned the true path." Now, however, he has been awakened:

> E come quei che con lena affannata,
> uscito fuor del pelago a la riva,
> si volge a l'acqua perigliosa e guata,
> così l'animo mio, ch'ancor fuggiva,
> si volse a retro a rimirar lo passo
> che con lasciò già mai persona viva.

> And just as he who, with exhausted breath,
> having escaped from sea to shore, turns back
> to watch the dangerous waters he has quit,
> so did my spirit, still a fugitive,
> turn back to look intently at the pass
> that never has let any man survive.[122]

As Richard Lansing has pointed out, nautical imagery was commonly used in medieval and early modern literature not only to signify Universal Man's journey through life but also a poet's experience in undertaking literary composition. Dante wrote his *Commedia* in part as a palinode, Lansing argues, to his earlier works – the *Convivio* and the *Monarchia* – which were "stained with a tincture of Aristotelian-Averroist philosophy." The "selva oscura," the forest roamed by the poet prior to his journey to Hell, thus represents a period of Dante's life as a knower and a writer, "a spiritual slumber in which Dante followed the calling of Lady Philosophy."[123] Critics such as John Freccero, David Thompson, Giuseppe Mazzotta, and Teodolinda Barolini agree, arguing that the figure of Ulysses in the *Commedia* personifies a presumptuous individualistic pride in philosophical independence and reflects "Dante's conscious concern with himself" as a poet.[124] Thus, in Canto XXVI, Dante's Ulysses laments, as Oviedo's Pánfilo de Narváez may have, his fateful decision not to return home to his wife, his artful persuasion of his comrades to follow him, and his final shipwreck beyond the Pillars of Hercules, demarcating the circle of knowledge:

> Quando
> mi departi' da Circe, che sottrasse
> me più d'un anno là presso a Gaeta,
> ...
> né dolcezza di figlio, né la pieta
> del vecchio padre, né 'l debito amore
> lo qual dovea Penelopè far lieta,
> vincer potero dentro a me l'ardore
> ch'i' ebbi a divenir del mondo esperto.

> When I sailed away from Circe, who'd beguiled me
> to stay more than a year there, near Gaeta
> ...
> neither my fondness for my son nor pity
> for my old father nor the love I owed to
> Penelope, which would have gladdened her,
> was able to defeat in me the longing
> I had to gain experience of the world[125]

Similar to Augustine's rejection of the neo-Platonic idea that the power of the individual's intellect was a sufficient vehicle for the attainment of Truth and the Absolute, Dante rejected the idea of Natural Philosophy as a means for the pursuit of Truth by sending his Ulysses into shipwreck, death, and eternal damnation, which the poet himself was able to escape only by his pilgrimage through Hell. For Dante, Ulysses' shipwrecked voyage beyond the Pillars of Hercules was an image of the "misguided philosophical Odyssey," the *via* that was revealed to the poet as *non vera* only through the eye-opening experience of shipwreck.[126] Dante's *Comedy* had thus inflicted upon the Classical epic tradition a "fundamental rupture between truth and a language which is caught up in the world of contingency... The text gives a remarkable exemplification of the inadequacy of knowledge and rhetoric to reach truth." Whereas the ancients, such as Virgil and Cicero, had systematically linked rhetoric and history, Dante directed his critique "against Cicero's sense of history as the world of man's own construction."[127]

Thus, if indeed Cabeza de Vaca, after reading Oviedo's moralizing commentary, made his curious amendments in his 1555 account of the Pánfilo de Narváez expedition in order to evoke Ulysses' captivity in Polyphemus' cave at the very place that marks his narrative's rhetorical inversion from an *historia de la conquista* to a spiritual autobiography and pilgrimage, it is not only an ethical commentary on his own transformation as a protagonist from conqueror to pacifier but also a poetological and meta-historical commentary on his role as a historian in the writing of a history of the New World. When inquiring into the content of this meta-historical commentary of Cabeza de Vaca's narrative, it must first be observed that the form of his own evocation of Odysseus is in striking contrast to that of the royal chronicler Oviedo. In Oviedo's *Historia*, the prominent figures of Classical rhetoric – Ulysses, Jason, Hercules, Medusa – recurrently function as metaphors to persuade the reader of Oviedo's moral interpretation of the demise of the Narváez expedition.[128] In Cabeza de Vaca's text, by contrast, the figure of Ulysses is evoked without ever being explicitly mentioned. Despite many readers' intuitive sense of the "epic" qualities of Cabeza de Vaca's narrative, there are no allusions to the Greek hero, his shipwreck, wanderings, or his alter-ego Polyphemus to be found anywhere in his narrative. This is significant because it sheds light on the role that the *Odyssey* and the epic tradition play as a subtext for Cabeza de Vaca's *Relación* as a whole: whereas in Oviedo the evocation of the Classical figure of Ulysses functions *metaphorically* in order to elaborate a certain moral lesson, in Cabeza de Vaca's narrative, the reference to Ulysses functions *metonymically*, never separating itself from the ethnographic "realism" of the narrative.[129] That is, Oviedo's metaphor apprehends the New World in terms of similitude, while Cabeza de Vaca's metonymy apprehends its subject matter by emphasizing difference and by reducing the general and the abstract to the concrete and particular. By effacing the author's awareness of the Classical tradition (the rhetorical power of which he nevertheless brings to act on the reader), Cabeza de Vaca's *Relación* renounces his role as historian and active creator of meaning and instead emphasizes his role as a passive, self-effaced recorder of things "experienced." It is through this modern rhetorical stance – the denial of Classical rhetoric – that Cabeza de Vaca's account has persuaded his (early) modern readers, who have privileged this as a documentary source about early North American native cultures and Natural History more "reliable" than the chronicles of the conquest. Moreover, it is in this context that Cabeza de Vaca's choice of "era tuerto" (rather than, say, Oviedo's "perdió un ojo") as well as Adorno and Pautz' translation as "blind in one eye," rather than López Morrillas' translation as "one-eyed," are significant. Whereas Oviedo's metaphor "familiarizes" his subject matter, thus drawing attention to the creative role of the historian as rhetor and the protector of virtue, Cabeza de Vaca's rhetoric "defamiliarizes" his subject matter, thus fashioning his own role as a transparent observer and deliverer of "facts." If Cabeza de Vaca inserted his oblique reference to the great Greek orator at the beginning of his narration of pilgrimage in order to signal the meta-historical interest of his account, he deliberately calls our attention to the form of his own epic and its rhetorical transformations. When answering to this call, however, we immediately observe (1) that *Relación* is not an epic in the *Classical* sense of the word, and (2) that it transforms, in the course of the narrative, from a history of conquest, to spiritual autobiography, and finally to ethnographic description.

It is again instructive here to see *Relación* in light of David Quint's argument about the correspondence between ideology and form in the transformation of the epic genre. Quint argued that, beginning with the *Aeneid*, the imperial politicization of the epic represented the beginning of the end of what had essentially been an aristocratic genre in the realm of *historia* that came to completion during the Renaissance: "The nobility of the sixteenth and seventeenth centuries found their traditional role and their identity undermined both from below, in competition with a newly powerful mercantile bourgeoisie, and from above, as their role and identity were absorbed as instruments into the war machinery of modern absolute monarchy."[130] Imperialism's anti-aristocratic tendency, already apparent in the ideological project promoted by the *Aeneid*, consists in the convergence of all power in the person of the emperor, as a result of which "the supporting cast became faceless... The suppression of politically suspect individuality was thus fitted into an ethos of self-sacrifice. And in the *Aeneid* this ethos becomes heroic."[131] It is thus not difficult to see here why the epic genre in general and the *Aeneid* in particular, with its plot of "just" conquests and rationalized violence in the western lands of the savage Turnus, would become the quintessential narrative model for the chronicles of the conquest of America. However, we can also see why the sixteenth-century Habsburg propagandists under Philip II should choose as the prototype for a Spanish imperial mythology not the *Aeneid* but rather the more marginal epic of Apollonius' *Argonautica*. For the *Aeneid*, in its centrifugal themes of exodus, settlement, and *translatio imperii* (which forbade the return to the site of Old Troy), was potentially subversive of the centralizing politics of Habsburg imperialism, while Jason's mission in the *Argonautica* was always the final return to Alexandria. For the same reason, the *Argonautica* would come to define the preferred narrative model for an emerging discourse of scientific objectivity and the fashioning of the modern scientific self – what Bronislaw Malinowski would call the "Western Argonaut": the modern golden fleece of empirical knowledge returned to a new Alexandrine metropolis by a new Jason.[132]

In this regard, Cabeza de Vaca's sixteenth-century account of his shipwreck in North America can be seen as a crucial text for the argument laid out by Quint not only about the connections between the epic tradition and imperialist ideologies but also about the gradual and permanent expulsion of the epic form from the realm of *historia* to the realm of *belles lettres* in the context of overseas imperialism and settler colonialism. In its ideological project of divorcing Classical rhetoric from (natural) historical discourse in the New World context, Cabeza de Vaca's *Relación* persuades the reader of its modern idea of "truth" by "asserting its self through self-denial." For the disavowal of Classical rhetoric *is* the rhetoric of modern scientific truth. "He who calls himself Nobody for his own sake and manipulates approximation to the state of nature as a means of mastering it, falls victim to hubris," write Horkheimer and Adorno; "The cunning of the clever man who assumes the form of stupidity turns to stupidity as soon as he surrenders that form. That is the dialectic of eloquence."[133]

Thus, the second rhetorical inversion in Cabeza de Vaca's *Relación* occurs at the end of Chapter XXIII, when, having completed his spiritual pilgrimage, the focus shifts once again from the story of his own transformation in pilgrimage to Native American culture and customs, as spiritual autobiography yields to ethnographic description. In chapters entitled "Chapter XXIV: Of the Customs of the Indians of That Land," "Chapter XXV: Of the Indians' Readiness to Use Arms," "Chapter XXVI: Of the Tribes and Their Languages," the narrative "I" recedes from the account, lending his eye to the service of the imperial historian authorized in the production of knowledge. "[T]heir way of cooking . . . is so novel," he writes, "that I wish to record it here, so that it can be seen and recognized how diverse and strange are the devices and tactics of human beings" (1555: López Morillas, 101). Interestingly, as Adorno and Pautz's reconstruction of the "Joint Report" shows, it was precisely these detailed naturalistic descriptions of terrain, the soil, the waters, the fauna, and Native culture – allegedly based on immediate first-hand observation – that were *absent* from the "Joint Report" filed by the survivors immediately after their return to Mexico and added only by Cabeza de Vaca when composing his published account eight years after he would have actually witnessed them.[134]

Those rescued from shipwreck, writes Hans Blumenberg in a commentary on Nietzsche's *The Gay Science*, "are astonished by their new experience of dry land. This is the fundamental experience of science, that it is able to establish things that stand from and provide solid ground for further discoveries."[135] Similarly, our New World author embarks on a spiritual journey which would transform the Renaissance maker of travel histories / histories of conquest, who "knew" the world through metaphor, into the self-effacing supplier of "all the other details that I could learn and know," subdued to the Baroque order of Catholic morality and to the historiographic authority of the imperial *cronista mayor*. While the early versions of Cabeza de Vaca's *Relación* – such as the "Joint Report" – would humbly serve as historical source documents in the vast archive of the royal chronicler Oviedo's monumental *Historia general y natural*, the subsequent revisions of *Relación*, published under Cabeza de Vaca's own name, stand as the meta-historical allegory of the making of the new "mercantilist" economy of knowledge production, which would monopolize "magic" in the *cronista mayor* at the monarchical court by dividing intellectual labor between imperial periphery and center and by demanding the documentary "transparency" of the colonial text. Indeed, Oviedo, in his belatedly added "seventh" chapter, insisted on the superiority of the "Joint Report" over Cabeza de Vaca's published account on the basis of the former's greater objectivity: "en alguna manera yo tengo por buena la relación de los tres, e por más clara que estotra que el uno sólo hace e hizo imprimir" ("In a way, I judge the account of the three [Cabeza de Vaca, Dorantes, and Castillo] as the correct one and the clearer one than this one which only one has written and published individually") (IV: 315). While Cabeza de Vaca's "factual" representation of reality pays homage to the incipient modern quest for "scientific" knowledge, the historical "truth" of first-person narratives like his will henceforth either be contained, assessed, and authorized by the royal court historian or otherwise be relegated into the realm of poetic truth, the realm of prose fiction.

Thus, if critics today sense the "modern," "picaresque," or even (proto-) "novelesque" character of Cabeza de Vaca's account of his North American epic journey,[136] it is because his translations of the New World bear no resemblance to the legendary lands familiar from the medieval and Classical textual traditions. A half-century before the *Quixote*, Cabeza de Vaca's account of his epic journey through North America chronicles the epistemic transformation described by Foucault, in which "magic, which [had] permitted the decipherment of the world by revealing the secret resemblances beneath its signs is no longer of any use except as an explanation, in terms of madness, of why analogies are always proved false."[137] Cabeza de Vaca evokes Odysseus' heroic account of one-eyed Polyphemus at the outset of his spiritual journey in order to incarnate the idea of conquest as a model of knowing, the wreck of which in the New World subsequently sends him on a meta-historical pilgrimage leading to the effacement of his human agency by displacing "magic" for "miracle" and, finally, for proto-scientific "objectivity." The motifs of shipwreck and naked pilgrimage in Cabeza de Vaca's account thereby narrativize the conqueror being "stripped" of his metaphor as a weapon of eloquence by the imperial state, which demands his transparency in providing the epistemic "raw material" in the mercantilist production of knowledge in trans-oceanic empires. While we will never know what Cabeza de Vaca "really" saw during his journey through North America, his claim to prominence rests on his rhetorical skill as a writer of a New World odyssey and a central text in the making of what Luiz Costa Lima has called "the control of the imaginary" – a modern "iron law of 'truth'" which "carved an abyss between the proponents of imitatio and Aristotle's Poetics."[138]

CHAPTER 3

The geography of history: Samuel Purchas and "his" pilgrims

History without that so much neglected study of Geography is sick of a half dead palsy.

Samuel Purchas

Truth is linked in a circular relation with systems of power which produce and sustain it, and to effects of power which it induces and which extends it. A "regime" of truth.

Michel Foucault[1]

CABEZA DE VACA'S ENGLISH CAREER

Nearly three quarters of a century had elapsed since Cabeza de Vaca's odyssey through North America when England succeeded in establishing its first permanent settlement in the New World in 1607. But because of the relative proximity of La Florida to the English colony at Jamestown in Virginia, his account was still of immediate interest to promoters of English imperialism. The earliest English notice of Cabeza de Vaca's *Relación* appeared in 1609, in the dedicatory epistle to a translation of the Count of Elbas' *Relaçam verdadeira* (1557), published by the Elizabethan collector of travel histories Richard Hakluyt under the title *Virginia Richly Valued by the Description of the maine land of Florida her next neighbor*. There, Hakluyt invoked Cabeza de Vaca's account as proof that "Florida was the richest countrie of the world" and claimed that the author had found "gold and silver, and stones of great value."[2] Hakluyt's note suggests that he may not have read Cabeza de Vaca's *Relación*, or at least not very carefully, before he wrote this;[3] for, as we have seen, his account had hardly substantiated the legends of gold and riches to be had in La Florida. If Hakluyt ever took a second look, it is hardly surprising that he never decided to publish it.[4] From the point of view of the private investors associated with the Virginia Company, who had sponsored much of Hakluyt's work, Cabeza de Vaca's account of sticks and stones in North America would have done little to

77

remedy the much-lamented lack of English entrepreneurship when it came to the building of empires.

By the time the first English translation of Cabeza de Vaca's narrative *was* published in English, in 1625, the Virginia Company had been dissolved, its charter revoked, and Virginia had become England's first royal colony in the New World. The editor was Samuel Purchas (?1577–1626), an Anglican minister, chaplain to the archbishop of Canterbury, and rector of St. Martin's Ludgate, who included it in his gargantuan four-volume collection of voyages entitled *Hakluytus posthumus, or Purchas His Pilgrimes*.[5] There entitled "A Relation of Alvaro Nunez called Capo di Vava" (XVII: 437), it was a very different text from Cabeza de Vaca's Spanish originals and from Purchas' direct source, the Italian translation contained in Giambattista Ramusio's *Navigationi et viaggi*.[6] Whereas Cabeza de Vaca's Spanish texts had narrativized, as we have seen, the supersession of the neo-feudalist empire of "conquest" by the absolutist Habsburg empire of "peace," Purchas' English version chronicled the supersession of the "Spanish" empire before the providentially advancing empire of the "British." Britain's rightful title to North America was "ratified," Purchas argued, "by the former Spanish disasters in the Expeditions of Pamphilo di Navarez" (XIX: 228). La Florida's impenetrable resistance to the Spanish rape evidenced God's determination to save the North American virgin land for the legitimate, English husband: she was "wooed by the Spaniards," as the Protestant minister had put it already in 1613, "almost wonne by the French, and yet remains a riche and beautifull Virgin, waiting till the neighbour Virginia bestows on her an English bridegroome, who as making the first love, may lay the justest challenge unto her."[7] As the author of the sixteenth-century Spanish originals would have been utterly surprised to find, in the hands of Purchas his account was made to re-enact the so-called "Black Legend" that had originated with the sixteenth-century Protestant translators of Benzoni and Las Casas. This Protestant propaganda campaign indicted Spanish cruelties against the Native Americans in order to create a philosophical pretext for English imperial ambitions: the English would "salvage the savage," as one critic has put it, from Spanish cruelties and the Catholic Antichrist.[8]

In what should more accurately be called a paraphrase rather than a translation of Cabeza de Vaca's account, Purchas had excised most of the early historical sections, which had detailed the confrontation between the author and the governor Pánfilo de Narváez, with the effect of minimizing the ethical conflicts so important in Cabeza de Vaca's original text. With regard to the middle sections, consisting mainly of Cabeza de Vaca's spiritual autobiography, Purchas annotated heavily, invoking writers as diverse as Benzoni, Las Casas, Acosta, and Ulrich Schmiedel in order to discredit Cabeza de Vaca's accounts of miraculous healings as a Catholic "superstition." "Let their holines pardon me," he wrote with regard to Cabeza de Vaca's claim of resuscitating a dead person:

I will easier believe that they killed foure living men then that they raised half one dead man to life . . . I permit some of these relations, more for knowledge of the Countrey, then for credit of Spanish cures in the Indies, which you shal find in Casas of another nature. These here challenge no Divine end to convert people to God, and therefore are not like to have any divine beginning, but are either falsely told, or falsly done, or falsly intended by the Father of falshood. And why may they not be ascribed to the Devill, either as lied, if never done; or if done, as devillish Arts to maintaine rapine and superstition, which are here mentioned the effects thereof? Acosta tells of the great miracle-worker in the Indies, a vicious man, and hanged for knaveries. This Cowes-Head ["Cabeza de Vaca"] the Author is also by Schmidel before recorded for a bad man in his acts at the River of Plate. (XVII: 482)

Purchas' cuts were slightest in Cabeza de Vaca's ethnographic and naturalistic descriptions. His marginal annotations draw the reader's attention to Florida's economic potentials – "Use of Horses," "Names of the Nations," "Plates of Plate," "South Sea," "A river," "Emeralds," "Great Deere." As Purchas explained elsewhere, his method was not to follow "the folly of the Spanish Authors which are more curious to set downe the names [of the actors] in the Indies" (XIV: 429). Instead he edited his materials with an eye to bare geographic and ethnographic information; for, he hoped, this information might still be "of use one day, when our Virginian Plantation . . . shall lift her head with more vive alacritie, and shake her glorious lockes, and disparkle her triumphant lookes, thorow in the inland Countries to the Western Ocean" (XVIII: 67–8).

For his tendency to paraphrase and summarize his sources, rather than let "His Pilgrimes" speak for themselves, Samuel Purchas has often been held in contempt by modern historians, who have unfavorably compared him in this regard to his Elizabethan predecessor Richard Hakluyt. As Richard Dunn has written, Purchas was "a much inferior editor to Hakluyt" because in Purchas there "is no clear distinction between his sources and his verbose running commentary." Similarly, Jack Beeching lamented that Purchas, "with the stay-at-home reader in mind," began to cut away at Hakluyt's conservatively edited documents to the effect of making them prone to "mislead" the readers. Travel and exploration were "being turned at his busy hands into national myth." Purchas' patent habit of manipulating his sources, abridging, and selecting them according to no discernible method except his own biases "irritates the user of *Pilgrims*" to such a degree, David B. Quinn complained, that he had to reserve his "comment on Purchas's action [as] liable to be unprintable."[9]

Significantly, however, the severe censure and neglect that Purchas has earned from modern historians sharply contrasts with the judgments of his own century, when his works were read widely and praised generously by historians, much surpassing in this regard both Hakluyt's *Principal Navigations* (1599–1600) and his earlier *Diverse Voyages* (1582).[10] Moreover, it is noteworthy that (as Quinn notes) Hakluyt, too, had abridged and edited his sources, though he did so, as Quinn put it, "more intelligently."[11] Unlike Purchas, Hakluyt had manipulated his sources tacitly and without further commentary, thus giving the *appearance* that the travel accounts he printed were the authentic manuscript sources. The differences between Hakluyt's and Purchas' roles as editors of travel narratives were thus less *methodological* than they were *rhetorical*: whereas Hakluyt had evoked the impression that the knowledge contained in the voyages he printed belonged to the individual travelers who, in his *Principal Navigations*, represented the English nation, Purchas' editorial rhetoric suggested that the knowledge brought home by the traveling pilgrims was ultimately "His."

The differences between Hakluyt's and Purchas' editorial rhetoric in imperial historiography are far from mere personal idiosyncrasies and point to things more interesting than the alleged superiority or inferiority of one editor over another when judged by the standards and assumptions of modern historicism. Rather, the rhetorical shift that modern historians have lamented in Purchas reflects significant ideological transformations with regard to the production, organization, and ownership of natural knowledge occurring in the context of imperial expansion in early seventeenth-century England. After Renaissance Neo-Platonists such as John Dee had synthesized the age-old Scholastic distinction, existing since Ptolemy and Strabo, between the separate disciplines of "geography" (the mathematical and rationalist mapping of the world) and what was then called "chorography" (the empirical description by travelers),[12] the post-Baconian seventeenth-century production of knowledge retained this marriage of rationalist with empiricist endeavors but aimed firmly to subordinate the empirical production of "effects" to the rationalist inquiry of "causes" by the natural philosopher. This hierarchical organization of knowledge responded to a growing anxiety in the late Renaissance about the need to police the proliferating empirical knowledge in order to make it useful for the "common wealth."

In this chapter, I explore the emergence of what we might call a "modern" historical epistemology in Samuel Purchas' collections in the dual cultural context of British inter- and intra-imperial development. Samuel Purchas' travel collections were one of the first – certainly the most comprehensive – attempts to implement the Baconian "scientific" division of intellectual labor between the producers of empirical effects and rationalist causes in distinctly territorial terms. They manifest the emergence of a "mercantilist" epistemic economy in British America that aimed to regulate the production of knowledge about the New World within the spatial hierarchies of imperial political power. Not unlike in sixteenth-century Spain, narratives of shipwreck contained in Purchas' *Hakluytus posthumus*, such as Cabeza de Vaca's "Account" and William Strachey's "A True Reportory," also performed thereby important cultural work in the formation of a "British" imperial ideology during the reign of the Stuarts by narrativizing not only Britain's inter-imperial rivalry with Spain and the Netherlands but also the supersession of Elizabethan aristocratic individualism by the mercantile subject under the Jacobean monarchy. Here, I investigate, first, how Purchas conceptualizes a territorialized order of knowledge production as an editor and collector of empirical travel accounts; second, I place Purchas' spatial organization of knowledge in the historical context of British imperial development during the first quarter of the seventeenth century, particularly the political developments leading to the dissolution of the Virginia Company in 1624, one year before the publication of *Hakluytus posthumus*; third, I explore the role that shipwreck narratives play in Purchas' collections and in the evolution of a "British" imperial ideology with the example of William Strachey's "A True Reportory"; and, fourth, I compare Purchas' historiographic project with that of his "friend" and nemesis John Smith and suggest that the relationship between the two historians of the New World manifests a divergence in models of historiographic authorship that will be of consequence for the evolution of colonial prose narrative discussed in more detail in subsequent chapters.

MATERIALS AND STRUCTURES

Samuel Purchas' literary career had begun in 1613 with the first edition of a travel collection entitled *Purchas his Pilgrimage; or Relations of the World. And the Religions observed in all Ages and Places. Discovered, from the Creation unto this Present*, additional and gradually expanding editions of which appeared in 1614, in 1617, and (posthumously) in 1626. The two subsequent works, *Purchas His Pilgrim. Microcosmus, or the History of Man*.

Relating the Wonders of his Generation, Vanities in his Degeneration, Necessity of his Regeneration, Meditated on the Words of David (1619) and *The King's Tower, and Triumphant Arch of London* (1623), were theological treatises that highlight the intensely religious framework of Purchas' interest in the history of travel. His *magnum opus* appeared only one year before his death and was entitled *Hakluytus posthumus, or Purchas his Pilgrimes, Contayning a History of the World, in Sea Voyages and lande Travells, by Englishmen and others* (1625). It was another collection of travels, though more comprehensive in scope than *Purchas his Pilgrimage*, beginning with the navigations of the early Jews, Ancients, and Christians, moving on to the Renaissance explorations of the Portuguese and Spanish in the New World, and culminating with the early modern travels of the English in the Americas and East India. In its gargantuan size – it was initially published in four volumes but filled twenty when republished by the Hakluyt Society in 1905–7 – *Hakluytus posthumus* resembled other Renaissance collections of travel narratives before and after Purchas, such as those of Giovanni Ramusio, Richard Eden, Richard Hakluyt, and Melchisédec Thévenot, all of whom eagerly compiled, printed, and re-printed the European record of new empirical information about the world, accumulating with each new voyage.

As the title suggests, however, *Hakluytus poshumus* was specifically intended to stand in the tradition of the now-deceased Hakluyt (1552?–1616), to whose manuscript collection Purchas owed 121 of the narratives included in *Hakluytus posthumus*, though only 14 of them had been included in the last edition of Hakluyt's *Principal Navigations* a quarter of a century earlier.[13] In the preface to *Hakluytus posthumus*, Purchas announced that his history of the world proceeded "by a New way of Eye-evidence," as prescribed by the new "inductive" method which was to govern the advancement of learning in modern times (1: xxxvii). Of course, this "New way of Eye-evidence" was not really new any longer in 1625, after Hakluyt had also been using empirical eyewitness accounts in modern geographical histories since the 1580s. What was still new, however, in 1625 was the theoretical and meta-historical formalization of Hakluyt's methods and practices, a historiographic meta-discourse that betrayed the strong influence of the Baconian reform of Natural Philosophy. The manuscripts he had inherited from Hakluyt, Purchas argued, provided him only with the raw materials for his own project in New World historiography. What made *Hakluytus posthumus* "new," and thus his "owne," was his scientific "method" in arranging, editing, and abridging. As for "Master Hakluyt's many yeeres of Collections," he wrote, "I will thus farre honour, that though it be but

Materials,...yet that stocke encouraged me to use my endevours in and for the rest." Whereas Hakluyt had presented "but Materials," it was Purchas' own achievement to "forme and frame those Materials to their due place and order in the Aedifice, the whole Artifice (such as it is) being mine owne" (I: xli).

When "form[ing] and fram[ing]" this edifice out of the material supplied by his pilgrims, Purchas targeted especially their rhetorical parts for excision but tended to retain empirically based descriptions of the natural environment and indigenous cultures. Typically, he justified these cuts by pointing out that (as in the case of a section selected for omission in Richard Whibbourne's narrative about Newfoundland) "the author useth reasons to perswade" and that therefore the passage was "omitted" (XIX: 438). More significant than these editorial practices in themselves, however, are Purchas' extended meta-historical discourses on his "method" to which they lend occasion. For, lest any of his readers failed to notice his heavy editorial hand, he pointed out who stood as the assembling and controlling mastermind behind the travels of "His" pilgrims in print: the narratives included in his collection were to be reduced, he said, to being as the "Brickes" are to the "Architects" when building their "Theoreticall structures" of modern knowledge. They were:

What a World of Travellers have by their owne eyes observed in this kinde, [which] is here (for the most part in their owne words transcribed or translated) delivered . . . as David prepared materials for Salomons Temple; or (if that be too arrogant) as Alex. furnished Aristotle with Huntsmen and Observers or Creatures, to acquaint him with their diversified kinds and natures; or (if that also seeme too ambitious) as Sense by Induction of particulars yeeldeth the premisses to Reasons Syllogistical arguing; or if we shall be yet more homely, as Pioners are employd by Enginers, and Laboureres serve Masons, and Bricklayers, and these the best Surveyers and Architects: so here Purchas and his Pilgrimes minister individual and sensible materials (as it were with Stones, Brickes and Mortar) to those universall Speculators for their Theoreticall structures. (I: xl)

By employing the language of divided labor – of pioneers and engineers, laborers, masons, brick-layers, surveyors, and architects – Purchas creates his own authority and license to commentate, excise, and paraphrase his sources. He fashions his editorial role as a Baconian collector who stands somewhere between the empirical pilgrim and the speculating historian, straddling the divide between the two professions in the production of modern knowledge. "[W]ell may the Author be ranked," he writes in reference to himself, with such Labourers (howsoever here a Masterbuilder also) for that he hath been forced as much to the Hod, Baroow and Trowel, as to contemplative survaying: neither in so many Labyrinthian Perambulations thorow, and Circumnavigations about the World in this and his other Workes, was ever enabled to maintaine a Vicarian or Subordinate Scribe, but his own hands to worke, as well as his head to contrive these voluminous Buildings; except in some few Transcriptions or Translations. (1: xl–xli)

In drawing a distinction between what he calls the "materials" and the "structures" in the writing of history, Purchas' meta-historical discourses manifest an important transformation in the epistemological status of the empirical travel account as a text in early modern historiography. As Jorge Cañizares Esguerra has explained, the attempt to separate "primary" from "secondary," and "archival" from "published," texts constitutes a "new art of reading" in the evolution of Western historiography that originated in an early modern debate over the question of "how to write the history of the New World" and that was at the epistemological foundation of modern historicism. Whereas textual criticism during the sixteenth century had primarily been a philological endeavor, geared toward an assessment of the authenticity of texts – as, for example, in the famous cases of Martin Luther, Lorenzo Valla, or Fray Luis de León, each of whom had proved Latin documents written by Church authorities to be anachronisms or corruptions of an earlier original – post-Renaissance historians became increasingly interested in texts not from a philological but from a factual point of view. For this purpose historians read empirical travel accounts for the "natural" information contained therein and subjected them to various sorts of factual criticism by comparing them to one another and by scrutinizing them for internal consistency.[14]

In England, the cultural anxiety about the need to "police" empirical travel accounts in an expanding world is manifest in a proliferation of manuals aimed at prescribing, formalizing, and regularizing the content and style of travel histories. As early as 1575, Jerome Turler, in his *The Traveiler*, had proposed recommendations on "the maner, and order of traveling...into straunge and forrein Countreys," in particular on "What things are to be considered in traveilinge," such as

the lande what maner one it is, and...the people that dwell therein, whether thy bee stronge or weake, many or fewe, the Lande good or bad; what Cyties there bee, walled or not walled; the soyle fertile or barreine; wooddie or champion; so That there bee five principal poyntes too bee considered in euerie Cuntruy: the fame, figure, binesse, jurisdiction, and situation.[15]

Similarly, in 1606 – one year after the publication of Bacon's *The Advancement of Learning* – Thomas Palmer published an essay entitled *Hovv to make our Travailes...profitable*, in which he addressed himself to remedying "the manifould errors and misprisions, that the greater sort of such as trauaile into forraine Countries, haue theretofore committed" and to giving a "perfect rule" on "how to make the trauailes of other men who for the good of this kingdom wherein they liue so happily, their better seruiue to his Maiestie." In his essay, he presented a quasi-scientific taxonomy of travel, prescribing moral conduct for travelers in various situations and things to be taken account of in their narratives. He especially calls upon the "General Voluntarie Trauailers" (meaning those who travel for curiosity, like aristocrats, not necessity, like soldiers) that before traveling they "counsaile and deliberate with themselves, whether they bee mooued with the iust pretence of doing good to the Common weale...or whether their owne lusts and affections pricke them not forward." He chastised those who traveled for "the disordinate appetite of man, corrupt and vnfauorie (as Ambition, Sensualitie, vaine glorie, couetousnes, vanitie of knowledge, and such like)". With regard to the content of travel accounts, he specified a number of topical heads in order to provide the traveler with an order to follow in making his (and in special cases her) observations, such as place names, population, situation, quantity, commodities, air, soil, rivers, springs, buildings, towns, fortifications, trade, farming, clothing, laws, religion, customs, government, and diplomacy.[16]

While Turler's and Palmer's prescriptions were still primarily intended as guides for the genteel traveler in Europe, who should have knowledge of the "Artes" such as astronomy, cosmography, geography, hydrography, geometry, arithmetic, and architecture for traveling in "ciuill" Italy,[17] in the course of the seventeenth century, these prescriptions in Natural Philosophy became confined to the recording of empirically observable facts.[18] Also, they were now increasingly addressed not to traveling aristocrats in Europe but rather to mariners and merchants traveling overseas in colonial territory, who were instructed to supply "particulars" rather than "generals," and topical first-hand observations rather than theories and rhetoric. In his "General Heads for a Natural History of a Countrey," for example, first published in the *Philosophical Transactions of the Royal Society of London* in 1665, Robert Boyle provided "Articles of inquisition about particulars" for travelers that would be instrumental for the natural philosopher to "superstruct" (as he put it) a "solid and useful Philosophy upon." Of particular interest were hereby (apart from the natural environment) "Natives and Strangers, that have been long settled there, And in particular, their Stature, Shape, Colour,

Features, Strength, Agility, Beauty (or the want of it), Complexions, Hair, Dyer, Inclinations, and Customs that seem not due to Education." This new historical inquiry encompassed not only climate, soil, flora, fauna, and animal world, but also man, "Natives" as well as "Strangers" who had been transplanted there.[19] Whereas Turler's and Palmer's instructions were still essentially pieces of moral and rhetorical advice to traveling authors for writing their histories, Boyle's are instructions to instrumental and faceless data-collectors whose empirical sensory perceptions would serve as the factual basis, the "materials," for the "superstructing" philosophical historian. The "primary" text is hereby increasingly seen as a transparent vehicle for bare and pre-textual "facts," thus becoming the subject of factual scrutiny and discipline by the historian.

There is then a certain irony in the circumstance that Purchas has become the subject of "denigration and contempt" by modern historians in comparison with Hakluyt.[20] From the point of view of the seventeenth century, criticisms that Purchas was "inferior" to Hakluyt as an editor because in Purchas there is "no clear distinction between his sources" and his own "commentary" are anachronistic, for the modern epistemological distinction between "primary" and "secondary" texts had not yet solidified in early seventeenth-century England but was only *in the process of doing so*. For Hakluyt, the individual voyage he printed was not a "source" and he was not a historian – the authors whose voyages he printed were. Historiographic authorship in Hakluyt's collections was essentially a Humanist one, modeled on the Greek example of Herodotus, who had also combined the role of the traveler and historian.[21] In Purchas, by contrast, we see the opening of an epistemological gap between the empirical traveler and the philosophical historian, between "primary" and "secondary" text, as the epistemological status of historical discourse was transformed from its previous existence in the realm of the Humanist rhetorical arts to a modern discipline aspiring to proto-scientific "objectivity." While Purchas' travel collections began to articulate this "new art of reading" that Cañizares-Esguerra sees at the root of the modern distinction between primary and secondary sources, Purchas himself is neither yet laborer nor master-builder, his texts neither yet historical source material nor modern historical discourse, still straddling the epistemological fault line in the making of which they were productive. Perhaps the severe censure that Purchas has received from some modern historians betrays a certain anxiety on their own part about what Peter Novick has called "the myth of historical objectivity" that has underwritten the cultural authority of the historical profession in modern times.[22] Purchas' texts still too imperfectly mask the modern ideology that "facts" can be isolated from texts, thus reminding us that this modern ideology itself has a history; that, from a pre-modern point of view, the historian's discipline was a branch of rhetoric; and that, from a postmodern point of view, there lurk specters (such as Hayden White), who would relegate the study of history to departments of modern languages.[23]

What caused this transformation in historical epistemology in early modern England? Historians of science have generally seen this shift in the light of seventeenth-century English social history, as a compromise solution in the attempt to accommodate while yet subordinating the rising "middling" classes in the scientific production of knowledge.[24] It is significant to note, however, that long before Boyle, Samuel Purchas articulates the new order of knowledge production not in the language of social space – of top and bottom – but of geographical space – of periphery and center – thereby formulating not so much a "sociology" but rather a "geography of truth." Thus, in the first edition of *Pilgrimage* (1613) he had still portrayed his role as an editor in the language of the metaphorical pilgrim who himself plowed the perilous seas of countless printed and manuscript travels in his "Paper-barke," toiling to bring them "home" to his English Ithaca:

I also begin to grow weary of the travell in an other World, willing to looke homewards; and therefore am now embarqued on the Peruvian coast, where the Peaceable Sea may free me of those former dangers whereto my Pilgrimage was subject,...and now by this commoditie of my Paper-barke, I may both direct my course homewards, and yet walke, as intending another contrary, or diuerse voyage. And euen as those heauenly Planets in their Wandering and yet most constant course, are guided by the generall motion of that vniuersall Wheele, and yet forget not their owne peculiar, so I, in my wandering Discoveries propound all an euery Place of the World, to be the place of my exercise and subject of my Labour, but yet the smoke of Ithaca is sweetest, and my knowing all would be but a melancholy maze, if I should not come home to fill English eares with the newes.[25]

In 1613 the "pilgrimage" was still his own, a "travail" that virtually took him to the "other World" in the act of reading, collecting, and editing. By the time he completed his later *Hakluytus posthumus* in 1625, by contrast, he had re-conceptualized his relationship to the travelers whose journeys he printed. He now drew on metaphors derived not from the language of virtual travel and fiction ("Paper-barke") but of science – of mechanics, geometry, and astronomy – in order to convey a new relationship between his traveling pilgrims and himself as a collector/historian: he now is the stay-at-home historian who boasts of having "never travelled two hundred miles from Thaxted in Essex...where he was borne" (xx: 130). Located at the "Centre" of the British empire, he holds "his Pilgrimes" by the "line" of his scientific authority on the imperial periphery (the "Circumference"). "We have now compassed the World," he concludes his *Hakluytus posthumus*,

[i]n the Course of so many Planets, every of which had a peculiar wandering, and yet noe erring from the publike benefit of the Universe. And as in Geometricall compasses one foote is fixed in the Centre, while the other mooveth in the Circumference, so is it with Purchas and his Pilgrimes, in this Geographical compassing: they have their owne motions, but ordered in this Circumference, from, for, and by hims which abideth at home in his Centre, and never travelled two hundred miles from Thaxted in Essex, where he was borne. All their lines tend to this Centre, and this Centre to the Basis and Ground thereof, that is to his Country, to the honour and benefit wherof, he and all his are due. (xx: 130)

Purchas' literary career as a collector and historian of the New World thus chronicles the beginning of what Mary Louise Pratt has called a "planetary consciousness" in the early modern Atlantic world, a thoroughly Euro-centric conception of the world which would culminate with its eighteenth-century rationalization by metaphors derived from the scientific theory of gravity.[26] Of course, Samuel Purchas' metaphors here do not yet draw on theories of gravity – a late seventeenth-century invention. His Pilgrims' travels, like those of seventeenth-century planets, are the "peculiar wandering[s]" of some mysterious will – a Cartesian "vortex" – held on the periphery ("Circumference") and revealed for the public to behold by his "art" as a man of science – the leash ("line") of his "Geometricall compasses." Thus, Purchas' work underscores that this cultural formation involved not only the image of the world that was being produced but also the methods of producing that image: a production of knowledge based on the division of intellectual labor between imperial periphery and center, with the former providing the "materials" and the latter the "structures" in New World historiography.

Apart from emphasizing his scientific method in "form[ing] and fram[ing]" his materials and his geographically stationary location at the "Centre" of empire, Purchas fashioned his authorial persona by professing his detachment and neutrality with regard to the events of his own time, typically suggesting that "appointed Commissioners... examine the Causes" in overtly political matters. As far as his own role as a historian and collector was concerned, he humbly announced that "I am no fit Relator of things ensuing, and farre unfitter Umpire in such differences" (xix: 170). But despite his claim that "I side no where" (xix: 217), it would be a mistake to see his professions of neutrality as evidence of the essentially "apolitical" character of Purchas' works.[27] As D. R. Woolf has shown, this posture was a new, though increasingly preferred, rhetorical model of historiographic authorship in Stuart England not only in natural but also in civil history, as in the works of John Selden. Its emergence marked a distinct and self-conscious "alternative to the older humanist notion" of the Renaissance and initiated a gradual shift in the relationship between scholarship and history in the course of which "the meaning of the word 'history'... evolved into something close to its modern sense." However, this new model of historiographic authorship, which has since solidified into a modern ideology, was still in competition with other models during the early seventeenth century, and the choice of one over another model had distinctly political implications. If the historiography written by the Stuart historians increasingly appears to resemble a model of "objective, modern scholarship," Woolf argues, it is not because it is less polemical but because it is "in some ways more so, for all its author's protestations of neutrality." When matters of politics were increasingly becoming reserved for the department of state and matters of science for the department of knowledge, the renunciation of political rhetoric in historiography *is* the political rhetoric that rationalizes the division of labor and the effacement of the political subject under an absolute monarchy.[28]

In order to understand the specific reasons why Purchas re-defined Hakluyt's project in imperial history in terms of spatialized hierarchies, it will be necessary to place his works in the historical context of the two and a half decades separating his *Hakluytus posthumus* from the last edition of Hakluyt's *Principal Navigations*, especially in light of the events of British imperial history as represented by Purchas himself in his works. In other words, we must see the logic of the *form* of his works in light of the logic of their historical *content*. Despite Purchas' protestations of neutrality, his selections and excisions of materials betray a number of distinct geo-political interests at stake in the first British colonial ventures in the New World that help explain his concern for the spatial control of knowledge, manifest in his conception of historiographic authorship.

"[L]ONG ROYAL ARMES": THE GEOPOLITICS OF *HAKLUYTUS POSTHUMUS*

When the first English settlement at Jamestown was attacked and nearly annihilated by the Powhowton confederacy in the so-called "Virginia Massacre" of 1622, Purchas composed a short treatise entitled "Virginia's Verger: Or a Discourse shewing the benefits which may grow to this Kingdome from American English Plantations" and later included it as the concluding piece on Viriginia in *Hakluytus posthumus*. "Virginia's Verger" offered an extended theoretical disquisition on what he called the "Law of Nature and Nations" that explained the reasons why Native Americans had forfeited their title to Virginia to the English. The English claim to the land had been established, he argued, by the rights of "first discovery, first actuall possession, prescription, gift, cession, and livery of seisin, sale for price natural Inheritance of the English their naturally borne, and the unnaturall outcries of many unnaturally murthered" (xix: 225). In order to preempt conceivable objections that the acts of violence committed by the Indians had been in legitimate self-defense, Purchas emphasized their allegedly natural savagery and barbarity:

[C]onsidering so good a Country, so bad people, having little of Humanitie but shape, ignorant of Civilitie, of Arts, or Religion; more brutish then the beasts they hunt, more wild and unmanly then that unmanned wild Countrey, which they range rather then inhabite; captivated also to Satans tyranny in foolish pieties, mad impieties, wicked idlenesse, busie and bloudy wickednesse: hence have wee fit objects of zeale and pitie, to deliver from the power of darknesse . . . God in wisedome having enriched the Savage Countries, that those riches might be attractives for Christian suters, which there may sowe spirituals and reape temporals. (xix: 231–2)

The ethno-historian Francis Jennings has perhaps been the harshest critic of Purchas' unflattering portrayal of Native Americans in "Virginia's Verger," arguing that it manifests the beginning of an insidiously racist "cant of conquest" that rationalized the English "invasion" of America and the systematic destruction of its Native peoples.[29] In a more nuanced reading, the anthropologist James Boon has further called attention also to some considerable inconsistencies in Purchas' ethnographic representations of Native Americans – inconsistencies that cannot fully be accommodated by Jennings' reading; rather, Boon argues, they must be seen in the context of the "domestic infrastructures" in which the historian/ethnographer Purchas wrote. For example, Boon sees Purchas' emphasis on Native American "vagrancy" not only as a rationalization for the appropriation of Native lands but also as a reflection of a Jacobean social politics in England, illustrating his larger argument that "cultures conceptualize their own diversity and the diversity of others, both positively and pejoratively, in related symbols."[30] Indeed, while there can be little doubt that Purchas' geographical histories had an underlying "interest" in imperial appropriation, the contest for power in the destabilizing cultural exchanges of the New World encounter was more complex than Jennings' account suggests; it was not a binary and static struggle between a monolithic English culture on the one hand and a Native American culture on the other but rather a complex cultural geography that engendered many unlikely alliances that often transcended divisions along racial lines.

Another aspect of Purchas' works has already become apparent in my brief introductory summary of Cabeza de Vaca's "English career" – the perpetuation of the anti-Catholic and anti-Spanish "Black Legend" that had originated with the Elizabethan translators of Spanish texts about the New World, such as Richard Hakluyt and Richard Eden. Thus, in addition to Cabeza de Vaca's narrative of the Pánfilo de Narváez expedition and the Count of Elba's narrative of the Hernando de Soto expedition, Purchas' coverage of Spanish America included the obligatory excerpts from the deprecatory histories of Las Casas and Benzoni, heavily edited selections from the Jesuit and court historians Acosta, Oviedo, and Herrera, as well as other Spanish and Portuguese authors who had criticized the practices of the Spanish conquerors. In the same spirit, Purchas published also the first edition of an ancient Mexican pictographic manuscript, the Codex Mendoza (xv: 412–504), which had been prepared in New Spain in 1541–2 and shipped to Charles V but was intercepted on the way by French privateers and later purchased by Hakluyt. Purchas called it the "choisest of my Jewels," there not being "an one History of this kinde in the world comparable to this, so fully expressing so much without Letters" (xv: 412, 414). Moreover, in his translations from the Inca Garcilaso de la Vega's *Comentarios reales* (1609) and *Historia general del Perú* (1617), he emphasized ethnographic information on Inca culture and the historical parts dealing with the murder of the warring Inca half-brothers Atahualpa and Huascar after the arrival of the Spaniards, as well as with the execution of the last Inca Tupac Amaru on the order of Viceroy Francisco de Toledo (xvii: 311–412). Already in his earlier *Pilgrimage*, he had argued that the Spaniards had given to the Americans "an Iron Age for a Golden":

imposing a heavy yoke of servitude which hath consumed worlds of people in this New World, and made the Name of Christ and Christians to stinke amongst them; yea they abhorre the Sea it selfe for bringing forth such monsters, as they thinke the Spaniards: whom for their execrable wickedness, they esteemed, not to come of humane generation, but of the froth of the Sea, and therefore call them Viracocha, or Sea-froth.[31]

Passages such as this one would thus seem to substantiate arguments by modern Spanish and Spanish American historians and philosophers of history who have detected a distinctly anti-Catholic geo-political agenda at the root of modern historical epistemologies, originating with Britain's early modern geo-political struggle against Spain for imperial hegemony in the New World. Purchas, in the act of translating the travel accounts of the Iberian discoverers, conquerors, and missionaries, appropriates the knowledge contained therein while yet discrediting the authority of their authors, and thus paving the way ideologically and epistemologically for Britain's physical annexation of American territory claimed by Spain.[32]

But the politics of Purchas' documentation of the history of the Spanish empire in the New World are still more complex than a monolithic English inter-imperial rivalry with Spain. Cabeza de Vaca's account of Spanish disasters in the New World joined in *Hakluytus posthumus* dozens of other shipwreck narratives also by English and Dutch adventurers in both east and west. Beginning with the account of the very first expedition sent out by the English East India Company – Sir James Lancaster's voyage of 1600 – one story after another told of English ships wrecked, cargoes destroyed, and investments lost; of Englishmen cast-away, captured, maimed, and killed by savage natives in far-away lands. One expedition sent out to India in 1608, for example, saw one of the two ships wrecked on Ascension Island, a bloody fight with the natives of Mozambique, the crew's captivity by the Portuguese and their escape, a mutiny on the homeward voyage, and – when the shores of England were almost in sight – shipwreck off the coast of France with the entire cargo lost. Of a crew of seventy-five, a mere ten survived (III: 355–7). Another account, written by the merchant John Milward, relates a voyage in 1610 in which the largest and most famous ship of its day, the *Trades Increase*, ran aground off the coast of Java, and "all her men died in the careening of her" (IV: 283). Indeed, these were not stories that would raise the stocks of the East India Company with joyful news about the profits to be made in the imperial rivalry with Spain. Their sum conveyed such an overall "dreary" picture of the European colonial enterprise that, as one reader has observed, it "may be wondered how they could serve as propaganda."[33]

In 1625, however, Samuel Purchas was no longer interested primarily in the promotion of the English imperial project as it had been conceived by his Elizabethan predecessor Hakluyt; his interest lay rather in an ideological re-definition of that project. The early English ventures to America conducted by the Elizabethans during the late sixteenth century had been inspired not by the English examples of Sir Thomas Smith and Walter Devereux in Ireland during the 1570s but rather by the Spanish model of the conquistadors in the New World – of subduing native cities and kingdoms, of establishing personal lordships, and of living upon rents and tributes.[34] As stridently as they had professed their hatred of the Spaniards and indicted their alleged cruelties, the Elizabethans had considered the Iberian model of universal conquest to be emulated and rivaled rather than to be superseded. For a Walter Ralegh, a Richard Hakluyt, or a Francis Drake, there was no essential difference between Spain's and England's New Worlds. Thus, although Ralegh could not report ever actually having *seen* its fabled riches upon his return from Guiana, he *knew* that Guiana held the "*same*" as or even "*more*" than what the Spaniards had found in Peru. The country had

> *more* abundance of gold than any part of Peru, and *as many or more* great cities than ever Peru had when it flourished most. It is governed by the *same* laws, and the emperor and people observe the *same* religion and the *same* form and policies in government as was used in Peru, *not differing in any part*, and I have been assured by such of the Spaniards as have seen Manoa, the imperial city of Guiana, that for greatness, for the riches, and for the excellent seat, it far *exceedeth* any of the world, at least so much of the world as is known to the Spanish nation. It is founded upon a lake of salt water of 200 leagues long, *like unto* mare caspium.³⁵

During the first couple of decades of the seventeenth century, however, this rhetoric of emulation and similitude in English historiography about the New World gradually gave way to a new rhetoric that identified a "British" imperial enterprise as being essentially *different* from the "Spanish" model of conquest, which became, as Jeffrey Knapp puts it, an example of "Elizabethan colonialism gone wrong."³⁶ While the gold of the Indies had made Spain the largest Christian empire the world had seen, so this Protestant narrative went, it had not reformed the world, indeed had sold the world into anti-Christian slavery. However, "Spanish" vanity and lust for American gold had been punished by God in the wreck of Spain's economy, in the humiliation of her haughty Armada in 1588, as well as in the defeat of her armies in the Netherlands by the forces of Protestantism, united since the alliance of Utrecht in 1581. The accessions of Philip III in 1598 and of Philip IV in 1621 to the throne of Spain seemed to have marked a steady decline in Spain's economic and geo-political might. In modern times, seventeenth-century English historians explained, God manifested Himself in history not by aiding human conquests with divine miracles – a Catholic "superstition" – but rather by the "natural" working of trade.³⁷ As one English writer pointed out, "miracle[s]" were now obsolete, because in international commerce the "sacred word will have a powerfull message throughout the world," so that all nations may be "reduced to the kingdom of grace."³⁸

This rhetorical shift from emulation and rivalry to differentiation and supersession with regard to the Spanish model in English imperial rhetoric in a period that was otherwise marked by considerable Hispanophilia in Stuart

England requires some explanation. In part, it may be seen as the product of a domestic political process that David Armitage has described as a transformation from an Elizabethan "English" to a Jacobean "British" imperial ideology. Not unlike in the Iberian case, with the union of the crowns of Castile and Aragon, England's imperialist expansionism also originated in a symbiotic relationship with dynastic consolidation – as the previously separate "kingdoms" of England, Ireland, and Scotland became united under one centralized composite monarchy with the accession of James I in 1603. Theorists of empire in Great Britain, like those earlier in Spain, increasingly turned in this context to religion as the ideological glue that was to bind the previously separate kingdoms together under the common umbrella of one imperial crown. According to Armitage, the differences between the Elizabethan Hakluyt and the Jacobean Purchas were thus paradigmatic: whereas the work of Hakluyt had "remained thoroughly English" in scope and owed "more to his classicism than to his Protestantism," Purchas placed England "firmly in the context of the history of the Three Kingdoms, of Europe, and of a wider world conceived within sacred time." Unlike orthodox Catholicism, whose Thomist foundation provided a congenial ground on which to build a political claim to earthly dominions, Protestantism, in its hampering tendency toward decentralized ecclesiastic authority and its metastasizing Augustinian chasm between the City of God and the City of Man, ultimately proved internally too divided and dogmatically unsuitable to serve as the ideological foundation for Great Britain's claim to foreign dominions. The ideology of British imperialism was therefore, Armitage concludes, "more negative in content than affirmative in structure." Mainly a secularist opposition to Spain's claim to a universal Catholic imperium, the ideological origins of the British empire were "identifiably Protestant only in so far as they related to rights of possession."[39] The secular principle at the root of British imperialist ideology – liberty, commerce, property, religious tolerance – thus originated in part in a north/south dialectic with what British empire builders such as Samuel Purchas imagined (or made out to be) the "Catholic" empire of Spain, as they aimed to define Great Britain's role in a cosmopolitan world in relation to other European empires, particularly Spain.

However, by 1625 – the year in which Purchas published *Purchas his Pilgrims* – the questions raised by modern empires were no longer confined in their geo-political scope to a European theater of action – the "triangular" relationship of the Three Kingdoms and Britain's rivalry with Spain. Another question increasingly vexing to British theoreticians of empire was how to define the relationship between Great Britain and her new colonies across the Atlantic Ocean. The British experience in working out a constitutional relationship between the Three Kingdoms on the British Isles seemed utterly inadequate to serve as a model to be followed in this unprecedented situation. While England had also founded colonies in Ireland, that island had been incorporated into the British empire not as an English "colony" but rather as a "Kingdom" that encompassed not only the English settlers there but also the native Irish population. Would the American colonies be "Kingdoms," equal to Scotland, Ireland, and England herself? Were the Native inhabitants of Virginia and New England "British" citizens?

If the Three Kingdoms were of limited exemplary value, the Classical examples of antiquity, Greece and Rome, proved equally problematic. Insofar as the ancient Greek colonies were largely autonomous settlements of surplus population that had started new polities in previously "barbarous" lands and that formed only a loose maritime confederacy with the homeland, they bore a certain resemblance to the modern English colonies in America during their inception. Indeed, in Renaissance England, from Thomas More's Utopian colonies to Richard Hakluyt's "Discourse on Western Planting," when England's New Worlds were still largely a futuristic fantasy, the ancient Greek model in Mediterranean colonies had held considerable currency.[40] However, the Hellenistic model of colonialism offered few advantages to the motherland – short of alleviating domestic population pressure. Increasingly, British theorists of empire therefore invoked the Roman model, with its mission to "civilize" the uncivilized in an *imperium* where all roads still converged in Rome. Yet the difference between the continental empire of ancient Rome and Britain's modern trans-oceanic empires was all too obvious in their respective relations to geographic space: whereas the challenge to the definition of the Roman empire had been how to *limit* political power to geographic space (*"Limes"*), the challenge to modern trans-atlantic empire was how to *connect* geographically disparate units under one polity, how to manage spatial distance across geographic divides. The unprecedented problem peculiar to modern trans-oceanic colonial empires was, as Jack Greene has observed, that of how a metropolitan government would "exert and maintain its authority within an extended polity, not every part of which was fully and formally incorporated into the central government." Soon after England's first footholds in the New World had been secured, therefore, the metropolitan authorities, not unlike the Spanish Crown a hundred years earlier, increasingly insisted on a territorial hierarchy between what they called the "inferior dominion[s]" of the New World and the "Dominion Superior" of the

Three Kingdoms under the "absolute obedience to the King's authority."⁴¹ To be sure, this territorial hierarchy would not become fully codified and enforced in British America until after the Restoration of the Stuart monarchy in 1660 – with the passing of several mercantilist Navigation Acts, the creation of the Lords of Trade, and a concerted effort to revoke the colonial charters earlier granted, in order to centralize political administration in the metropolis. But the question of how to define the relationship between Great Britain and her New World colonies had been latent since the founding of Jamestown in 1607 and first emerged on the British imperial political landscape precisely during the years of Purchas' activity as a theoretician of empire – with the debate leading up to the revocation of the Virginia Company's charter in 1624, one year before the publication of *Hakluytus posthumus*.

If the political history of British imperialism in America after the middle of the seventeenth century would increasingly revolve around the question of how to "reconstruct the political relationship between the monarchy and the colonies in a way that would both significantly enhance the power of the crown at the center and weaken the effective authority of legal institutions in the peripheries,"⁴² this political history had its first theoretician in Samuel Purchas. In search for an answer, Purchas turned, however clandestinely, a curious eye not to Britain's Protestant neighbors – the colonial ventures of the Dutch republics – but rather to Spanish imperial history in the New World. Not unlike the first Spanish conquest of America a hundred years earlier, the early English conquests had also been conducted on the basis of contractual agreements between the agents of colonization and the monarchy in which the former were granted by the latter a generous amount of latitude to pursue their own personal objectives in return for expanding the national dominions overseas. Of course, whereas in Spanish America this relationship had been articulated in the grants of native tribute labor to individual conquistadors (*encomienda*), in the British context this relationship came to be articulated in the royal grants not of vassals but of land "chartered" to private individuals or joint stock companies.⁴³ In his attempt to re-define the English colonies in the new context of a British American empire, Samuel Purchas, not unlike his sixteenth-century counterparts in Habsburg Spain, also promoted a "demythification" of the illustrious Elizabethan figures of the sixteenth-century discovery and conquest. It is in this context that Purchas' apparently contradictory and ambivalent positions on the Spanish empire in the Americas – "consistently anti-papal but only incidentally anti-Spanish" (as Armitage observes) – must be seen. While Purchas aimed to define a "British" empire of Protestantism and commerce in distinction to a "Spanish" empire of Catholicism and conquest, he also aimed to define a "British" empire of mercantilism and absolute monarchy in distinction to the "English" empire of pirate sea dogs and aristocratic power. When Purchas wrote "I question not the Right of the Spanish Crowne in those parts...I quarrell the Pope only," he did so because Spanish imperial history in the New World offered a concrete modern pretext for the questions that now also concerned British theorists of empire – questions of how a colonial empire can be made profitable not only to the particular wealth of the colonists abroad but also to the "common wealth" at home.

To be sure, from the vantage point of 1625, the historical record of England's first colonial ventures provided Purchas with ample ammunition in his endeavor. The first attempt to establish an English colony, by Sir Humphrey Gilbert in Newfoundland in 1583, had literally ended in a storm; the first English colony actually established in America, by Ralegh in 1585, had inexplicably vanished at Roanoke; and the first colony that had lasted so far, Jamestown in Virginia, had barely survived in the face of recurrent disasters. Meanwhile, in 1620, a second colony had been established by a band of religious Separatists to the north who had arrived, via the Netherlands, at Plymouth. However, that particular brand of permanent "pilgrims" seemed more preoccupied with their own spiritual salvation in the New World than with making profitable returns on their investors' money in the Old. The aristocratic regime that had been improvised at Jamestown in 1607 was still in 1616 remembered by John Rolfe for its "dissentions and jarres [that] were daily sowne amongst them, that they choaked the seed and blasted the fruits of all men's labors."[44] The Virginia Company had reacted to these disasters by blaming the depravity of the English colonists, for the "licence, sedition, and furie, [which] are the fruits of a headie, daring, and vnruly multitude," as John Smith put it in 1610.[45] The colonists' depravity was, of course, not much to be wondered at, since they had come out of England as "the very excrements" of a "full and swelling State," as the minister to the Middle Temple William Crashaw wrote. In a place "wanting pleasures" and subjected to "some pinching miseries," he supposed, they would still become "good and worthie instruments and members of a Commonwealth."[46]

By the second decade of the seventeenth century, the "plain truth" was being spread that Virginia was not a Peru or Mexico, as the early settlers had falsely been made to believe by the early promoters such as Hakluyt. Writers now busily adjusted the story by pointing out that profits depended on the "improvement" of the land, so as to produce something of sufficient value in trade. What was required was not glory or gold won in conquest but rather work and toil for the "common" wealth of the British empire. In order to turn these English "excrements" abroad still into "worthie instruments" of empire, the Company re-formed under the second charter of 1609, creating a military regime under the strong authority of one commissioned governor, who ruled the settlement with an iron hand by enforcing the infamous Virginia Code, or *Lawes Diuine, Morall and Martiall*, authored by Sir Thomas Gates and Sir Thomas Dale and published by William Strachey in 1612. When, despite the implementation of these draconian new measures, profits were still elusive a decade later, English investors ran out of patience. In 1619, Sir Edwin Sandys organized an opposition among the stockholders and gained control over the Company. He proposed abandoning the military regime and revoking the martial laws. Meanwhile, the general enthusiasm that had initially prevailed with regard to England's first colonial enterprise had notably abated. Not only had the horror stories about the abysmal condition of the colony – spread from the lips of some malcontented returnees – begun to take effect; but also, cries could increasingly be heard that England, by joining the newfangled frenzy about New Worlds to be seen, traveled, and conquered, had strayed from her traditional national virtues, which were best guarded by staying at home. "How much more desperate must it then needs bee to send forth our children into those places which are professedly infectious, whose every goodnesse is either impietie, or superstition," Joseph Hall asked in 1617, "Whether it be the enuie, or the pusillanimitie of vs English, we are still ready to vnder-value our owne, and admire forrainers; whiles other Nations haue applauded no professors more then those which they haue borrwed from vs."[47] In order to counter-act the effects of perfidious slanderers of the colony as well as old stick-in-the-muds such as Hall, Sandys published a new pamphlet, written by Edward Waterhouse and entitled *A Declaration of the State of the Colonie and Affaires in Virginia*, informing prospective settlers that the "rigour of Martiall Law, wherewith before they were gouerned, is reduced within the limits prescribed by his Maiesty: and the laudable forme of Iustice and gouernment used in this Realme, established, and followed as neere as may be."[48] Indeed, he was able to rally up several thousand new settlers and sent them off to Virginia. Having arrived there, they died by the hundreds, ill-equipped to sustain themselves, in the Massacre of 1622.

As a result, company officials adopted an increasingly militant "discourse of conquest" that was reminiscent of the early Spanish chronicles of the sixteenth century.[49] Edward Waterhouse, trying to find the positive side in things, even argued that the massacre had much improved the situation of Virginia in the long run – "[b]ecause our hands which before were tied with gentlenesse and faire vsage, are now set at liberty" and "the way of conquering them is much more easie than of ciuilizing them by faire meanes."[50] The Church, on the other hand, called for the patience and sacrifice necessary on every hard path with a glorious end: "Be not you discouraged," John Donne exhorted, "if the promises which you have made to yourselves, or to others, be not so soon discharged; though you se not your money, though you see not your men, though a flood, a flood of blood have broken in upon them, be not discouraged . . . Only let your principal end be the propagation of the glorious Gospel."[51] The Crown, finally, blamed Virginia's failures on the Company leadership, for its continual internal dissensions debilitating the kind of forceful action necessary in running a commonwealth.[52] Soon after the news about the Virginia massacre had reached London, officials at court were quick to discern the vengeance of God, suggesting that the massacre was a just punishment of the Company's infatuation with vain commercial gain and its inability to police the emigrant riffraff in its "enormous excesses of apparel and drinking, the cry whereof cannot but have gone up to heaven, since the infamy hath spread itself to all that have but heard the name of Virginia."[53] When the Crown announced its plans to dissolve the Company, its members petitioned Parliament on 21 April 1624 to intervene on its behalf. The sympathetic Members responded promptly and convened on the matter on 28 April but were, the next day, ordered by James not to meddle in the affair any further. Here was finally a clear case that incontrovertibly demonstrated the superiority of a strong monarchy over Republican government in the attainment of the national "common good." What was required in the affairs of empire was a strong hand that could act independently of the dissensions and quibbles of legislative bodies. About a month later, on 24 May 1624, the Court of King's Bench issued a decree that voided the Company's charter and declared Virginia royal property.[54]

Samual Purchas had been keeping busily abreast of these developments as he was completing his *Hakluytus posthumus*, attending the Company's courts six times between 1622 and 1624. The narratives he included in the section on Virginia betray a keen sensitivity to Jacobean imperial politics. Apart from his own "Virginia Verger," he selected manuscript accounts that had previously been in the possession of Hakluyt but that had remained unpublished – probably in consideration of the Virginia Company's interests – such as Master Thomas Canner's narrative of Bartholomew Gilbert's unsuccessful attempt to penetrate the Chesapeake Bay (the narrative having been concluded by one of Canner's partners after he himself had been killed by Indians), and George Percy's "observations" about Virginia in 1606, which Purchas abridged, breaking off the relation of events in September 1606 (XVIII: 403, 419). From these texts, there emerges a most distinct version of the history of the first English colony. Insofar as a single individual was recognized for the discovery of Virginia, the Elizabethans (such as Hakluyt) had credited Ralegh. This remained the position taken by the Virginia Company throughout its existence in its records and promotional tracts. In the semi-official Company tract *Nova Britannia* (1609), for example, Robert Johnson, while acknowledging John Cabot's voyage, asserts that "we now intend to ground [our title] upon... a more late Discovery and actuall possession, taken in the name and right of Queen Elizabeth, in Anno 1584."[55] Still in 1613, Samuel Purchas himself, in the first edition of *Purchas his Pilgrimage*, had acknowledged Ralegh as the discoverer of Virginian lands, although accrediting Cabot with the discovery of the Virginian seas and slandering Ralegh for making "frivolous" claims:

And well may England court her [Virginia], rather than any other European Lovers, in regard of this long continued amitie, and first discoverie of her Lands and Seas: this [sea] by Sebastian Cabot with his English Mariners, a hundred and fifteene yeares since, and the other [land] by Sir Walter Raleighs charge and direction, Anno Domini one thoussand five hundred fourescore and foure... but hee... [Ralegh] performed nothing, but returned with friuolous allegations.[56]

In its last year of operation, the Virginia Company, in a symbolic act reaffirming its members' essentially Elizabethan and aristocratic understanding of the English overseas project, granted Ralegh's son special membership in the company, since "his father was the first discoverer of Virginia."[57] Purchas, by contrast, undergoes a curious change of mind in this regard. In *Hakluytus posthumus*, he drops his earlier distinction between the discovery of the seas and the discovery of the lands and unequivocally affirms that Virginia was "then discovered by Sir Seb. Cabot" (XIX: 226). Ralegh is now mentioned only as the person who had "sent thither with two Barkes furnished" Captain Amadas, and Captain Barlow, who "in those times [took] formal and actual possession... for her Majesty" (XIX: 226–7).

The position Purchas took on these issues may, incidentally, also explain the final break between Hakluyt and Purchas. We know that the two collectors – who had initially been in close collaboration and even shared an almost-familial relationship, with the older man generously opening his archives to Purchas – later became estranged from each other. Purchas even had to go to great lengths in order to obtain Hakluyt's immense collection when the latter failed to leave it to him at his death in 1616. While the actual reason for the break between the two men must remain speculation here,[58] there can be no doubt that questions of New World history, such as who had first discovered Virginia, increasingly assumed concrete polit-ical implications during these years and exposed the clearly fundamental ideological differences between the Elizabethan Hakluyt and the Jacobean Purchas. Whereas the former had celebrated the aristocratic individualism of the Renaissance explorers and promoted imperial expansion, the latter rewrote the history of the Elizabethan discovery and conquest of the New World from the point of view of Stuart centralizing imperial geopolitics. While Purchas still pays, in this context, tribute to Elizabeth – whom he calls the "Centre of the Centre" and who represents, next to James himself, one of the two "Starres" by the light of which "our Pilgrimes beganne their Progresse" (xx: 131) – it was James alone who "hath combined a Trinitie of Kingdomes into an Unitie," and who "hath rooted out" the feudal prac-tices of "Scottish Fewds, of English Duells, of Irish Bogges" and therefore who ultimately stands "Beyond our victorious Debora not in sex alone, but as Peace is more excellent then War, and Salomon then David" (xx: 131). James emerges in these pages as a new Aeneas or Augustus whose masculine *clementia* prevails over Elizabeth's feminine *furia*.

Not unlike the Habsburg historians a hundred years before, then, the Stuart historian Purchas "demythified" an aristocratic ideology of conquest that had informed the Elizabethan imperial project in the New World with the rhetoric of a Jacobean empire of peace. The Elizabethan aristocrats such as Ralegh, by contrast, become in the pages of Purchas a new version of the Spanish "Iron mindes," "Alchemysts," and "Impostors" who "gave Gold or Silver the Monopoly of wealth" (xix: 232). Indeed, his invectives against the Spanish "Iron Age" of the New World seem conceived largely as a prelude to his immediately subsequent treatment of certain "Mine-mindes" among the English, who, in their greed for gold, have entirely neglected Virginia's other natural resources of potential economic value. "Neither speake I this," he writes, "as if our hopes were blasted, and growne deplorate and desperate this way, the Country being so little searched, and the remote in-land-Mountaines unknowne: but to shew the sordid tincture and base alloy of these Mine-mindes" (xix: 232). His discussion of English colonial history in Virginia is in this way often reminiscent of the indictments of the "greed," "tyranny," "alchemy," and "imposture" of Spanish conquerors:

And if successe hath not been correspondent to English hopes: who seeth not the causes of those disasters? Division that taile-headed Amphisbæna and manyheaded monster, deformed issued of that difformed old Serpent, in some of the Colony there and Company here, hath from time to time thrust in her forged venomous tongue, whereby they have swolne ... A long time Virginia was thought to be much encombered with Englands excrements, ... whence not only lazie drones did not further the Plantation, but wicked Waspes with sharking, and the worst, that is beggerly tyrants, frusted and supplanted the labours of others. (XIX: 236)

Luckily, however, James has decided to come to the rescue of the colonial ship in trouble and with his "long royal armes" has assumed administrative control and responsibility over colonial Virginia: "it hath pleased his Majesty to have a Royall care, as likewise the Honorable Lords of his Majesties privy Councell" by "reach[ing] his long royal armes to another world" (XIX: 237, 238). In time, Purchas hoped, "Virginia may performe as much with equal manuring as ever Britannia and Ireland could promise" (XIX: 238). With the Elizabethan empire of conquest overthrown by the Jacobean empire of commerce, Purchas was confident that Virginia would still yield the promised profits by regulated commercial exchange between England and Virginia. After England had depleted its own supplies of timber after centuries of exploitation, Virginia would become "by divine bounty," the "Magnæ spes altera Britanniæ": "yeah, as England hath wooed and visited Virginia, so herein Virginia will be glad and rejoyce to visit England, in her there-built ships, and to dwell here with us in thence-brought Timbers, and esteeme her selfe advanced to adorne our Towres, and take view of our Pomps and Spectacles" (1: 247). Wood, fish, cattle, fowl, sugar, and spices, Purchas proposes, will be Virginia's exports. In turn, Virginia would become, he hoped, the future market for "our Wools and Clothes, both to the English and civilized Indian, as the Spaniards doe in their Indies by their Wines and Oyle, of which I have already said that they permit not the generall growth in their Indian plantations for the continuance and necessitie of commerce with Spaine" (1: 252).

For his advocacy of commerce rather than conquest as Britain's imperial program Purchas has sometimes been seen as a precursor of economic liberalism. Thus, Richard Helgerson has seen the works of Purchas as a pivotal step in a long-term ideological process, manifest already in Spenser's *The Faerie Queene*, Camões' *Lusiads*, and Richard Hakluyt's *Principal Navigations*, in which the cultural values of a landed aristocracy gradually gave way to those of a merchant class. In Purchas' work, he argues, "as was never possible in Hakluyt or in the work of those Elizabethan contemporaries of Hakluyt, the popular writers who praised merchants, men of trade are preferred to nobles, and they are preferred not for their magnanimity and valor, but for qualities intrinsic to their commercial activity, for diligence, thrift, and worldly knowledge." This gradual transformation from an aristocratic to a commercial value system during the late sixteenth century was accompanied, Helgerson argues, by important generic transformations in literary form. "Though recognized by no system of poetics," he writes, "commerce, like conquest, has its genres." On one pole Helgerson sees here the epic poem, with its elaborate narrative structure and its careful hierarchical ranking of gods and heroes; on the other, the commercial letter, with its bare lists of commodities to be bought or sold in some distant part of the world. The collections of Hakluyt, Helgerson argues, had performed important cultural work in this transformation by bringing "merchants into the nation and gentry into trade," thus representing "a fundamentally new alignment of power in England, one in which merchants and mercantile activity had an ever increasing share." While Hakluyt was hereby the first to make England the champion (as he himself put it) of "free trade of merchandise," Purchas' collections manifest the final triumph in this conflict, a triumph that would later lead to the economic theories of Thomas Mun and Adam Smith.[59]

However, despite the insightfulness of Helgerson's argument about the connections between literary form and ideological content in early modern travel collections such as those of Purchas, it is important to note that Purchas, unlike Hakluyt, was emphatically not an advocate of "free trade of merchandise" and the liberal state but rather of economic mercantilism and political absolutism. While his idea of a regulated system of balanced trade indeed foreshadows the mercantilist theories formulated in Thomas Mun's *Treasure by Foreign Trade* (which was written in the mid-1620s, though not published until 1664), both Mun and Purchas were advocates of the very "mercantile system" later singled out for critique by Adam Smith, who argued that the military protection of colonial trade monopolies wrecked state budgets and ultimately proved "to the great body of the people, mere loss instead of profit."[60] Thus, if historians have often taken exception to Purchas' "windy religiosity" and his "sycophantic adoration of James I" in works that were obviously "licensed by the Crown,"[61] it is due, perhaps, to the fact that they expose, all too clearly for modern liberal sensibilities, that the rise of middle-class culture in seventeenth-century England did not result in a liberating and "fundamentally new alignment of power"; that, rather, the political power of the nobility was not so much supplanted as merely reconstituted on a higher, national level, as Perry Anderson has argued, as baronial courtiers gathered under the royal ensign the monarchical state after their power had been under assault at the local level.[62]

For Purchas, there was, as with unregulated conquest, a dark side also to unregulated commerce. His thoroughly negative view of free trade and Republicanism couldn't be more evident than in his treatment of the confrontations of the English East India Company with the Dutch, whose commercial ventures he saw as being inspired by no higher moral purpose than the gratification of personal greed and checked by no higher authority than that of the individual merchant. While the ill effects of this lack of authority among the Dutch were aggravated by the East Indian climes, the natives – better acquainted with human infirmities in a state of nature – immediately recognized the inferiority of the Dutch in their lack of a strong monarchy. In the account of John Davis, for example, the author records a Dutchman's experience with a native king, who:

> did often demand of him, if he were not of England, which he did strongly denie, using some unfit speeches of our Nation [Purchas' marginal note: "Englishmen abused by Hollander"] ... he was not of England but of Flanders, and at the King's service. I have heard of England [Purchas' marginal note: "England famous"], said the King, but not of Flanders; what Land is that? He further enquired of the King, State, and Government; whereof our man made large report, refusing the Authoritie of a King, relating the government of Aristocratie ... Again [the King] required to show if there were no Englishmen in the ships: he answered, there be some English [Purchas' marginal note: "Diverse Englishmen in this Voyage"] in the ships, but they have been bred up in Flanders. I understand, said the King, that there be some that differ both in apparell, language, and fashion: what are those? he answered, English. of which my chiefe Pilot is one. Well, said the King, I must see those men. (II: 313)

When the natives were informed by the English that the Dutch "had no King, but [that] their Land was ruled by Governors," they immediately discern that "the English men are good, [and that] the Hollanders are naught" (II: 486, 457). The making of imperial diplomacy, international commerce, and national fame required a strong monarchy, such as the one to which James I aspired. In this regard, Englishmen should not emulate their Protestant compatriots, the Dutch, but rather surprisingly, the Spanish monarchy! Then the king "enquired much of England, of the Queene, of her Basha's, and how she could hold warres with so great King as the Spaniards? (for he thinketh that Europe is all Spanish)" (II: 314). However, after being better advised, another native king accounted it "one of their greatest happinesses to have commerce with so great a King as his Majestie of England" (II: 522).

For Jacobeans such as Samuel Purchas, settler colonialism based on mercantilist trade between Britain and her colonies was thus the key to solving the apparent conflict between imperialism and international commerce and to preventing the inflation that English trade with the Spanish Indies had brought about. By international commerce, John Hagthorpe wrote in his *England's Exchequer* (published in the same year as *Hakluytus posthumus*), "there goes out of this land in mony, and valewable commodities, 2. or 3. millions yearely." In order not to "lie exposed to the malice, and reage of such enemies," it is necessary, "by reuvuing trades decayed, [to] find[] out new, and cherish[] the Plantations."[63] Almost forty years before the publication of Mun's influential treatise in mercantilist theory, Purchas' "Virginia's Verger" was one of the earliest and most comprehensive English articulations of the mercantilist economic program that functioned on the principles of inter-imperial economic protectionism, a regulated system of balanced trade, and an intra-imperial division of labor aimed at the unequal economic development and co-dependency of colonial periphery and center: a program that would govern British imperial policy for nearly two centuries to come.

"TEMPESTS OF DISSENTION": WILLIAM STRACHEY'S "A TRUE REPORTORY"

The travel accounts relating to Virginia and preceding Purchas' own "Virginia's Verger" narrativize his political program in imperial consolidation and centralization. One narrative of particular relevance to the political controversy surrounding the dissolution of the Virginia Company included in *Hakluytus posthumus* was William Strachey's "A True reportory," an account of the events surrounding the wreck of the *Sea Venture* on the Bermudas on its way to Virginia in 1609, the survival of the shipwrecked men on the island, the building of pinnaces, and the passing to Jamestown. There, the survivors found the colonists so destitute and desperate that they were convinced of the irredeemability of the situation and resolved to abandon the colony and return to England. Just as they were sailing down the James River en route for the Atlantic Ocean, however, they encountered the fleet of Sir Thomas West, the Lord De-La-Warre, who had been sent as the new governor vested with the strong powers that the second charter of 1609 had established for that office. The ships returned to Jamestown, De-La-Warre assumed official authority over the colony, and soon the situation was restored.

The author of the narrative, William Strachey, had been one of the losers in the cultural transformations occurring over the course of his lifetime (1572–1621). A country gentleman descended from a minor aristocratic family in decline, he had come to London in search of advancement and success. After attending Cambridge, he proceeded to Gray's Inn, then one of the largest Inns at court. Soon, however, he found himself in debt, with the expenses of courtly life exceeding what his modest family estate afforded him. Like many other men of his background, he was forced to consider the only remedy suggested by his friend, the playwright Ben Jonson: to "repair itself by Constantinople, Ireland, or Virginia."[64] This is precisely what Strachey did. In 1606, he accompanied the new representative of the Levant Company, Thomas Glover, to Constantinople in the function of Company secretary. Soon, however, he fell into Glover's disfavor and returned to England in 1608, now "further out of pocket... and debtors' prison correspondingly closer."[65] With his "remedies" in Constantinople having vanished, he soon turned his interests to the New World. The next year, in 1609, he embarked for Virginia as a gentleman settler with the fleet of Sir Thomas Gates, who had been appointed deputy governor until the arrival of Lord De-La-Warre.

The textual history of Strachey's narrative reflects the cultural transformations that it chronicles. It is addressed to an unnamed "excellent Lady" – most likely Sara Smith, wife of Sir Thomas Smith, treasurer of the Virginia Company.[66] Written during Strachey's stay in Virginia and delivered to the Company in London by Sir Thomas Gates in 1609, it circulated in various manuscript copies, one of which came into the possession of Richard Hakluyt and another into that of William Shakespeare, who is generally assumed to have based *The Tempest* on Strachey's account.[67] However, despite having been described as "probably the finest piece of writing we have from an Englishman of his time on the Americas,"[68] the narrative was not published until its inclusion by Purchas in *Hakluytus posthumus* in 1625. Historians have generally assumed that Strachey's account was not published earlier because of the reluctance of the Virginia Company to allow information to be circulated that was unfavorable to its interests.[69] While this seems plausible, Strachey's only biographer to date, S. G. Culliford, has argued that "A True reportory" was intended to be only a fragment of a much larger projected work designed to cover the whole history of the settlement of Virginia.[70] This larger work, however, was never finished and its fragments not published until 1849, when it appeared under the title *The History of Travaile into Virginia Britannia*. Another likely reason why Strachey never finished the work was that he was anticipated by Purchas, who had acquired Hakluyt's manuscript copy of "A True reportory" sent from Virginia. Strachey, when learning about Purchas' impending publication after his return to England on board the *Prosperous*, sent a manuscript copy of the expanded history to Francis Bacon in a "last despairing effort" to publish his own history; though to no avail. "Had Strachey not been thus forestalled," Culliford speculates, "we might have had from his pen a better, a more detailed, and a more accurate and balanced account of the early history of Virginia than has been provided either by John Smith or by that extremely bad editor, Samuel Purchas."[71] As the record stands, however, only the version printed by Purchas remains of Strachey's "A True reportory" – as is the case with so many other narratives first printed and edited by Purchas. In the context of Purchas' collection, Strachey's narrative assumed meanings that would have been unintended by the original author, thereby meeting a fate that strikingly resembles that of Cabeza de Vaca's narrative of "shipwrecks" in the hands of Purchas. Strachey had written "A True reportory" in the context of the reform of the Virginia Company in 1609; and it was, in its original version, almost certainly intended to lend support to the second Virginia Charter and the laws written by Gates and later published by Strachey himself (in 1612). Again not unlike Cabeza de Vaca's narrative, "A True reportory" chronicles the breakdown of the imperial social order in the New World due to individualistic ambition and insubordination. However, when edited and published by Purchas in 1625, it was intended to lend support not to the reform but rather to the dissolution of the Company one year before.[72]

Whereas in Cabeza de Vaca's account the narrator's immediate superior, Pánfilo de Narváez, was blamed for the ensuing disaster, in Strachey's narrative, the governor, Sir Thomas Gates, strove and succeeded to uphold the social order in the face of the insubordination of his rebellious colonists. Soon after the wreck of the vessel in the Bermudas, a certain Stephen Hopkins "began to shake the foundations of our quiet safety":

And sure it was happy for us who had now runne this fortune, and were fallen into the bottom of this misery, that we both had our Governour with us, and one so solicitous and carefull, whose both example (as I said) and authority, could lay shame, and command upon our people: else, I am perswaded, we had most of us finished our dayes there, so willing were the major part of the common sort (especially when they found such a plenty of victuals) to settle a foundation of ever inhabiting there; as well appeared by many practises of theirs (and perhaps of some of the better sort)? Loe, what are our affections and passions, if not rightly squared? how irreligious, and irregular they express us? (XIX: 28)

While these "dangerous and secret discontents [that] nourished amongst us" first begin with the mariners, they soon affect also the "land-men," who, contemplating the "wretchedness and labour" to be expected once they arrive in Virginia, find that the shipwreck was not so disagreeable after all and therefore decide to "repose and seate" themselves on the island, where "pleasure might be injoyed" (XIX: 29).

Modern historians of the events chronicled by Strachey generally agree that the underlying conflict during the first decade or so of England's colonial enterprise was essentially a socio-political one. "The English poor," writes Nicholas Canny, "did not accept the arguments of English social and cultural superiority that were expounded by their betters, and that their failure to do so had drastic consequences in a colonial setting."[73] In Purchas' edition of Strachey's narrative, by contrast, the conflicts that rock the boat of the British imperial order are not imputed to the common sort alone (XIX: 67). In fact, none of the three mutinies that actually occur on the island are specifically ascribed to individuals of low birth. The first one is ascribed to a religious sectarian – a "John Want,... an Essex man of Newport... both seditious and a sectary in points of Religion, in his owne prayers much devout and frequent, but hardly drawne to the publique, insomuch as being suspected by our Minister for a Brownist" (XIX: 30). Another is ascribed to "a Gentleman" by the name of Henry Paine, who is "full of mischiefe, and every houre preparing something or other, stealing Swords, Adises, Axes, Hatchets, Sawes, Augers, Planes, Mallets, and c. to make good his owne bad end" (XIX: 33). When being summoned to order by the governor, he "replyed with a setled and bitter violence... that the Governour had no authoritie of that qualitie, to justifie upon any one (how meane soever in the Colonie) an action of that nature, and therefore let the Governour (said hee) kisse, and c" (XIX: 34). The governor, not humored by Paine's invitation, sentenced him to death by hanging. Paine, however, "earnestly desired, being a Gentleman, that hee might be shot to death, and toward the evening he had his desire, the Sunne and his life setting together" (XIX: 34). In Purchas' edition of Strachey's "A True reportory," the class distinction between gentry and commoners is thus less significant than the distinction between subordinate loyalists and insubordinate individualists – a distinction that transcends class lines. In fact, it seems that simple laborers who might steal food or weapons are less subversive to the social order on the island than are those who are educated and, thus, in possession of the dangerous weapon of rhetoric. Yet another mutiny was instigated, Strachey reports, by one Stephen Hopkins, a "fellow who had much knowledge in the Scripture, and could reason well therein," producing substantial arguments, both civill and divine (the Scripture falsly quoted) that it was no breach of honesty, conscience, nor Religion, to decline from the obedience of the Governor, or refuse to goe any further, led by his authority (except it so pleased themselves) since the authority ceased when the wracke was committed, and with it, they were all then freed from the government of any man; and for a matter of Conscience, it was not unknowne to the meanest, how much we were therein bound each one to provide for himselfe, and his owne family. (xix: 30–1)

When the governor, not persuaded by Hopkins' eloquence, sentenced that mutineer to death as well, the latter begged, full of "sorrows and teares," for mercy by pleading "simplicity and denial" (xix: 31). What was required in the colonial project was not a gentleman's art of rhetoric, Strachey's account suggests, but rather a soldier's blind obedience and a farmer's simplicity. A "Colony," he writes, "is therefore denominated, because they should be Coloni, the Tillers of the Earth" (xix: 68–9).

Once the shipwrecked party succeeds in making their passage to Virginia, they find the colony a "headlesse multitude." The miseries they are suffering, however, had been "brought upon them by their owne disorders" and their "misgovernment" (xix: 47, 45, 44). "If it should be examined from whence, and by what occasion, all these disasters, and afflictions descended upon our people," he writes, the cause was to be found in "the forme of government of some errour," which "was not powerful enough among so headie a multitude, especially, as those who arrived here in the supply sent the last yeere with us: with whome the better authoritie and government now changed into an strong command, came along, and had beene as happily established, had it pleased God, that we with them had reached our wished Harbour" (xix: 46). Thus, Strachey's narrative about tempests and shipwrecks on uninhabited islands illustrated that the "ground of all those miseries" haunting the English imperial enterprise to date was that in the New World "the head" had become separated "from the bodie" as a consequence of eloquent rhetoric in the hands of self-interested subjects disinclined to obey. Whereas the party had survived the shipwreck on the Bermudas, the survivors found "a greater shipwracke in the Continent of Virginia, by the tempest of Dissension: every man over-valuing his owne worth, would be a Commander: every man underprizing anothers value, denied to be commanded" (xix: 67). Strachey's eye-witness testimony thus lent support to the absolutist political philosophy later articulated in Thomas Hobbes' *The Elements of Law, Natural and Politic* (1650), which was circulating in England as early as the 1640s and made ample use of the texts of empire such as Purchas' *Hakluytus posthumus* as evidence for his political theory of absolutist power.[74] In Purchas' *Hakluytus posthumus*,

Strachey's plain account of shipwreck, providing only the "facts" in the new rhetoric of philosophical history, allegorized, in form and content, the transformation of English imperialism predicated on an ideology that held that "man" in the state of "nature" answers to "Strong command." Out of the experience of shipwreck brought about by the "tempests of dissention," however, a new *passo* in the life of the British empire is born in Strachey's narrative. The arrival of the Lord De-La-Warre, the new governor and captain general of Virginia, is marked by a shift in Strachey's discourse from accounts of shipwreck and failures to descriptions of the rituals of power. After De-La-Warre makes a speech in which he laid "many blames upon them for many vanities, and their Idlenesse," he continued to "give place of Office, and charge to divers Captaines and Gentlemen, and elected unto him a Counsell, unto whom he did administer an Oath, mixed with an oath of Allegiance, and Supremacy to his Majesty" (XIX: 60).

While Strachey's De-La-Warre was, of course, sent on behalf of the Virginia Company, in the context of Purchas' collection, published after the dissolution of the Company, Strachey's arguments for a strong hand assume a new meaning, now becoming synonymous with the "long royal arme" of James I. The "late alteration of Virginia Government is unknowne to none," Purchas writes in his own commentary on the Company government, "and most know of the frequent complaints, both by private Letters, and by Petitions to his Majesty." As evidence, he includes, following Strachey's narrative, an "Intelligence from Virginia" (dated 1624) that he had received in the form of "one of the Planters private Letters" and in which are "transcribed a few words of grievances" (XIX: 207). The letter is dated, he informs the reader, "Dec. 22 last past" – 1623, thus just *before* the "late alteration" – and details the settlers' grievances with the colonial government. "Thus, you see," Purchas addresses his reader, "(I neither warrant, nor except against the truth, but present the worst quarelled paralelled with the best) complaints of great prizes of things, not arising from plenty of money, as you reade before in the conquest of Peru, but from I know not what ill habit and indisposition of that Colony." In order to demonstrate his disinterestedness, he produces a "commendation of the Country" out "of the same mans Letters," which is, incidentally, dated "22 March 1624" (and thus *after* the "late alteration of Virginia Government") (XIX: 208). "God prosper his Majesties care," Purchas concludes, "and make those which are therein emploied not to seeke their owne good by hasty returnes, much less other their fellow adventurers evill by calumnies and undermining, but Virginians prosperity" (XIX: 208). By bringing into connection the king's patrimonial care for his "good Subjects" with first-hand accounts chronicling the "failures" of the Company to make Virginia yield what it had promised but failed to deliver, Purchas' "form[ing] and fram[ing]" of his materials lent support to the royalist argument for centralized control of the colonial project. By focusing on the past failures of the colony, and by appealing to God and king for a remedy, Purchas makes a case for reform in the government of Virginia and for centralization of colonial administrative authority without making direct recourse to political rhetoric. The royalist argument for political centralization is thus couched in the language of "prosperitie" and the common good of the nation in the imperial enterprise abroad:

My Prayers shall be to the Almightie for Virginias prosperitie; whose Dwarfish growth after so many yeeres, convulsions by dissentions there and heere, lamentations in the complaints of both sides (a Plurisie Stich in her sides, continuing after so much boud taken from her) weaknesse . . . But what doe I in plaints, where some perhaps will complaine of my complayining? I will expect better from God and his Majestie. (XIX: 170–1)

With regard to his coverage of "north Virginia" (New England) in *Hakluytus posthumus*, Purchas mentions having several manuscript sources at hand but chose to include only John Stoneman's relation of the voyage of Henry Challons in the *Richard*, which ended in the ship's capture by the Spanish in the Florida Strait, and the crew being "slaine, drowned, hanged or pittifully captived" in Spain before the author's escape from Seville to Lisbon, and final passage back to Cornwall (XIX: 296, 284–98). Purchas mentions owning other relevant manuscripts but excluded them, he claimed, for aesthetic reasons – because their "voluminousness makes me afraid of offending nicer and queasier stomaches" (XIX: 296). They are today lost from the records of history. Instead, he reprinted sections from texts that had already been published during the 1620s, such as John Smith's *New Englands trials* (London, 1620, 1622; rpt. XIX: 297–311), *A Relation* by Edward Winslow (alias "G. Mourt") (1622; rpt. XIX: 312–43), and Winslow's *Good news from New England* (1624; rpt. XIX: 344–93), all of which related the initial hardships then gradual improvements of the state of affairs in the colonies. His selection of New England narratives was arranged to dramatize the gradual triumph of the English nation against all odds through sacrifice in pilgrimage. The shift from the East Indian to the West Indian activities represents a transition from failure to success: "We have bin long enough perplexed with viewing Easterne Tragedies," Purchas writes, "Let us now turne our Eyes Westward" (X: 521). The Virginia accounts, and particularly Strachey's "A True reportory," inhabit hereby a strategic place in the collection, representing a rite of passage in articulating an ethics and poetics of renunciation, a rhetoric of sacrifice and self-effacement of the individual will and interest in the name of the "common good" of a nation represented by one crown.

LITERARY "FRIENDS": SAMUEL PURCHAS AND JOHN SMITH

One year before the appearance of Samuel Purchas' *magnum opus*, a work was published with the title *The General Historie of Virginia, New England, and the Summer Isles* (1624). It was written by a man named John Smith, sponsored by the Duchess of Richmond and Lennox, and printed by a Michael Sparkes, an English Puritan who was made free of the Stationers' Company in June 1610. Though a commoner, Smith was not unknown in the circles interested in England's colonial enterprise, as well as to the general public. He had been one of the original colonists at Jamestown in 1607, had been elected – on merit of distinctions earned in earlier military missions in Hungary – to the Council of the Company in London, and had even risen to be president of the Council in the colony before his return to England in 1609. In 1614, he had gone on a second venture to America, this time to "north Virginia," which he named "New England." Smith's previously published works, beginning with *A True Relation* (1609), had primarily consisted of short accounts about these travels, most of them patronized and published by the Virginia Company. His *General History*, by contrast, was of an entirely different nature. It was not a particular eyewitness account but rather a definitive and official history of British America to date, rivaling the works of Purchas, with whom he had shared a friendly relationship for some time.

There are many similarities between Purchas and Smith, in their personal backgrounds, their affiliations, and their works. Smith, like Purchas, was of humble origins, born in the West country, and had made a name for himself in England's budding imperial enterprise. Like Purchas, he had been associated with the Virginia Company but later took the royalist position in the controversy surrounding its dissolution, writing in his Preface that "This plaine History humbly sheweth the truth; that our most royall King James hath place and opportunitie to inlarge his ancient Dominions without wronging any" (II: 41). He voted that the Charter be surrendered to the king though being himself a Council member of the Company at the time. Although his book was exclusively confined to America, as its title suggests, it nevertheless shared several common features with *Hakluytus posthumus*. It was a "general history", like *Hakluytus posthumus*, a collection of empirical eyewitness accounts. In Book I of *General History*, Smith, like Purchas, drew on many earlier travel accounts derived from Hakluyt's collection; in Books II and III, he re-edited his own account previously included as a portion of *Map of Virginia* (1612), but expanded it by adding new ethnographic details about Native American culture – which he presumably recalled after more than ten years. In Book IV he related the principal events from the second Charter to its revocation; in Book V, he worked from an unpublished manuscript in order to compile the history of Bermuda; and in Book VI, about New England, he reprinted his two earlier, "particular" relations on the region, *A Description of New England* and the *New Englands Trials*.

In his later *A Sea Grammer*, published after Purchas' death, Smith shed some light on the peculiar nature of his friendship with Purchas. In a discourse concerning the depth of the ocean he cited Plutarch, Pliny, Aristotle, and other authorities but then acknowledged his real source: "If you desire any further satisfaction," he wrote:

reade the first part of *Purchas His Pilgrimage*, where you may reade how to find all those Authors at large. Now because he hath taken neere 100. times as much from me, I have made bold to borrow this from him, seeing he hath sounded such deepe waters for this our Ship to sail in, being a gentleman whose person I loved, and whose memory and vertues I will ever honour. (III: 95–6)[75]

The literary "friendship" between the two men had consisted in a mutually profitable exchange of two different types of knowledge: whereas Smith had supplied Purchas with his accounts based on first-hand experience, he now appropriated Purchas' knowledge of the rhetorical arts. It was a fair deal. Yet, there is a hint of irony, so characteristic of Smith's style, in his nautical metaphor showing Purchas in the vanguard sounding the "deepe waters" for Smith's own literary enterprise. Possibly, it is Smith's sly reference to the fact that his own *magnum opus*, the *General History*, had preceded Purchas' work by one year (after the latter had anticipated Strachey with the publication of his own account). Smith's irony here suggests also his awareness of a certain epistemological tension between the two works of Purchas and those of Smith. For Smith, empirical knowledge was primary, not secondary, to Classical rhetoric in the making of history.

Smith has often been criticized for his unpolished style and lack of rhetorical refinement. In *Notes on the State of Virginia*, Jefferson found Smith's style "barbarous and uncouth."[76] Twentieth-century historians agree that "no one would claim that Smith was a great stylist," and there is a sense that "Smith produced a book quite different from anything that preceded him" because he avoided the "moralizing" of previous historians and instead "concentrated on recording the facts."[77] Philip Barbour even argued that the "*General History* is not a history; it is not even a journalistic narrative"; it is rather John Smith's personal "Memoirs, his Apologia, and his Defense, rounded out with information from others bearing on what he considered *his* colonies." This "'I was there' technique," Barbour writes, "has become so familiar to us that we fail to credit Smith with working it out for himself."[78] Indeed, Smith invoked a model of historiographic authorship that markedly differed from those in other available histories of the New World. Unlike Purchas, for example, who called attention to his scientific "art" as an editor, collector, and historian, Smith incessantly reminded the reader that he was not a "historian" in the conventional sense at all and even prided himself on his unpolished style as evidence of a man who could handle a weapon better than a pen. As in Cabeza de Vaca's account, ethnographic descriptions and first-hand accounts of captivity are a powerful literary device that enhances the sense of immediacy that his works as a whole aim to evoke. Throughout, Smith portrays himself as a principal actor in the history of the colony, one who dwells in the realm of the arts not of rhetoric but rather of action. "This History," he began,

might and ought to have beene clad in better robes then my rude military hand can cut out in Paper Ornaments. But because, of the most things therein, I am no Compiler by hearsay, but have been a reall Actor; . . . That, which hath beene indured and passed through with hardship and danger, is thereby sweetned to the Actor when he becometh the Relator. (II: 41)

Despite the elaborate appearance botched together for his first edition of *General History*, Smith fashioned himself as an author for whom writing was of importance only insofar as it recorded action. "History," he wrote in his later *Advertisement for the Unexperienced Planters of New England, or Any Where* (1631), is the "memory of time, the life of the dead, and the happiness of the living" (III: 288). Yet, as Bradford Smith points out, "if Smith had been wholly successful in action he might never have turned to writing."[79] This is a crucial point to keep in mind when reading John Smith. For all its pretension to authorial humility, his *General History* was written with a purpose more cunning than merely to record his memories – it was supposed to vindicate his own actions in the colonial enterprise and to earn the credit that he felt he deserved but had not yet received. Although Smith had succeeded in winning the presidency for himself, the other councilors, according to Smith, had allied themselves with the dissidents in the colony "to regain their former credit and authority." With the arrival of De-La-Warre in 1609, however, he was himself overruled by newly appointed officers of higher social standing than himself, after which he returned to England. In this context, Smith did what he could to persuade his readers. Smith's authorial stance in *General History* as "Actor... becometh...Relator" by the use of unadorned language is therefore itself a rhetorical device that is supposed to lend his history persuasion. It is not, however, a persuasion in the older Renaissance sense of verisimilitude – the assertion of the primacy of language in the art of history – but rather in the sense of mimesis, thereby invoking a rhetorical tradition that had an equally long history in Western culture.[80] Indeed, the very aphorism in which Smith defines the writing of history not as a rhetorical art but merely as secondary to experience ("memory") rings, as Philip Barbour has pointed out in his annotations to Smith's works, of John Florio, who had written in a 1578 comment on Cicero: "History...is the testimony of Tyme, the light of veritie, the life of memory, the guide of tyme, the messenger of antiquity" (III: 288). In Smith's *General History*, the disavowal of the Classical art of rhetoric in the writing of history becomes the rhetorical figure that constitutes the historian's authority. Thus, while the title of *General History* invoked as possible rhetorical models texts such as Knolles' *Generall Historie of the Turkes*, John Speed's *Historie of Great Britaine*, Walter Ralegh's *History of the World*,[81] Smith consciously rejects these models and instead fashioned himself as the travelled "participant-historian" in antithesis to contemporary stay-at-home historians such as Purchas.

It would be wrong to assume, however, that John Smith, lacking any English precedents, had "no handy models to go by,"[82] that he somehow invented this authorial stance in writing the New World history *ex nihilo*. As we have seen, Spanish authors such as Oviedo and Acosta had employed the authorial claim to first-hand experience since the sixteenth century, the latter calling his work a "natural and moral history," and the former a "natural and general history." Unlike Smith, however, Oviedo, a royal chronicler (the last one actually to have set foot in America), and Acosta, a Jesuit monk, had been vested with the authority of State and Church. Smith, a social upstart who ranked, as Philip Barbour has put it, "but a little higher in Elizabethan society than a Hindu 'untouchable' in Akbar's India,"[83] resembled more closely in this regard the Inca Garcilaso de la Vega, a Peruvian mestizo historian who had descended from a Spanish conqueror and Inca noblewoman. When Smith designated his text as a "general history" but at the same time invoked as a rhetorical model the Classical example of the *Commentaries* of Julius Caesar – "whose atchievments shine as cleare in his owne Commentaries, as they did in the field" (I: v) – there was in fact a more immediate and modern precedent than Caesar's *Commentaries* for his "general history": the Inca Garcilaso's *Comentarios reales* and *Historia general de Peru*, written after his permanent relocation to Spain and partially translated (as well as "formed and framed") into English by Purchas in *Hakluytus posthumus*. Smith, when priding himself on writing in the "stile of a Souldier [which] is not eloquent, but honest and justifiable" (II: 42), followed the Inca's authorial strategy of writing a "general history" based on what he had "seen." Thus, Garcilaso introduced his history with the autobiographical comment that he had grown up as "un indio, nacido entre los indios, criado entre armas y caballos" ("an Indian, born among Indians, bred among arms and horses"). The Spanish historians of Peru such as Pedro Cieza de León, Agustín de Zárate, or Francisco López de Gómora, from whom he quotes extensively, may impress in the "buen tono" ("elegant style") of their eloquent language and Classical rhetoric, but their accounts were flawed for their lack of understanding of Inca language and culture – "haberles faltado *relación* entera" and "ignora[n] de diez partes las nueve" ("they have failed to give a full account" and "ignore nine out of ten parts"). His history, by contrast, was based on the authority of "mis ojos" ("my eyes") – the authority of first-hand observation and understanding of Inca culture, his rhetorical eloquence secondary to the authority of experience.[84]

Smith's fashioning himself in the tradition of New World historians such as Garcilaso – as historians who had *been there* – thus illuminates a crucial difference between Smith's and Purchas' respective ideas about the writing of history. While both would agree that history had to be based on an empirical foundation, Smith's "general history" undercuts the division of intellectual labor which Purchas aims to implement. "I am no compiler by hearsay but have been a real actor," Smith wrote. "I have not spared any diligence to learne the truth of them that have been actors, or sharers in those voyages. Had I not discovered and lived in the most of those parts, I could not possibly have collected the substantial truth from such a number of variable Relations" (II: 41, 43). No doubt, this authorial statement was made in part with his old friend and fellow historian Samuel Purchas in mind, who had prided himself upon "never [having] travelled two hundred miles from Thaxted in Essex ... where he was borne." Smith was precisely the sort of historian that Purchas was not – the amateur historian on whose effacement the scientific authority of Samuel Purchas as a historian depended in the historical context of early modern settler colonialism: the maker of "general history" on the "Circumference," rather than the "Centre," who commanded the powers of natural knowledge without being tied to the "line" of Purchas' scientific authority underwritten by the patronage and approbation of the monarchical court. But who could assure the loyalty of a man of action to his God, King, and Country? While Purchas, in subjecting the production of knowledge about the New World to the Baconian method, became the founder of a long tradition of English imperial historiography about the Americas, Smith, though not a Creole himself, introduced a rhetorical model into English writing about the New World that would, as we will see in the following chapters, become foundational in the emergence of a Creole tradition in colonial historiography and prose narrative.

CHAPTER 4

"True histories": the captivities of Francisco Núñez de Pineda y Bascuñán and Mary White Rowlandson

If a little group of pious Christian laymen were taken captive and set down in a wilderness, and had among them no priest consecrated by a bishop, and if there in the wilderness they were to agree in choosing one of themselves, married, absolving and preaching, such a man would be as truly a priest as though all bishops and popes had consecrated him.

Martin Luther, *Open Letter to the Christian Nobility*

Few speculative subjects have exercised the passions more or the judgment less, than the inquiry...Whether in point of intellect we are equal to Europeans, or only a race of degenerate creoles.

Fisher Ames[1]

In the previous two chapters, I have suggested that the early modern reorganization of knowledge must be seen as a response not only to the socio-political but also to the geo-political questions raised by European expansionism in the New World. In the historical context of the "second conquest" of America, imperial administrators, historians, and travelers aimed to articulate a "mercantilist" model of science that structured the production of knowledge about the New World in trans-atlantic networks of divided intellectual labor between peripheries and centers, with the former producing the "effects" and the latter the "causes" in scientific inquiry. The following chapters shift in geographic focus from Europe to the Americas in order to explore the consequences of these imperial geographies in early modern science on texts written in the colonies, particularly those written by colonial "Creoles" ("criollos") from various parts of the early Americas, such as New England, Chile, New Spain, New York, and Peru.

Creoles were European by descent and citizens of empire; but, unlike the European imperial functionaries traveling in and writing about the New World, their cultural location within the empire was defined by what Benedict Anderson has called the "fatality of trans-Atlantic birth." Whereas the imperial functionary traveled for social advancement back in the metropolis, in a modern-day form of "lateral and vertical pilgrimage,"

Anderson suggests, the mobility of the Creoles was "blocked" by the geographic, social, and even legal boundaries placed upon their cultural location – by a wrong place of return, so to speak, not to the center but rather to the periphery of imperial power.[2] But why and how did an American birth become a "fatality" and marker of difference in early modern settler empires? And how did the cultural location of a Creole writer affect the form of his or her text? The following chapters investigate how the basic scientific theorem in early modern Natural History – the environmental determination of human faculties – rationalized the Creoles' cultural location at the geographic semi-periphery of trans-atlantic settler empires not only in political administration but also in historiographic and scientific authorship. In early modern debates over creolization, European "colonists" became American "colonials," constituted as the objects rather than subjects of science.

But despite the efforts of early modern natural philosophers to control and regulate the production and exchange of knowledge in prescriptive scientific systems, the social and geo-political dynamics, as well as the actual literary practices, of European expansionism often proved more unwieldy and recalcitrant to metropolitan control than the theoreticians of empire would have wished. Excluded from the "vertical" and "lateral" pilgrimage as imperial citizens, colonial Creoles appropriated and transculturated the European narrative models as powerful platforms of geo-political resistance that could be as subversive ideologically as colonial manufacture, contraband, smuggling, and inter-colonial trade were economically to the imperial order. In the writing of history about the New World, the authorial rhetoric of eyewitness experience, in particular, could confer considerable cultural authority onto non-traditional social sectors in the production of natural knowledge, such as soldiers, merchants, mariners, and even colonial women, on whose first-hand testimony the production of knowledge in an increasingly complex and trans-regional modern world depended.

The next two chapters discuss the special role that the colonial captivity narrative played in negotiating the geo-political tensions in early modern settler empires. Here, I compare two narratives written during the seventeenth century in colonial Chile and New England by the soldier and *encomendero* Francisco Núñez de Pineda y Bascuñán (1607–82) and the Puritan woman Mary White Rowlandson (*c.* 1637–*c.* 1711) respectively. Both narratives were written in the aftermath of a severe colonial crisis resulting from frontier warfare – the so-called "rebelión de 1655" in Chile and "King Philip's" War in New England (1675). However, I want to argue that what's at stake in these two narratives is not so much the confrontation between

European colonists and Native Americans as the geo-political confrontation between European imperial states and the Creole elites over administrative centralization in the context of a "Second Conquest." Despite the tremendous differences between these two narratives – differences with regard to gender, culture, and the personal experience of each captive – both captivity narratives were in this context of crisis self-consciously designated as "true histories" not only in a historiographic polemic about imperial geo-politics but also in a meta-historical polemic about the question of "truth" and the writing of history. Both narratives similarly exploit the rhetorical power of eyewitness experience and invert the subordination of empirical testimony to the authority of the imperial historians. Finally, in both narratives the story of Indian captivity powerfully narrativizes the breakdown of imperial patronage and the need for colonial self-sufficiency.

MONSTROUS BOOKS

Although Mary White was born in Somerset, England, around 1636 (and was thus not technically a Creole), she came to America at the early age of two, when her family emigrated and eventually settled in the frontier village of Lancaster, thirty miles west of Boston. In 1656, she married a prominent New England clergyman, Joseph Rowlandson, and subsequently had three children. Her husband had been away in Boston when Lancaster was suddenly attacked in 1676 by Narragansett Indians, who had rallied behind Metacomet ("King Philip") in a general uprising along the New England frontier resulting from a land dispute with the English colonists. She, her three children, and a number of other surviving villagers were taken into captivity by the Indian war party, who retreated in flight from the pursuant English army. During her captivity she traveled over 150 miles and was exposed to severe hardships, including the death of her youngest child in her arms; gradually, however, she was able to stabilize her extremely vulnerable position somewhat by trading her needlework with the Indians. In one instance, she even met Metacomet, who "spake to me to make a shirt for his boy, which I did, for which he gave me a shilling" (337). After having spent eleven weeks and five days in captivity, she was finally redeemed in exchange for guns. Some time after her redemption, she wrote a narrative in which she recounted her experience in captivity. Critics today are in agreement that the narrative, which is cast in the form of a spiritual autobiography of pilgrimage and conversion, was edited, and its composition perhaps even assisted, by Increase Mather, one of the most prominent Puritan ministers of the seventeenth century in New England. It first appeared in New

England in 1682 – in two successive editions published in Boston and Cambridge – under the title *The Soveraignty and Goodness of God* and later the same year in London under the sensationalist title *A True History of the Captivity and Restoration of Mrs. Mary Rowlandson, A Minister's Wife in New-England. Wherein is set forth, the Cruel and Inhumane Usage she underwent amongst the Heathens, for eleven Weeks time: And her Deliverance from them*, together with one of her husband's sermons and a "Preface to the Reader," signed "Per Amicum" and written most likely by Mather (see Illustrations 4.1 and 4.2).[3]

Francisco Núñez de Pineda y Bascuñán was born in 1608, the son of one of the original conquerors of Chile, Álvaro Núñez de Pineda y Bascuñán. He grew up among the colonial *encomendero* elite and followed in his father's footsteps by inheriting his *encomienda* and becoming an officer in the Spanish army. In 1629, he was taken captive in the battle of Cangrejeras, one of the many Spanish *entradas*, or raiding expeditions, against the *mapuche* Indians on the southern frontier, who would not be "pacified" until after Chilean independence in the nineteenth century. Pineda spent some four months in captivity, during which he served his rather benevolent captor Maulicán on his travels from Native village to village before being granted his freedom. Unlike Rowlandson, who wrote her account within a few years of her redemption, Pineda did not begin writing his narrative until 1655 and did not finish it until 1672. During the almost twenty years he spent in composing it, the narrative of his captivity turned into an immense manuscript of over 600 pages, including lengthy excursions into colonial history, politics, philosophy, and theology. Unlike Rowlandson and most other colonials in the seventeenth-century Americas, he portrayed the Indians in a curiously positive light, celebrating the valor and virtue of the Araucanians and blaming the reasons for the "protracted wars" in Chile not on the Indians but rather on the Spaniards – an aspect of his work that has been called by one critic a "pequeño misterio" ("small mystery").[4]

A conspicuous tendency in the critical reception of both colonial captivity narratives has been the attempt by literary historians to establish a link, historical or geographical, to the rise of the novel. Thus, while the Anglo-American literary historian Roy Harvey Pearce argued in the 1940s that the "significance" of colonial captivity narratives lies in the role that these texts played as "precursors" to the (belated) rise of the American novel in the nineteenth century, during the 1990s Nancy Armstrong and Leonard Tennenhouse made a provocative argument for colonial captivity narratives such as Rowlandson's as the "American origin of the English novel." Most recently, James Hartman, building on Michael McKeon's account of the rise of the

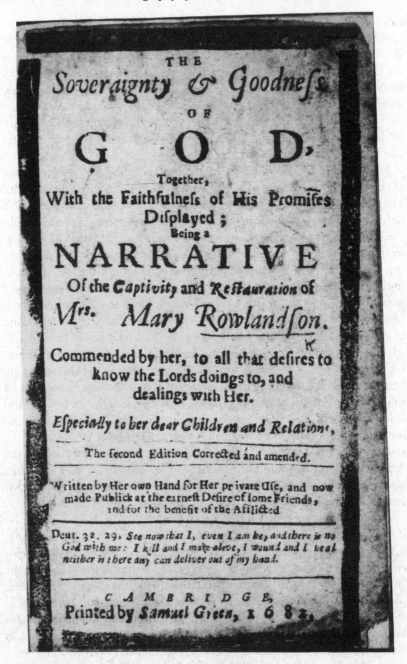

THE
Soveraignty & Goodness
OF

GOD,

Together,
With the Faithfulness of His Promises
Displayed;
Being a

NARRATIVE

Of the *Captivity* and *Restauration* of
Mʳˢ. Mary Rowlandson.

Commended by her, to all that desires to
know the Lords doings to, and
dealings with Her.

Especially to her dear Children and Relations,

The second Edition Corrected and amended.

Written by Her own Hand for Her private Use, and now
made Publick at the earnest Desire of some Friends,
and for the benefit of the Afflicted

Deut. 32. 29. *See now that I, even I am he, and there is no
God with me: I kill and I make alive, I wound and I heal
neither is there any can deliver out of my hand.*

CAMBRIDGE,
Printed by *Samuel Green*, 1682.

4.1 Mary Rowlandson, *The Soveraignty and Goodness of God* (Cambridge, MA, 1682).

A TRUE

HISTORY

OF THE

Captivity & Restoration

OF

Mrs. *MARY ROWLANDSON*,

A Minifter's Wife in *New-England*.

Wherein is fet forth, The Cruel and Inhumane
Ufage fhe underwent amongft the *Heathens*, for
Eleven Weeks time: And her Deliverance from
them.

*Written by her own Hand, for her Private Ufe : And now made
Publick at the earneft Defire of fome Friends, for the Benefit
of the Afflicted.*

Whereunto is annexed,

A Sermon of *the Poffibility of God's Forfaking a People that have been near and dear to him.*

Preached by Mr.*Jofeph Rowlandfon*, Husband to the faid Mrs.*Rowlandfon:*
It being his Laft Sermon.

Printed firft at *New-England :* And Re-printed at *London,* and fold
by *Jofeph Poole,* at the *Blue Bowl* in the *Long-Walk,* by *Chrifts-
Church* Hofpital. 1682.

4.2 Mary Rowlandson, *A True History of the Captivity and Restoration* (London, 1682).

English novel, has argued that the colonial captivity narrative, as a popular variation of early modern "Providence Tales," played an important "role in the rise of the American novel ... similar to the role that McKeon posits for his English tales in the development of the English novel."[5] However, while such arguments about the "significance" of colonial captivity narratives as a proto-type or source material of the (early) modern novel have provided interesting insights about European or nineteenth-century American literary history, they have begged the question why colonial American writers, though productive of the source material for the novel, did not themselves produce any novels. American literary historians operating within a Formalist critical paradigm have typically answered this question by lamenting the apparent cultural "lag" of their colonial ancestors who, unlike their European ones, seemed somehow incapable of simply writing a "good" story such as a "real" novel. The critical reception of Pineda's narrative presents here a particularly illustrative case in point. Unlike Rowlandson's narrative, which was published numerous times during the seventeenth and eighteenth centuries, *Cautiverio feliz* circulated during colonial times only in manuscript form and was not published until the nineteenth century, in an edition by Diego Barras Arana (1863). At a time when Chileans were attempting to cement their sense of national identity, Pineda's portrayal of the heroic, unconquerable Araucanian warrior, immortalized already by Ercilla's sixteenth-century epic *La Araucana* and Alvarez de Toledo's *Purén indómito,* served as the perfect image of a pre-national past in the making of a Chilean national literary history after independence from Spain.[6] However, as literary critics soon found, from a formal point of view, *Cautiverio feliz* left much to be desired as a "precursor" to the Chilean novel. They were exasperated by Pineda's lengthy "digressions" into history, politics, philosophy, and religion, which had swelled the perfectly palatable captivity narrative to monstrous proportions. Vicente Aguirre described Pineda's work as a "monster similar to a man with two heads"; instead of the "two separate books that he should have written," he complained, "he wrote only one with two titles" – "Happy Captivity" and "Reasons for the protracted Wars."[7] This notion still persisted in the twentieth century when the eminent Venezuelan critic Mariano Picón-Salas lamented that "the obligatory tedious moral reflections, quotations from the Gospels and from the lives of the saints ... [had] aborted a potentially excellent novel."[8] Even before then, the Chilean historian Amunategui y Solar therefore suggested that the "grave defects" would disappear if an abbreviated edition were made, including only "the principal scenes and descriptions" of Pineda's experiences among the Indians. "No doubt," he announced, "the book would then read just as nicely as a novel, while yet preserving its great intrinsic merit."[9] Finally, Pineda's work was abridged – some may say, mutilated – and re-published in various editions: as a biography by Alejandro Vicuña, who thought it advantageous to drop the "political, moral, and religious digressions";[10] as an approximately 150-page captivity narrative by the literary critic Angel González, who pointed out that Pineda "did not pretend to writing a work of art";[11] and as an English translation by William Atkinson – also an abridged captivity narrative.

More recently, however, historians such as Sergio Corréa Bello have reclaimed "*Cautiverio* as history," reminding readers that Pineda himself had deemed the historical discourses to be the main and most important part of his work.[12] José Anadón has therefore spoken of Pineda's narrative as an example of colonial "literary historiography," as history couched in the form of a personal narrative and written based on personal experience. Yet, as were earlier critics, Anadón was puzzled by the "pequeño misterio" of Pineda's favorable portrayal of Native Americans in this text, entirely absent from his earlier writings and correspondence. It is "curious," he wrote, "that early on there appears no trace at all of this change, manifest later in *Cautiverio*, where pro-Indian sentiments prevail over belligerence." He therefore speculated, in one place, that Pineda's impressions of *mapuche* culture "did not mature in his conscience" until a later time;[13] and, in another, that the positive image he portrayed of his captors in his *Cautiverio* manifested the psychological effect of a "Stockholm syndrome" – a sort of emotional bond developing between captor and captive in captivity situations.[14]

The confusion over Pineda's "change" points to the limitations not only of a Formalist attempt to see this narrative as a proto-novel but also of a biographical approach that attempts to make sense of Pineda's historical discourse in light of the path-breaking personal experiences of captivity that he relates in his narrative.[15] Rather, it underscores the need for an investigation of the rhetorical function of the captivity narrative – of the "interrelation of the digressions and the account of the captivity," as Raquel Chang-Rodríguez has put it – and of how the captivity narrative served as a "trampolín" for reinforcing the verisimilitude of the historical arguments presented in the text.[16] Here, I want to pursue this line of inquiry from a comparative angle; but I also want to go one step further and suggest how such an approach to colonial captivity narratives challenges the universalizing Formalist narratives of literary history and exposes the metropolitan geo-politics of the epistemic formation that gave rise to "the novel" in Europe. Why is it that, while in seventeenth- and eighteenth-century

Europe picaresque and novelistic prose fiction was becoming a discursive vehicle in the fermentation of nationalist ideologies in the realm of the aesthetic, the privileging of this genre has proved so problematic in the Americas, where, as Jean Franco has written, "literary genres and styles are inevitably hybridized"?[17] The "colonial rise" of the European novel consisted not only in that genre's commodification of racial otherness and exotic consumer goods,[18] but also in its complicity with the emergence of the hierarchical division of intellectual labor that separated historical truth from the experiential travel account by relegating the latter into the realm of the aesthetic and the former into the realm of the "philosophical" traveler and historian whose authority was underwritten by metropolitan institutions of knowledge production and authentication, such as the Royal Society of London or the Spanish Royal Academy of History.[19] On the colonial periphery, by contrast, the experiential rhetoric of the testimonial (*testimonio*) retained an important rhetorical function in authorizing political discourse in the context of intra-imperial conflict with the metropolis, by enabling colonial writers "writing back" to the imperial metropolis.[20] The captivities related in both Pineda's and Rowlandson's narratives must therefore be seen as an integral part of their rhetorical structure, as the literary strategy of "primitive eloquence" for authorizing a political discourse that articulates a new and distinctly Creole vision of history as it arose in Chile and New England during the middle of the seventeenth century.

THE IMPERIAL SYNTHESIS AND THE INVENTION
OF THE CREOLE

As already suggested by the original title of Pineda's manuscript – "Cautiverio felis Del M. de Campo, jeneral D. Fran. Nuñes de Pineda y rason individual de las guerras dilatadas del Reyno de Chile" – his purpose in writing was two-fold: his narrative was to rectify, he wrote, "the gross distortion of the facts" about his personal "cautiverio" as well as about the "affairs of Chile" concerning the "reason of the...wars." Although his "historia verdadera" is formally a personal narrative, Pineda repeatedly emphasizes that the lengthy historical "digressions I make and not the succinct story" are the "principal purpose of this book" (160). In his narrative, the "distortions" concerning his personal identity are intimately bound up with the "reasons for the protracted wars" in Chile in the historiography of which he meant to intervene. On the one hand, his narrative is partially a response to a comedy that had been staged in 1634 by the theater company Los conformes in Lima about his captivity among the Araucanian Indians.

In the dramatic convention of the Baroque stage during the *siglo de oro*,[21] the comedy had portrayed Pineda's captivity as a pastoral adventure among bucolic noble savages, detailing his capture in battle and spicing up the plot with a love affair between the Spanish captive and an Indian "princess," who is finally converted to Christianity and taken in by her lover after his redemption. In his own narrative, Pineda is therefore careful to present himself in steadfast resistance to Native women, pagan religious rites, and "fiestas" during his pilgrimage in the Araucanian wilderness. When, once, he nevertheless finds himself tempted by a Native beauty, he virtuously commands her to "be off": "anda, vete por tu vida, y no vengas mas acá, porque me tengo de esconder de tí en no viniendo acompañada" (149) ("be off now, on your life, and don't come back, for I shall hide unless I see you come accompanied" [Atkinson 77]). Then he interrupts his narrative and addresses his reader:

He significado este amoroso subceso con todas circunstancias, por haber sido los informes que hicieron en el Perú a quien hizo una comedia de las cosas de Chile, mui a la contra del hecho; porque representó estos amores mui a lo poético, estrechando los afectos a lo que las obras no se desmandaron. (149–50)

I have dwelt in detail on this half-amorous interlude because of the stories that later got as far as Peru, and there into a play on the affairs of Chile which romanticized them to the gross distortion of the facts and carried the relationship far beyond its true outcome. (Atkinson 77)

On the other hand, the suspicion of *mestizaje* and "indianization" that rested on the personal identity of the captive was only a part in a larger set of historical and political issues that had rested upon Creole character in general and the reasons for the "protracted wars" in Chile in particular. In order to understand why, in 1656, Pineda sat down to rewrite Chilean history in the form of a narrative of captivity that had occurred some twenty-five years earlier, it is necessary to see his account in the specific historical context of the political issues concerning the colony in 1656, as well as in its inter-textual relationship to a tradition of Chilean historiography.

By the middle of the seventeenth century, colonial Chile had long been notorious throughout the Spanish empire for its continual social unrest. Imperial expectations for its economic development as a supplier of commodities such as meat, wine, and copper had continually been frustrated by the colony's remoteness and the perpetual failure of all attempts to "pacify" the Araucanian Indians.[22] In a constant state of war, Chile had mainly exported slaves captured on the frontier and sold on the Peruvian slave markets. When, in 1655, yet another Indian uprising erupted on the

Araucanian frontier – the so-called "rebelión de 1655" – the colony was plunged into the severest crisis of its history. Not only did the new Indian offensive leave thousands of people dead and hundreds of colonial settlements in ruins (Pineda's own *encomienda* among them); but also a discontented white populace, who had long felt that the imperial officials in charge of Chile's provincial government had been provoking the Indian wars in order to cater to the powerful economic interests at stake in the slave trade with Peru, rose up in arms against the government and elected their own governor. Not surprisingly, the count of Alba, viceroy of Peru, reacted swiftly to this unprecedented event in the history of the Spanish empire by having the democratically elected governor arrested and brought in chains to Lima while (illegally) appointing a replacement. Thus, the "rebelión de 1655" split colonial society along clear geo-political lines and pitted the imperial authorities against the Chilean locals, who were heard yelling, "Long live the King! Death to the bad governor."[23]

When reading Pineda's narrative, written in the midst of these turbulent affairs, we must therefore see it primarily as a historical discourse deeply invested in the social and political issues of the colonial crisis of the 1650s, and not simply as the private memoirs of his captivity among the *mapuche* in 1629. When, in 1656, Pineda announced that he would reveal the true "reasons for the protracted wars" in Chile, his subject already had a long and extremely polemical literary history.[24] As we have seen in Chapter 2, as early as the middle of the sixteenth century, the new imperial discourse of "pacification" had stripped the conqueror of his messianic myth. When in Chile the southward progress of "Universal Empire" was suddenly and inexplicably put to a halt in 1556 by the stubborn resistance of the Araucanian Indians (who had already kept the Incas at bay before the European invasion) historians were quick to discern in these events the wrath of God. Hardly could there have been a more vivid illustration of the Spanish conquerors' fall from divine grace than the fate of Pedro de Valdivia – the would-be Cortés of Chile: having planted his new capital "La Imperial" on the utmost extremes of the Araucanian frontier – which would only be, as he still wrote to the emperor in 1545 with providentialist self-assurance, the "first step" by which to "populate all these lands for your majesty from the straits of Magellan to the Northern seas" – before finding a gory end at the hands of the Araucanians, who quenched his proverbial "codicia" ("greed"), as legend has it, by pouring a gallon of melted gold down his throat.[25]

Then, as now, historians asked the same question: what had gone "wrong" with the Spanish empire in America? The answer given by the seventeenth-century *cronistas mayores*, the court historians of the Habsburg monarchs, was to blame what they perceived to be the degeneracy of the conquerors and their Creole descendants. In 1567 the *licenciado* Lope García de Castro reported from New Spain to the president of the Council of the Indies that Spanish society in America was now "different from that before" and that "these lands are full of Creoles, who are those that are born there and, as they have never known the king nor ever hope to know him, are quick to hear and believe those who are mal-intentioned."[26] Originally, the word "Creole" was, according to the Inca Garcilaso de la Vega, invented "in order to . . . distinguish between those blacks born in the Indies and those born in Guinea because the latter are more honest and of better quality having been born in their native country."[27] Increasingly, however, the term "Creole" came to be applied by sixteenth-century historians mainly to European-descended colonials born in the Americas as distinct from Peninsular Spaniards, assuming, as Bernard Lavallé has shown, "thoroughly negative" connotations.[28] What could be the reason for this apparent difference between Spaniards in America and Spaniards in Spain? Based on the information supplied by European travelers, who had provided countless topographic descriptions of America and Native Americans in a state of "savagery," European natural historians began to advance theories and "laws" of the influence of the natural environment in the Americas upon humans.[29] After descriptions of the American environment, the alleged savagery of Indian cultures, and accounts of the conquest by the Spanish redeemer nation, these historians proceeded to relate the decline of colonial societies into cruelty and tyranny in historical narratives that bore little resemblance to the European literary utopias of the sixteenth century. Instead, the Creoles came to assume in these accounts many of the abominable qualities of the barbarous Indians due to the unrelenting influences of the American environment. "I do not marvel at the great defects and imbecility of those who are born in these lands," the disenchanted Franciscan missionary and ethnographer Bernardino de Sahagún exclaimed in the 1580s,

because the Spaniards who inhabit them, and even more those who are born there, assume these bad inclinations; those who are born there become like the Indians, and although they look like Spaniards, in their constitution they are not; those who are born in Spain, if they do not take care, change within a few years after they arrive in these parts; and this I think is due to the climate or the constellations in these parts.[30]

It is significant that already Sahagún makes a distinction between Peninsular Spaniards residing in America ("españoles que en ella [tierra] habitan") and Creoles who are born there ("que en ella nacen"). The effect of the

New World environs, on the latter more so than on the former, was a "declension" from the allegedly superior standards of European civility. Similarly, the *cronista mayor* Juan López de Velasco, apparently first to use the term *criollo* in print,[31] claimed in the 1570s that the Spaniards born in the Indies, "who are called Creoles, turn out like the natives even though they are not mixed with them [by simply] declining to the disposition of the land." The effect of this "declension" was that "general manners and conversation are vanishing" and that European "strength of virtue" had yielded to barbaric shiftlessness, greed, licentiousness, and lawlessness.[32] This theory would be echoed again and again by Peninsular historians such as the *madrileño* Juan de la Puente, who claimed that "the heavens of America induce inconstancy, lasciviousness and lies: vices characteristic of the Indians and... of the Spaniards who are born and bred there."[33] Thus, in European eyes, creolization in America resulted, as Anthony Pagden has written, in an essentialized "single, if varied, character... It became possible to ascribe to the criollos all those supposed shortcomings of the Indians that were thought to derive from psychological weakness or deformation, above all their moral and social instability."[34]

The theory of creolization became a powerful proto-scientific paradigm underwriting the centralizing politics of the Habsburg crown and the imperial histories produced by the *cronistas mayores*, such as López de Velasco, Antonio de Herrera y Tordesillas, Gil González Dávila, and Antonio de Solís, who carefully synthesized the polemical and contradictory discourses of the conquest dating from the first half of the sixteenth century.[35] On the one hand, these *cronistas mayores* tended to fall in line with the early sixteenth-century defenders of violent conquest in their providentialist justifications of Iberian overseas expansionism; but, on the other hand, they were also eager to rationalize Madrid's centralizing imperial policies that had begun, as we have seen in Chapter 2, during the 1540s with the New Laws and which had gradually centralized the allocation of the spoils of conquest (i.e. Indian labor) away from the local colonial elites and into the hands of the royal *corregidores* (chief magistrates). The *cronistas mayores* therefore made implicit and explicit use of the sixteenth-century chroniclers who had denounced the "cruelty" and "tyranny" of the conquistadors and their descendants toward the American Natives after the first conquests had been completed. In the early seventeenth century, Antonio de Herrera y Tordesillas, official historiographer of the Habsburg crown, for example, drew his sources from sixteenth-century chronicles as politically divergent as Las Casas, Oviedo, Bernal Díaz, and López de Gómara.[36] He discussed at great length the "inclination" on the part of the conquerors and their descendants toward enriching themselves, epitomized by the rebel Gonzalo Pizarro, who was "possessed by ambition and fury... [and] lost no opportunity to execute his cruelty." In order to protect the Indians, he wrote, from the colonials, who with "stout carnivorous dogs" forced the Indians "to work more than they were accustomed," Madrid dispatched royal officials to the New World. The conquerors and their descendants had failed (and even resisted) their colonial mission of converting and protecting the Natives. This, Herrera concluded in his monumental history of America, was "legitimate reason to deprive them of their encomiendas; wherefore the King ordered that care be taken to find out whether the encomenderos complied with the obligation with which they were charged."[37] Thus, the "Black Legend" and the "myth of the Noble Savage" became the two interconnected parts of a political "propaganda tool" in the Atlantic world.[38] While this tool would later get, as we have seen in Chapter 3, into the hands of Spain's imperial rivals during the seventeenth century, it was first employed during the sixteenth century by Spanish imperial historians who suggested that the American Creoles had succumbed to the "American" disorder and immorality which the Spanish conquerors had been sent to redeem; they had, in effect, succumbed to the very "America" invented in the discourses of the First Conquest as a place where the Devil's unrestrained force had turned upside down God's natural order.

When writing the history of his captivity in the aftermath of the "rebelión de 1655," Francisco Núñez de Pineda y Bascuñán was keenly aware of the political implications that a determination of the "reasons for the protracted wars" might have for the future of colonial Chile. He agrees with the imperial historians that the frontier uprising, the war, and the ruin of the settlements were the "azote con que Dios, nuestro Señor, nos ha castigado" (112) ("the whip with which God, our Lord, has chastised us"). However, he is quick to clarify that by "nos" he does not mean *all* Spaniards in Chile. Not only is he careful to portray himself (and his paternal ancestors) as the Indians' best friend when emphasizing how much he was loved and respected by the people of his captor and master Maulicán as well as other friendly tribes; but he also points out that the protracted wars in Chile were not the result of the alleged deficiencies of an "American" character – Indian or *criollo* – but rather God's punishment for the abuses of "los que gobiernan" (132) ("those that govern") – the (Peninsular) Spanish governors and "foreign" imperial administrators, who had provoked the wars with their perpetual slave raids. "[A]lgunos alborotos y alzamientos que ha habido en las fronteras", he informs his reader, "se han orijinado todos por malos ministros y gobernadores cudiciosos, sin temor de Dios ni respeto a la justicia ni a los mandatos del Rei N. S." (162–3) ("Some disturbances and uprisings on the frontier have originated entirely because of bad ministers and greedy governors who have neither fear of God nor respect for the justice and mandates of His Majesty"). In his narrative, he thus accepts the historiographic commonplace that distinguishes between two kinds of Spaniards: the Chilean local natives (born in America) and the recent Spanish immigrants and imperial administrators, whom he calls the "habitadores" or "estranjeros." However, he inverts the moral evaluation attributed to each by the imperial historians: the Creoles, such as his father, appear as morally superior while the "habitadores," or Peninsular Spaniards who now govern Chile, imitate the "primeros conquistadores" ("first conquerors"), such as Pedro de Valdivia and García Hurtado de Mendoza, whose corruption stood implicated by the histories written by clerical chroniclers such as Alonso de Ovalle and Diego de Rosales and in Peninsular belletristic literature, such as Ercilla's *La Araucana*. The imperial officials and recent Peninsular immigrants had turned the world, formerly governed by justice and reason but now by corruption and vice, upside-down.

Porque nuestros habitadores siguen los pasos de aquellos primeros conquistadores, imitando sus acciones y aun aventajándose en ellas, con insaciable cudicia y con extraordinarios modos de ejecutarlo, atropellando la justicia y desquiciando la razon de su conocido asiento, cuyo vacío es forzoso que la disension le ocupe, la traicion se apodere dél, la mentira se atreva, el apetito ande suelto, vivan los malos y los vicios prevalezcan, con que la paz se sepulta, la concordia se sujeta, la lealtad queda abatida, la verdad acobardada, presa la razon, los buenos oprimidos y finalmente destruidas las virtudes. (54)

Because our recent arrivals follow in the footsteps of those first conquerors, imitating their actions and even surpassing them, with their insatiable greed and with their extraordinary ways of executing them, trampling justice and tearing reason from its throne, a gap is left which is filled by dissension, taken over by treason, and allows lying, lets appetites loose, lets the bad ones live and vices prevail, with which peace is buried, harmony is bound, loyalty is vanquished, truth frightened, reason is imprisoned, the good are oppressed and finally (all) virtues are destroyed.

Thus, the proverbial Spanish crimes and abuses in Chile, past and present, become, in Pineda's narrative, an essentially Peninsular affair. After all, Valdivia and the original conquerors had not been Creoles but were also Spanish-born. The victims of the First Conquest had been the Native-born Indians; analogously, the victims of the more recent Second Conquest by Spanish "foreigners" are the native-born Creoles, who are, like the Indians, just, peace-loving, and valorous – due, presumably, to the salubrious effects of a Chilean birth. Thus, Pineda wrote his autobiographical history as the apologia of the Chilean locals who felt that they had defied corrupt imperial officials on behalf of the superior justice of the monarch. Writing in the context of political friction between a colonial frontier society and the centers of imperial administration, Pineda attributes the Indian wars in providentialist terms to God's punishment for Spanish "declensions" and makes a case for Chile's political equality with the Peninsular centers of imperial administration. His "verdadera historia" (133) was his appeal to his king that Chile should be governed by native Chileans, not corrupt strangers. The "pequeño misterio" of Pineda's positive portrayal of Native Americans must thus not be mistaken for the result of his "cautiverio feliz" but rather taken as a rhetorical ploy in his polemic with the proto-scientific imperial historians of the New World in the political context of the 1650s.[39]

MONSTROUS BIRTHS: THE TRANSLATION OF THE CREOLE

Not unlike in Pineda's captivity narrative in Chile, in Mary Rowlandson's New England narrative, there was also more at stake than an individual's personal memories during war and captivity. Her narrative, whose composition and promotion were assisted by Increase Mather, one of the colony's shrewdest political lobbyists during several trips to London, had distinct implications for colonial political relations with the imperial metropolis in British America. Specifically, the title of the London edition – "The True History of…" – establishes a dialogue with the historiography commissioned by imperial administrators in Whitehall, whom Cotton Mather called the "late oppressors of New England" for their continual assaults on the colonial charter, which was indeed revoked in 1684.[40] Not unlike colonial Chile, colonial New England, too, had held a rather singular status in the imperial realm, remaining of little economic value to its imperial metropolis by the second half of the seventeenth century. In British America, the West Indies had supplied sugar and Virginia and Maryland revenue from the tobacco trade. The colonials there were accustomed to abundant consumption of English manufactured goods. By contrast, the New England colonies, with their economies based on farming, fishing, and trade, had not only failed to furnish the metropolis with raw materials but also continuously sought to decrease their economic dependency on England through the creation of local manufacture and inter-colonial trade. Instead of supplying the empire with raw materials, New Englanders were competing with the metropolis in the export of manufactured goods to the West Indies and even on foreign markets.[41] Not surprisingly, English mercantilists such as Josiah Child did not look favorably upon the fact that half of the colonies' credits came from their merchant fleets. New England was, he complained in the 1660s, "the most prejudicial Plantation to this Kingdom." In 1671, the earl of Sandwich, president of the Council for Plantations, observed that New England was soon likely to become so "mighty rich and powerfull" as to be "not at all carefull of theire dependence upon old England."[42] Moreover, New England had been a special case within the larger history of British America also with regard to its constitutional, religious, and social character. A series of charter colonies through much of the seventeenth century, New England had retained an atypically high number of political liberties, such as the election of governors and the local regulation of the body politic in terms of congregational church membership. As a New World culture where radical Protestant religious dissent had become the new orthodoxy in a thoroughly theocratic state, it did not, like other colonies, attempt to replicate Old World culture but rather to reform it, to return to a more "ancient" or "primitive" state of Old World history.[43] For these reasons, New England societies have sometimes appeared to historians as comparatively anti-modern, as anachronistically stable and coherent "communities" in their early years, only later evolving into "societies" resembling other parts of the early modern Atlantic world.[44]

An important consequence of this relatively large degree of political and cultural autonomy maintained by New England during the first part of the seventeenth century was that much of its literary production and historiography had been largely independent from metropolitan imperial politics. With the possible exception of its ethnographic missionary literature, much of which was addressed to the London-based Society for the Propagation of the Gospel in the hope of sponsorship,[45] colonial Puritan prose was predominantly religious in nature and typically directed "inward" and "downward," not "outward" and "upward" in the socio-spatial hierarchies of the British empire. Rowlandson's narrative, published as it was in New and Old England under two different titles during the early 1680s, manifests a transition in this regard, triggered by the metropolitan attempt to convert a "plantation" into a "colony." After the Restoration of the Stuart monarchy in 1660, the Privy Council, not unlike the Spanish Consejo de Indias (Council of the Indies) in the 1540s, grew increasingly determined to bring colonial administration more closely into line with metropolitan interests. Although Parliament had begun to enact a series of Navigation Acts designed to re-define the economic relationship between England and its colonies – by stipulating the elimination of colonial trade with foreign powers and the subordination of the colonial economies to that of the metropolis – it did not see to its actual enforcement until 1664, when sending a delegation of Royal Commissioners to ensure that the colonials were in compliance. In 1675 – the year of the outbreak of "King Philip's" War – the Lords of Trade were created, a permanent committee to the Privy Council responsible for overseeing the colonies. This measure represented a decisive step by the imperial government toward a "vigorous and systematic metropolitan supervision over the colonies." The *intended* effect of these "centripetal" measures was the reconstruction of the "political relationship between the monarchy and the colonies in a way that would both significantly enhance the power of the crown at the center and weaken the effective authority of local institutions in the peripheries."[46] The *real* effect of these measures, however, has been the subject of much dispute among historians. Thus, while Stephen Saunders Webb has described the impact on New England as an effectual "end of American Independence,"[47] the consistent failure on the part of the metropolis to subject these colonies to dependence has led others to the more qualified argument that the conflict was negotiated in a perpetual dialectic that was at the foundation of the "constitutional development of the early modern British Empire."[48]

It was, not coincidentally, in this context of intra-imperial geo-political tension since the beginning of the 1660s that metropolitan charges could increasingly be heard to the effect that the New England colonials had failed in their imperial mission – a mission that was made explicit on the seal of the Massachusetts colonial charter in the form of an Indian figure begging Englishmen to "COME OVER AND HELPS US."[49] As early as the 1640s, even Puritan historians in England such as William Castell had suggested that New Englanders, not having amounted to much with regard to their apostolic mission, remove to Barbados, where, hopefully, they would be of more service to the Commonwealth.[50] Not surprisingly, non-Puritan historians were hardly more generous toward the New England saints. Peter Heylyn wrote that "I finde not any great increase of Christianity amongs the Natives...our English Undertakers think it sufficient if they and their houses served the Lord without yearning what became of the souls of the wretched People; which hither have sate in darknesse and the shadow of death, notwithstanding those New Lights which have shined amongst them."[51] Another historian, George Gardyner, indicted the New Englanders' cruelty in their treatment of the Indians when he sarcastically remarked that "They punish sin as severely as Jews did in old time, but not with so good a warrant. And they have brought Indians into great awe, but not to any Gospell knowledge."[52] English imperial historians such as John Ogilby lambasted the American Puritans for having "made themselves Masters of their own opinion" against the imperial interest of the Crown.[53] Shortly after the outbreak of "King Philip's" War, Samuel Groom attacked the Puritan oligarchy for their constant "quarrels which you have brought upon yourselves, through your pride and unequal dealing with dissenters in matters of religion, and by your treacherous practices toward the Indians, all which crieth very loud for vengeance." Like the Spanish critics of Creole character a century before, he argued that the American colonials had succumbed to greed, barbarity, and cruelty from their original English virtues and wondered whether New Englanders, "since ye fled out of Old England into the Wilderness of New England, ... have not brought forth many monstrous births, like bruit beasts, like dragons, like Cockatrices, like roaring lyons and Devouring Wolves?"[54] Joseph Mede claimed that the English colonists "themselves are become exceeding rude, more likely to turne Heathen, then to turne others to the Christian faith."[55] The colonials' inability to convert, and tendency to destroy, the Indian subjects of His Majesty were, according to Morgan Godwin, a "crime of such degenerate English, who with that air [of America], have imbibed the Barbarity and Heathenism of the countries they live in."[56] If the English colonials depicted in metropolitan historiography after the Restoration increasingly resembled the Spanish colonials familiar from earlier accounts, the scientific paradigm of Natural History readily provided the plausible explanation in terms of the natural "law" that the environment determined the form of all observable phenomena. The men in Jamaica, travelers such as Ned Ward wrote in 1698, "look as if they had just knock'd off their Feters, and by an unexpected Providence, escap'd the danger of a near Mis-fortunes; the dread of which, hath imprinted that in their Looks, which they can no more alter than an Ethiopian can his Colour." Moreover, the women in New England, he wrote a year later, had "contracted so many ill habits from the Indians, that 'tis difficult to find a Woman cleanly enough for a Cook to a Squemish Lady, or a Man neat enough for a Vallet to a Sir Courtly Nice."[57] In the accounts of imperial historians and travelers, European *colonists* who had removed to the New World had at last become American *colonials*.

Rowlandson's 1682 narrative of a colonial Englishwoman's extraordinary suffering at the hands of cruel American savages was to counter metropolitan notions that "King Philip's" War was the story of the slaughter of the king's nobly savage subjects provoked by degenerate Creoles. "Little do many think," she cries, "what is the savageness and brutishness of this barbarous enemy, aye even those that seem to profess more than others among them, when the English have fallen into their hands" (326). As in Pineda's narratives, issues of colonial history and Creole character are inter-connected with the personal identity of a returned captive also in Rowlandson's text. Like Pineda after his return from the frontier, the returned

New England captive purifies herself from unauthorized "other versions of what had happened in the wilderness" in her captivity narrative.[58] As if she somehow had to dispel her readers' suspicions that "I speak it for my own credit," she asserts that "not one of them [the Indians] ever offered me the least abuse of unchastity to me, in word or action...I speak it in the presence of God, and to His Glory." Ironically, as she is anxiously laboring to convince us, her exculpatory discourse is betrayed by the very print face of her narrative, which bears the marks of creolization left by the idiosyncratic spelling of an Indian typesetter.[59] Thus, both colonial captivity narratives were designated as "true histories" in order to rectify and critique not only other versions of the colonial captive's individual experiences in captivity but also other versions of colonial history in a moment of intra-imperial conflict. But in order to discern the rhetorical significance of this generic designation within the context of this imperial dialogue in Natural History about creolization in the American environment, it will be necessary to investigate its epistemological and ideological underpinnings in more detail.

"TRUE HISTORIES"

Two years after Increase Mather had assisted in the writing and publishing of Rowlandson's narrative, he published his *Essay for the Recording of Illustrious Providences* (1684), in which he wrote that "I have often wished that the Natural History of New England might be written and published to the World, [according to] the Rules and method described by that learned and excellent person, Robert Boyle, Esq."[60] Yet, Mather never produced such a natural history; indeed he and his contemporaries among the New English Puritan elite, such as John Winthrop, Jr., consistently resisted all requests by the Royal Society of London to provide an inventory of New England's natural resources.[61] When Mather did write a history of New England, it was his own account of "King Philip's" War, *Relation of the Trouble occasioned by the Indians of New England*. This sheds light on the nature of the Puritan divine's special interest in a Puritan woman's personal account of Indian captivity. Jim Egan, in his study of the politics of the rhetoric of experience in seventeenth-century New England, has argued that in the second half of the seventeenth century, when the Puritan colonial oligarchy gradually lost its monopoly on political and cultural authority in New England and English political authorities threatened to revoke colonial charters, New English writers increasingly "turn[ed] away from the corporate spiritual body that served as the figure linking colonial subjects to the ideal English social body." Instead, Egan argues, New England writers in the final decades of the century turn to a "rhetoric of experience" in order to show how colonial political self-government "derives from a body politic that grows out of the colonial ground itself and, as such, is separate from the English communal body."[62] New England's radical Protestant culture had hereby privileged individual experience as a legitimate way of knowing, and experiential accounts such as Rowlandson's narrative of captivity could bear considerable weight as authentic testimony that New English experience was different from that of Old England. As a sub-genre of the Protestant "Providence Tale," the Puritan captivity narrative betrayed, as James Hartman has argued, an "overall concern with truth – scientific, empirical, Baconian truth."[63]

Of course, as we have seen in the previous chapters, there was nothing essentially New English, Puritan, or even Protestant about this new "over-all concern with truth" and the rhetorical power of eyewitness testimony. Rather, this concern had originated in the context of European expansionism in the New World during the sixteenth century and is manifest also in Catholic captivity narratives such as that written by the Chilean Creole Pineda. Yet, there are, to be sure, several important differences between Rowlandson and Pineda with regard to their respective relationships with this "New World" of science. One such difference is fairly obvious in regard to gender. As critics such as Carolyn Merchant and Denise Albenese have argued, colonialist language frequently employs a gendered hierarchy that casts the female embodiment of "America" at the "border zone between nature and culture in the colonial fantasy," thus constituting women as the natural objects of the male scientific gaze.[64] While Rowlandson was therefore hardly in a subject position of authority to speak on matters of history and politics, her identity as a woman could lend her testimony the *authenticity* particular to what Stephen Shapin has called the "antiauthor" in the experimental narrative, whose self-effacing transparency negated "the egotistical and fame-seeking manner ascribed to the dominant tribe of philosophical authors."[65] This anti-author's identity as "a Minister's wife" is therefore not only explicitly emphasized in the title of the London edition of the Rowlandson account but reiterated also in Mather's "Preface" to that edition, which contains her narrative, as "that worthy and precious Gentle-woman," who had suffered so severely "under such Captivity, travels, and hardships (much too hard for flesh and blood)," before telling her story. If her story was published, it was only because "some friends" persuaded the reluctant author, whose "modesty would not thrust it into the Press, yet her gratitude unto God, made her not hardly perswadable to let it pass":

"I hope by this time none will cast any reflection upon this Gentlewoman, on the score of this publication of her Affliction and Deliverance. If any should, doubtless they may be reckoned with the nine Lepers, of whom it is said, Were there not ten cleansed, where are the nine?" (320). In the light of Mather's manifest interest in the New Sciences propagated by the Royal Society, it is significant that he stresses the "affliction" to which the Puritan gentlewoman had been subjected before writing her "true" history. The authenticity claimed by the "afflicted" captive had long been a common rhetorical figure in the natural histories of the New World. In his *Historia natural*, Oviedo, for example, had stressed that Europeans who had been captives among the Indians were "more trustworthy" than those who had "never known anyone but their neighbors" and that the chronicler of "these things over here" lived with "much thirst and hunger, with exhaustion, in warfare with his enemies, and in both war and peace, he struggles with hostile elements and great needs and dangers."[66] Rowlandson, in her own narrative, also exploits this rhetoric reserved for the lone afflicted witness in the New World of experience. "All was gone," she laments, "my husband gone...my children gone my relations and friends gone, our house and home and all our comforts" (324). She "wondered at [her son's] speech" when he told her that he "was as much grieved for his father as for himself" because "I had enough upon my spirit in reference to myself, to make me mindless of my husband and everyone else" (344). Her husband (like England) has not "been there" and experienced what she has. "Now is the dreadful hour come, that I have often *heard of* (in time of war, as it was the case of others)," she writes, "but now *mine eyes see* it" (323; my emphasis). During her captivity, she was deprived of all comfort. Like a "swine," she must "lie down on the ground" (346). But it is only through the experience of affliction, when human idols and illusions vanish, that God's Truth and mercy are revealed to her, when even the Indians' food – "their filthy trash" – gradually becomes "sweet and savory to my taste" (333).

Apart from emphasizing her afflictions during captivity, she also aims to lend her history authenticity by resorting to (proto-)journalistic, sensationalist language in her descriptions of the "cruelty of the heathen." For example, her account of the death of Goodwife Joslin gives the impression of dramatic immediacy: "[They] stripped her naked, and set her in the midst of them: and when they had sung and danced about her (in their hellish manner) as long as they pleased, they knocked her on the head, and the child in her arms with her: when they had done that, they made a fire and put them both into it" (332). The "significance" of this sensationalist description is, as some critics have already noted, that Rowlandson could

not have actually witnessed this scene herself but wrote it based on the accounts of other captives.[67] Although Rowlandson appeals to her status as an eyewitness, she admits that she knows of this incident only second-hand, from "some of the company…in my travel" (331). Her appeal to eyewitness experience must therefore be read less as the epistemological basis of her account than as a rhetorical strategy in the New World genre of the "true history." Although she mentions that "twenty-four of us" were taken "alive and carried captive" (325), her authority depends on an erasure of twenty-three other potential narratives. Thus, she asserts ("with Job") that "*I only am escaped alone to tell the news*" (325). What makes her colonial American "true history" extraordinary in literary history is therefore not the unusual amount of violence that she experienced *in reality* – a violence sometimes presumed to be exceptional to the "American experience"[68] – but rather the graphic and proto-scientific *realism* with which her narrative represents this reality of frontier warfare from the point of view of the eyewitness observer. It is a difference not of ontological reality that makes the American captivity narratives "exceptional" but rather the new epistemic circumstances in which they were produced: the imperial fantasy of an extra- or pre-textual objective absolute, accessible in a "New World" of "experience."

While the colonial *encomendero* Pineda lacked the natural authenticity conferred onto "anti-authors," in his narrative it is also the experience of affliction that authenticates the contents of his narrative. For "Mas de cuarenta anos" ("More than forty years"), he laments, he has

continuado esta guerra…padecido en un cautiverio muchos trabajos, incomodidades y desdichas, que aunque fue feliz en el tratmiento y agasiajo, no por eso me excuse de andar descalzo de pie y pierna, con una manta o camiseta a raiz de las carnes, lleno de pulgas y otros animalejos que me daban fatidio; que para quien estaba criado en buenos panales y en regalo, el que tenia entre ellos no lo era. (467)

continued this war…suffered in captivity much hardship, inconvenience, and misfortune, for although I was happy in the treatment and gracious regalement that I received, I was not on that account exempt from going about bare of foot and leg, with a blanket or under-shirt next to my skin, full of fleas and other little animals that pestered me. For one who was reared in good swaddling clothes and in dainty comfort, the life I led amongst them was far from convenient.

Also not unlike Rowlandson, he, too, uses extremely graphic and sensationalist language – despite his essentially sympathetic attitude toward the Indians, who became brutal and savage, he reminds us later, only as a result of Spanish injustice. Thus, shortly after having related the battle in which

he was taken captive, and after having crossed the Bío-Bío River, Pineda witnesses the gory sacrifice of his fellow captive:

le dió en el celebro un tan gran golpe, que le echó los sesos fuera con la macana o porra claveteada, que sirvió de la insignia que llaman toque. Al instante los acólitos que estaban con los cuchillos en las manos, le abrieron el pecho y le sacaron el corazon palpitando, y se lo entregaron a mi amo, que despues de haberle chupado la sangre, le trajeron una quita de tabaco, y cojiendo humo en la boca, lo fué echando a una y otras partes, como incensando al demonio a quien habian ofrecido aquel sacrificio... Acabado este bárbaro y mal rito, volvió el corazon a manos de mi amo, y haciendo de él unos pequeños pedazos, entre todos se lo fueron comiendo con gran presteza. (43)

was dealt such a blow on the head with the studded club he dashed his brains out. Straightway the other two with the knives cut open his breast, ripped out his still quivering heart and handed it to Maulicán. He sucked its blood, was handed a pipe of tobacco and drew in a mouthful of smoke which he then blew in every direction, as though wafting incense to the devil in whose honour the youth had been sacrificed... The barbarous rite ended at last when the heart was given back to my master, who cut it into pieces which the others devoured. (Atkinson 27–8)

Due to the growing rhetorical power of first-hand testimony, imperial historians of the New World, such as Oviedo, Herrera, and Samuel Purchas eagerly collected, edited, and reprinted the accounts and letters by first-hand witnesses in their histories. The colonial Creole historian Pineda, however, distinguishes himself from the European historians in two important regards: first, most of the *relaciones* he provides as evidence of his historical and political arguments are based on his *own* first-hand accounts. Not unlike a John Smith in this regard, he is historian *and* witness at the same time, thus undermining the division of intellectual labor between the eyewitness and the historian that constructed early modern historiographic authority. He invokes his "ability to bear witness," to mark off those who have "been there" from those who had not, as Anthony Pagden has written in regard to another New World author, in order "to sharpen the boundary which divided the Old World from the New, and the 'them' from the 'us,'" thus articulating what Jorge Cañizares-Esguerra has called a "patriotic epistemology" in writing the history of the New World that opposes that of the imperial historians.[69] Second, Pineda's "historia verdadera" differs from the imperial histories in the structural relationship between narrative eyewitness accounts and historiographic discourse. In the imperial history the *relación* is contextualized, edited, and commentated by the scientific authority of the detached historian, who organizes the material with scientific method into the topically distinct discourses constituting the totality of knowledge in natural and "general" history (i.e. geography, climate, culture). Similarly, Pineda's "true history" is structured into five historical "discursos" (each of which is itself divided into twenty-six "capítulos"); but none of the different "discursos" (nor the "capítulos") are topically distinct from the others in content. Instead, the content of his "true history" is entirely structured by the narrative of his experiences in captivity, into which are inserted his lengthy historiographic "digresiones." In his "true history," eyewitness testimony contains historiographic discourse, not vice versa. However, since pure experience continued to be considered somewhat "unstable because of its novelty" during the seventeenth century,[70] Old World doctrinal foundations had to be found to reinforce the legitimacy of this authority. Pineda therefore seems compelled to provide endless Scriptural and Classical precedents and analogues for every page of narrative. He begins, for example, by emphasizing the validity of empirical knowledge with an invocation of the first chapter of Genesis, where God created light and dark and "vió" ("saw") that it was good. Hereby, Pineda goes on to argue, God had provided a principle to be followed also by worldly rulers when governing: "no juzgar sin haber visto" (56) ("not to judge without having seen"). The narrative of his captivity serves then as testimony that he – unlike those who write "sin haber asistido en las fronteras de guerra cuatro dias" (132) ("without having served on the frontiers of war for even four days") – has seen and therefore is qualified to judge.

As in Pineda's narrative, in Rowlandson's narrative there is also a certain tension between two opposing models of historiographic rhetoric: the rhetorical appeal to eyewitness experience on the one hand and to theological doctrine on the other. When, for example, Rowlandson relates the death of her eldest sister during the raid she interrupts her narrative in order to insert a brief account of her sister's conversion experience, which likens her seemingly senseless death to her "reaping the fruit of her good labors" (324). In Rowlandson's "true History," interpretative discourse "punctuates" narratives of personal experience with the effect of subverting the authorial division of labor that constitutes the institutionalized "dichotomy between the voice telling the plot details and the voice interpreting them."[71] In particular, Rowlandson invokes, in a distinctively Protestant fashion, the rhetorical figure of the traveling book – the Bible which was allegedly given to her by an Indian and which accompanies her as she "removes" ever farther from the social centers of interpretative authority. She claims that she randomly opened her Bible whenever an event left her at a loss for meaning and, providentially, is invariably guided to just the right passage that gives meaning to her apparently meaningless suffering. Meaning and truth cannot be dissociated from empirical experience in her narrative, nor historiographic rhetoric from first-person narrative. Christianity is, as Anthony Pagden has noted, a "religion of observance." The Martyr (as Pagden notes, a word whose original Greek root means simply "witness") is a Christian hero who has "seen" but failed to persuade others of the unique authenticity of his or her vision, a pilgrim who has not returned.[72] While our two colonials did return, both exploit their experiences as the suffering castaway/captive. Although our two colonial Creole historians lacked the cultural authority of their European counterparts, their appeal to first-hand experience becomes in their histories an important rhetorical tool and literary device in giving voice to a colonial identity. "Writing back" to the center of imperial authority in this fashion, American colonials could appropriate, manipulate, and transform European conventions of historiographic rhetoric and notions of "truth."

HETEROLOGIES

Besides appealing to the authority of the eyewitness, of having *seen*, our two colonial captives also enlist what Michel de Certeau has called the rhetoric of "heterology," the representation of Native primitive or "savage babble" in European historiographic discourse about the New World. It is an authority which resides in the truth value of the Savage voice as God's unconscious vehicle of revelation; a voice that is itself unaware of the implications of its testimony for "civilized" society, Indian language acquires a "double function," De Certeau writes, "of being the way by which a substance (the effectivity of primitive life) happens to uphold the discourse of a European knowledge":

[It is] a fable, a speech which is unaware of what it expresses before decipherment can provide it with meaning and practical usage. The being which authenticates the discourse is no longer directly received from God; it is made to come from the foreign place itself, where it is the gold mine hidden under an exotic exteriority, the truth to be discerned beneath primitive babble.[73]

In Pineda's "true history," the authority of "primitive babble" – the disinterested speech of the Savage – authorizes his historiographic reflections on the reasons for the war. By employing this rhetorical tool, Pineda's "historia verdadera" transfers the revelation of meaning and truth from center to the semi-periphery in the imperial geography of historiographic authority by establishing himself as the collector/historian who contextualizes the Indians' oral testimonies. His representations of the *mapuche* orators are stylizations of Montaigne's Cannibals, whose fictitious voice of nature he mobilizes for his social critique of Spanish imperial administration. For the testimony of the Cannibal, Montaigne had written, is to be much preferred to that of the "subtile" travelers. The "Cannibal" was

a simple and rough-hewn fellow: a condition fit to yield a true testimony. For subtile people may indeed mark more curiously, and observe things more exactly, but they amplify and gloss them: and the better to persuade, and make their interpretations of more validity, they cannot choose but somewhat alter the story. They never represent things purely, but fashion and make them according to the visage they saw them in; and to purchase credit to their judgment, and draw you on to believe them, they commonly adorn, enlarge, yea, and Hyperbolize the matter. Wherein is required either a most sincere Reporter, or a man so simple, that he may have no invention to build upon, and to give a true likelihood unto false devices, and be not wedded to his own will.[74]

Pineda's Native witnesses bear a striking resemblance to Montaigne's Cannibals in this regard. In order to authorize his corrective history, he presents as his superior "evidencia" the personal *relaciones* of the old Indians who were actually alive to witness those events, as a kind of legal testimony:

[P]ara que se conozca con evidencia que lo que digo y escribo en este volumen, es por ciertas relaciones adquiridas de los propios antiguos naturales, he fundádolos en historia de mi captiverio dichoso y feliz, por referir experimentado lo que adquirí cuidadoso entre los indios mas ancianos, criados y nacidos en aquellos tiempos de los primeros conquistadores. (246)

In order for it to be known that what I say and write in this book is based on the authentic relations of the old Indians themselves, I have included them in the history of my blessed and happy captivity, in order to provide experienced reference of what I carefully acquired among the oldest Indians, who were born and brought up in those times of the first conquerors.

Frequently, these accounts are presented in the form of proto-Rousseauian confessional apologias, in which a notorious (Indian) "enemy of man" relates how he was transformed from friend to foe. After relating all the injustices and cruelties suffered at the hands of the Spaniards, the Indian enemy typically concludes: "'Esta fué la causa, capitan y amigo, de mi tranformación y mudanza de amigo vuestro a enemigo declarado. Mirad, por vuestra vida, ahora si tuve razon o no'" (52) ("'And that, captain and friend, is why I changed sides and, from being the Spaniards' friend, became their enemy. Say, on your life, if I had cause'" [Atkinson 34]). It is the "natural" or "authentic" truth of the Savage voice as God's unconscious vehicle of revelation which is enlisted here in the cause of Pineda's political rhetoric.

While Rowlandson makes less frequent (and quite different) use of heterology as an authorial strategy, in her narrative the content of Native speech also frequently assumes unexpected significances. For example, though her Indians are in the service of the Devil – of "him who was a liar at the beginning" – when speaking with intent, truth about New England history, and the causes of the Indian wars, are revealed in the speech of the unintentional Indian witnesses. Thus Rowlandson is struck with the Indians' blunt reply that they would "break my face" at her announcement that she would rest on the Sabbath day (333). She interprets her captivity as God's just punishment for violating, in her inward wilderness, the Sabbath. Her subsequent captivity is her chastisement by God, who casts her into the corresponding outward wilderness, in which she is – an awful irony – excluded from the Sabbath. In the Indians' "primitive babble" is revealed God's justice, truth, and Providence – but also, of course, her personal election.

Rowlandson often accentuates the effect of this rhetorical tool by pitting primitive babble against "civilized" readers' "reasonable" expectations, thereby conveying a distinctly Protestant feeling of cosmic rupture between man's reason and objective cosmic truth. The unorthodoxy of Indian behavior, the encounter of two mutually alien discourses, and the disruption of European cultural expectations thereby often result in what Michelle Burnham has called the "dialogism" of her account,[75] which renders her narrative grimly comical. When, for example, she appeals, as an English woman, to the expected comforting chivalric sensitivities of her male captors – to lighten the burden of her pack because "the skin was off my back" – she "had no other comforting answer from them than this: That it would be no matter if my head were off too" (342). Moreover, the dialogism of Rowlandson's narrative not only consists in the upsetting of cultural expectations; rather it is often raised to another plane of complexity in the cross-cultural "mimicry" of discourses about the Other. Thus, the Indians even frequently parody European colonial discourses of cross-cultural representation by enacting colonialist stereotypes in jest. When, for example, Rowlandson asks an Indian about the whereabouts of her son, he answered that "such a time his master roasted him, and that himself did eat a piece of him, as big as his two fingers, and that he was very good meat" (342).

Thus, both colonial writers of "true history" enlist the authenticity of what Europeans imagined to be the Savage's primitive eloquence in order to authorize their historiographic reflections on the reasons for colonial war. However, Pineda's Indians lack the Gothically grotesque and horribly surprising caprices of Rowlandson's Indians. His Indian's voice does not derive from the perverted tongue of the Devil but from a natural language, as yet uncorrupted in an innocent Golden Age. Pineda's is the rational, inclusive, and symmetrical universe of the Catholic culture of the Baroque, which even the Indian Savage inhabits. His Savages are not natural creatures of the Devil but turned to evil either as a result of the Devil's seduction and perversion or as a result of Spanish cruelty, abuses, and injustice.

BAROQUE DREAMS AND GOTHIC NIGHTMARES

The two colonial histories of captivity reflect this difference in religious ideology both in their language and in their narrative structure. Pineda's narrative about his experiences in captivity resembles here the "horizontal" architectural designs of the Baroque aesthetic, based on a neo-Thomist epistemology that resisted the fragmentation of knowledge by subordinating all of its increasingly diversifying branches to one "queen" of sciences – theology – and a hermeneutic that celebrated ornate signs as mediators between the worldly and the otherworldly. The form of his 600-page narrative vividly chronicles man in his eternal struggle for Truth – a struggle as futile as it is imperative in its compulsion to glorify God – through human reason and art. Hence his endless disquisitions on philosophy, theology, and history that fill his "digressions" from his first-person narrative.[76] Rowlandson's language, by contrast, resembles in this regard the "vertical" architectural design of the Gothic, an aesthetic of profound cosmic incoherence and Augustinian distrust of worldly forms and reason. Her narrative is intended to impart upon the reader the awe and horror felt when God's Truth is suddenly revealed to the passive Protestant human subject in the moment of apocalyptic rupture. In her Puritan "plain style" all signs are turned upward to point away from this world, into the supernatural, to God and heaven: "On the twentieth of February 1676 came the Indians with great number upon Lancaster," her narrative begins, "several houses were burning, and the smoke ascending to heaven." While at "another time" the English dogs would have come to their help, this time "none of them would stir." In her narrative, it is in the suspension of the laws of nature that the Protestant God "would make us the more to acknowledge His hand, and to see that our help is always in Him." For Pineda, the perversion of God's order is due to man's fall from reason, with which he was endowed by God, while for Rowlandson reliance on human reason *is* the cause of God's order being perverted.

These cultural differences between Pineda's Baroque and Rowlandson's Gothic representations of reality are evident also in their diverse notions regarding the Indian's role in the social, cultural, and religious body politic.

For Pineda, the converted Indian is an integral subject in the heavenly City of God. Unlike Rowlandson's Augustinian redemption theology, which equates the state of nature with a state of sin, Pineda, educated in a Counter-Reformation Jesuit school, believes (after Thomas Aquinas) that the dispensation of divine grace perfected, rather than destroyed, nature. Human corruptions are not evidence of a Calvinist innate depravity but manifest that "con nuestros delitos y maldades borrábamos la perfeccion con que fuimos criados" (107) ("by our offences we blotted out the perfection that was ours at birth" [Atkinson 58]). For Pineda, therefore, Indian "Devil worship" is not the natural state of the Savage but rather the Devil's (reversible) perversion of God's natural order, and he therefore feels obligated to convert the Natives to Christianity through persuasion and reason. In Pineda's Counter-Reformation fusion of a Classical with a Book-of-Genesis philosophy of history, which stresses humanity's unity as Adam's descendants, Indian "gentile" cultural practice operates, as Rome had in Europe, as a preparatory step to the final triumph of Christ in the redemption of humanity. Rowlandson's Puritan incorporation of America into Old World history, by contrast, is based on a Book-of-Exodus theology of history, where there is no room in heaven for American "Canaanites."

These distinct religious attitudes toward cultural difference finally imply important differences also between Catholic and Protestant notions of the "Creole." Pineda finds space for praise of certain aspects of Araucanian culture, such as their humility, valor, bravery, and love of freedom, which birth in Chile's vast and wild beauty supposedly furthered and from which the Creoles also benefited. The Spanish idea of empire, which largely derived from the Roman model, rested on the medieval theory that existing regional cultures could be incorporated within the Baroque structure of the absolutist state. There was, then, in the Spanish empire, a certain positive space for regional cultural diversity into which a Spanish American Creole patriotism could be inscribed. The Creoles' resistance to the inferior colonial status of the Americas in relation to the *peninsulares* could therefore be grounded in an assertion of the equality of the Americas among the kingdoms comprising the empire (i.e. the Spains, the Netherlands, Italy, etc.). By contrast, in the Anglo American empire, colonial settlements that did not resemble England were, by definition, un-English and thus "American." As Kenneth Burke has put it, "In contrast with the [Catholic] church's 'organic' theory, whereby one put a going social concern together by the toleration of *differences*, the Protestant sects stressed the value of *complete uniformity*. Each time this uniformity was impaired, the sect itself tended to split, with a new 'uncompromising' offshoot reaffirming the need for a homogenous community, all members alike in status."⁷⁷ Whereas Pineda's captivity narrative therefore shows a Creole returning from America's Otherness in order to assert a Creole identity different from but *equal to* the metropolitan Self, Rowlandson's narrative must insist on a colonial identity that is asserted through the preservation of her pure English body.

WRITING IN COLONIAL SPACE

These hermeneutic differences notwithstanding, both Rowlandson's and Pineda's accounts illuminate not only the epistemological and political but also the important semiotic role that colonial captivity narratives played in emerging Creole cultures. By imagining a new "place of return," the colonial captivity narrative translated the European New World narrative of shipwreck and pilgrimage into a colonial context, thereby mimicking the narrative structure of the European travels into "Other" worlds but re-inscribing the boundaries of colonial space in terms of both spatial and racial economies. When, for example, in the nineteenth "Remove" of Mary Rowlandson's narrative, her Indian master asked her "When I washed me?" she answered him, "not this month," whereupon he "gave me the glass to see how I looked" (351). Rowlandson's look in the mirror occurs one stage before her final and, according to the structure of her narrative, farthest removal from the Christian community, the city, and human civilization itself, from which she will ultimately be removed twenty times before her eventual return.

By the second half of the seventeenth century, the image of Rowlandson looking into the mirror while on the American frontier had already become a recurrent trope in the literary history of the New World. While she herself refrains from a detailed description of "how I looked," we may speculate how her early modern readers' imagination would have filled her descriptive gap. On the one hand, the imaginations of her seventeenth-century readers would still have been colored by medieval popular legend, in particular the tradition of the "Wild Man." According to this legend, the Wild Man is a semi-human creature who lives outside the medieval human community of the City. As Hayden White has explained, the Wild Man/Woman in these legends represented a threat to civilized society and the "civilized" individual, "both as nemesis and as a possible destiny, both as enemy and as representative of a condition into which an individual man, having fallen out of grace or having been driven from his city, might degenerate." Black and disfigured in appearance, sexually promiscuous, the Wild Men/Women live in the forest or the desert outside the city, occasionally carrying off civilized women and children.⁷⁸ On the other hand, however,

Rowlandson's contemporary readers would have recalled images of Europeans living beyond the edges of the civilized world from the many New World narratives reproduced by early modern print technology. Unlike in medieval oral tradition, where the Wild Man had lived "just out of sight, over the horizon," the early modern New World ethnographies extrapolated and projected his realm onto the new trans-atlantic geographic periphery, thus inventing the "idea" of Europe as a distinct geo-cultural entity during the sixteenth century. Hans Staden's narrative of 1554 about his captivity among the Tupinimbá in Brazil is paradigmatic. His captivity narrative went through a total of sixteen editions, including its original 1557 edition in German and all its translations into six European languages. Entitled *The True History and Description of a country of wild, naked, and furious man-eating people of the New World of America*, it tells an outrageous tale of American cannibalism and other "unnatural" cultural practices. In one particularly grotesque scene Staden relates, for example, how the Indians "tied my legs on top of each other and made me hop through the cabins, while they were shouting: 'There runs our dinner.' "[79]

Of particular interest and appeal in this literary history of the New World, however, were images of Europeans themselves being "Indianized" into "wild men" while living on the western edges of the known world. We might recall here Cabeza de Vaca's narrative, where he describes the bewilderment on the faces of the first Spaniards he encountered toward the end of his eight-year odyssey in northern New Spain: "The day after I overtook four of them on horseback, who were astonished at the sight of me, so strangely habited as I was, and in company with Indians. They stood staring at me a length of time, so confounded that they neither hailed me nor drew near to make an inquiry."[80] Ten years later, the soldiers of Hernando de Soto found another shipwrecked Spaniard captured during the Narváez expedition, Juan Ortiz, who was tattooed, unable to speak (Spanish), and, according to the Inca Garcilaso in his *La Florida del Inca*, "like the natives with nothing but some loin clothes on his body, a bow and arrows in his hand, and for ornament, plumage half a fathom in height upon his head."[81] Various versions of Juan Ortiz' encounter with the Spanish soldiers were later republished in England during the seventeenth century.[82] Similarly, the Spanish redeemed captive Jerónimo de Aguilar, shipwrecked and found in Yucatán, was, according to Bernal Díaz del Castillo, "not in his appearance to be distinguished from a native, ... his colour was dark as a native, and he was marked like them; he had a few rags about his shoulders and waist, an oar in his hand, and the remnant of an old book of prayers tied in a bundle on his shoulder."[83] Finally, in the famous story of Pedro Serrano, as related by the Inca Garcilaso in his *Comentarios reales*, the shipwrecked European protagonist caught "crabs, shrimps, and turtles, ate them raw," and "drank [their] blood instead of water." After two months on the island, Serrano "was as naked as when he was born, for the great rain, the heat, and the humidity of the region rotted the few clothes he had." Interestingly, however, this story has already turned into a grotesque parody of the European shipwreck narrative in the hands of the Peruvian chronicler Garcilaso. Because of the alleged "inclemencias" ("harshness") of the American climate "his hair grew all over his body till it was like an animal's pelt, and not just any animal's, but a wild boar's. His hair and beard fell below his waist." When another European is shipwrecked on his island and

they saw one another, it would be hard to say which was the more surprised. Serrano thought it was the Devil come in human form to tempt him to some desperate act. His guest thought Serrano was the Devil in his true form, he was so coated with hair, beard, and hide. Each fled from the other, and Pedro Serrano went off crying: "Jesus! Jesus! Oh Lord, deliver me from the demon!"

When, finally, they were redeemed years later, they no "longer looked like human beings."[84]

Within the context of what has been called the "specular" literature of European colonialist expansion, which dwells on descriptions of Native alterity "as a mirror that reflects the colonialist's self-image,"[85] these moments in the literary history of the New World – of Europeans transformed into "Savages" at the edges of the earth – are of particular interest because they underline the geo-cultural Euro-centrism (rather than "racism") of this early modern ethnographic imagination in the scientific paradigm of Natural History. Early modern ethnography projected what Michel de Certeau has called the "split that divides the universe" in the medieval mental world of ordinary experience and the world of fable onto the Atlantic as a "breakage of space into two worlds." A "rift between the Old and the New World," the Atlantic becomes an ideological axis in the European geo-cultural imagination that separates "over here" from "over there" and that re-affirms Europe as geo-cultural center in countless reenactments in travel narratives, novels, and histories during the early modern period. Ethnography functions in these New World narratives as "a form of exegesis" that articulates Europe's identity through a relation with its past and future, with foreign lands and nature, its fears and desires. The return to Europe – the re-integration into the *civitas* of the human community – asserts identity in a movement "from the self to the self, through the mediation of the other."[86]

In a narrative ritual of purification, both of our colonial captivity narratives parody the structure of the European New World shipwreck narrative – of removal to "over there" and return to "over here." However, whereas the European New World pilgrims had projected the cosmic "split" onto the Atlantic, the colonial narratives, engaged in the continual semiotic process of re-inscribing "America" for "Europe," re-locate the cosmic divide in the European geo-cultural imagination from the Atlantic into the American landscape – the "frontier." Both captives' treacherous journeys thus begin with a providentially guided "removal" by crossing a vast spatial divide – through a "vast and desolate wilderness," in Rowlandson's case. Her entire subsequent narrative is structured by a series of spatial "removes" during which historical time is suspended and measured in terms of spatial distance to the final place of return (335).[87] As if semiotically to reenact the European traveler's crossing of the Atlantic divide, both colonial captivity narrators attribute special significance to their crossings of bodies of water as spatial divides.[88] Thus, Pineda's capture is immediately followed by the crossing of Chile's Bío-Bío River, which marks the Araucanian frontier and his entry into the conceptual space of "America." Echoing the many exotic accounts of hurricanes during the trans-atlantic crossing in the European New World shipwreck narratives, Pineda describes the "copiosas y abundantes aguas despedidas del cielo con violencia, y de furiosos vientos sacudidas, mezcladas con relámpagos, rayos, truenos y granizos" (34) ("swirling waters of the Bío-Bío, by when a tempest had been unleashed so fierce that it seemed the elements were in league against us" [Atkinson 17]). The colonial narrative of an individual crossing spatial divides – removing to, and returning from, the "frontier" – re-negotiates colonial space by engaging in a compulsive "identification of the self-same," as Walter Mignolo has written, which sets it apart from the focus on "otherness" in the account of the European traveler, whose journey to the New World ends in his return to the geographic center. The narrative anxiety that critics have sensed in many colonial texts may therefore provide an insight into the semiotic labor of those narratives that had to construct what Mignolo calls "alternative loci of enunciation in a colonial space" – spaces "in-between" where writers, though returned from the frontiers to become authors, are still, as it were, running when writing.[89]

More important than natural boundaries in this production of "alternative loci of enunciation" for Creole culture, however, is the emphasis on racial boundaries in the colonial text. Unlike the metropolitan natural historians – for whom colonial "difference" was the consequence of environmental influences – both colonial captivity narrators anxiously compensate for the geographic absence of the Atlantic divide through an intense focus on racial difference. They openly debunk, for example, their missionary predecessors in colonial ethnography, such as the Jesuit Luis de Valdivia (in Pineda's case) or John Eliot (in Rowlandson's case), who had dreamed of all-inclusive Christian Commonwealths and utopias unifying all of humanity. Rowlandson, especially, de-emphasizes Christianity as a unifying force and emphasizes racial difference for an identification of a colonial Self by exposing the "true" nature of the "praying Indians" who seem to undermine the imaginary "hedges" and "walls" that a Puritan frontier ideology built around (white) New England: "Those seven that were killed at Lancaster the summer before upon a Sabbath day, and the one that was afterward killed upon a week day, were slain and mangled in a barbarous manner, by One-eyed John, and Marlborough's praying Indians, which Captain Mosely brought to Boston, as the Indians told me" (326). At a time when Indians were becoming "Red Puritans" and when Creole Englishmen were regarded as "White Indians," racial difference remained the only objective bastion that kept New Englanders apart from "Americans" and thus "fabricated," as Michael Zuckerman has argued, colonial identity by compensating for the anxieties involved in the colonials' sense of their own transculturation.[90]

Pineda, too, would insist on the institutionalized social division in colonial society – between a *república de los indios* and a *república de los españoles*. On the one hand, he is appalled by the "degeneracy" of those (unreturned) Spaniards who voluntarily live and mix with the Indians and whom he finds during his captivity:

reparé con cuidado que en algunas habia españoles antiquísimos entre ellos, y no los solicitaban para este sacramento; y inquiriendo la causa, me sacó de esta duda un indio antiguo y en nuestro lenguaje ladino, que me mostraba amor y buena voluntad, y este me dijo, que los españoles que habian quedado entre ellos, no eran captivos, sino era de los que por su gusto entre ellos estaban viviendo a su usanza, y no como cristianos, gozando del vicio y del ocio que los demas infieles. (219)

I discovered that in some [districts] there were Spaniards who had been living there for many years but had never sought to lead anyone to baptism. I asked the reason, and was given it by one old Indian who spoke my language [...] [and] showed himself particularly friendly and well-disposed towards me. These Spaniards, he said, were not captives but lived among the Indians by choice, following their ways and abandoning themselves to the same vices and sloth, to the forgetting of their Christian upbringing. (Atkinson 98; my insertions)

On the other hand, he debunks, like Rowlandson, the inclusive utopias of the (Jesuit) missionaries, who attempt to convert the Indians by giving them:

regalos de chaquiras, agujas, listones, añil y otras menudencias que para ellos eran de alguna estimacion, por cuyo interes se baptizaban muchos dos y tres veces; y ocasion hubo que un cacique principal hizo que se baptizasen todos los de su casa, por el interes de lo que a cada uno se le daba, y no teniendo otra persona que pudiese baptizarse, llevó un gato o perro al padre que los cristiniaba, y le dijo que le baptizase tambien aquel perro, y le daria unas chaquiras. (218)

gifts of beads, ribbons and the like baubles, so that many would come for baptism two or three times... there was even a cacique who had his entire household baptized just to collect what he could get, and when there was nobody left he took a dog to the priest and asked him, for the sake of a few more beads to baptize it too. (Atkinson 97)

However, there are also a number of important differences between Pineda's and Rowlandson's attitudes toward race and *mestizaje*. Most notably, Pineda's narrative allows for a certain degree of erotic attraction to the American tribals. His description of the "venereal insignia" – the Indian headdress – for example, is an ambivalent composite of American exotic eroticism and savage wildness: it was

un hocico de zorra desollado, *abierta la boca* manifestando los dientes y colmillos, y las orejas mui *tiesas y levantadas para arriba*, cubierta a trechos de muchas llancas y chaquiras de diferentes colores mui bien adornadas. (203; my italics)

a skinned vixen's skull, its *jaws gaping open* to show its teeth and fangs, its ears *very stiff and erect* and draped in beads of different colors. (Atkinson 91–2; my italics)

The eroticism of Pineda's description of the *mapuche* women is sanctioned by the colonial order, where *mestizaje* with Indian women is sanctioned if it promotes the objective of conquest. Pineda, in his narrative, once even confesses that he was tempted:

encontramos algunas muchachonas desnudas en el agua, sin rebozo, y entre ellas la mestiza, hermana de mi compañero (que tambien por su parte me insistia y solicitaba para que la comunicase a lo estrecho), entre las demas muchachas se señalaba y sobresalia por blanca, por discreta y por hermosa. Confieso a Dios mi culpa, y al lector aseguro como humano, que no me ví jamas con mayor aprieto, tentado y perseguido del comun adversario; porque aunque quise de aquel venéreo objeto apartar la vista, no pude. (296)

There were several girls already in the water, swimming naked among them the one in question stood out from the whiteness of her skin, her beauty and her obvious air of discernment. Her brother had already been urging me to be more responsive to her, and may God forgive me – I know the reader will, as a fellowman – but never had I known myself in greater danger or temptation from the evil one. When I would have averted my gaze from that so desirable object I could not. (Atkinson 113)

After his return, Pineda appeals to his reader for absolution regarding his inability to resist gazing at his "desirable object" with the cavalier reference to the fact that she was, after all, exceptionally "white." Nevertheless, when a local *cacique* offers his daughter to Pineda as a wife, he informs him that "no podíamos ofender a Dios N. S. tan a las claras, y mas con mujeres infieles y ajenas de nuestra profesion, porque era pecado doble y de mayor marca" (137) ("It was impossible for a Christian to offend God in this manner, especially with an infidel, which would make it doubly sinful" [Atkinson 70]). Pineda's "double" resistance to biological *mestizaje* appears as a rational reservation originating in his sense of obligation to God, *patria*, and civility. Rowlandson's account, by contrast, displays a particularly Protestant disgust for humanity's innate depravity in the state of nature. When invited by an Indian – "What, will you love English men still?" – she recoils into a description of the fiendish "roaring, and singing and dancing, and yelling of those black creatures in the night" (333). Despite these differences, however, both colonial captivity narratives imagine new "loci of enunciation" for colonial Euro-American Creole cultures by re-negotiating colonial space and re-imagining the Atlantic divide on the frontier in terms of geographic or racial boundaries.

FROM CONQUEROR TO CREOLE

By enunciating a new "place of return," the colonial captivity narrative, finally, re-writes not only the European New World pilgrimage but also the narratives of New World removal (without return) of their conqueror and settler ancestors for a new generation of Creoles. Pineda, in his colonial seventeenth-century narrative reenactment of New World removal, for example, appropriates the theme of "shipwreck" rather than that of *translatio imperii* governing the Spanish chronicles of conquest of the sixteenth century. When he arrives on the "other" side, he does not stand in the proud and imperial pose of a Virgil or as a *Christum ferrens* (a "Christ-Bearer") of the Catholic World empire – as had a Columbus, a Cortés, or a Pedro de Valdivia. Pineda is not the harbinger of empire but the castaway, who stands humbled, naked, and "Indianized" in America. When finding himself obliged by his captor Maulicán to exchange his Spanish for Indian clothes, Pineda reflects upon the image of his present condition: "dándome vueltas y mirándome por una y otra parte," he writes, "vestido como uno de los mas desdichados indios, descalzo de pié y pierna, representándoseme la poca estabilidad de las cosas humanas" (105) ("preoccupied as I turned this way and that, looking at myself transformed into a down-and-out Indian, barefoot, barelegged, eloquent testimony to the instability of all things human" [Atkinson 57]). The captive Pineda is the American version of the Cervantesque seventeenth-century "lonely individual," not the confident Renaissance man conquering New Worlds.[91]

Rowlandson's narrative also presents interesting variations upon the narratives of removal derived from her cultural tradition. However, as Andrew Wiget has observed in his comparison of Spanish and British American "origin stories," first-generation New Englanders had interpreted their New World removal not in terms of the expansion of the Holy Empire but in terms of the Biblical Exodus, as "a people set apart" from the worldly empire of Anti-Christ and as a restoration of the primitive church in their American "exile."[92] Unlike William Bradford's *Of Plymouth Plantation* or John Winthrop's *Journal*, however, Rowlandson's narrative of Western exodus does not tell the experience of a community "closely knit together," but rather the experience of the modern individual all alone out in the wilderness of the world.[93] Rowlandson's narrative of exodus moreover counterpoints the Biblical subtext, which would put Egyptians in pursuit of Israelites. In her narrative, the Egyptian pursuers become the English redeemers, and she is taken across the watery divide not by a Moses leading his people into the Promised Land but by Savage heathens, who would drag her into an American wilderness in order to strip her of her English identity. At a time when second-generation New England divines called out against community "dispersal" (spatial, but also ideological and social), Rowlandson's "gendered" narrative of removal thus operates as a metaphor of defining "place" *against* the centrifugal cultural dynamics of a people moving out into the "Promised Land" under the patriarchal guidance of perennially proliferating types of Moses.[94]

While there are, then, significant similarities between Pineda's and Rowlandson's "true histories" with regard to the historical context in which each was written, as well as with regard to their cultural geography in transatlantic settler empires and the epistemological, ideological, and semiotic role that each played within its colonial culture, there are also important differences between these two texts. First, while Rowlandson's narrative asserts a particularly Protestant version of (Baconian) empiricism, Pineda's narrative was informed by Jesuit and Baroque learning, which strove to find ways of incorporating the new empiricism but resisted the increasing fragmentation of knowledge that characterized Baconian science. Second, the differences between these two narratives also illustrate larger cultural differences between Catholic Spanish and Protestant English concepts about the "frontier," as they had in turn partially resulted from the very different political structures of the Spanish and the British empires.[95] As one historian has noted, while we typically find in the former a "frontier of inclusion," with the Church, Crown, and settlers all having active though varying interests in the Indian population, in the latter we typically find a racially and culturally sharply defined "frontier of exclusion,"[96] with Protestantism having in part originated as a rejection of Catholic "paganism" (or rather syncretism). It is, perhaps, for this reason that overall, the motif of *Indian* captivity lacked the tremendous significance in Spanish American literary history that Roy Harvey Pearce and others have claimed for it in Anglo American literary history. In Spanish America, as we shall see in the next chapter, colonial Creoles more frequently narrativized the geo-political tensions of early modern settler empires in narratives not of Indian but of Pirate captivity. Finally, then, I want to submit that it is significant that Pineda's Spanish American narrative was never published during colonial times and circulated only in manuscript, while Rowlandson's British American narrative went through no less than fifteen editions by 1800. In the next chapter, I will explore some of the reasons for this, including the cultural geography of print ideologies that gave rise to a "public sphere" as a particularly Protestant phenomenon during the eighteenth century, while in Catholic Spain the idea of the "public" remained strongly tied to that of "officialdom" represented by the state.

CHAPTER 5

"Friends and compatriots": Carlos de Sigüenza y Góngora and the piracy of knowledge

On 12 September 1682 – the year when Rowlandson's narrative was published in New and Old England – Increase Mather, soon to become president of Cambridge College (Harvard), and his two sons Nathaniel and Cotton (later to be elected fellow to the Royal Society of London) could be seen gazing into the night sky through a brand new telescope that had just arrived from England for deployment at Cambridge. In the early 1680s, a series of comets had begun making their appearance in the Western hemisphere, which had elicited great interest and wonder not only among the New England divines but also among English natural philosophers, such as Isaac Newton. Cotton subsequently wrote about these events in *The Boston Ephemieris* (1683) and supplied his observations to Isaac Newton in England, while Nathaniel, still an undergraduate at Harvard, published in the same almanac for 1685 a list of astronomical discoveries which demonstrated that he was keeping abreast of the latest scientific inventions as reported in the *Philosophical Transactions*. Increase, finally, who had preached a sermon on the occasion of the comet of 1680, published two of these sermons as *Heaven's Alarm to the World* (1682) and a longer treatise entitled *Kometographia, or A Discourse Concerning Comets* (1683). In this treatise on the comet – later known as "Halley's Comet" – Increase conceded that comets proceeded from natural causes and that they moved, like planets, on orbits but insisted that their appearance had to be interpreted as God's providential signs of evil.[1]

As the New Englander Increase Mather was relishing the terrestrial calamities and cosmic disasters that seemed to him portended by the comets in the Western skies, another American colonial witnessed the great celestial spectacle 3,000 miles southwest of Boston, in Mexico City. But in the lens of Carlos de Sigüenza y Góngora (1645–1700), professor of mathematics and astrology at the University of Mexico, as well as one of the few colonials to hold the position of "Royal Cosmographer" of New Spain, "Halley's" comet apparently presented itself less ominously than it had in that of the

Puritan divine; for in his *Manifiesto philosóphico contra los cometas, despojados del imperio que tenían sobre los tímidos* (1681), the Catholic scholar discredited the age-old notion that comets forebode evil, thereby refuting some of the most learned men of science in his day.[2] While Sigüenza y Góngora shared Mather's scientific interest in supernatural apparitions, he did not attribute "things preternatural" to the Devil, as had the Puritan divine;[3] rather, he became one of the principal seventeenth-century propagators of "guadalupanismo," Mexico's syncretist cult celebrating the miraculous appearance of the Virgin of Guadalupe to the Indian Juan Diego in 1531.[4] Like Mather, Sigüenza y Góngora was a colonial oligarch and Creole patriot, wary of less illustrious elements in the colonial social order as well as vigilant of the rights and reputation of what he called "nuestra criolla nación."[5] He therefore had an interest not only in science and religion but also in colonial history and politics; and, like Mather, he had a hand in the writing of one of the first colonial captivity narratives published in the Americas. Unlike his Protestant counterpart, however, the Mexican scholar found such a narrative not in the story of a minister's wife captured by Savage American Indians but rather in the story of a poor Puerto Rican ship's carpenter captured by Protestant English Pirates who belonged, most likely, to the fleet of William Dampier, author of *A New Voyage around the World* (1697) and a good friend of Hans Sloane, then president of the Royal Society of London.[6]

The narrative published in Mexico City in 1690 under the title *Los infortunios que Alonso Ramírez natural de la Ciudad de S. Juan de Puerto Rico padeció assi en poder de Ingleses Piratas* (The Misfortunes that Alonso Ramírez, native to the city of San Juan of Puerto Rico, suffered while in the power of English Pirates) was the first-person account of the life of Alonso, who had set out from the economically depressed Caribbean island to go west in search of fame and fortune, as once had a Cortés 150 years before him. However, having arrived on *tierra firme*, he soon found himself not the conqueror of fabulous cities but rather a down-and-out stranger in a land of millions like him. Pressed by economic hardship, he saw no other remedy than to enlist as a mariner in service to the Crown. During his first tour en route from Acapulco to Manila, he was captured by English Pirates and compelled to accompany the Englishmen on their voyage around the world – across the Pacific and Indian Oceans, up the coast of southern Africa, and across the Atlantic to Brazil. Finally, he was released in the Caribbean on a small vessel and landed under difficult circumstances in Yucatán. Eventually, he returned to Mexico City, where his "círculo de trabajos" ("circle of travails") comes to an end at the house of the royal cosmographer Sigüenza y Góngora, who transcribed and published the story.[7]

For the most part, the story is told as the first-person account of Alonso in the plain style of a *relación de méritos*. In the final paragraph, however, the text takes a curious turn, as the Mexican historian/transcriber Sigüenza y Góngora parenthetically intrudes into Alonso's first-hand account, thus alerting the reader to the hybrid and collaborative character of the narrative:

Mandóme [el virrey a Alonso] (o por el afecto con que lo [Alonso] mira o quizá porque estando enfermo divirtiere sus males con la noticia que yo [Sigüenza y Góngora] le daría de los muchos míos) fuese a visitar a Don Sigüenza y Góngora, cosmógrafo y catedrático de matemáticas del Rey nuestro señor en la Academia mexicana, y capellán mayor del hospital Real del Amor de Dios de la ciudad de México (títulos son estos que suenan mucho y valen muy poco, y a cuyo ejercicio le empeña más la reputación que la conveniencia). Compadecido de mis trabajos, no solo formó esta Relación en que se contienen, sino que me consiguió con la intercesión y súplicas que en mi presencia hizo al Excmo. Sr. Virrey, Decreto para que D. Sebastián de Guzmán y Córdoba, factor veedor y preveedor de las cajas reales me socorriese, como se hizo. (83)

He [the viceroy] sent me [Alonso] (either because of the affection he felt for him [Alonso] or perhaps because, being ill, he might be diverted from his pains by my [Sigüenza y Góngora's] story) to visit don Carlos de Sigüenza y Góngora, cosmographer and Professor of Mathematics of the King our master in the Mexican Academy, and First Chaplain of the Hospital Real del Amor de Dios in the City of Mexico (titles which have a ring to them but are of little real value and the exercise of which is obliged more by reputation than by convenience). Sympathizing with my troubles, he not only wrote a volume in which they are contained but secured for me through the intercession and pleas which he made in my presence to the Most Excellent Viceroy, a decree by which don Sebastián de Guzmán y Córdoba, agent overseer and purveyor of the royal coffers, should help me, and so it was done. (103–4)

In this chapter, I want to inquire into the nature of the Creole cosmographer's "sympathy" for the man whose tale of piracy and captivity he transcribed. On the one hand, Alonso's captivity narrative about his sufferings at the hands of imperial enemies, not unlike the colonial captivity narratives discussed in the previous chapter, exposes the utopian fiction of a trans-atlantic patrimonialist empire.[8] Specifically, the tale about the "misfortunes" of an impoverished Creole subject of empire critiqued Madrid's mercantilist economic policies in the New World, which had deprived the colonials, they feared, of their de-jure status as free imperial citizens equal to those residing on the peninsula. In Sigüenza y Góngora's transcription of Alonso's tale, I want to show, this Creole critique is narrativized in a curious homology that the text creates between Protestant piracy and Peninsular administration – a homology that undermines the ideological oppositions in official imperial representations of the Protestant Pirate (English/Spanish, heretic/Catholic) and that exposes Spanish mercantilist policy as being but another form of piracy. On the other hand, however, the meta-historical irony manifest by the self-referential ending of Alonso's plain tale draws attention to the discrepancy between the American Creole's de-jure status and his social reality not only with regard to the imperial city of material exchange but also with regard to what Angel Rama has called the Baroque "lettered city," the patrimonialist literary culture of royal and ecclesiastic patronage.[9] I would therefore argue that this narrative may be seen as a critique not only of Spain's economic politics but also of her epistemic politics in the Americas, which were of immediate concern for the Creole cosmographer himself. In other words, there are *two* narratives of piracy and captivity in *Infortunios de Alonso Ramírez*: a tale primarily about the piracy of knowledge – the "contraband" of epistemic mercantilism – *Infortunios de Alonso Ramírez* alerts the reader to the marginal socio-political location not only of lower-class Creoles but also of the elite Creole cosmographer, who, disenchanted with the courtly city of letters, subsequently sells Alonso's plain tale about piracy on the literary marketplace.

SIGÜENZA Y GÓNGORA: CREOLE COSMOGRAPHER OF THE BAROQUE

Because of its social "realism," formalist critics have long seen in *Infortunios* a sort of missing link in the evolution of the Spanish American novel, connecting the seventeenth-century Spanish picaresque tradition of *El Lazarillo de Tormes*, Mateo Alemán's *Guzmán de Alfarache*, or Quevedo's *El Buscón* on the one hand with the rise of the novel in Latin America during the nineteenth century on the other.[10] However, although no documents corroborating Alonso's historical existence have been found, recent linguistic and literary scholarship suggests that it is unlikely that Sigüenza y Góngora had simply invented the story.[11] Historicist critics, in their turn, have seen in Sigüenza's use of plain language – in *Infortunios* as well as in some of his other journalistic narratives such as *Trofeo de la justicia española*, *Relación de lo sucedido a la Armada de Barlovento*, and *Mercurio volante* – a first step toward the Enlightenment and to Latin American nationalism. In his seminal biography of the "Mexican Savant," Irving Leonard, for example, saw these texts as evidence of Sigüenza's "progressive" spirit in the regressive time of the Baroque:

[H]ere we may see Don Carlos at his best as a prose writer, and we may hazard a guess as to how great a writer he might have been if circumstances had permitted him to write fiction. The style is simple and unaffected, conspicuous for the lack of ponderous Latin quotations which make so much of his available work so unpalatable to the modern reader.[12]

Gone were the Baroque literary excesses, the hyper-intellectual *conceptismo* emulating the revered Spanish model of a Quevedo, and the artificial *culteranismo* of Sigüenza y Góngora's distant Cordoban relative Luis de Góngora, thus pointing forward to the Enlightenment and the Age of Reason.

More recently, however, Kathleen Ross has shown that it is a mistake to see Sigüenza's use of the plain style in *some* of his writings as evidence of his *general* distaste for the Baroque literary style – a critical anachronism that has resulted, she suggests, from the anti-Baroque bias in nineteenth- and twentieth-century aesthetic mentalities rather than from a firm grounding in historical evidence.[13] If Sigüenza abandoned the use of the Baroque for the plain style in these transcriptions, she argues, it was rather in order to authenticate a new discourse of history that includes, though in a sub-ordinate position, non-traditional subjects of historiographic representation, such as women (in his *Parayso occidental*) and lower-class Creoles (in *Infortunios*).[14] But while Ross' argument against Sigüenza's alleged preference for the journalistic plain style over the Baroque rhetoric of history is persuasive, it raises the question of where precisely Sigüenza's interest lay in authenticating this new discourse of history in the first place, especially in Alonso's narrative about his captivity at the hands of Protestant Pirates. One answer, I want to suggest, may be found in the royal cosmographer's own ambivalent social location within the imperial order of Baroque culture in vice-regal New Spain.

By the end of the seventeenth century, the great upheavals accompanying the confrontation between the first settlers and the imperial bureaucracy that had raged in New Spain during the sixteenth century had abated, making way for a period that the literary historian Hernán Vidal has called a time of "colonial stabilization," which he loosely dated from 1580 to about 1700.[15] In seventeenth-century New Spain, the new viceroys sent from the peninsula were welcomed by the Creole population with grandiose processions and extravagant triumphal arches inscribed with Aztec pictographs representing Mexico's ancient past. The vice-regal court stood at the center of an extraordinarily vibrant cultural life by promoting the arts in grand literary competitions. It was a period that saw the flowering of a culture that Mariano Picón Salas has called the "barroco de indias" ("the Baroque of the

Indies") – the transplantation of the Baroque cultural forms of Europe to the Americas, where they were filled with specific Mexican contents, thus becoming, Picón argues, the vehicle for a distinctly Creole expression in Spanish America in the works of writers such as Sor Juana Inés de la Cruz, a good friend of Sigüenza y Góngora's. Although this period does not offer the historian, Picón writes, "the same abundance of external history as does the time of the Conquest," it nevertheless was "one of the most long-lasting and deeply rooted elements of our cultural tradition . . . It carries weight in our aesthetic sensibility and in many complicated forms of our collective psychology."[16]

The newly found political stability in which the Spanish Baroque could flower in New Spain was, in part, the product of a new alignment of imperial power devised with the intent of resolving the initial conflict between the settlers and the imperial state through better integration of the Creole elite in the rule of the vast colonized masses of deject Indians and mestizos. Indeed, educated Creoles from the (male) elite held offices more frequently now than they had before in the imperial bureaucracy and especially in the more permeable ecclesiastic establishments of vice-regal New Spain. Nevertheless, there still remained what might be called a "glass ceiling" as a result of a lingering pro-Peninsular bias in the selection of functionaries for important imperial offices. There had yet to be, for example, a single viceroy of Mexican birth; only two archbishops of Mexico had been American-born in its almost 150-year history; and all of the judges presiding over the Audiencia in Mexico had been *peninsulares*, despite a petition by the Mexican City council in 1637 demanding that at least half of the seats should be reserved for American-born Creoles.[17] For all the rhetoric of imperial reforms, there was, as Jonathan Israel has written, "a social, cultural, and even ethnic dimension to the estrangement between bureaucracy and colonists in that the former was staffed mainly by peninsulars while the latter were predominantly Creole."[18]

One of the reasons for the social stability in which Baroque culture could flower in seventeenth-century New Spain may thus be seen in the *ambivalence* of the elite Creoles' socio-cultural location in the vice-regal order – in the fact that their resentment at being treated as second-class citizens in the Spanish empire was outweighed only by their fear of the third-, fourth-, and fifth-class citizens of mestizos, mulattos, zambos, and *indios*; by the terror that they felt when pondering the consequences if imperial power ceased to keep the colonized masses in check. Indeed, while the seventeenth century did not see any serious challenges to Spanish imperial rule on the part of the Creole elites in New Spain – as had the sixteenth century and as would again the nineteenth century – it did not lack in social upheavals. In 1692, for example, Mexico City was shaken by a corn riot in which the local population, mostly Indians and mestizos, vented their anger at the government for its mal-distribution of food supplies after incessant rains had destroyed the year's harvest and famine had become rampant throughout the City. Sigüenza y Góngora was on that day seen rushing through the burning city in order to make his way to the municipal archives, where he and his helpers seized the ancient Mexican "codices and capitulary books here and there amidst the flames...until not a monument was left that had not been devoured by the fire."[19] While he thus saved the invaluable documents testifying to Mexico's ancient glory, in his own account of the event, entitled *Alboroto y motín de los indios de México*, he described the present Mexican population as "plebe tan en extremo plebe" ("plebs, so extremely plebeian"), prone to tyranny, mob violence, and barbarism.[20] In Sigüenza's eyes, the plebeians that he beheld among the heterogeneous masses in the streets of Mexico City were not the legitimate heirs of the great Aztec empire. The antiquarianism for which the Creole patriot became famous with twentieth-century historians must thus be seen primarily as an ideological appropriation of Mexico's indigenous past by the Creole elite for the invention of an aristocratic lineage that would have an air of legitimacy in the Habsburg imperial order. As Jacques Lafaye has written, New Spanish Creoles:

Incapable of establishing a mixture of the races on viable socio-juridical bases, incapable of creating an Indian clergy,...achieved with the help of Sigüenza y Góngora (among others) a spiritual hybridization without which they must have remained a group of exiles in a country which rejected them...the Creoles had to invent it anew after they had frightfully mutilated it.[21]

Sigüenza y Góngora's historical works in verse and prose, such as *Primavera indiana* (1662), *Oriental planeta evangélico* (1700), *Glorias de Querétaro* (1680), *Teatro de virtudes* (1680), *Triunfo parténico* (1683), or *Piedad heroyca de Don Fernando Cortés* (1663), were precisely such an act of patriotic reinvention and celebration of New Spain and its glorious history. In accordance with his position as cosmographer of the realm, they were written in the Baroque historiographic tradition of the seventeenth-century Peninsular court historians of the Habsburgs. The most important one of them with regard to the historiography of Mexico contemporary to Sigüenza was the royal cosmographer, playwright, and poet Antonio de

Solís y Rivadeneyra, whose *Historia de la Nueva España* was published in Madrid in 1684 and subsequently went through no less than twenty-three editions in five languages by 1748. Solís praised the moral righteousness of Cortés and generally emphasized the justness of Spanish rule in New Spain, in order to control the increasing damage being done by the popularity of Las Casas and Benzoni abroad, among "the strangers, who cannot tolerate the glory of our nation." Reflecting the influence of the new Natural Sciences on Baroque historiographic method, Solís erected a lavish rhetorical edifice upon an empirical apparatus of eyewitness accounts that mirrored the social order of the empire. Thus, the emblematic title page of his *Historia* shows his bust encased in an ornamental, circular shrine upheld by two female figures, one naked and wearing a headdress, allegorizing New Spain, and the other wearing European costume, allegorizing Spain, united under the imperial crown of the Habsburgs (see Illustration 5.1). In its hierarchical architectural conception of history as an empirical base subordinate to a rhetorical edifice, Solís' Baroque history continued the seventeenth-century tradition of stay-at-home royal chroniclers such as Herrera who built their "general histories" on the "particular" accounts of eyewitness testimonies. Thus Solís faulted the Renaissance chronicler López de Gómara for his lack of "inspection and exactness" ("poco examen y puntualidad"), and for giving too much credit to hearsay rather than eyewitness testimony. More so than Herrera, however, the royal chronicler Solís clearly accorded primary importance to rhetorical eloquence over empirical detail. Thus, he heaped contempt upon Bernal Díaz' primitive style, in which he saw evidence of the "danger of permitting discussion to those who are born to obey" ("peligro que se permita el discurrir a los que nacieron para obedecer"). Thus, Solís' marvelous eloquence transformed even the most exotic aspects of Mexican culture into variants of the Classical model. His imperial authority thus rested on the fiction of his scientific "detachment" as a stay-at-home historian, who was devoid of the "passion" that characterized the accounts of those, like Bernal Díaz, who actually took part in the events.[22]

Sigüenza y Góngora's historical works in verse and prose emulated those of the royal cosmographer Solís with regard to their Baroque appeal to the arts of poetry and rhetoric. His published works display on their title page as his personal insignia the Pegasus, the mythic winged horse who had opened the well of poetry on Helicon, the mountain of the muses (see Illustration 5.2). But we know that today only a small fraction of Sigüenza's entire literary production survives, most of which has been lost in manuscript due to his difficulties in publishing his works. These difficulties were due less to existing infrastructures of printing (in Mexico the first

5.1 Frontispiece of Antonio de Solís y Rivadeneyra, *Historia de la Nueva España*
(Madrid, 1684).

INFORTVNIOS
QVE
ALONSO RAMIREZ
NATVRAL DE LA CIVDAD DE S. JUAN
DE PVERTO RICO
*padeciò, aſſi en poder de Ingleſes Piratas que lo apreſaron
en las Islas Philipinas*
como navegando por ſi ſolo, y ſin derrota, haſta
varar en la Coſta de lucatan:
Conſiguiendo por eſte medio dar vuelta al Mundo
DESCRIVELOS
*D. Carlos de Siguenza y Gongora
Coſmographo, y Cathedratico de Mathematicas,
del Rey N. Señor en la Academia Mexicana.*

CON LICENCIA EN MEXICO
por los Herederos de la Viuda de Bernardo Calderon: en la calle de
S. Aguſtin. Ano de 1690.

5.2 Title page of Carlos de Sigüenza y Góngora, *Los Infortunios de Alonso Ramírez* (1690).

press had been introduced in 1576),[23] than they were to the imperial geography of historiographic authorship within the established patrimonialist venues of patronage in state and church.[24] Despite the illustrious titles conferred upon the Mexican Creole, Sigüenza lacked the support available to most of his European counterparts in cosmography, such as Solís. Irving Leonard's classic 1929 biography still provides the best account of Sigüenza's marginal location as a colonial Creole in the Baroque Lettered City. His marginalization had begun with his fateful expulsion from the Jesuit Order as a young man and continued with his life-long, though futile, effort to gain re-admittance. (The reasons for his expulsion are not entirely clear, but they seem to have involved a nightly escapade during which the young Creole was missing from the monastery.) Despite his later appointment as a professor of mathematics and astronomy at the University of Mexico, as well as "Royal Cosmographer of the Realm" by Charles II in 1680, and for all his internationally famous erudition, Sigüenza y Góngora remained on the fringes of the Baroque world of science throughout his life. While he cultivated a number of literary and scientific "friendships" with some of the most influential men of science of the seventeenth century, he was frequently consigned to the role of provider of information to other cosmographers with institutional support from secular or ecclesiastic institutions. His friendship with the renowned Peninsular Franciscan friar and historian Agustín de Vetancurt is a case in point. Vetancurt, later appointed official chronicler of his Order, had shared Sigüenza's interest in the early Indian history of New Spain and published in 1698 a book entitled *Mexican Theater*, which dealt with all aspects of life in New Spain, including its economic, social, and religious history, its natural wealth, people, and monuments. His authority vested in the authenticity of his sources, Vetancurt referred to numerous original maps, books, and manuscripts which "my friend and compatriot, Don Carlos de Sigüenza y Góngora, . . . a diligent investigator of old papers and anxious that the greatness of this new world be uncovered and published, has shared with me." In fact, Sigüenza had himself begun to write just such a book before 1690, to which he refers with the title "Theater of the Magnificent Mexico" in the Prologue of his *Libra astronómica*. Leonard speculated that "Considering the fact that Vetancurt published his book shortly after this date (1698) and the chronic inability of Don Carlos to publish his own writings, it is not unlikely that the unselfish scholar not only withdrew in favor of his elderly friend but even supplied the latter with many of the valuable data which appeared in the Mexican Theater."[25] Indeed, in his scientific relations with Peninsular men of learning, it was the lot of the colonial "friend and compatriot" Sigüenza chiefly to give, lest the knowledge he accumulated was to be doomed to oblivion in the drawers of his desk. Leonard saw Sigüenza's stoic humility as an expression of his "noble" character and "willingness to sacrifice personal ambition and fame for the sake of making knowledge known to the world."[26] But even Don Carlos' "nobility" of character and willingness to "sacrifice" had its limits. In 1681, the renowned Austrian Jesuit scholar and explorer of northwestern New Spain (today the southwestern USA) Eusebio Kino published his *Exposición astronómica*, an implicit attack on Sigüenza's earlier *Manifiesto philosóphico* – after having borrowed (and failed to return) the Mexican's charts and celestial maps (and after having been introduced by him to the circles of the vice-regal court). Worse than Kino's scientific attack, however, was the condescending tone in which the European scholar had called into question the Mexican professor's "wits" when obliquely referring to him (without mentioning him by name) as having "trabajosos juicios."[27] Sigüenza immediately sat down to write his counter-attack in his *Libra astronómica* – which was not published until 1690, at the personal expense of the Inspector of the Royal Funds, Don Sebastián de Guzmán y Córdoba (a personal friend of Sigüenza's who had owed him a favor). The bitter tone of Sigüenza's response to Kino is revealing of the sting that Sigüenza felt when reading the attack: "Those who understand it know that in the Castilian language to say someone has 'trabajoso el juicio' is the same as to call him crazy;...I say 'long live the reverend father for the singular elegy with which he honors me.'"[28] There was, however, more at stake in Sigüenza's counter-attack than his personal revenge on a backstabbing friend. Kino's failure to acknowledge him by name, as well as his condescending dismissal of the Mexican professor's "wits," was only the latest affront to the Mexican Creole's hurt patriotic pride. As he refuted Kino's treatise point by point, Sigüenza remarked with bitter sarcasm that:

Piensan en algunas partes de la Europa y con especialidad en las septentrionales,... que no sólo los indios, habitadores originarios de estos países, sino que los que de padres españoles casualmente nacimos en ellos, o andamos en dos pies por divina dispensación o que aun valiéndose de microscopios ingleses apenas se descubre en nosotros lo racional.

In some parts of Europe, and especially in the north,...it is commonly thought that not only the Indians, original inhabitants of these parts, but also those born of Spanish parents here, walk on two feet by divine dispensation and that even with the use of English microscopes they can hardly discover anything rational in us.[29]

Thus, one of the most important scientific treatises of seventeenth-century New Spain was written as a defense of the intellectual faculties of the Creole elite. Sigüenza's ironical identification of an extreme empiricism as a particularly English way of knowing ("English microscopes"), as well as his reference to European scorn of Creole intellectual faculties, suggests that he was keenly aware of the new branch of Natural Philosophy that had expanded the empirical investigation of nature into human psychology, thereby involving Baroque scientific reason in the division of intellectual labor along geographic lines. Moreover, Sigüenza was also aware of the superb irony posed by the fact that Spain's mercantilist economy of knowledge had ultimately benefited not Spain or Spanish America, but rather her Protestant enemies, as English and Dutch Pirates were pouncing upon the valuable intelligence in the shipholds en route from the Americas to the Iberian peninsula. Once diverted north, it aided the Protestants' military campaigns against the Spanish colonies, was refined into the "Black Legend" by their historians, and then came into the possession of their rare book merchants, museums, and libraries, where it remains to this day. Thus, in his *Teatro de virtudes políticas* (1680), Sigüenza cites Volume III, Book v, Chapter 7 of Samuel Purchas' *Hakluytus posthumus*, in which the Creole patriot encountered for the first time what Purchas had called the "choisest of my Jewels" – the "Codex Mendoza," the Mexican pictographic history, whose manuscript had been prepared in New Spain in 1541–2 and shipped in Spanish translation to the court of Charles V, but was on its way intercepted by French privateers and later purchased by Hakluyt.[30] As the Mexican Creole Sigüenza was reading (in English!) about the ancient history of "nuestra nación criolla" ("our Creole nation") in Purchas' collection,[31] the "círculo de trabajos" of the "Codex Mendoza" had come to completion at the Mexican's house. If little was known of the true glories of the Mexican past, he complained,

El defecto es nuestro pues cuando todos nos preciamos de tan amantes de nuestras patrias, lo que de ellas se sabe se debe a extranjeras plumas... No hablo de la explicación de los caracteres o jeroglíficos mexicanos, que algunos tendrán por trivilidad despreciable y, por el consiguiente, indigno objeto de sus estudios sublimes,... porque (por vergüenza nuestra) ya fue empeño de Samuel Purchas, de nación inglesa, en sus Peregrinaciones del mundo.[32]

The fault is our own because all the things that we pride ourselves on loving so much about our fatherlands we know from the pens of foreigners... I speak not of the explication of the characters of the Mexican hieroglyphs, which some will dismiss as a triviality and, therefore, as an unworthy subject of their sublime studies,... because (to our shame) it was already done by Samuel Purchas, of the English nation, in his *Pilgrimages of the World*.

It is as a vehicle for his critique of Peninsular mercantilist ideologies, I would argue, that a plain tale about the sufferings of a poor Puerto Rican ship's carpenter, who had turned up on his doorstep after his own "círculo de trabajos" during his captivity among Protestant Pirates, was of interest for the Creole Cosmographer of the Baroque, Sigüenza y Góngora.

PIRACY AND KNOWLEDGE IN *INFORTUNIOS*
DE ALONSO RAMÍREZ

By the time that Sigüenza transcribed Alonso's narrative, the Protestant
Pirate and his Catholic victim had already had a long and extremely politi-
cized literary history in Spanish America. Thus when, in 1850, the editors
of the Biblioteca de Autores Españoles de Rivadeneyra were preparing the
first complete edition of the longest poem in the Spanish language, the
Colombian Juan de Castellanos' *Elegías de varones ilustres de Indias* (1589),
they were surprised to find that in Part III of the work, which dealt with
the history of Cartagena, an entire section had been torn from the original
manuscript of the poem. The missing section was announced on the last
page of the previous section as the "Discurso del Capitán Francisco Draque,
de nación ingles," but the page was crossed out, and in the margin was written: "from this place onward, must erase." Likewise, on the first page of the
subsequent section, also crossed out, the censor had written, "up to here
is the discourse about Drake which must be erased" (see Illustration 5.3).
Both marginalia were signed "Pedro Sarmiento," whom twentieth-century
historians have identified as Pedro Sarmiento de Gamboa, a Peninsular
Spaniard who had been commissioned by the Holy Office of the Inquisition to oversee, censor, and license the publication of texts dealing with
the Indies.[33] Apparently, Gamboa was wary of the subversive Creole politics in Castellanos' epic poem, in which the dreaded poet asked: "Did
Adam decree in some testament that only Spaniards should profit [from
the Indies]? Show me that clause, and I will immediately renounce my
right, but if it is not so, let him take the most who is the most able."[34] In
light of the Creoles' well-known dissatisfaction with the unequal distribution of "profit" in the Spanish empire, the word "Spaniards" threatened to
assume a dangerously ambiguous meaning in the ventriloquist mouth of
the English villain – "Spaniards" not only in opposition to "Englishmen"
but also in opposition to "Americans." After the imperial state had in effect
stripped the American conqueror of his arms, thus replacing the man of
arms with the man of letters, the colonials were left the defenseless prey of
foreigners: "we, without fences or walls, but entirely unprepared," Castellanos wrote, "few of us knowing the business of war for lack of practice and
exercise."[35] Thus, as Nina Gerassi-Navarro has shown, while the official
Peninsular representations typically demonized the Protestant Pirate in a
"discourse of morality," the colonial Creole historians frequently exposed
the weakness of the Spanish empire in a "discourse of amazement" about
his stunning feats.[36] This literary polemic encompassed other epic poems,

5.3 Manuscript of Juan de Castellanos' *Primera Parte de las Elegías de varones ilustres de Indias* (1589) without the missing canto about Drake.

such as Silvestre de Balboa Troya y Quesada's *Espejo de paciencia* (1608) and Juan de Miramontes y Zuázola's *Armas antárticas* (1608); official broadsides, such as Pedro de Baño's *Verdadera Relacion de la Maravillos Vitoria que en la Cudad de Manil, el las Filipinas, han tenido los Espanoles contra la poderosa armada de los Cosarios Olandeses* (1603); Spanish translations of Protestant collections of Pirate narratives, such as Alexander Olivier Esquemeling's *Píratas de la América, y luz a la defensa de las costas de Indias Occidentales* (1681); and picaresque tales about the experiences of captives, such as José de Acosta's *Peregrinación de Bartolomé Lorenzo* (1586).

The foreign Pirate posed a threat not only to Spain's material exchange with her American colonies but also to the imperial production, dissemination, and control of knowledge about the New World. Imperial officials such as Gamboa, who had himself been captured by a famous Protestant Pirate in the Straits of Magellan, were highly conscious of this. Thus, Walter Ralegh remembers, in his *History of the World*, that his captive responded to his demand for information with a "pretty jest":

when I asked him, being then my prisoner, some question about an island in those straits, which methought might have done neither benefit or displeasure to his enterprise, he told me merrily, that it was to be called the Painter's Wife's Islands; saying, that whilst the fellow drew that map, his wife sitting by desired him to put in one country for her; that she, in imagination, might have an island of her own.[37]

As early as the sixteenth century, the Pirate's most valuable booty had been knowledge – the letters, notes, accounts, charts, and maps in the holds of ships as well as the oral intelligence of the crew on board.

By the time that Sigüenza y Góngora met Alonso Ramírez, he had himself written several accounts relating to piracy in the Americas. In his *Trofeo de la justicia española* and *Relación de lo sucedido a la Armada de Barlovento*, he had related the Spanish extirpation of the French settlement on Hispañola, frequently used by Caribbean Pirates as a home base.[38] However, whereas these texts had been focused on the historical events and displayed the triumphalist tone that characterized the official Spanish versions of these encounters, *Infortunios* was the history of an individual captive and distinctly counter-utopian in tone, emphasizing the humiliation of Spain and her imperial subjects. Significantly, Alonso is captured not for the supplies he was to deliver but rather for the knowledge he and his crew carried about the empirical particulars of the Philippines' geography. The English captain, immediately after taking Alonso's ship, "Prometióme a las primeras palabras la libertad, si le noticiaba cuáles lugares de las islas eran más ricos, y si podría hallar en ellos gran resistencia" (31) ("promised me my freedom in return for news about which of the islands were more wealthy and if one could expect much resistance from them" [29]). Alonso, loyal to the mercantilist system of trusting, answers him that he "no podía satisfacerle a lo que preguntaba" ("could not satisfy his desire for information") and, when pressed harder, decides to give him a piece of fiction:

dijele no haber allí población alguna y que sabía de una bahía donde conseguiría fácilmente lo que deseaba. Era mi intento el que, si así lo hiciesen, los cogiesen desprevenidos no sólo los naturales de ella, sino los españoles, que asisten de presidio en aquella isla, y los apresasen. (31)

I told him that there was no village there at all and that I knew of a bay where he could easily secure what he needed. It was my intention, if he should go there, that he should be seized unexpectedly not only by the natives but by the Spanish who serve on the prison staff on that island. (29–30)

His boatswain, by contrast, "quien por indio jamás se podía prometer cosa que buena fuese" (33) ("who being Indian could not be expected to do things properly" [32]), surrenders the valuable empirical information.

Despite the afflictions he endured in defending the imperial network of trusting, Alonso is ill rewarded for his loyalty by an empire that is in a state of utter decay and that offers him neither opportunities nor protection. When he first departed from his native San Juan in order to seek fame and fortune on a western *tierra firme*, he still marveled at the symbols of Spanish imperial power – "lo incontrastable del Morros que la defiende; las cortinas y baluartes coronados de artillería que la aseguran" (18) ("the invincible Morro Castle which defends [the island]; the walls and bulwarks crowned by artillery assuring her safety" [8]). Soon enough, however, the sobering reality becomes apparent when he finds Spain's former possessions to be "un monte de ruinas, a violencias de los estragos que en ella hicieron los franceses y holandeses por poseerla" (27) ("a mound of ruins caused by the struggle between the French and Dutch" [25]). What has not been ruined is now owned by Protestant heretics:

debajo de cuyo yugo gimen los desvalidos católicos que allí han quedado, a quienes no se permite el uso de la religión verdadera, no estorbándoles a los moros y gentiles sus vasallos, sus sacrificios. (28)

under whose yoke groan the destitute Catholics that have remained there and are not permitted the exercise of the true religion even though Moors and gentiles are not disturbed in their vassals and sacrifices. (25)

When the ill-equipped royal vessel that was put into his charge is attacked and boarded by the foreign invaders, they

celebraron con mofa y risa la prevención de armas y municiones que en ella hallaron, y fué mucho mayor cuando supieron el que aquella fragata pertenecía al rey, y que habían sacado de sus almacenes aquellas armas. (30)

mocked us with loud laughter at the sight of the arms we had and even more when they discovered that the frigate belonged to the king and that the arms had been taken out of the royal storehouse. (28)

The humiliation and emasculation of the loyal Spanish subject, disarmed by his own Crown, are painfully illustrated by the grotesquely homoerotic masochism that Alonso and his crew must endure during their captivity:

Era para nosotros el día de lunes el más temido porque haciendo un círculo de bejuco en torno de la mesana, y amarrándonos a él las manos siniestras, nos ponían en las derechas unos rebenques, y habiéndonos desnudado nos obligaban con puñales y pistolas a los pechos a que unos a otros nos azotásemos. (50)

Monday was for us the most feared of days for it was then that they made a circle of reeds about the mizen-mast and tying our left hands to it and putting ropes in our right hands they obliged us while in the nude to whip one another. (56–7)

Alonso's defiance in the face of these humiliations allegorizes a struggle between the forces of good and evil, between Catholic morality and the modern Protestant renegade spirit. However, while this struggle appears at first to be clearly defined in national terms – Spaniards versus Englishmen (Alonso even witnesses Englishmen committing acts of cannibalism) – we soon learn that this is a false appearance, as many of the Pirates turn out to be not nominal heretics but rather renegade Catholics. In fact, one of the most degenerate and cruel among Alonso's captors is not an Englishman but rather a Peninsular Spaniard, "que se preciaba de sevillano y se llamaba Miguel" (53) ("who boasted of being from Seville and whose name was Miguel" [60]):

No hubo trabajo intolerable en que nos pusiesen, no hubo ocasión alguna en que nos maltratasen, no hubo hambre que padeciésemos, ni riesgo de la vida en que peligrásemos, que no viniese por su mano y su dirección haciendo gala de mostrarse impío y abandonado lo católico en que nació por vivir pirata y morir hereje. Acompañaba a los ingleses, y esta era para mí y para los míos lo más sensible, cuando se ponían de fiesta, que eran las Pascuas de Navidad, y los domingos del año, leyendo o rezando lo que ellos en sus propios libros. Alúmbrele Dios el entendimiento, para que enmendando su vida consiga el perdón de sus iniquidades. (53)

There was no intolerable work which they made us do, nor any occasion in which they mistreated us, nor hunger which we suffered, nor risk of life in which they placed us which did not come from his hand and order. He gloried in his impiety and abandoning the Catholicism in which he was born he chose to live as a pirate and die a heretic. He accompanied the English when there were festivities, which were on Christmas and the Sundays during the year, reading and praying with them out of their own books which for us was the most lamentable of all. May God enlighten his understanding so that his life may be reformed and he may be pardoned for his iniquities. (60–1)

It is significant that Miguel is identified as being not only Peninsular but specifically from Seville – the seat of the Spanish Casa de Contratación and the citadel of Spanish economic imperialism in the New World. In the course of the narrative, Miguel becomes increasingly homologous with the quasi-piratical Peninsular officials whom Alonso encounters after his return to New Spain, who are like "most experienced pirates" when it comes to enriching themselves at the expense of the colonials during their tenure in imperial office. When Alonso attempts to retrieve his belongings still on board his stranded ship, for example, the town mayor Ziphirino de Castro notified him that:

debajo de graves penas no saliese de la villa para las playas, porque la embarcación y cuanto en ella venía pertenecía a la cruzada, me quedé suspenso, y acordándome del sevillano Miguel, encogí los hombros. (79)

there would be a severe penalty should I leave town for the beach because the ship and everything belonging to it now belonged to the government. Thus I suspended my plans and remembering the Sevillan Miguel, I shrugged my shoulders. (98)

The Sevillan Miguel thus illustrates that the mercantile spirit that is now threatening to undermine the Catholic "Universal Empire" has taken possession not only of Protestant heretics but also of Peninsular officials in their greedy raids upon the American colonies. They represent two sides of the same coin for which New Spain has been sold into captivity, into a "New" world of bourgeois modernity, in which the old familial relationships and values of chivalry break down, leaving the individual subject helpless, exposed, and naked.

To be sure, Alonso also finds golden cities as he sets out on his westward enterprise; but they are not *his* cities – not fabulous Aztec cities he *knew* were for his taking, but rather impenetrable Spanish citadels from which he, an American Creole, was excluded as a stranger in his own land. Upon his arrival at Puebla, for example, he marvels at the riches he beholds but laments that "[l]ástima es grande el que no corran por el mundo, grabadas a punta de diamante en láminas de oro, las grandezas magníficas de tan soberbia ciudad" (20) ("it is a great pity that the greatness and magnificence of such a superb city should not spread through the world engraved by a glazier's diamond on plates of gold" [12]). The glamorous cities of viceregal New Spain afford the Creole no opportunities for socio-economic advancement. While his narrative begins on a note that evokes the tradition of the Renaissance chronicles of conquest – as he hopes to discover a "moda para ser rico" (20) ("way to become rich" [11]) – his actual experiences in the New World are cast in the Baroque language of bitter disillusionment (*desengaño*):

Desengañado en el discurso de mi viaje de que jamás saldría de mi esfera con sentimiento de que muchos con menores fundamentos perfeccionasen las suyas, despedí cuantas ideas me embarazaron la imaginación por algunos años. (26)

Disabused in the course of my voyage that I would ever escape from my sphere and thinking about those who with few qualities had managed to improve their lot, I dismissed from my mind those ideas which had been perplexing my imagination for several years. (23)

In its social realism and Baroque theme of *desengaño*, *Infortunios* resembles many narratives written in the Spanish picaresque tradition, particularly José de Acosta's *Peregrinación de Bartolomé Lorenzo* (1586), in which the main character Lorenzo leaves home because he was in trouble with the law, is captured and about to be killed by a group of "luteranos piratas," but then is providentially redeemed by another Pirate (a Catholic himself), upon which the protagonist thanks God, repents his sins, and enters the Jesuit Order as a monk.[39] Like *Infortunios*, Bartolomé's story of Pirate captivity asserts the re-dedication of the humbled subject to Catholic morality after facing the Protestant Pirate as the ultimate manifestation of the modern renegade spirit. Unlike Acosta's *Peregrinación*, however, *Infortunios* does not tell the story of an individual's moral and religious pilgrimage. *Infortunios*, by contrast, emphasizes the historical exteriority of material strife between groups of people demarcated by social and racial boundaries. His afflictions are not the providential punishment for his former depravities but, ironically, for his very loyalty to the Catholic order as a good imperial subject:

no faltaron ocasiones en que por obedecer a quien podía mandármelo hice lo propio, y fué una de ellas la que me causó las fatalidades en que hoy me hallo, y que empezaron así. (28)

carrying out orders did not always spare me trouble and one occasion caused me the ill-fortune in which I find myself today and which began as you will hear. (26)

What was once possible for all (whites) even with "few qualities" is now possible only for Peninsular Spaniards, who are able to enrich themselves in imperial office or by marrying the daughters of wealthy Creole landholders. Impoverished Creoles such as Alonso, by contrast, are left with a morality of self-abnegation, subordination, and sacrifice, the resignation to the irreconcilable rift between New World utopia and New World reality in seventeenth-century vice-regal New Spain.

The differences between *Peregrinación* and *Infortunios* may be seen in light of the disparate cultural locations of their respective authors. While both Acosta and Sigüenza held university appointments – the former as rector of the Jesuit college of the University of Salamanca and the latter as professor of mathematics at the University of Mexico – the Peninsular historian enjoyed the life-long patronage of his Order and institution, while the latter was faced with a choice of private donors or the commercial book market for sponsorship. By the end of the seventeenth century, Acosta's *Historia natural y moral de las Indias* had gone through four editions in Spanish, one in Italian, two in Dutch, five in French, two in German, one in Latin, and one in English, while many of the historical works of Sigüenza had remained in the drawers of his desk or were published under the name of his Peninsular "friends," such as the Franciscan monk Vetancurt.[40] Thus, while the elite Creole scholar Sigüenza had no love for the "plain style" of plebeians or the commercial marketplace of print, his marginal position in the patrimonialist Lettered City of the Spanish empire offered his patriotic literary activism few alternative venues.

It is in light of the Creole historian's ambiguous social and geographical location that we must see the ideological *tension* between the "patrimonialist" relationship in which Sigüenza transcribed Alonso's tale and the "public" form in which we read this text today. Indeed, it is unlikely that we would be reading this text at all had it remained the "brief summary" that was prepared for the viceroy upon Alonso's return to Mexico City (103). A *relación de méritos*, Alonso's summary was an "official" but not a "public" document in the Baroque Lettered City. It was intended not for the eyes of strangers, for a public of readers, but rather for the private viewing of his patrimonial superiors, a viewing as intimate as the pain inflicted by the inquisitor extorting a confession from the accused. But the viceroy sent Alonso – "o por el afecto con que lo mira o quizá porque estando enfermo divirtiere sus males con la noticia que yo le daría de los muchos míos" (83) ("either because of the affection he felt for him or perhaps because, being ill, he might be diverted from his pains by my story" [103]) – to don Carlos de Sigüenza y Góngora, so that the narrative might be written down. When Sigüenza subsequently decided to publish it, the nature of the text fundamentally transformed. No longer addressed to monarch, imperial official, or royal chronicler, it is now supposed to speak to whoever "se entretenga el curioso que esto leyere por algunas horas con las noticias de lo que a mí me causó tribulaciones de muerte por muchos años" (17) ("is curious [to] read this book [and] may entertain themselves for a few hours with the incidents which caused me mortal anguish for many years" [7]). Moreover, as this text transformed from an official into a public document, even the *ways of reading* change, as the narrator points out to the reader in the beginning:

Y aunque de sucesos que sólo subsistieron en la idea de quien los finge, se suelen deducir máximas y aforismos que, entre lo deleitable de la narración que entretienen, cultiven la razón de quien en ello se ocupa, no será esto lo que yo aquí intente, sino solicitar lástimas que, aunque posteriores a mis trabajos, harán por lo menos tolerable su memoria, trayéndolas a compañía de las que me tenía a mí mismo cuando me aquejaban. (17)

[A]lthough we are concerned only with events which subsisted in the mind of a man who invented them, maxims and aphorisms may be deduced which together with the pleasures of the narrative may cultivate the reason of those persons who occupy themselves here. However, this will not be my main intention but rather to arouse sympathy, even though long after my ordeals, which will make their memory tolerable, thus coupling the reader's feelings with those which vexed me at that time. (7–8)

It is for the purpose of eliciting "sympathy" from a reading public of strangers in the literary marketplace that this narrative is published, not to secure a pension in exchange for the information offered behind the closed walls of patrimonial officialdom and the archive.[41]

Thus, form and content in Sigüenza's transcription of Alonso's plain tale of Pirate captivity operate metonymically as an allegory of Sigüenza's own abduction as a historian from the baroque Lettered City of vice-regal New Spain and seduction by the literary marketplace. There is a certain irony in the fact that Sigüenza has come to be celebrated by modern historians as an important figure not only in the history of the Latin American novel but also in the related history of Latin American print journalism.[42] If colonial Spanish America was "late" in developing a permanent periodical press of the sort that Protestant scholars such as Jürgen Habermas have seen as foundational in the formation of bourgeois modernity at large, of a "print ideology" that Michael Warner has seen as underwriting these new discursive practices, and of communal imagination that Benedict Anderson has seen at the root of modern nationalism,[43] it was due not to the fact that colonial Spanish America lacked the material infrastructures of print but rather to the fact that elite Creoles such as Sigüenza were highly ambivalent about the introduction of liberal media into their colonial societies. While they resented their exclusion from the patrimonialist Lettered City, they also dreaded opening a public forum to the colonized masses on a liberal marketplace of print. With respect to modernity, their dilemma was that, unlike their Protestant contemporaries, they had failed to exclude philosophically (or exterminate physically) the social sectors they had colonized and upon whose labor and land that culture of modernity was being built in the increasingly globalized networks of exchange. Faced with a relative lack of the social and racial cohesion that characterized the societies of Europe and the neo-European outposts of British America, elite Spanish American Creoles could not agree all to be "equal" for they had failed to disqualify their non-equals as "men."

CHAPTER 6

"Husquenawing": *William Byrd's "Creolean humours"*

[M]ake a tour of the world in books, he may make himself master of the geography of the universe in the maps, atlasses and measurements of our mathematics. He may travell by land with the historians, by sea with the navigators. He may go round the globe with Dampier and Rogers and kno' a thousand times more doing it than all those illiterate sailors.

Daniel Defoe, *The Compleat English Gentleman* (1730)

On 6 March 1719, William Byrd II of Westover, a Virginia planter and fellow of the Royal Society of London, wrote a letter to his English friend Charles Boyle III, in which he gratefully acknowledged Boyle's hospitalities during one of Byrd's extended stays in England. They stuck so "fast in my Memory in all Clymates," he wrote, that "I believe I could go thro' the Ceremony of *Husquenawing* without forgetting them." "*Husquenawing*," Byrd explains, is a Native American rite of passage performed by young men during puberty, which involves extended confinement, drugging, and fasting. It "makes them perfectly mad for Six Weeks together," but afterwards leaves them "return[ed] to their Understanding," though having "forgot everything that befell them in the early part of their Lives."[1] Moving into the "Clymates" of the New World, Byrd suggests, slightly tongue-in-cheek, is a rite of passage not unlike that of *Husquenawing* – the erasure of cultural memory leaving the mind a *tabula rasa*, ready for inscription by pure New World experience.

As we have seen in the previous chapters, Creole patriots throughout the Americas frequently assumed or appropriated this rhetorical posture of *Husquenawing*, of a "primitive eloquence," vis-à-vis the imperial metropolis. Byrd's irony here, however, manifest in his simile likening his own to Native American rites of passage, suggests a new attitude toward the epistemological status of New World experience. Late seventeenth-century developments in British Natural Philosophy, such as the publication of Isaac Newton's *Mathematical Principles of Natural Philosophy* in 1687, had begun to challenge the "naïve empiricism" underwriting the rhetorical power of eyewitness testimony.[2] While the scientific practice of Natural History during the seventeenth century had largely consisted of collecting and cataloguing new empirical phenomena, ascribing their causes to God's mysterious Providence, it now became an increasingly explanatory endeavor that greatly enhanced the authority of speculative Natural Philosophy by offering a universal theory of nature in terms of mathematical rationalism. "I have laid down the principles of philosophy," Newton had written, "principles not philosophical but mathematical: such, namely, as we may build our reasonings upon in philosophical inquiries."[3] Thus, whereas Cartesian science had been able to explain why bodies in circular or elliptical motion were not carried off by centrifugal force only by postulating a quasi-mystical "vortex" at the center, Newton's revolutionary "invention" (as he called it) of a theory of gravity fully rationalized centripetal force acting upon bodies as a principle of nature. Newton hereby laid the scientific groundwork for a new geo-political imagination that Mary Louise Pratt has characterized as a "planetary consciousness" emerging in the age of Linnaean taxonomies.[4] But Newtonian Natural Philosophy had rationalized this "planetary consciousness" not only conceptually but also epistemologically, as the producer of "effects" lost cultural authority in comparison with that of the producer of invisible "principles" and "laws." He who became a natural philosopher, as Newton famously (though probably sarcastically) put it when charged with plagiarism, stood "on the shoulders of giants."[5] Whereas the seventeenth-century historians of the New World, such as Samuel Purchas, had still rationalized their scientific authority in appeals to their superior rhetorical "art" – their scientific "form[ing] and fram[ing]" – now metropolitan natural philosophers sought to ground their scientific authority in the laws of nature itself. Consequently, the historical debate about the natural influences of the environment upon human faculties took an increasingly meta-historical turn that subjected the traveling historian to the scientific gaze in a particular sub-discipline that I want to call the "natural history of scientific authorship" – the censorship and criticism of empirical testimony based on an assessment of its author's physical and mental constitution as conditioned by his or her natural habitat.

These last two chapters explore the implications of these transformations for the evolution of colonial prose during the eighteenth century. This chapter returns to the Chesapeake Bay region of British America about a century after Samuel Purchas, William Strachey, and John Smith had written their histories of Virginia (discussed in Chapter 3). As historians have noted, a distinct "Creole consciousness" did not emerge in the Chesapeake until almost the end of the seventeenth century.[6] By that time, the British empire was rapidly undergoing far-reaching economic transformations in the course of which the Old Empire – a "trans-atlantic" European settler empire based on small-scale farming and indentured labor – was rapidly beginning to overlap with a new style of empire that Philip Curtin has described as a "plantation complex," encompassing not only Europe and the colonial Americas but also Africa in a "circum-Atlantic" system of production based on slave labor.[7] Here, I place William Byrd's *History of the Dividing Line Betwixt Virginia and North Carolina* in the context of this emerging "circum-Atlantic" empire and its post-Newtonian economies of knowledge production. In particular, I read the textual evolution of Byrd's *History* in its dialogues and interferences with Peter Kolb's *The Present State of the Cape of Good Hope* (1731), one of the first and most important early modern natural histories about sub-Saharan Africa. I argue that Byrd's *History* may in part be read as a satirical response to his ambivalent location as an American Creole within the cultural geography of Enlightenment historiographic authorship. On the one hand, his imperial metaphors, derived from what V. Y. Mudimbe has called a discourse of "Africanism," invent Virginia as a geographical entity in terms of Newtonian mathematical rationalism in the knowledge of colonial space. On the other hand, however, Byrd's satire parodies the imperial taxonomies of the Second Conquest, as the "dividing line" between Virginia and North Carolina turns into what Homi Bhabha has called a "boundary" – the hybrid and in-between location of colonials "building" and "dwelling" on the colonial frontier.[8]

WILLIAM BYRD II AND THE "ORDEAL" OF COLONIAL VIRGINIA

The lifetime of William Byrd II of Westover (1674–1744) spanned the heydays of the colonial planter oligarchy in the history of colonial Virginia. The son of one of the principal landowners in the colony, Byrd was born two years before Bacon's Rebellion (1676), the last serious challenge to the social ascendancy of the emerging planter elite during the seventeenth century; and he died in a decade of the eighteenth century when religious and political transformations had begun to erode the monopoly his class had held on colonial public and political life.[9] Like many of his fellow American-born plantocrats, Byrd spent the greater part of his youth in England, where he was sent at a young age to be educated. When, in 1705, Byrd inherited his father's estate – one of the largest along the James River – he took up residency in Virginia and assumed many important colonial offices, such as a seat in the Virginia House of Burgesses, Councilor, Auditor and Receiver

General, as well as Indian trader. In 1715, he returned to London as the representative of the House of Burgesses and remained there, with some interruptions, until 1726. At age 52, he returned permanently to Virginia, continuing to serve the colony's political interests, expanding his father's substantial library, and corresponding with his friends in London. After his final return to the colony, Byrd described his new life in the colony in a letter to Boyle:

we abound in all kinds of Provisions without expence (I mean we who have Plantations). I have a large Family of my own, and my Doors are open to Every Body, yet I have no Bills to Pay, and half-a-Crown will rest undisturbed in my Pocket for many Moons together. Like one of the Patriarchs, I have my Flocks and my herds, my Bond-men and Bond-women, and every Soart of Trade amongst my own Servants, so that I live in a kind of Independence on every one but Providence.[10]

But reality corresponded only superficially to the aristocratic myth with which Byrd and his kind surrounded themselves. As Lewis Simpson has observed, theirs was a class based on the master–slave relationship that exposed "all the contradictions of the Southern reality: a pre-bourgeois ruling class with a solidly bourgeois religion, a patriarchal social structure in a market economy; a flesh-peddling chivalry."[11] Indeed, the Virginia elite had crystallized mainly as the result of the transformation of the colonial labor force from European indentured servants to African slaves, after indentured labor had increasingly come into short supply during the second half of the seventeenth century.[12] This shift toward capital-intensive slave labor had disproportionately benefited large landholders, who were able to monopolize large tracts of available land at the expense of the economic opportunities of recently freed servants. The result was the rise of a new class of landless and dissatisfied ex-servants that the historian Edmund Morgan has called "terrible young men," who caused considerable social unrest and violence on the frontier as they encroached upon Native American lands.[13] However, even the wealthy planters were hardly immune from the "ordeals" accompanying a colonial economy, being subject to the caprices of circum-Atlantic mercantile capitalism. Thus, colonial estates, such as the Byrds', were consistently in debt with the London merchants, who frequently threatened to confiscate the plantations.[14] Nevertheless, by the middle of the eighteenth century, "the image of the independent Virginian lodged in his plantation fortress," writes Timothy Breen, "had become something of a cliché, a self-deception that contained a good measure of defensiveness."[15]

The aristocratic pretensions of the colonial elite were regarded with extreme suspicion, even derision, by the Old World aristocracy. In Virginia, as elsewhere in the Americas, the devastating wars on the frontier, such as Bacon's Rebellion, which killed thousands of royal subjects, were attributed to colonial maladministration and gave occasion to a "full-scale reconsideration" of the relations between the American provinces and central administration.[16] Initially, this "deep skepticism" about the legitimacy of the colonial elite had been implicit in occasional disparaging remarks by imperial officials about the lowly social origins of the planters.[17] However, as Caroline Shammas has observed, in the course of the seventeenth century, when second-generation colonials born in America were replacing their immigrant parents, the implications of an American birth rather than of non-aristocratic lineage became increasingly of interest to English officials, travelers, and natural historians, who referred to the colonials as "natives," "Creoles," and "country-born."[18] As was the case in other parts of the Americas, nature's undesirable effects upon bodily "humors" in the New World were thus seen as a plausible explanation for the "extreme choler and passion" that seemed to characterize the way in which the inhabitants of Virginia handled their affairs. In the 1690s, Governor Francis Nicholson, for example, wrote back to England that practice should become policy, and only men sent from England should occupy the positions of governor and lieutenant governor. When Nicholson sent an emissary back to London in order to keep in check the influence of the colonial agent William Byrd II with imperial authorities, he emphasized that his courier, unlike Byrd, was an "old Englander" and therefore could be trusted.[19]

The life of William Byrd II had frequently been marked by friction with imperial officials, such as Governor Alexander Spotswood, who had made it his mission to remedy what he saw as the essential flaw of colonial administration: the excessive power of the colonial Council and other institutions of colonial self-government, such as the Virginia House of Burgesses, which, he felt, was gradually usurping the authority of the Crown.[20] Byrd was, as biographer Kenneth Lockridge writes, "one of the central figures in a vastly larger political event," which was Virginians' more "general resistance to their governor" in an effort to "gain greater control over their own affairs."[21] Yet, like their contemporaries in other parts of the colonial Americas, elite Creoles in Virginia such as Byrd clung to the notion that they were "gentlemen" of European stock who had more in common with the aristocratic classes of Europe than with what they perceived to be the low-class "rabble" that inhabited the colony around them. Thus, Lockridge chronicles Byrd's life-long frustration in trying to overcome the social and political barriers placed on American Creoles: "The dilemma was always that, despite his longing, England never accepted him enough to give him the place...aspired to, while Virginia never seemed to offer the scope he felt his English education and ambitions deserved."[22] Creoles such as Byrd always had to prove that they were in fact what they could not assume to be: English gentlemen. The very Enlightenment education that they paraded to this end led to profound insecurities about their own identities after having imbibed its Eurocentrism. Lockridge documents, for example, Byrd's "deep-seated fear of his own emotional and sexual impulses" on which he blamed his rejections and failures. "When rejected by genteel society in England" Byrd "would never know whether his colonial status or his character were to blame. They were inseparable."[23] Byrd's psychological dilemma was that he could not help but look at himself with a peculiar "double-consciousness" – through the scientific lens of Natural History. His obsessively methodical entries in his diaries, containing information about what he ate, what he read, about the weather's effects upon his body as well as about his neglect of his nightly prayers, may thus be seen as his pathological exercise in scientific self-objectification.[24] A Creole transplant to the New World neither "European" nor "American," he was his own specimen as a natural historian. Byrd bore America in his "humours."

WILLIAM BYRD, COLONIAL MAN OF SCIENCE

Despite Byrd's continued failure to penetrate English aristocratic society through marriage or imperial office during his extended stays in England, he was nevertheless afforded the rare distinction of becoming one of the few American colonials to be elected, at the young age of twenty-two, a fellow to the Royal Society of London. Here was an avenue for the young Creole to gain acceptance by the London aristocratic circles. Not surprisingly, Byrd quite consciously fashioned himself after the images of aristocratic men of science, such as that of Sir Isaac Newton, whose portrait he quite patently emulated in his own portrait of 1705 (see Illustrations 6.1 and 6.2). More significant than the strong similarities between Newton's and Byrd's portraits, however, are their differences in detail: whereas Newton points to an as yet unopened letter, which will momentarily be subjected to his scientific gaze, Byrd points not to a textual source but rather to a Virginia landscape, emphasizing his immediate access to nature through first-hand observation and suggesting his keen understanding of this special mission as a colonial in the trans-atlantic Republic of Science: he would "collect data in the field, the minute particulars of natural history."[25] While still in England, he regularly participated in the Society's meetings and, when

D. ISAACVS NEWTON EQVES
REG. SOCIETATIS PRÆSES, AN°. 1702.

6.1 Portrait of Isaac Newton by Charles Jervas.

back in Virginia, remained in constant correspondence with the famous botanist Sir Hans Sloane, the secretary of the Royal Society from 1693 to 1741, following Newton.[26] Once, Byrd sent an account of a young boy who was born of two black parents and was himself black until, at age three, he became "dappled in several Places of his Body with White Spots." The Society published Byrd's account in their *Philosophical Transactions* in 1697.

6.2 Portrait of William Byrd II of Westover.

Following the prescriptions of Boyle's "Heads" (discussed in Chapter 3), his short account was confined to empirical observations of the superficial phenomena.[27] Still in 1706, he eagerly wrote to Sloane that "no body has better inclinations to promote natural knowledge than my self, and if you will direct me after what manner I may be most serviceable to the society and to the common wealth of learning, I will readily obey you."[28] Indeed,

Byrd dutifully sent specimens of plants and minerals to Europe for several years. Eventually, however, he had to realize that "men of science" were made in London, while non-aristocratic colonial providers of specimens and particulars like himself, being far removed from the centers of the trans-atlantic scientific community, would remain confined to a provincial status.[29] When in 1709, for example, he asked Sloane to send some mineral samples from England so that he could compare them to the variety he found in Virginia, he was informed that it was not "practicable" to send specimens to the colony; instead Sloane encouraged Byrd to send the samples he wanted to be informed about to England.[30] Thereafter the promising young colonial did not contribute another report to the *Transactions* for publication. When, some thirty years later (in 1741), the secretary of the Society omitted his name from the list of fellows in the *Proceedings*, Byrd's reaction reveals that he was still sensitive to the hurt of an old sting: "I take it a little unkindly Sir," he wrote to Sloane, "that my name is left out of the yearly list of the Roial Society, of which I have the honour to be one of its ancientest members. I suppose my long absence has made your Secretarys rank me in the Number of the Dead, but pray let them know I am alive."[31]

While this suggests a sense of disenchantment with the Royal Society during his later years, Byrd did retain his life-long interest in the Natural History of Virginia and in imperial service. In 1728, he had been appointed to a delegation charged with determining the colonial borderline between Virginia and North Carolina, which had been in dispute since 1665, when King Charles II had signed a new charter that conflicted in its geographic specifications with the original charter of 1663.[32] In accordance with their instructions and the surveying method commonly known as a "chain survey,"[33] the party, composed of seven commissioners, four surveyors, forty laborers, and a chaplain from both colonies, met at Currituck Inlet on the Atlantic coast and proceeded due west in a straight line until they arrived at the Dismal Swamp, about eighty miles inland, where they decided to postpone the remainder of the mission until the following autumn, when they completed it by proceeding all the way to the Appalachian mountains. During the surveyors' progress toward the Appalachians, Byrd kept a diary that later became the basis for three separate narratives about the expedition surviving today: his "Commissioners' Report," the so-called "Secret History," and the "History of the Dividing Line betwixt Virginia and North Carolina." Whereas the "Commissioners' Report" was intended for the official record, the "Secret History" was his private account, intended only for circulation in manuscripts among his friends. By the mid-1730s, however, Byrd was at work on a new narrative that seemed to be conceived for public consumption – though it was never actually printed until 1841. When, in 1736, the famous English naturalist Peter Collinson asked to see the manuscript, Byrd regretfully declined but offered to send the earlier account, the "Secret History," calling it his "Indian Scribble." It is "only the Skeleton and Ground-work of what I intend," he wrote, "which may sometime or other come to be filled up with vessels, and Flesh, and have a decent Skin drawn over all, to keep things tight in their places and prevent their looking frightfull."[34] Indeed, the "History of the Dividing Line" only faintly resembled the earlier version. Whereas in "Secret History" Byrd had appeared as a traveling character and participant expeditionary named "Steddy," as a frontiersman guide through rugged terrain versed in "particulars," in the expanded "History" he promoted himself to the status of the "general" historian of Virginia, who "clear[ed] the way," as Robert Arner has observed, "by blazing a trail through books."[35] No longer the man of action and experience, Byrd invoked Pliny and Herodotus and wrote in the voice of a natural and moral philosopher of Virginia.[36]

Because of its greater "immediacy," the "Secret History" has frequently been preferred to the "History" by modern critics and anthologizers, who deemed the latter's "artificial embellishment" a "comparative failure" from a mimetic point of view. As one critic has observed, "Despite variations of distance the published *History* maintains the illusion of an orderly movement through the wilderness" – a sense of order absent from the "Secret History."[37] Especially the prominence of the borderline dividing Virginia from North Carolina was much accentuated in the "History" through an increased emphasis on the cultural differences between genteel English Virginians and degenerate North Carolinians.[38] The "History" thus invented Virginia as a distinct geocultural entity that could henceforth definitively be *known* in counter-distinction to North Carolina, hereby manifesting the hand of the self-creating imperial historian Byrd.

Yet, this "illusion of order" in "History" always remains an ambivalent one, its utopianism being invoked deliberately *not* to be maintained but rather to be exposed by the colonial author's meta-historical satire. While the imperial natural historian Byrd creates the illusion of order, the colonial satirist Byrd frequently disrupts this illusion, as the straight line separating Virginian English gentlemen and North Carolinian Hottentots continuously seems to bend, quake, and shake in his text on the shifting sands and swamps of an apparently chaotic American wilderness. Thus, as one critic has written, in Byrd's *Histories* "boundaries can frequently cloud distinctions that they pretend to clarify," for his writing manifests a "persistent interplay between containment and resistance – between an appetite for order and the irrepressible mutability of experience."³⁹ The final product of his revisions was a far cry from a serious Natural History in the manner of John Banister's *Natural History of Virginia* or Mark Catesby's *Natural History of Carolina, Florida, and the Bahama Islands*. How can we explain this satirical ambivalence toward the order represented by the Line? In order to appreciate the meta-historical significance of Byrd's colonial satire, we must see his revision from "Secret History" to "History" in the context of the geo-politics of scientific authorship in eighteenth-century Natural History.

WILLIAM BYRD, PETER KOLB, AND THE GEOPOLITICS OF GINSENG

One of the most interesting aspects of Byrd's creation of this illusion of order in the process of revising his earlier narratives about the survey into the "History" is the metaphoric construction of the line dividing Virginians and North Carolinians. On the one hand, he reports in a passage still absent from "Secret History" that the men of North Carolina are "just like the Indians, impos[ing] all the Work upon the poor Women":

They make their Wives rise out of their Beds early in the Morning, at the same time that they lye and Snore, till the Sun has run one third of his course, and disperst all the unwholesome Damps. Then, after Stretching and Yawning for half an Hour, they light their Pipes, and, under the Protection of a cloud of Smoak, venture out into the open Air ... To speak the Truth, tis a thorough Aversion to Labor that makes People file off to N Carolina, where Plenty and a Warm Sun confirm them in their Disposition to Laziness for their whole Lives.⁴⁰

Byrd employs here the "Occidentalist" scientific discourse, about the influences of the environment in the American paradisiacal "Lubberland" upon the human faculties, familiar enough from sixteenth- and seventeenth-century Natural Histories about the New World. Unlike the European Natural Histories of America, however, Byrd's "History" re-inscribes the geocultural Atlantic frontier not as an east–west but rather as a north–south dichotomy whose axis corresponds to the "dividing line" between Virginia and North Carolina:

I am sorry to say it, but Idleness is the general character of the men in the Southern Parts of this Colony as well as in North Carolina. The Air is so mild, and the Soil so fruitful, that very little Labour is requir'd to fill their Bellies, especially where the Woods afford such Plenty of Game. These Advantages discharge the Men from the Necessity of killing themselves with Work, and then for the other Article of Raiment, a very little of that will suffice in so temperate a Climate. (304)

On the other hand, however, Byrd frequently employs also a new class of colonialist metaphors that evidences the distinct influence of contemporary eighteenth-century comparative ethnology and that places his "History" firmly in the context of an emerging "circum-Atlantic" imperial geopolitical imagination. Thus, Byrd argues that since "People uninstructed in any Religion are ready to embrace the first that offers, it is natural for helpless man to adore his Maker in Some Form or other, and were there any exceptions to this Rule, I should expect it to be among the Hottentots of the Cape of Good Hope and of North Carolina" (68–70).

Most likely, Byrd was hereby inspired by Kolb's *Present State of the Cape of Good Hope* (1715), one of the first scientific books in Natural History about sub-Saharan Africa available in English and immensely popular throughout Europe after its translation into most Western languages.[41] Byrd had become aware of Kolb's *Present State* as a result of his interest in the cultivation and marketing of American ginseng. Encouraged by the famous natural historian of the Carolinas, Mark Catesby, Byrd had hoped to profit hugely from persuading some of the fellows of the Royal Society that the American variety of the plant was the same that Europeans imported at great expense from Asia.[42] Unfortunately, the American ginseng that Byrd had sent across the Atlantic appears to have lost its salutary vigor, for his English friends remained skeptical. On 28 December 1730, John Percival enclosed in a letter to Byrd "a picture of the kanna root that grows among the Hottentots," which he believed to be the same species as the American ginseng, based on a description extracted from Kolb's *Present State*, due to be published in English translation later that year.[43] Some time between 1731 and 1736, as he was at work on revising his "Secret History" into the "History," Byrd obtained a copy of the first English edition of Peter Kolb's Natural History of southern Africa.[44] On 5 July 1737, he wrote a letter to Peter Collinson in which he affirmed that the North American ginseng "is like the ginseng of the Cape of Good-Hope, which the Hotentots call kanna."[45] For Byrd, Kolb's Natural History of the Cape of Good Hope confirmed the "Doctrine of Signatures," according to which the aspect of every plant suggested to man its uses as a remedy for the very "distempers" with which he had been afflicted by the climatic zone he inhabited.[46]

In his ethnographic descriptions of the Khoikhoin (as the "Hottentots" were in the habit of referring to themselves), Kolb had declared that he "made it a Rule not to believe any Thing I did not see of which a Sight could be had"; but in the very next sentence he affirms "that Negroes are born White" and change color several days after their birth.[47] For Kolb, the reasons for the observable differences between Europeans and

Hottentots had little to do with inherent racial difference – an invention of the nineteenth century – but rather with the influence of the environment upon the bodily "humours." This influence affected not only the natives of the Cape of Good Hope but also the Dutch and English "inhabitants," and even the travelers, who, like himself, entered the "torrid zone." The effect of the natural environment upon him was evident as soon as he left Europe on his sea journey on a Dutch vessel. Not knowing low-Dutch, but "wanting the Reliefs of Conversation there," he fell into "a deep Melancholy; by means of which and the extremeley piercing Cold I suff'd in the Northern Climates I fell dangerously ill. My Blood was in a Manner frozen in its Channels." Soon enough, however, they

were got into a pretty warm Climate, which gave me wonderful Relief; and it was with the highest Satisfaction I perceiv'd, that as I advanc'd towards the Line, and within the Sun's Activity, my Health and Vigour were augmented. The Phlegm and Melancholy that oppress'd me vanish'd as I approached the Sun, insomuch that under the Torrid Zone I found my self perfectly freed from every Incumbrance of either kind, and in Possession of as much Health and Chearfulness as a Man can with. I shall not trouble the Reader by accounting for this, since, if he is any Thing of a Philosopher, he will easily do it himself.[48]

The English translation of Kolb's *Present State* as Byrd read it was published with a preface by the English natural historian Guido Medley, who admitted that his edition is "not so properly a Translation as an Abridgement of Mr. Kolben's History." For, although "the Original is in great Esteem abroad, as the exactest History of the Hottentots the World has yet seen," the author tends to be "very tedious in some Relations, and here and there runs out in Reflections that are neither very entertaining, nor very much to the Purpose."[49] The reason for Kolb's shortcomings, which rationalize the need for an editorial preface, are for Medley not far to seek: a historian's faculties, like those of other human beings, are determined by his or her physiological "constitution." "All Ages, since the Writing has been known in the World," he argues, "have produc'd, as does the present, and as doubtless, will every one to come, Swarms of the Ignorant and Designing to plague the World with mutilated Fact and Historical Fiction. But few People, I believe, dream of the Evils that are often deriv'd upon History from the *Constitutions* of Authors." By "constitution" Medley meant the composition of a historian's bodily fluids, his "Four Humours" regulated by the peculiarities of the natural environment (ix): "He must never set up for Discernment, who has liv'd any considerable Time in the World, and not discover'd his Variations from himself merely by Virtue of Alterations in his Fluids...In a moist Air, or in rainy Weather, his Humours rise, and his Spirits sink; his Mind languishes; his Ideas fade" (x–xi). For example, the "Melancholic Humour" makes "the devil of an Historian," predisposing him to "deal[] in Omens, Apparitions and Haunted Houses" and to "dwell[] for ever on the dark Side of Things" in a "Style... plaintive, thick, set with Interjections, as the *Ah*! the *Alas*! and the *Oh me*!" The "Sanguine Temperament," by contrast, makes the historian "very awkward at exhibiting ugly Truth; but very handy at a beautiful one." Finally, the "Historian of the Choleric Complexion, who had not the Art of Guarding against its Deceptions, neither shews nor sees any Thing that despleases him in a true Light" (xv).

Thus, just as Kolb's rhetoric of first-hand experience constructed his authority as natural historian in representing the Khoikhoin, Medley's prefatory Natural History of historiographic authorship rationalized his own role as natural philosopher editing, abridging, and authorizing Kolb's eyewitness testimony. The reason for Kolb's tediousness, Medley pointed out, was that the author was a German, residing in Nuremberg, and (due to the climatic conditions prevailing in southern Germany) predisposed to a "phlegmatic" constellation of humors that determined his faculties as a natural historian, especially his accuracy in observation. One of the less commendable traits of those humans subject to the ascendancy of phlegm, however, was their lack of judgment and insight into things:

[While] the Phlegmatic Writers certainly excel all others in Accounts of Fact, [they]... have no Eyes, indeed, for the Inside of Things; but they have excellent ones of the Outside; and give a Detail of a Thousand Particulars there which escape Men of other Complexion. They relate every Thing they see and hear, with the most religious Exactness, not omitting the smallest or most indifferent matter or Circumstance, they remember, tho' it be of neither Use nor Entertainment, nor any Thing at all to the Purpose... Their Phlegm keeps that Faculty under so tight a Rein, that it never runs away with 'em, or throws em out of their Road. The Mischief of 'em is, that they are dull and tedious, and, in Point of Reasoning, apt to forget and involve themselves in Tautology and Contradiction. (xiii–xvi)

While the German Kolb was therefore naturally predisposed to providing the "authentic" information about the Khoikhoin people and the Cape of Good Hope, the English gentleman Medley must extract from it the facts that are important in order to convey to the reader the "Inside of Things" – the secret laws of nature hidden from the empiricist's eye and discernible only to the rationalist.

This theory of scientific authorship would have struck a melancholic chord in the aspiring Creole natural historian William Byrd from Virginia. Was he, by his American birth and habitat, doomed to play the role of the wit-less provider of tedious particulars, incapable of discerning Nature's "laws" and "principles" at the "Inside of Things"? Some of his modern readers seem to have read his *Histories of the Dividing Line* in this way – as a humbled colonial's capitulation to the cruel laws of Nature that made him an American Creole and not an English gentleman. Thus, Kenneth Lockridge writes that by "1728 he became a man capable of facing his limitations. He learned to deal with his actual place in the world":

William Byrd was virtually never again to exercise any of the witty genres which had characterized his adult life to that point. Here, as in politics, sheer loss forced him to abandon the compulsive behaviors of his youth, and he drew the right lesson . . . It was a sign of great maturity that in the ultimate histories Byrd took anything so humble as a daily journal as the genre of his most sustained literary efforts. Gentlemen had long kept travel journals, but journals were by definition relatively mundane affairs, as much record as art . . . But the new Byrd had a sense of context which enabled him to see that this was the appropriate genre for his country.[50]

While it seems plausible that Byrd rid himself of the "obsessive pursuit" of becoming an English gentleman by pleasing those to whose status he had in vain aspired, I would propose a different reading of his *Histories of the Dividing Line*. They were hardly humble daily journals devoid of wit; and their "main value" lies not in the "scrupulous application of the methods recommended by the Royal Society in description or analysis, particularly in the realm of natural science" (as another of Byrd's biographers has claimed),[51] but rather in their literary and meta-historical parody of the Natural History of historiographic authorship prescribed by the Royal Society.

SCIENCE AND SATIRE IN *HISTORY OF THE DIVIDING LINE*

While more attention is paid to the scientific aspects involved in the surveying of the Line in "History" than there is in "Secret History," the entire enterprise of imposing a geometric abstraction upon the American landscape appears from the very beginning as a quixotic endeavor. This ambivalence is created through the introduction of a playful dialogue between two ways of knowing space: one in terms of Newtonian mathematical rationalism, the scientific surveying instruments, and the logo-centric letter of the law; and another in terms of empirical observation and description by the traveler's eye and pen. As the surveying party advances west in the name of empire, the direction of the scientific gaze frequently turns, as the locals – the objects of the natural historian's descriptions – become the subjects who gaze upon the imperial travelers as a sort of curiosity: "They lookt upon us as a Troop of Knight Errants, who were running this great Risque of our Lives, as they imagin'd, for the Public Weal; and some of the gravest of them question'd much whether we were not all Criminals, condemned to this dirty work for Offences against the State" (50). While Byrd's satire is here ostensibly directed at the simplicity of the American colonials when seen through the imperial eyes of European science, it is also directed at the inadequacy of the logo-centric methods of the European knowledge production that would "know" America not by empirical experience but rather by the methods of mathematical rationalism. Thus, while American colonials appear to the surveying team as a degenerate lot, the surveying team appears to the locals as a "Troop of Knight Errants." While the author ostensibly insists on the reality of the dividing line, his meta-historical satire frequently undercuts its straightness and, thus, the clear distinction between colonial Virginians and North Carolinians.

Even as the expedition commences its westward journey, the American landscape resists the utopian reason of the Line, as local knowledge of the landscape conflicts with the logo-centrism of imperial geography. After the commissioners from North Carolina finally arrive at the agreed meeting spot – they were, in keeping with their natural predisposition, late – "the first Question was, where the Dividing Line was to begin" (44). A heated debate between the two parties ensues. The Virginians, "with a great deal of reason," argue that the line should begin on the low-lying sandbank of the northern shore of the Corautck inlet, according to the letter of the law. The North Carolinians, by contrast, argue that the line should begin on the High Land, "because that was fixed and certain, whereas the Spitt of Sand was ever Shifting, and did actually run out farther now than formerly" (44–6). Whereas in "Secret History," Byrd details how he persuaded the North Carolinian commissioner (aptly named "Plausible") to acquiesce by blackmailing him, in "History", he merely states that "Mr. M . . . to convince us he was not that Obstinate Person he had been represented, yielded to our Reasons, and found Means to bring over his Collegues." Finally, however, "Reason" (as defined by the Virginia party) has to yield to North Carolinian unreasonableness, after some locals testify that the sandbank had indeed shifted since 1712, when the agreement between the two governors had been fixed in writing. The experiential reality of the ground shifting beneath the feet of the expedition even as the surveying team sets out on its journey opposes the idea of a perfectly straight line in "History" with the effect of rendering the entire project humorously quixotic.

Once propelled westward, the Line seems to advance well enough, like a *perpetuum mobile* in a Newtonian vacuum, through space without resistance. "The Surveyors enter'd Early upon their business this Morning and ran the Line thro' Mr. Eyland's Plantation, as far as the Banks of North River. They passt over it in the Periauga, and landed in Gibbs' Marsh, which was a mile in Breadth, and tolerably firm. They trudg'd thro' this Marsh without much difficulty as far as the High Land" (52). Increasingly, however, the author clashes the utopian conception of space represented by the Line against local knowledge of ontological location. It gradually becomes evident that America is not a Newtonian vacuum, in which the laws of dynamics can be enacted without local resistance, but that settlers had been *dwelling* and *building* on the colonial frontier, despite the un-orderly and law-less appearance of their settlements in imperial eyes: "The Line cut William Spight's Plantation in two, leaving little more than his dwelling House and Orchard in Virginia. Sundry other Plantations were Split in the same unlucky Manner, which made the Owners accountable to both Governments" (104). The steady westward advance of the dividing line, drawn straight across hundreds of miles of American landscape for the purpose of imperial taxation and spiritual supervision, represents here the "Second Conquest" of America by the imperial state, the triumph of ordered reason and planned empire over the individualistic, pragmatic, and unsystematic settlement of the First Conquest. While the Biblical metaphors of Byrd (the "historian") still aim here to rationalize the Line, the local disorder and disarray it leaves behind, in the form of split properties and farms, undercut this very reason. Increasingly, however, the historian's metaphors render the methodical advance of the expedition in a perfectly straight line at once troublesome and ridiculous. "[L]ike Norway-Mice," he writes, "these worthy Gentlemen went right forward, without suffering themselves to be turned out of the way by any Obstacle whatever":

We are told by some Travellers, that those Mice march in mighty Armies, destroying all the fruits of the Earth as they go along. But something Peculiar to those obstinate Animals is that nothing stops them in their career, and if a House happened to stand in their way, disdaining to go an Inch about, they crawl up one side of it, and down the other: or if they meet with any River, or other Body of Water, they are so determin'd, they swim directly over it, without varying one Point from their course of the Sake of any Safety or Convenience. (100)

The progress of the journey is slowed down by the party's blind reliance on the data supplied by scientific instruments (as though the American landscape was a navigable ocean – a "green sea" [84]) – instead of their pragmatic sense supplied by their empirical faculties. Thus, whereas in the "Secret History," Byrd put on the mask of the empirical traveler, in "History," he assumed that of the natural philosopher and rationalist.[52] However, his satirical wit – his "Creolean humours" – purposely undercuts the very credibility of the masks he adopts.

Pierre Marambaud has argued that Byrd's "History" was not written for Virginians; instead, it "aimed at giving some idea of the colony to the English public, and perhaps attracting some of them as settlers."[53] However, while this might be true for Byrd's "Journey to the Land of Eden" and "A Progress to the Mines" (the former of which was written in German in order to attract Swiss settlers to Byrd's newly acquired land),[54] the European audience in "History" is implied *only ostensibly*. In fact, the (imperfect) fiction of an English natural historian talking to an English reader in "History" is an integral part of a meta-historical satire that is very much intended for communicating specifically with a *colonial* audience. Unlike Jonathan Swift's meta-historical satire, which would have been readily apparent to his English reader by the plainly fantastic qualities of the pseudo-travel accounts "collected" in *Gulliver's Travels*, in Byrd's "History" the English reader could never quite be sure. It is the suspicious "double-take" the *colonial* reader could imagine on an *English* face when reading Byrd's tall tales that would have rendered his "History" superbly humorous to a colonial audience. For example, in his description of the American alligator – an animal utterly unfamiliar to Englishmen but very much familiar to Americans – the butt of the joke is the English reader: "They swallow great Stones, the Weight of which being added to their Strength enables them to tug a Moderate Cow under Water, and as soon as they have drown'd her, they discharge the Stones out of their Maw and then feast upon the Carcass" (300). The audience with whom the author is communicating here is a *colonial* one, who, familiar with the empirical actualities of the land, would have recognized Byrd's parody. Thus, while the figure of the traveler – called "Steddy" in the "Secret History" – is still an occasional presence in "History," he now provides only "naked" ethnographic description:

The Prisoners they happen to take alive in these expeditions generally pass their time very Scurvily. They put them to all the Tortures that ingenious Malice and cruelty can invent. And (what shows the baseness of the Indian Temper in Perfection) they never fail to treat those with the greatest Inhumanity that have distinguish'd themselves most by their Bravery; an, if he be a War-Captin, they do him the Honour to roast him alive, and distribute a Colop to all that had a Share in stealing the Victory. (220)

The annotator to his own narrative, however, Byrd provides – as in Medley's "Preface" and annotations to Kolb's ethnography – the rhetoric that familiarizes Native American cultural practices. In a note to the above-quoted passage, Byrd's annotator reflects:

Tho' who can reproach the poor Indians for this when Homer makes his celebrated hero, Achilles, drag the Body of Hector at the Tail of his chariot for having fought gallantly for the defense of his Country. Nor was Alexander the Great with all his Fam'd Generosity, less inhuman to the brave Tyrians 2,000 of whom he ordered to be crucified in cold Blood, for no other fault but for having defended their City most courageously against Him, during a Seige of Seven Months. And what was still more brutal, he drag'd alive at the Tail of his Chariot thro' all the Streets for defending the Town with so much Vigour. (220)

Byrd's parody of the imperial production of knowledge resembles here that of his Maryland contemporary Ebenezer Cook, who, in his mock epic *The Sot-Weed Factor*, masquerades as an English traveler who is appalled by the depravities of the American colonials but who is immediately recognized by the colonial audience as a travel liar. Into the mock-epic poem are inserted footnotes that are ostensibly intended to close the hermeneutic gap between the experienced traveler and his English stay-at-home audience, producing a layered, though inverted, hierarchy of authorship in the scientific production of knowledge about America that includes, in ascending order, the quoted voices of the American degenerate Creoles, the (mock-)epic narrative of the English traveler, the English editor/collector annotating his narrative, and finally the parodic voice of the colonial author. Thus, the traveler-character relates how

> Wearied, yet pleas'd, we did escape
> Such ills, we anchor'd at the Cape
> But weighing soon, we plough'd the Bay,
> To Cove it in Piscato-way,
> Intending there to open Store,
> I put myself and Goods a-shore:
> Where soon repair'd a numerous Crew,
> In Shirts and Drawers of Scotch-cloth Blue.
> With neither Stockings, Hat, nor Shooe.
> These SOTWEED Planters Crowd the Shoar,
> In Hue as tawny as a Moor.[55]

The fictional annotator explains in a footnote, which is an integral part of Cook's meta-fictional satire, that "By the Cape, is meant the Capes of Virginia, the first Land on the Coast of Virginia and Maryland"; but the author also evokes here the Cape of Good Hope and the "Africanist" discourse of contemporary scientific accounts about the Hottentots ("tawny as the Moor"). The author, Cook, finally parodies not only the annotator/collector but also exposes the epic travel-character as a liar when he shows him, in a famous scene, as standing upright in his canoe:

> I boldly put myself afloat:
> Standing Erect with legs stretch'd wide,
> We paddl'd to the other side:
> Where being Landed safe by hap,
> As Sol fell into Thetis Lap.[56]

As Leo Lemay has first pointed out in his pioneering study of early Maryland literature, a colonial reader would have immediately recognized the impossibility of standing "erect" in a canoe without capsizing. Thus, the English traveler–narrator is exposed by the author as a liar.[57] Yet, while the English travel-character is the butt of the joke, most of his observations about the "degeneracy" of colonial society would have struck a chord of recognition with the elite Creole reader, who not only resented English arrogance but also despised American difference. Not unlike in twentieth-century African American stand-up comedy, in Cook's *The Sot-Weed Factor* and Byrd's *Histories*, the "difference" of the author's marginal community is the object of his satire while the perspective from which colonial difference appears as inferior is the object of his parody.

Thus, the "second" conquest of Virginia – like the first and all conquests – was then an ambivalent one. But while the written documents of the First Conquest only rarely evidence ambivalence with regard to the European claim to knowledge and title to Indian land, the documents of the Second Conquest, as far as they were produced by European colonials themselves, frequently do. The reason for this is, as I have aimed to show, that colonials such as Byrd, who were English gentlemen as well as American Creoles in a circum-Atlantic empire, inhabited an ambivalent socio-political position in this utopian enterprise of Second Conquest, their attempts at Natural History frequently turning into hybrid meta-historical satires of the imperial production of knowledge and division of intellectual labor in Baconian and, especially, Newtonian Natural Philosophy. Byrd's meta-historical satire may thus be seen as the product of two conflicting ways of knowing space on the colonial "boundary." Homi Bhabha, influenced by Martin Heidegger's essay "Building, Dwelling, Thinking," has theorized this cultural "location" on the colonial boundary not as an absolute limit, as a dividing line, but rather as "the place from which something begins its presencing."[58] A "boundary," in Heideggerian terms, thus denotes a space restructured through "building," a "bridge," as it were, that transforms the natural terrain along the divided banks of a river into the locus of new cultural formation. It exists only through man's relation to space; it "inheres in dwelling" (as Heidegger had put it).[59] Similarly, in "Natural Histories" written by colonial Creoles such as Byrd, two opposing ways of knowing space frequently stand in playful dialogue with each other: one in terms of Newtonian dynamics, increasingly privileged by eighteenth-century scientific rationalism; and another as a "location" on the boundary, as experienced and transformed by colonial Creoles "building" and "dwelling" on the colonial frontier.

CHAPTER 7

Dismembering the empire: Alonso Carrió de la Vandera and J. Hector St. John de Crèvecoeur

When Hermes took the post of messenger of the gods, he promised Zeus not to lie. He did not promise to tell the whole truth. Zeus understood. The ethnographer has not.

(Vincent Crapanzano)

If I die a martar to Botany Gods will be done

(John Bartram)

...but all colonies inherit their empire's sins.

(Derek Walcott, *Omeros*)[1]

In 1783, the English index maker of the British Museum, Samuel Ayscough, published a polemical pamphlet entitled *Remarks on the Letters from an American farmer; or a detection of the errors of Mr. J. Hector St. John; pointing out the pernicious tendency of these letters to Great Britain*. In this tract, he debunked a book that had been published in London a year before by a "J. Hector St. John" and which was rapidly becoming popular throughout the Atlantic world. The book, entitled *Letters from an American Farmer*, was "a fraud, artfully disguised," Ayscough charged, and "sets history at defiance" by apparently having relied on "disquisition rather than experience and fact." Worse, its author was not at all "American born, as he pretends"; he "never was a farmer there" but rather a "Frenchman, born in Normandy." His "style is by no means that of a simple cultivator of the earth," and parts of the book were plagiarized from "old womens stories" with some added "scraps of Latin, which though they shew no depth of erudition, yet they evince that the author has assumed a character which he ill supports...A simple cultivator of the earth, ought to have told a plain tale, without the brilliancy of imagination, or the ornament of figures." In short, *Letters from an American Farmer* represented "a new species of forgery, imported from the continent of America," a "Transatlantic imposition" which had once more disturbed the "peace of the literary world" to the effect of "produc[ing] a total dismemberment from the British empire."[2]

What was so disturbing to Ayscough, we may wonder, about a simple literary hoax? Building on Jürgen Habermas' work on the "structural transformation of the public sphere" in eighteenth-century Europe, Grantland Rice has argued that in its blurring of the "conventional distinctions" that rendered intelligible "the line between fact and fiction," *Letters from an American Farmer* threatened to effect a "transformation of authorship" that subverted the vesting of a text's authority in the social standing of its author, thus signaling the bourgeois egalitarianism of an emergent Republican print ideology.[3] Ayscough's anxiety about the "dismembering" effects of Crèvecoeur's text upon the body of the "British empire," however, suggests that this transformation of authorship occurring during the late eighteenth century was precipitated not only by a historical dialectic of changing sociopolitical relations in Europe but also by a geographic dialectic changing the geo-political nature of modern empires. If this period would finally see the collapse of the old socio-political arrangement between the monarchy, the aristocracy, and the middling classes in Europe, it was due in part to the erosion of the economic and geo-political foundation that had facilitated this arrangement in the first place – the mercantilist economies of the old settler empires of Spain, France, and England in the Americas.

This geo-political change held important implications also for the ways in which knowledge was produced and organized in Western culture. Thus, the cultural authority of the genteel European "Man of Science" – sitting in his armchair in the detached seclusion of his study, clad in a banian, and surrounded by his books – was slowly yielding to that of the modern "scientist" of the nineteenth-century imperialist nation states, who rejected "Nature" as a unifying and self-contained paradigm explaining the diversity of all empirical phenomena, who wanted to see *beneath* the surface of the phenomenological world, and who, most of all, wanted to *go there and see* for him/herself.[4] The results were a collapse of the scientific division of intellectual labor between Euro-American Creoles and Europeans, a general epistemological crisis in what has been called the "lost paradigm" of Natural History in the late eighteenth century,[5] and the rise of a new scientific paradigm that increasingly privileged rationalizations of colonial difference in terms of racial essentialism.[6]

We are alerted to the geo-political dialectic transforming the organization of Western knowledge in the late eighteenth century if we reflect upon the origins of the more recent "dilemma" in the human sciences in the decolonization of the so-called "Third World" during the twentieth century. Ayscough's outrage curiously anticipates that of many twentieth-century professional anthropologists when former colonial "friends" turned upon the authority of modern ethnography and exposed the imperialist poetics and politics of its epistemological foundations.[7] The "ill supported" fiction of authenticity in *Letters from an American Farmer* dismembered the imperial body of knowledge in the old settler empires by exposing the utopian ideologies of detachment and objectivity upon which its mercantilist epistemic economy had rested. It thus participated in a larger "breakup" of the scientific authority of the eighteenth-century aristocratic natural historian not unlike that occurring during the twentieth century with respect to the scientific authority of the cultural anthropologist in the geo-political context of the de-colonization of the "Third World."[8]

In this last chapter, I want to compare how two late eighteenth-century American texts participated in this breakup of Natural History and in the rise of the modern sciences during the nineteenth century. In his troublesome tendencies toward the "dismemberment" of the cultural authority of the eighteenth-century Man of Science, J. Hector St. John de Crèvecoeur resembles not only the debunkers of ethnographic authority during the late twentieth century but also one of his eighteenth-century contemporaries on the southern part of the Western hemisphere whose book has come to be regarded as one of the major texts of early Spanish America: Alonso Carrió de la Vandera, author of *El lazarillo de ciegos caminantes* (A guide for inexperienced travelers) (Lima, 1776). Both Crèvecoeur and Carrió assumed in their texts a narrative mask intended to lend their texts the "authenticity" that would afford them entry into the Lettered City of Enlightenment historiography – Farmer James in *Letters* and the mestizo "guide" Concolorcorvo in *Lazarillo*. Having constructed this narrative mask, however, both (post-)colonial authors deconstruct the fiction of authenticity and break through the various levels of scientific authorship to the effect of exposing the imperialist geo-politics of Natural History and its institutionalized geographic division of intellectual labor.

EMPIRE AND INSURGENCY

Michel Guillaume Jean de Crèvecoeur (1731–1813) was born near Caen and educated in France. He had come to America as a soldier in the French army and served during the Seven Years' War under the Marquis de Montcalm against the British army and the British American colonial militia. After the war had been lost by the French, in 1765, he became a British subject, changed his name to J. Hector St. John de Crèvecoeur, settled on a farm in Orange County, New York, in 1769, and married the daughter of a well-to-do colonial family. The sketches that were later revised and published as

Letters from an American Farmer under the pseudonyms "Hector St. John" (the alleged editor of the letters) and "James" (the alleged author) probably originate from this period in Crèvecoeur's life as a farmer in New York.[9] However, *Letters* was not published until Crèvecoeur's temporary return to Europe and after a period of severe personal distress at seeing his family and farm torn apart by Revolutionary factionalism. Moreover, this publication only included a small and careful selection from the entire body of sketches he had written, the remainder of which appeared only during the twentieth century in two separate stages.[10] After the publication of *Letters from an American Farmer* in 1782, Crèvecoeur was appointed French consul to the United States, lived in New York City from 1783 to 1790, and died in France in 1813.

Although the exact date of Alonso Carrió de la Vandera's birth in Spain is unknown, he states that he arrived in Lima in 1746 at age thirty, which would put his date of birth in 1716. He came to America as a government official in approximately 1736, spent ten years in Mexico, and then moved to South America to settle down in Lima, marrying Petronila Matute y Melgarejo, the daughter of a socially prominent Creole family. In Peru, he held government offices such as Indian agent, supervisor of mines, and sub-delegate of estates, helped defend the coast against Pirates, and, in 1767, accompanied a number of Jesuits to Europe, after their general expulsion from the Americas had been decreed earlier that year.[11] The journey during which he took the notes that would later be revised and published as *Lazarillo* was undertaken in the service of one of the reform projects initiated by the Bourbons, who had come to the Spanish throne in 1700: the inspection of the royal postal system in South America for the purpose of improving the intra-imperial networks of communication. Carrió's journey thus began as a classic example of the absolutist "pilgrimage" in both of Benedict Anderson's senses: a "lateral" or centripetal movement through space from the province of La Plata to the vice-regal metropolis of Lima – the opposite direction from the centrifugal course of the First Conquest of South America during the sixteenth century – and a "vertical" movement on the ladder of Spanish absolutist officialdom.[12] After having spent nearly a year in the field, however, Carrió returned only to find that postal administrators had already made, without ever seeing his report, some perfunctory changes which satisfied the imperial officials who had recently arrived, but generally left things as they were. The published version of *Lazarillo* is Carrió's disenchanted response to learning that his efforts had been in vain and that they would not be rewarded with the hoped-for advancement of his career as an imperial functionary, and to suddenly finding himself outside the walls of the Lettered City of Spanish officialdom.¹³ The book went to press in Lima in 1776 and was published the following year under the authorial pseudonym of "Concolorcorvo" ("with the color of a raven"), allegedly the name of a mestizo native of the city of Cuzco. The title page deceptively misidentified the place and date of publication as "Gijón" (in Spain), 1773, and the press as "imprenta de la rovada" ("the press of her who was robbed") (see Illustration 7.1).

Thus, in both instances we have an immigrant author who came to the Americas in the service of an imperial crown in the dual historical context of inter-imperial rivalry and mounting intra-imperial conflict. In both cases, the authors spent a considerable time living in the New World, apparently reaping the benefits of the imperial order, but became, for various reasons, disenchanted with the compact of imperial pilgrimage. Each of our authors thus represents a New World social type that has been called the "new Creoles" – Europeans who "migrated to the New World and married into traditional Creole society."¹⁴ In both cases, these "new Creoles" began the composition of their texts in the service of the imperial production of knowledge before a period of personal and political crisis but published them only thereafter in the name of thinly disguised fictional authors – with "Farmer James" being the alleged author of *Letters* and the mestizo Concolorcorvo being the alleged author of *Lazarillo*.

Letters from an American Farmer was published in 1782, at the end of the Revolutionary War, which was, as many historians today agree, only the culmination of a much wider conflict that had been crystallized by the Seven Years' War (1756–63) but was latent as far back as the seventeenth century.¹⁵ On the one hand, the Seven Years' War had reaffirmed the patrimonial relationship between England and her colonies, with the former providing imperial protection by sending a standing army against an outside enemy and the latter providing loyalty and militia service to the Crown. However, when imperial reformers after the war attempted to capitalize on this situation by translating the wartime balance of power into an economic policy that threatened permanently to increase the dependency of the colonies at a time of trans-atlantic economic slump, they met with fierce colonial resistance. It became ever more apparent, writes Stephen Saunders Webb, "that the anti-imperial forces of acquisitive capitalism, individual liberty, provincial autonomy, and Anglo-American oligarchy had won lasting social and political influence for the local elites who were the eventual authors of the American Revolution."¹⁶ The crisis that ensued over the new laws passed by Parliament after the Seven Years' War, such as the Stamp Act of 1765, signaled an increasing colonial skepticism about the

✠

EL LAZARILLO
DE CIEGOS CAMINANTES

desde Buenos-Ayres, hafta Lima
con fus Itinerarios fegun la mas pun-
tual obfervacion, con algunas noticias utiles á los Nuevos Comercian-
tes que tratan en Mulas; y otras
Hiftoricas.

SACADO DE LAS MEMORIAS QUE
hizo Don Alonfo Carrió de la Vandera en
efte dilatado Viage, y Comifion que tubo
por la Corte para el arreglo de Cor-
reos, y Eftafetas, Situacion, y
ajufte de Poftas, desde
Montevideo.

POR
*DON CALIXTO BUSTAMANTE CARLOS
Inca*, *alias* CONCOLORCORVO *Natural
del Cuzco, que acompañò al referido Comifio-
nado en dicho Viage, y efcribiò fus Extractos.*

CON LICENCIA.
En Gijon, en la Imprenta de la Rovada. Año
de 1773.

7.1 Frontispiece of Alonso Carrió de la Vandera's *El lazarillo de ciegos caminantes*
(Lima, 1776).

mutuality of the "common good" and economic benefits derived from the mercantilist economic order.[17] On the other hand, this disagreement over economic policy quickly escalated to a higher, political plane, revealing, as Jack Greene has written, a "deep rift... never to be bridged within the structure of the empire," a rift, reaching back to the Glorious Revolution and beyond, with regard to the very constitutional role that colonies play in the "balance of authority between the center and the periphery" in the administration of empire. Whereas most people in the metropolis thought the empire a unitary body with sovereignty vested in Parliament, most people in the colonies thought the empire to be "'predominantly federal in practice,' with the authority of the center limited by the authority it had delegated to the peripheries."[18]

Although, in Spanish America, the wars for independence did not erupt until several decades after the publication of *Lazarillo*, the political origins of the military struggle for independence reach back at least to the Bourbons' "Second Conquest" at the beginning of the eighteenth century.[19] Having succeeded to the throne of a second-rank power in decline able to compete only with Prussia and Austria, the Bourbon dynasty under Charles III re-acted to the alarming state of the Spanish empire with the conservatively enlightened reform measures in the Americas that aimed at the fortifi-cation of Spain's remaining colonial possessions against foreign intrusion and at strengthening Spain's position in Europe by maximizing its profits from colonial trade through a reform of its mercantile economy. On the one hand, the Crown therefore attempted to improve enforcement of the mercantilist policies that the Habsburgs had implemented but gradually compromised over. They reinstated, for example, the "general visitation" (an imperial inspection seeing to the execution of imperial law) though with the difference of cautioning against the excessive power that the church had exercised earlier in the Habsburg state. Unlike their Habsburg predeces-sors, who had tried to accommodate the Creole elites to some degree, the Bourbons went about colonial administration not through compromise but rather by categorically excluding colonials from any imperial office – a policy that one historian has characterized as a "difference between abso-lutism and despotism."[20] On the other hand, the Bourbons' advisers such as Jerónimo de Ustariz also looked abroad for practical guidance – to the English Navigation Laws, the French tariffs of 1664–7, and especially to the economic theories of Jean-Baptiste Colbert, French comptroller gen-eral of finance under Louis XIV. The effect was "a radical reorganization of the imperial commercial system in the interest of tapping the potential of Spain's American possessions as suppliers of raw materials to the mother

country and consumers of Spanish manufactures."[21] Internal colonial economic development and diversification, which had inevitably happened by
the end of the seventeenth century, was hereby increasingly eyed as incom-
patible with the metropolitan demand for American minerals and colonial
markets for its consumer goods. "The security of the Americas must be
measured by the extent of their dependence on the metropolis," the Bourbon monarch Charles III concluded in the 1760s, "and this dependence
is founded on their need of consumer goods. The day they can supply
all their needs themselves, their dependence will be voluntary."[22] The reform programs implemented by the Bourbons included the abolition of
the fleet system, the establishment of the new vice-royalty of La Plata in
1776 (which comprised what today is Argentina, Uruguay, Paraguay, and
Bolivia), the expulsion of the Jesuits in 1767 (many of whom had become
eloquent spokesmen for Creole political interests), the enlistment of colonial militias under the direct command of royal officers, and the levying of
new excise duties. In the La Plata region especially, the Bourbon crown's
efforts at centralizing the empire "had a disruptive effect on existing Spanish institutions and tended to break the unity of colonial government at a
critical period."[23] The result of this "new style of government" was a series
of riots and uprisings throughout Spanish America which the "New State"
took harsh measures to suppress and which continued to mount until the
Revolutionary ruptures during the early nineteenth century.[24]

The perhaps greatest Creole intellectual of colonial Peru, the limeño
Pedro de Peralta Barnuevo (1663–1743), scathingly satirized the state of the
Spanish empire and its pretense to authority over the American colonies
in a fictional dialogue between Charon, the mythic boatsman of souls on
their way to Elysium, and Menippus, Greek satirist recently arrived at the
River Lethe with news from Peru. "I clearly saw the entire world through
the telescope," the latter reports to a Charon eager for news:

But it was a sad sight for me to recognize the devastation of the nations of Europe,
the most notable spot on earth . . . I saw the great monarchy of Spain reduced to the
narrowness of its peninsula. In the Indies, the only colony it has left, I saw Peru.
It was full of leeches stuck to its shores, grabbing hold of its ports; after a while,
they would separate, swollen with the blood they had gently sucked from them.
The operation was performed every year by the barbers of Saint-Malo, Brest, and
Marseilles, who kept the vermin in the water. They appeared to be a relief but have
been a ravage because of the copious drain.[25]

Thus, the "outburst of defiance" characterizing late eighteenth-century
colonial attitudes toward the imperial metropole throughout the Americas

must be seen, as Lester Langley has written, in the historical context of the "hemispheric imperial debate" that had erupted in the aftermath of inter-imperial warfare and in the course of which the metropole attempted to "alter or, at least, redefine the political and economic role of colonies in the national agenda, a reassessment that occurred in an era of accelerating social and economic reform."[26] It is in the context of this wider hemispheric debate about empire, I would suggest, that both *Letters from an American Farmer* and *El Lazarillo de ciegos caminantes* must be read. While neither Carrió nor Crèvecoeur was a nationalist patriot in favor of American political independence – Carrió did not live to see (and probably could not imagine) colonial independence, and Crèvecoeur was even vocally opposed to the secession of the thirteen colonies when it did occur during his lifetime – both texts engage in a critique of the unequal status of imperial citizens in America and Europe, and particularly of the effacement of the colonial subject in the Enlightenment production of knowledge.

"LIKE A FISH BETWEEN TWO WATERS": THE QUESTION OF GENRE

Formally, *Letters from an American Farmer* consists of a collection of twelve letters supposedly written by a simple colonial American farmer named James to his English acquaintance, the "great European man" Mr. F. B., an apparently aristocratic Man of Science who had met the farmer during his earlier travels in America and who has now assigned James to provide first-hand information about his home-land. The subject matters of James' twelve letters range from descriptions of the natural environment, to colonial life and character in the country and cities such as Nantucket and Charleston, to a visit to the farm of a colonial botanist, "John Bertram" (a reference to the historical botanist John Bartram). The final letter deals with the effects of the American Revolution on the American farmer, who resolves to remove from colonial society, politics, and civilization altogether and to live with the Indians – even though the real author, Crèvecoeur, moves in the opposite direction, becoming a prominent figure in the political world of the post-Revolutionary nation states as French consul to the United States.

At first sight, *El lazarillo de ciegos caminantes* appears to be an itinerary of two men's journey from Buenos Aires to Lima – a *gachupín* (European Spanish) inspector of the colonial postal system named "don Alonso" and his mestizo "guide" named Calixto Bustamente Carlos Inca or "Concolorcorvo," who is supposedly also the author of the itinerary. The text consists of travel anecdotes, observations on the postal system, descriptions of colonial life in various South American cities such as Buenos Aires, Montevideo, and Tucumán, as well as on the rural pampas; statistical tables, information on geography and commerce, as well as what seem to be long digressions on literature and history, often presented in the form of dialogues in conversations taking place between Concolorcorvo and don Alonso. Although both characters are loosely based on historical figures, it is important to separate them from the literary characters in the text. Concolorcorvo is based on a historical person of racially mixed background who actually accompanied Carrió during his inspection tour of the postal system, although the duration of their common voyage does not correspond with that in the narrative.[27] The inspector don Alonso matches in some ways the biographical profile of Carrió; but the narrative preserves a crucial distance between the author and the literary figure he creates. Indeed, as J. G. Johnson has noted, the latter is in some ways a satirical portrait of himself in his former role as an agent of Spanish imperial officialdom.[28]

A persistent problem in the critical reception of these narratives has been how to categorize them generically. Because of the separation of the narrator from the author and the attribution of authorship to an "American" character, each text has often been read as an American "novel in embryo."[29] However, in both texts, this authorship is only a thinly disguised fiction, which is consistently and, it seems, deliberately exposed as such by the authors.[30] Thus, in the course of the twelve "letters," Crèvecoeur's James gradually transforms from the simple American "cultivator of the earth" of the early letters into the narrative voice characterized by Ayscough as using "brilliancy of imagination" and "ornament of figures." While some modern critics, not unlike Ayscough, have considered this to be an aesthetic flaw that shows that Crèvecoeur "loses control of the initial contrast between the farmer and his learned friend,"[31] *Letters from an American Farmer* has nevertheless become a classic in American literary studies for apparently giving an early expression to an emerging American national identity as a cultural "melting pot," especially in the much-anthologized third letter entitled "What is an American?" which celebrates the pastoral, multicultural, and secular virtues of colonial American life.

Carrió de la Vandera was apparently more artful in disguising the fiction of authorship than Crèvecoeur – if we may take the number of prominent critics that have fallen into his literary trap as an indication. While critics have generally pointed to the all-too-obvious picaresque tradition of *Lazarillo de Tormes*, all through the nineteenth century, and even into the early twentieth, critics as eminent as Ricardo Palma, in his famous

Tradiciones peruanas (1923), have mistaken Concolorcorvo's mestizo voice in *Lazarillo* for a truly authentic specimen of what they saw as the essentially indigenous spirit of Peru's national identity, latent already during colonial times. While readers were occasionally disturbed by the fact that the fiction of Concolorcorvo's mestizo authorship is frequently disrupted in the text, revealing another voice beneath the mestizo's words, only since 1960 has Carrió's authorship been firmly established, due to the incontrovertible evidence presented by the eminent French Hispanist Marcel Bataillon.[32] While some critics have dismissed this imperfect fiction of authorship in the text as the result of Carrió's "often carelessly applied paintjob," which supposedly illustrated the author's lack of "artistic refinement,"[33] more sympathetic readers have shown it to be an intricate narrative technique, effecting an ambivalent interplay of voices characteristic of Creole writing in early Spanish America.[34]

Thus, in both cases recent criticism has moved away from anachronistic Formalist assumptions about "the literary" and seen these texts in the tradition of other, non-belletristic discursive practices. Pamela Regis, for example, has shown that the "framework for Crèvecoeur's representation of America" is that of the Enlightenment rhetoric of Natural History in the tradition of Linnaeus and Raynal.[35] Similarly, Emilio Carilla and Evaristo Penha have each observed that the title of *Lazarillo* is reminiscent not only of the picaresque tradition of *Lazarillo de Tormes* but also of an eighteenth-century Natural History written by the limeño viceregal cosmographer Cosme Bueno entitled *Lazarillo de ciegos*, whose scientific rhetoric Carrió "imitated," they argue.[36] Yet, the fiction of authorship in both texts suggests that our colonial authors imitated this rhetoric of Natural History not in order to emulate but rather to parody the scientific authority of the natural historian. In order to appreciate the peculiar geocultural location of these two colonial authors within eighteenth-century metropolitan discursive practices, "literary" as well as "scientific," it is helpful to recall here François Charlevoix's proposal in 1744 that an author may write one of "two kinds of history." First, "a serious, dignified, factual kind" when dealing with the ancient civilizations of the European homeland; and second, a "lighter, more entertaining kind" when treating the remote and new countries.[37] Both colonial authors – treating "remote" countries that were "home" to them – found themselves thus on the in-between of this generic dichotomy. Crèvecoeur has James compare himself as an author to the European historians but humbly assume a subordinate position when comparing them to "eagles [which] soar high." A colonial author like himself, by contrast, is like "a feebler bird, [who] cheerfully content[s] [him]self with skipping from bush to bush and living on insignificant insects."[38] The North American Farmer James resembles here the South American mestizo Concolorcorvo, who refers to the historian as "el Plomo" ("Mr. Lead") on the one hand and to the traveler as "el Corcho" ("Mr. Cork") on the other. His own position, by contrast, is in this regard akin to a "peje entre dos aguas" ("fish between two waters"), neither "tan pesado" ("as ponderous") as the historian nor "tan liviano" ("of as little weight") as the traveler.[39]

The meta-historical irony apparent in both texts suggests that Natural History and prose fiction are not so much their generic *medium* as they are their *subject matter*. More specifically, as I want to show, both texts are a parody of the Enlightenment *methods of production* in the making of Natural History – "epistolary commerce" in the case of *Letters* and "polite conversation" in the case of *Lazarillo*.[40] Each text consists of a meta-fictional dialogue between two representative types in the geographic hierarchy of Baconian science governing the production of knowledge about empire: the American "Farmer" James and the Baconian natural historian, appropriately named "Mr. F. B.," in *Letters*; and the Native "guide" Concolorcorvo and the traveling imperial "inspector" don Alonso in *Lazarillo*. In both cases, formal authorship is attributed to the colonial American character, who appears to speak in the "primitive eloquence" of a Baconian "miner" (farmer; Native Indian), while the educated metropolitan type appears as a character that is distinct from the narrative persona. What is conspicuously absent from the surface of both texts is the voice of the (post-)colonial American intelligentsia living in America and educated in or by the European metropolis. It is precisely the group to which both authors belonged and which represents, as Enrique Pupo-Walker has pointed out, the voice upon which a "new context of values" would be founded in the newly/future independent American nation states.[41]

CRÈVECOEUR AND THE ECONOMY OF EPISTOLARY COMMERCE

The creation of the narrative mask of self-effacement assumed by the fictional American type vis-à-vis the European historian begins in *Letters* already with the Dedication to the abbé Raynal, who is reverently addressed as an "F. R." (Fellow of the Royal Society of London) and who had "viewed these provinces," J. Hector St. John writes in the Dedication, "in their true light as the cradle of future nations and the refuge of distressed Europeans" (37). While readers have noted that, in the later parts of *Letters*, Crèvecoeur overtly debunks the utopian portrayal of British America by the French *philosophe*,[42] few have questioned the "sincerity of the motives which urge

[Crèvecoeur]" to profess his love and respect for the "man whose writings I so much admire" (37). Crèvecoeur's *Letters* are not "the purest tribute of reverence and affection" to the French historian, as J. Hector St. John ostensibly professes here. In reading *Letters*, we must often heed the advice of James' wife about Mr. F. B.'s motives in requesting his epistolary "friendship": "thee must read this letter over again," she says, "paragraph by paragraph, and warily observe whether thee canst perceive some words of jesting, something that has more than one meaning" (41).

Readers have long wondered about Mr. F. B.'s "rather implausible attitude" in needing James as his informant on things American when, obviously, he had traveled to America himself.[43] Their confusion here resembles the bewilderment of James himself over the curious fact "that in the course of your [past] American travels you should not have found out persons more enlightened and better educated than I am" (38). Of course, the Baconian natural historian Mr. F. B. never desired to find an "educated" man while traveling through America. It was precisely James' lack of refinement that made him useful to Mr. F. B. as an observer with (in the words of James' minister) a "mind . . . we called at Yale college a *tabula rasa*, where spontaneous and strong impressions are delineated with facility" (46). The minister dispels the farmer's self-consciousness as a worthy correspondent of the "great European man" by reminding him that the rudimentary appearance of his letters, which will seem "like one of our wild American plants," will be "no detriment to them, take my word for it." The minister, educated at Yale and presumably familiar with the poetics of Enlightenment Natural History, knows that the refined Mr. F. B. could not simply write down his own observations, made during his stay in America, and subsequently call them a "Natural History." Rather, as the Enlightened minister would have known, the scientific authority of the natural historian rested precisely on his "detachment" in following a strict grid of Bacon's "rules" that had divided the "two professions" in the making of Natural History into the producer of Nature's "effects" through first-hand observation on the one hand and the producer of Nature's "causes" through scientific conjecture on the other. As I have aimed to show in Chapter 1, the best producer of effects was an individual whose observation was unmediated by the corruptive influences of European book learning, whose sensory perception would represent an authentic impression of the "volumes of the world," not of the "volumes of man." Thus, when "J. Hector St. John" addresses the abbé Raynal, in the guise of a "humble American planter, a simple cultivator of the earth," he ostensibly assumes the role that the Baconian poetics of history have carved out for him: he would be the miner, not the speculator.

Farmer James learns his lesson in the Enlightenment poetics of history swiftly and immediately fashions himself in the role that the metropolitan politics of authorship in Enlightenment historiography have assigned to him: he vows that he will record only "the spontaneous impressions which each subject may inspire" (49). He has neither the capacity nor the ambition to become a historian, who would inquire into the causes of things, but confines himself to his role as the American informant producing Nature's effects: he is the natural historian's eye, "so habituated to draw all my food and pleasure from the surface of the earth which I till that I cannot, nor indeed am I able to, quit it" (90). In compliance with his role as a transparent observer, he will report "nothing... but what lies within the reach of my experience and knowledge" (51).

The value of James' testimony for Mr. F. B. thus derives in part from its "authenticity" as oral speech. "What he requires of you is but simple," the minister instructs James, "what we speak out among ourselves we call conversation, and a letter is only conversation put down in black and white" (44). The fiction of James' early letters as transcribed oral language is intensified by his short sentences, broken up by semi-colons, and his paratactic style, which was, as Barbara Stafford has noted, the "preferred mode for achieving an impression of directness... of description or 'demonstration'" in the eighteenth-century "factual travel narrative," which was based on the "ideal of linguistic or representational transparency and primitive terseness."[44] James' voice, unlike the voices of "several histories" Mr. F. B. may have "read," has retained its direct relationship to "things."

The Creole Farmer James, then, appropriates not the voice of the Enlightened "philosophical" traveler but the "primitive eloquence" of Montaigne's nobly Savage Cannibals. It is therefore not entirely accurate that Crèvecoeur (the author) "wanted to be an *intellectual* savage," as D. H. Lawrence once famously argued.[45] Rather, Crèvecoeur used the narrative persona of the uneducated farmer as "an innocent mouthpiece," as Albert Stone has written, which sets up the "ironic interplay between naive actor and knowing narrator that... is characteristic of many American novels and autobiographies."[46] Crèvecoeur exploits the possibilities of this narrative mask in order to create a space for himself in the historiographic production of America and, ultimately, as Mary Rucker has noted, to critique Enlightenment theories of man, Nature, and America from the vantage point of colonial British American subjectivity. It is the primitive eloquence of the noble Savage, which had fascinated European utopists about the New World – from Peter Martir to Montaigne and to Crèvecoeur's contemporary Rousseau – that James enlists also in his famous third letter, "What is an American?," where he appears in his Cannibalesque role as social critic of Europe by invoking the customary contrast between Europe's corruption and a utopian American Golden Age.[47]

However, as early as the Dedication to Raynal, J. Hector St. John already undermines the fiction of his self-effacing humility – and, thus, the foundation of the Baconian division of labor – in his reflection on the "secret communion" of all men espoused by Enlightenment doctrine and the "mental affinity connecting them by a similitude of sentiments": "Why," he asks, "though an American, should not I be permitted to share in that extensive intellectual consanguinity? Yes, I do," he asserts, because, despite the fact that he "possesses neither titles nor places," nor "rose above the humble rank of a farmer," he is still "a man" (38). The letters following the Dedication to Raynal dramatize Crèvecoeur's rebellion against his subordinate position as a colonial in his relation to European Men of Science such as Raynal. In the course of *Letters*, he recreates a discursive space for his Euro-American colonial subjectivity which had been effaced by eighteenth-century metropolitan poetics of Natural History.

Initially, the disruption of the fiction of authorship is primarily effected by an ironic distance between the simple James and the author, audible not only in the Menippean satirical dialogue between the Farmer and the minister but also in the "double meaning" of words that James' wife cautions against. Crèvecoeur's satire of the "scientific" maxim that climate determines the development of human faculties rings, for example, behind the exclamation of James' wife: "What!...James, would'st thee pretend to send epistles to a great European man who hath lived abundance of time in that big house called Cambridge, where, they say, that worldly learning is so abundant that people get it only by breathing the air of the place?" (38). Indeed, it often seems that James is either parroting what he has been told by the book-learned minister, or that the transcription of his voice was manipulated by an editor, perhaps the author of the "Advertisements to the First Edition, 1782," who claims that the letters were "the actual result of a private correspondence" and contain "authentic information" about America recorded by an "eye-witness" (35–6).[48] When James, for example, professes his complete ignorance of scientific rules in his vow that the "only line I am able to follow [is] the line which Nature has herself traced for me" (49), his very use of the idioms of Baconian poetics contradicts his professed ignorance of their "scientific rules." The claim of James' authenticity is, then, as Robert Lawson-Peebles has observed, a "complex fiction" of authorship, which "manipulates personae and carefully arranges the individual letters."[49] However, this fiction, unlike supposedly more "refined" metropolitan prose fictions, is deliberately "imperfect" (because apparent as such) from the very beginning. While employing the authentic voice of the simple American farmer on the one hand, Crèvecoeur parodies the metropolitan historian's quest for the authentic transparent American voice when he undermines the reliability of his narrator James. Thus, when later, in Letter XII, James feels compelled to enumerate the reasons why exactly he "prefer[s] that [Indian] life for which we entertain such dreadful opinions," he confesses, after being able to list only two, that "I have forgot" the many other reasons for arguing as he does (214). This suggests that his voice, too, is a text and that the authentic American voice does not exist except in the metropolitan historian's utopian imagination.

In the course of the twelve letters selected for publication, Farmer James breaks through the various levels of historiographic authorship involved in the writing of Natural History, thus deliberately transgressing against the division of labor that constructs its scientific authority.[50] Gradually, James hereby breaks out of his role as F. B.'s informant in the early letters and assumes that of the biographer in his narrative about the immigrant Andrew. As he leaves his provincial domain, he feels the need to justify his transgression and reaffirms his commitment to humility and self-effacement before the authority of the historian:

Let historians give the detail of our charters, the succession of our several governors and of their administrations, of our political struggles, and of the foundations of our towns; let annalists amuse themselves with collecting anecdotes of the establishment of our modern provinces . . . All I wish to delineate is the progressive steps of a poor man, advancing from indigence to ease, from oppression to freedom, from obscurity and contumely to some degree of consequence. (90)

However, all the biographies he relates are allegories of his own auto-biography as an author in the becoming. Thus, by Letter XI, in the account of "Mr. John Bertram," he no longer appears in the role of the transcriber of "conversation put down in black and white"; but rather has promoted himself to the collector of eyewitness testimony, for the letter is written, the reader learns, by a self-effacing "Russian gentleman" identified by the farmer only as "Mr. Iw – n Al – z" (187). The "John Bertram" portrayed in this letter represents a self-sufficient "Man of Science," a model for Crèvecoeur himself in his project to collapse the Baconian division of labor. Thus, the Russian traveler, upon arriving at Bertram's farm, finds the colonial scientist returning from his manual work in the field before sitting down at his desk to write, classify, and theorize.

As James emancipates himself as an author in the poetics of eighteenth-century historical discourse, all references to the epistolary partner, Mr. F. B., vanish from the text. On the plane of the text's meta-historical commentary, then, the plot of *Letters* is the story of the gradual displacement of Mr. F. B. and of "James" becoming the "Hector St. John" who displaces the abbé Raynal in the Dedication. While, in Letter IV, "Description of the Island of Nantucket," James still establishes his authority as an eyewitness observer (106–7), this seeing "I" recedes into the background in the subsequent letters as he gradually becomes, as Pamela Regis has illustrated, the natural historian of Nantucket.[51] Thus, the "speculating" historian–philosopher takes over, who inquires into the causes of his observed effects and praises the superior experiential value of his Nantucketeer observers:

They have all, from the highest to the lowest, a singular *keenness of judgement, unassisted by any academical light*; they all possess a large share of *good sense*, improved upon the *experience* of their father; and this is the surest and best guide to lead us through the path of life, because it approaches *nearest* to the *infallibility* of *instinct* ... university knowledge would ... pervert their plain judgement, it would lead them out of that useful path which is so well adapted to their situation. (142–3; my emphasis)

Thus, the American observer James begins to speculate. He openly debunks the determinist theories of a William Robertson, a Comte de Buffon, a Cornelius de Pauw, and a Raynal, all of whom had claimed that the American natural environment and climate are averse to the development of culture. "Famine, disease, elementary convulsions, human feuds, dissensions, etc.," James declares, "are the produce of every climate." While European natural historians had claimed that the American Indians' reproductive organs were smaller than those of Europeans, James counters, "Let us say what we will of them, of their inferior organs, of their want of bread, etc., they are as stout and well made as the Europeans" (215). However, he also counters the scientific maxim that the natural environment of America in particular effects a degeneration of all things Native and transplanted with the theory that it is the distance from the equator, rather than from Europe, which determines the nature of human "vices and miseries" (a theory which James also supports with his comparison between Charleston and Lima) (175). The newly baked *philosophe* James resuscitates here the sixteenth-century scientific theory proposed by Jean Bodin's *Methodus ad facilem historiarum cognitionem* (1566), which had, based on Aristotle, conceptualized the world in different zones from north to south. This division had put the New World and the Old World in an exact parallelism, not in the essential opposition that contemporary *philosophes* had drawn between the western and eastern hemispheres.[52]

Thus, if Crèvecoeur constructs James "as an aspiring New World author, a would-be-man of letters,"[53] he begins his career as a sign of transparency and authenticity, as a self-effacing narrative mask which yields him entry into the production of Natural History. He professes to speak in the "primitive eloquence" of a "new man" of pure experience, not in the refined eloquence of the European whose perceptions have been corrupted by the medieval "idols of the marketplace," as Bacon had famously called the reliance on language as a key to truth in *Novum organum*.[54] In the course of the twelve letters Crèvecoeur selected for publication, however, Farmer James gradually transforms from a Baconian miner into a Baconian speculator, thereby subverting the geo-political order of the imperial production of knowledge – a subversion that Crèvecoeur announces in his meta-historical satire conveyed through the Menippean dialogues between Farmer James, his wife, and his minister in the introductory letter of the text that was published as *Letters from an American Farmer*.

GUIDES, TRAVELERS, AND THE PLAGIARISMS OF HISTORY

As in *Letters from an American Farmer*, in *El lazarillo de ciegos caminantes* the very title signals the text's interest in epistemology. First, and most obviously, "lazarillo" establishes an inter-textual dialogue with a long tradition of picaresque narratives, such as *La vida de Lazarillo de Tormes* (1554), Francisco de Quevedo's *Historia de la vida del Buscón* (1626), or Mateo Alemán's *Guzmán de Alfarache* (1599, 1604).[55] Told from the perspective of a lowly, itinerant narrator, these Baroque narratives represented a radically disenchanted social world with a distinctly modern critical "realism."[56] By the eighteenth century, however, this tradition had turned, as Karen Stolley has shown, on language itself, and *Lazarillo* must be read, she argues, in the tradition of the Enlightenment genre of linguistic "criticism."[57] Similarly, Mariselle Meléndez has argued that the "most significant aspect of the voyage" lends *Lazarillo* "its epistemological character" and reveals its distinct interest in the "structure of knowing."[58]

It is the European production of knowledge about the New World, however, in particular, I want to submit, that is singled out as a target of epistemological critique in *Lazarillo*, particularly the colonial relationship between the (Native) "guide" and the (European) discoverer/traveler. As Chris Tiffin and Alan Lawson have observed in their analysis of twentieth-century British narratives about the first conquest of Chomolungma (Mt. Everest), the native guide inhabits a peculiar space in the European discovery narrative. He must "know and yet not know," for the European can "discover" a place only if it is not already known. This paradox of modernity is resolved, Tiffin and Lawson argue, by "textualizing the event [and] rendering the guide's knowledge pragmatic rather than conceptual and strategic. The guide has the practical knowledge . . . but not the conceptual knowledge to see its 'true' significance."[59] While Tiffin and Lawson are concerned with twentieth-century European geographic discourse about the Third World, the rationalization of the appropriation of local colonial knowledge in the imperial production of scientific discovery holds true also for the case of eighteenth-century Natural History in the historical context of European settler colonialism in America. As we have seen, however, unlike in nineteenth- and twentieth-century scientific discourse (geography, ethnography, etc.), eighteenth-century Natural History distinguishes not only between the Native guide and the traveling discoverer but also between the discoverer/traveler and the natural historian as separate subjectivities in the production of knowledge, thereby reflecting the geography of power distinctive to early modern settler empires. This separation was crucial in constructing the authority of eighteenth-century natural historians such as the abbé Raynal, who prefaced his *Histoire philosophique et politique de deux Indes* (1776) with the remark that "I have interrogated the living and the dead. I have weighed their authority. I have contrasted their testimonies. I have clarified their facts." Here was an "objective" Man of Science who, from the scientific detachment of his armchair, was so entirely "raised above all human concerns" as to be "disengaged from all passions and prejudices."[60] It is this ideology of scientific detachment, the natural historian's "blindness," that is the object of satire in *El lazarillo de ciegos caminantes*. Like Crèvecoeur, Carrió stages a meta-historical dialogue between two of the principal agents involved in the production of knowledge in Natural History – the Native "guide" Concolorcorvo and the imperial "inspector" don Alonso. Like Crèvecoeur's Farmer James, Carrió's Concolorcorvo serves as a narrative mask, as a utopian sign of authenticity, which is gradually exposed in the Menippean dialogues between the inspector and the mestizo, thus disrupting the authority of Natural History at its epistemological foundation.[61]

From the beginning, Concolorcorvo makes European historiography about the New World the explicit concern of his narrative, asserting the crucial role of travel and empirical knowledge:

Si fuera cierta la opinión común, o llámase vulgar, que viajero y embustero son sinónimos, se debía preferir la lectura de la Fábula a la de la Historia. No se puede dudar, con razón, que la general extractó su principal fondo de los viajeros, y que algunas particulares se han escrito sobre la fe de sus relaciones. (17)

If the common, or shall we call it popular, opinion were true, that the words traveler and liar are synonymous, then the reading of fables should be preferred to that of history. It cannot be doubted, and with justification, that history in general drew its principal sources from travelers, and that certain historical works have been written which accept the accounts of travelers as authoritative. (47)

Concolorcorvo subsequently embarks on a philosophical reflection on the significance of Ulysses, wondering why his son Telemachus sought his famous father in the Elysian fields if it was obvious that the latter was a "héroe algo bellaco" (18) ("villainous hero" [49]). In the process, he inverts the hierarchical and imperial relationship of dependency that subordinates the traveler to the historian and the colony to the metropolis. The historian, he claims, is utterly dependent on the travelers, who are like "guide boys" to the "blind":

Los viajeros (aquí entro yo), respecto de los historiadores, son lo mismo que los lazarillos, en comparación de los ciegos. Éstos solicitan siempre unos hábiles zagales para que dirijan sus pasos y les den aquellas noticias precisas para componer sus canciones, con que deleitan al público y aseguran su substancia. Aquéllos, como de superior orden, recogen las memorias de los viajeros más distinguidos en la veracidad y talento. (19)

Travelers (and here I come in) are, with respect to historians, just as guide boys are to the blind. The latter always solicit skillful youths to direct their steps and to supply them with necessary tidbits for composing the songs with which they entertain the public and assure themselves a living. Historians, of a higher order, collect the memories of travelers most distinguished for their talent and veracity. (50)

Like Farmer James, Concolorcorvo "come[s] in," or enters into, the production of knowledge about the New World by ostensibly filling his slot as a supplier of empirical information. The writing of history about America, he argues, is different from the writing of history about Europe because America lacks Europe's "roídos pergaminos, carcomidos papeles, inscripciones sepulcrales, pirámides, estatuas, medallas y monedas" (17) ("worn parchments and moth-eaten papers, sepulchral inscriptions, pyramids, statues, medals and coins" [47]). In Natural History, unlike in Civil History, the traveler's empirical first-hand observation is therefore vital as the only reliable source of information (17/47).

Significantly, however, in *Lazarillo* the socio-spatial order governing the production of scientific knowledge is complicated vis-à-vis *Letters*. Although Concolorcorvo is a mestizo, he fashions himself as an "indio neto" (13) ("Indian pure and proud" [41]), in order to establish the authenticity of the information he provides. He thus assumes a space that had had a long tradition in Spanish American historiographic authorship since Bernardino de Sahagún's *Historia general*, Felipe Guaman Poma de Ayala's *Nueva corónica y buen gobierno*, and the Inca Garcilaso de la Vega's *Comentarios reales*, all of which had made use of literate Native American testimonies, whether they were Mexican pictographs or Peruvian Quipus.[62] Similarly, Concolorcorvo appeals to indigenous "texts," such as the Peruvian "quipus, o nudos de varios colores, los jeroglíficos o pinturas de los mexicanos, la tradición de unos y otros, vertida en cuentos y cantares y otros monumentos" (17) ("*quipus*, or multicolored knots, the Mexican hieroglyphics or paintings, and the oral traditions of one or another peoples, translated into stories, songs, and other memorials" [47]). In their greater antiquity, the European documents of history, he argues, "no merecen más crédito" ("are not more worthy of merit"] than the indigenous Quipus (as some had argued), for "así como no estorban las barbas para llorar, no impiden las canas para mentir" (17) ("just as a beard does not prevent one from weeping, neither do white hairs keep him from lying" [47]). Indeed, Concolorcorvo immediately qualifies his initially stated purpose of writing a travel memoir, "distinguished for [its] talent and veracity," by adding that:

No pretendo yo colocarme en la clase de éstos [los viajeros], porque mis observaciones sólo se han reducido a dar una idea a los caminantes bisoños del Camino Real, desde Buenos Aires a esta capital de Lima. (19)

I make no pretext of placing myself among these [the travelers] because my observations have been reduced to giving to inexperienced travelers an idea of the royal road from Buenos Aires to this capital, Lima. (50)

His role is not, then, that of a traveler supplying first-hand observations for the historian but rather to serve as the (Indian) "guide" for the (Euro-American) "inexperienced traveler," who will then supply the "blind" European historian with observations. Concolorcorvo's testimony is thus twice "reducido" in authority – at twice the distance from that of the metropolitan historian of the "higher order" on the socio-spatial scale of the imperial production of knowledge. But despite its lowly location at the very bottom of the social hierarchy of knowledge production, the testimony of the "Indian" does find an integral place in the inclusive hierarchy of the Catholic/Baroque Lettered City. It is in this, more intricately graduated hierarchy of subjectivities that *Lazarillo* distinguishes itself from its North American counterpart, where Native American knowledge is not being represented at all (not even as a parody).

However, not unlike in *Letters from an American Farmer*, the degree of historico-poetical awareness of the first-person narrator – here the "Indian" Concolorcorvo – when dramatizing himself as a sign of authenticity belies his very credibility and manifests the interference of the ironic voice of the author. As does Crèvecoeur, then, Carrió, too, parodies the hierarchical socio-spatial stratification in the production of scientific knowledge by disrupting the utopian fiction of Concolorcorvo's authenticity and by hybridizing the voice of the Native informant with the ironical voice of the Creole intelligentsia. Thus, the mestizo's appeal to his identity as an authentic "Indian pure and proud" is suspect from the very beginning. And the (not at all) "inexperienced" travelling inspector, too, does not buy it: "Dejemos lo neto para que lo declare la madre que lo parió" (167) ("Let's leave off this pure business until the mother who gave birth to you declares it" [237]), he tells him. Even Concolorcorvo himself undermines his own authenticity by warning the reader:

Cuidado con mestizos de leche, que son peores que los gitanos aunque por distinto rumbo. Yo soy indo neto, salvo las trampas de mi madre, de que no salgo por fiador. (13)

Be careful of tricky *mestizos*, for they are worse than gypsies, although in a different way. I am an Indian pure and proud, except for the malpractices of my mother, for which I do not stand security. (40–1)

By revealing himself as a fraudulent sign of authenticity, Concolorcorvo often infuses a racialized color symbolism in his association of mixture with deceit. "En todo hay trampa menos en la leche," he says, "que le echan agua, y alguna veces se halla un bagrecillo que la manifiesta" (158) ("There is something deceitful in everything except milk, and even into that water may be poured; and sometimes a fish is found to prove it" [225]).

Concolorcorvo's authenticity is ridiculed, finally, by the obviously false bibliographic information given on the title page of *Lazarillo*. Both fictions – that the book was published in Gijón (Carrió de la Vandera's birthplace in Spain) by a press called "de la Rovada" – signal his critique of the plagiarism of colonial Creole knowledge in the metropolitan geo-politics of historiographic authorship. The reader gradually learns that Concolorcorvo's voice is not transparent after all, that his discourses are indebted to what Bacon had called the "volumes of men," and, worse, that they are motivated by pecuniary interests: like the "Dos primas mías collas [quien] conservan la virginidad a su pesar en un convento del Cuzco, en donde las mantiene el rey nuestro señor" ("Two cousins of mine [who] are preserving their virginity, to their sorrow, in a convent in Cuzco, where the King our lord supports them"), Concolorcorvo informs the inspector:

me hallo en ánimo de pretender la plaza de perrero de la catedral del Cuzco, para gozar inmunidad eclesiástica, y para lo que me servirá de mucho mérito el haber escrito este itinerario. (13)

I have in mind to try for the post of beadle of the Cuzco cathedral in order to enjoy ecclesiastical immunity and my having written this itinerary will serve me well in this. (41)

Thus, Concolorcorvo is gradually exposed as a "tricky *mestizo*," a conman playing his assigned role in the poetics of Natural History in order to gain material favors in return.

Not only is Concolorcorvo's supposedly authentic voice revealed to be "interested" like that of "prejudiced" Creoles, but also, like Farmer James' observations, his testimonies turn out to be nothing more than parroted phrases, instilled into the "*tabula rasa*" of his natural mind by Europeans who had a distinct interest in having the voice of Nature prove their theories. Although he supposedly wrote his itinerary "en Dios y en conciencia" ("in the eyes of God and of my conscience"), he admits that:

lo formé con ayuda de vecinos que a ratos ociosos me soplaban a la oreja, y cierto fraile de San Juan de Dios, que me encajó la introducción y latines, tengo a lo menos mucha parte en haber perifraseado lo que me decía el visitador en pocas palabras. Imitando el estilo de éste, mezclé algunas jocosidades para entretenimiento de los caminantes, para quienes particularmente escribí. (13)

I wrote it with the help of the neighbors who whispered in my ear in idle moments, and of a certain friar of San Juan de Dios who inserted the introductory remarks and the Latin phrases, at least I had a large part in having paraphrased what the inspector said to me in a few words. Imitating his style, I included some jocularity for the diversion of the travelers for whom I wrote it in particular. (40)

Not enough that the contents of his narrative originate from inauthentic sources, but the entire itinerary was, the reader learns, edited and cut by the inspector, by the representative of the metropolitan imperial order in America. "Me hago cargo" ("I realize"), he says,

de que lo substancial de mi itinerario se podía reducir a cien hojas de octavo. En menos de la cuarta parte le extractó el visitador, como se puede ver de mi letra en el borrador que para en su poder, pero este género de relaciones sucintas no instruyen al público, que no ha visto aquellos dilatados países, en que es preciso darse por entendido de lo que en si contienen, sin faltar a la verdad. (13–14)

that the essence of my itinerary could be reduced to 100 pages in octavo. The inspector cut it to less than one quarter of the present length, as can be seen from my writing in the rough draft, which I have in my possession, but this kind of short narrative does not instruct the public who have not seen these vast countries, and it is necessary to give attention to what is contained therein, without violating the truth. (40–1)

The imperial inspector has acted, like the scientific "collector," as the ultimate author of the text while invoking Concolorcorvo's "authentic" voice as primitive observer. The "noble Savage" says, Carrió implies in this metahistorical satire, what you want him to say – as long as you pay him. He is a metropolitan fiction, the phantasm of Enlightened *philosophes* imagined to yield authentic truth about the secrets of the "volumes of the world." "Hágame Vm. el gusto" ("Do me the pleasure"), Concolorcorvo asks the inspector, "de decirme alguna cosa sobre las virtudes, calidades y circunstancias de los indios" ("of telling me something of the virtue, character, and circumstances of the Indians"). The inspector, however, responds only with a sarcastic reference to the common European notion that the Indian's inability to blush is an outward sign of their inability to lie: "Eso mejor lo puede Vm. saber, señor Inca, retratando su interior e inclinaciones; pero porque no se ponga Vm. pálido, ya que no puede rubicundo" (164) ("You could divulge this better, Señor Inca, depicting your inner state and inclinations, but not in a way that would cause you to turn pale (since you cannot blush!)" [232]). Thus, Carrió de la Vandera's ironical voice consistently breaks through the dialogue between the mestizo Concolorcorvo and the imperial inspector don Alonso at the surface of the text, exposing the narrative mask of Concolorcorvo's fraudulent authenticity as an "Indian pure and proud."

Carrió's meta-historical satire is finally manifest also in the inter-textual relationships that *Lazarillo* establishes with earlier histories of Peru, such as the *Comentarios reales* (1607) by the famous Inca humanist Garcilaso de la Vega. Carrió frequently uses Concolorcorvo in order to parody European images of the noble Savage, as well as indigenous attempts to cultivate an Inca mystique fashioned after Garcilaso's portrayals of Peru's past. The author hereby parodies the claim to authenticity not only of his own narrator, the mestizo Concolorcorvo, but also of Garcilaso himself. When Concolorcorvo, upon reaching the old Inca metropolis of Cuzco, finds that the streets that his Inca ancestors built were like those of "todas las demás naciones del mundo antiguo" (144) ("all the other nations of the ancient world" [204]), he echoes the Inca Garcilaso's Renaissance universalistic descriptions of the city in the image of Rome. Equally, in his remark that the "naturales decimos Cozco. Ignoro si la corruptela será nuestra o de los españoles" (143) ("natives of this city call it Cozco. I do not know whether the variation in this word is a thing of our own doing or the work of the Spaniards" [203]) he echoes the Inca's etymological discourse, at the beginning of *Comentarios*, on the origin of the word "Peru," which was, the Inca Garcilaso argued, a Spanish corruption of a Quechua word.[63] Satirizing the claim to authenticity in

Concolorcorvo's Indian voice, Carrió frequently has him make ridiculous mistakes when recounting historical facts commonly known to readers as familiar with Spanish American histories of the discovery and conquest as Carrió de la Vandera. When, for example, Concolorcorvo instructs the reader that "que luego que los españoles saltaron en las tierras del Virú, supieron que se hallaba en Cajamarca...Cápac" ("as soon as the Spaniards set foot in the lands of Virú, they learned that there was in Caxamarca... Manco Capac"), he does not only mean to say "Atahualpa" (for "Cápac"), but seems to be unaware of the damaging implications to his political cause when continuing that this man was an "ascendiente mío bastardo, que se había levantado con la mitad del Perú, y que pretendía destronar a su hermano, legítimo emperador" (148) ("bastard ancestor of mine, who had revolted with half of Peru at his side, in an effort to dethrone his brother, the rightful emperor" [211]). In Concolorcorvo's upside-down version of Inca history, Manco Capac, the mythical founder of the Inca dynasty, becomes a "hombre de mala fe(e)" ("man of bad faith") and a "traidor y aleve" (148) ("perfidious traitor" [212]). The fact that the references to the Inca Garcilaso are put into Concolorcorvo's mouth illustrates that *Lazarillo* is not only a "parody of this distinguished mestizo writer's work," as Julie Greer Johnson has observed,[64] but also a parody of contemporary appropriations of Garcilaso in the idealizations of the Inca image by Indian rebels as well as by Las Casas' Enlightenment descendants, such as Jean François Marmontel in his popular *Les Incas, ou La destruction de l'empire du Perou* (1777).

Without seeming to notice the ramifications for his own political cause, Concolorcorvo obviously attempts to please the inspector when criticizing European promoters of the legendary noble Savage and of the *leyenda negra*. European historians produce their authoritative "General Histories" of America, he argues, frequently based on false travel accounts written by anti-Spanish Frenchmen and ignoring the American writers:

Así como los monsiures se jactan del honor de su idioma, por ser el que más se extendió en este siglo en toda la Europa, y se escribieron en él tantas obras excelentes.

Just as the *monsieurs* boast of the honor of their language, since it is the one of most extensive use in this century in all Europe with so many excellent works being written in it.

He refers here to French *philosophes* such as Raynal, who had disparaged the Spanish empire in America at length and whose *Histoire* was therefore received with outrage in Spanish America.[65] The European historians in general, he argues, should be aware of the

agravio que hacen a los españoles los viajeros que, en su idioma, pretenden denigrar a unos vecinos tan inmediatos como los españoles, ... pero estos monsiures, o sean milords o ilustrísimos, a la francesa, inglesa o italiana, sólo piensan en abatir a los españoles, publicando primeramente en sus brochuras, que pasan después a sus historias generales, ignorancias y defectos que cuasi hacen creer a los españoles poco advertidos, y dar motivo a los sabios a un concepto injusto por falta de práctica de los ingenios americanos, que generalmente están reducidos a sus libros y particulares meditaciones. (155)

wrong done to Spaniards by travelers who try, in their language, to defame such immediate neighbors as the Spaniards ... but these *monsieurs*, milords or illustrious Frenchmen, Englishmen, and Italians think only of debasing the Spaniards, publishing in their pamphlets (which afterwards become general history) follies and faults which are almost convincing to Spaniards of little intelligence, and give wise men an unjust concept, due to the lack of acquaintance with creative Americans who are usually occupied with their books and private meditations. (220)

The conquerors, he asserts, were "injustamente ... perseguidos de propios y extraños" ("unjustly ... persecuted by strangers as well as by their confreres"). And, with a reference to Las Casas, he continues:

A los primeros no quiero llamarlos envidiosos, sino imprudentes, en haber declamado tanto contra unas tiranías que, en la realidad eran imaginarias, dando lugar a los envidiosos extranjeros para que todo el mundo se horrorice de su crueldad. (145)

I do not wish to call the latter envious, but rather indiscreet for having declaimed so loudly against tyranny which was really only imagined, giving rise to the stories of begrudging outsiders who soon caused the whole world to be horrified at the cruelty of the Spaniards. (206)

Of one of these "estranjeros" in particular (namely Rousseau), he writes: "quisiera preguntar yo a este crítico naturalista por qué influjo se convirtieron estos hombres feroces en tan humanos" (146) ("I would like to inquire of this nature-loving critic by what influence were these ferocious men converted into the humble creatures" [208]). Thus, while Concolorcorvo often becomes the mouthpiece of colonial Creole politics, the constant disruptions of the fiction of his authorship also draw attention to the distinction between the (rather foolish) "Indian" narrator of Concolorcorvo and the Euro-American author Carrió de la Vandera. Not unlike Crèvecoeur, who adopts the narrative mask of Farmer James, Carrió adopts the mask of Concolorcorvo as a "trap" into which more than one critic has fallen.[66] Both (post-)colonial authors similarly speak in a ventriloquist's voice that hybridizes the unconscious naked eloquence of a "primitive Native" with the conscious voice of the Euro-American colonial intelligentsia.

By gradually breaking through the fiction, both subvert the socio-spatial stratification governing the production of historiographic authorship in Natural History and thus create an authorial space in the production of knowledge for the Euro-American whose subjectivity had been effaced by the Enlightenment poetics of history.

A "STRANGE ORDER OF THINGS!"

As Ivette Malverde Disselkoen has argued, the playful dialogue between the European inspector and the American mestizo in *Lazarillo* creates a "heterogeneous discourse," a "hybridism which generates a liberating and restraining discourse at the same time."⁶⁷ However, while the narrative produces "a hierarchical inversion" in the imperial order between the metropolitan historian and colonial traveler, this hardly has the effect of "giv[ing] voice to [the] marginalized perspectives" of the Indian (as Disselkoen goes on to argue), which would "make room for his [the Indian's] discourse." Less than agreeable to our current political and cultural sensibilities, Carrió's eighteenth-century colonial satire represents, as Marcel Bataillon has pointed out, the very "antipodes of indigenism."⁶⁸ His satire must be seen in the context not only of metropolitan centralizing reform movements but also of the constant threat of indigenous Indian uprisings in Peru.⁶⁹ Thus, if I have so far emphasized the liberating and unsettling aspects of the colonial satire at work in *Letters from an American Farmer* and *El lazarillo de ciegos caminantes*, it is also necessary to take into consideration the profoundly ambivalent and conflicted nature of the Creoles' rebellion against their colonial status manifest in these texts.

In eighteenth-century Peru, the frequent Creole rebellions against the imperial reforms of the Bourbons had failed to escalate into a full-blown revolution due only to the terrifying specter of Indian uprisings that had haunted colonial Creole society since the sixteenth century (and continues to haunt it to this day). Indeed, in the decade following the publication of *Lazarillo*, Peru would experience numerous devastating Indian rebellions under the leadership of self-styled heirs of the ancient Inca dynasts, such as Juan Santos Atahualpa and José Gabriel Condorcanqui Tupac Amaru II, who would have expelled from Peru not only the Peninsular Spanish imperialists but also (and especially) the hated *criollo* settlers, had they not been subdued in an extremely bloody and long-lasting war by a coalition of *gachupín* (Peninsular) and Creole forces. Similarly, the British American colonies had experienced serious Indian uprisings such as that led by Chief

Pontiac, who had mobilized an alliance against the European settlers that included tribes from Lake Superior to the Gulf of Mexico. It was not a coincidence that Native tribes frequently sided with the British in the Revolutionary War. For, as Native leaders were aware, their interests were guarded better under an imperial rather than a national order. As Stephen Slemon has observed, Euro-American settler colonials have "always been complicit in colonialism's territorial appropriation of land, and voice, and agency, and this has been their inescapable condition even at those moments when they have promulgated their most strident and most spectacular figures of post-colonial resistance."[70] When, in Spanish America, the wars for independence did erupt during the early nineteenth century, it was only after Spain had itself been invaded by Napoleon. The struggle was carried on mainly by the Creole elites who had cobbled together an uneasy alliance with the various subordinated social sectors of the colonial Americas (mainly mestizos). From this point of view, the American "revolutionary" wars that brought about the separation from the old European imperial systems present themselves, as Jorge Klor de Alva reminds us, not so much as de-colonizing efforts (like the struggles for de-colonization in twentieth-century Africa and South Asia), but rather as civil wars between different interest groups of Englishmen or Spaniards mostly over economic and political issues; but not over cultural ones.[71] For this reason, Lester Langley has characterized the Anglo American rebellion against imperial patrimony as a "Revolution from Above" and the Latin American independence movements as a "Revolution Denied." Revolutionary British Americans, who "lacked a pervasive sense of class consciousness," refused and therefore failed to deal with issues of social disparity in wealth, Langley argues: "Statistically, the United States remained a society of disparities in wealth. Income and wealth were as inequitably distributed in the United States in 1800 as in British America in 1776 – this despite the confiscation of loyalist estates, the elimination of primogeniture and entail, and the opening up of the West to settlement."[72] Moreover, the revolution and the postwar definition of the worth of labor left slavery intact as an economic foundation at the same time as it prompted Anglo Americans to "perceive [slavery] as anomalous or to find more scientific means to justify its retention in a republican society." Similarly, in Spanish America, where Bourbon reform policies, such as the sale of "certificates of whiteness" to mestizos, had "blurred social distinctions based on race, instinctively fearful Creoles clung to racial categories to justify their social positions" at a time when traditional descriptions of social status "no longer served to guarantee one's place in the social order." In fact, the racially and socially volatile situation

in Spanish America, Langley suggests, may have been one of the principal reasons why the Creole elites remained loyal to the imperial crown
even after the thirteen British colonies in North America had succeeded in
securing their independence.[73]

To what ends did Revolutionary American writers use their new roles as
self-empowered authors in the production of knowledge after they had "dismembered" themselves from the body of imperial knowledge production?
What was the new constellation of knowledge resulting from the breakup
of the "lost paradigm" of Natural History? And what was the relationship of
this modern knowledge to the new socio-political order in the former settler
colonies in the Americas? In order to answer this question, it will be instructive to investigate how "J. Hector St. John de Crèvecoeur" acted in his new
role as collector/editor in the selection of sketches published as *Letters from
an American Farmer*. For this purpose, I want to bring into consideration
also some of those sketches he chose to exclude from publication in 1782
that have recently been published in an edition by Dennis Moore, who
reproduces the unpublished sketches in an unedited form that includes
Crèvecoeur's strikethroughs and reproduces in brackets what the author
had scribbled above or below the line in place of the strikethroughs.[74] In
"A Snow-Storm," for example, Crèvecoeur describes a cozy winter evening
at the home of the American farmer in New York with his extended family
that includes also his "servants" (145):

the Negroes friends to the fire, smoakes & Cracks some Coarse Jokes, ~~they sweat~~,
& well fed ~~& well~~ Clad, they Contentedly makes their Brooms & Ladles without
any farther Concerns on their Minds, [they] the Industrious family, all Gathered
together under one Roof Eat their wholesome supper, Drink their Mugg of Cyder
& grows [Imperceptibly] less talkative ... finally they Go to bed, not to that bed of
slavery or sorrow as is the Case in Europa with people of ~~his~~ [~~our~~ their] Class but
on the substantial Collection of Honnest feathers picked & provided by ~~his~~ [~~our~~
their] Industrious wife ... the almighty has no Crime to Punish in this Innocent
family – why shou'd he permit ominous Dreams & Terrifick Visions to disturb the
Imagination of these ~~worthy~~ Good people. (146)

Who does "~~his~~[~~our~~ their] Class" refer to in this passage, we must wonder?
And who are the people of "~~his~~ [~~our~~ their] Class" in Europe? While "his"
and "our" seem to refer to himself and all people like him (American
farmers and their families), "~~his~~ [~~our~~ their]" signals the acknowledgment
of difference between the farmer and his slaves. As someone living in the
colonies, Crèvecoeur knows that "his" or "our" class is not the same as
"their[s]"; and as someone born in Europe, Crèvecoeur knows that there
are no people of "their Class" in Europe, but only in America. The dual

equation New World = liberty / Old World = slavery, which had still prevailed in the famous Letter III, "What is an American?" in *Letters from an American Farmer*, breaks down here with regard to his slaves. The faltering prose of this passage (quite atypical of this sketch up to this point) therefore begs Crèvecoeur's question in a way that deconstructs its rhetorical structure: why *should* God afflict the family with "ominous Dreams & Terrifick Visions"? Was the decision not to publish this sketch just another form of erasure, intended to mystify the social foundation of the white American's "liberty" ("~~they sweat~~")?

There is a striking difference between this scene of uneasy happiness and the farmer's unequivocal outrage in his observations on slavery in the South in Letter IX of *Letters from an American Farmer*, entitled "Descriptions of Charles Town; Thoughts on Slavery; on Physical Evil; A Melancholy Scene," which *was* published in 1782. "[H]ow different their lot, how different their situation, in every possible respect!" (171), he exclaims; and in order to illustrate his point, he includes a Gothically horrific description of

a cage suspended to the limbs of a tree, all the branches of which appeared covered with large birds of prey, fluttering about and anxiously endeavouring to perch on the cage. Actuated by an involuntary motion of my hands more than by any design of my mind, I fired at them; they all flew to a short distance, with a most hideous noise, when, horrid to think and painful to repeat, I perceived a Negro, suspended in the cage and left there to expire! I shudder when I recollect that the birds had already picked out his eyes; his cheek-bones were bare; his arms had been attacked in several places; and his body seemed covered with a multitude of wounds...I found myself suddenly arrested by the power of affright and terror; my nerves were convulsed; I trembled; I stood motionless, involuntary contemplating the fate of this Negro in all its dismal latitude. (178)

This impression triggers the reflection that "were I to be possessed of a plantation, and my slave treated as in general they are here, never could I rest in peace; my sleep would be perpetually disturbed by a retrospect of the frauds committed in Africa in order to entrap them, frauds surpassing in enormity everything which a common mind can possibly conceive" (170). Of course, the sleep-disturbing "frauds" committed upon the slaves "in Africa" (and, we might add, during the Middle Passage) are in essence the same with regard to those that end up left to die in cages in South Carolina and those who end up "sweat[~~ing~~], & well fed ~~& well~~ Clad" on farms in New York. The uneasiness and confusion apparent in the unpublished passage surrounding the Farmer's assertion of the slaves' lack of any "Concerns on their Minds" can therefore be assuaged only by a "redoubling" assertion of an *absolute* and *essential* difference between slavery in the North and in the South, a difference in the way that slaves are "treated" by their masters.

How can such an essential difference between Northern and Southern slavery in the New World be explained within the paradigm of Natural History, when European historians such as López de Gómara had since the sixteenth century argued slavery seemed to be "natural" to the Americas? In part, Crèvecoeur suggests, it is due to the degenerative influences of the environment particular to the South, to the "rays of their sun [which] seem to urge them [the South Carolinians] irresistibly to dissipation and pleasure" (167). However, the decrepit state of society in South Carolina seems to be not entirely explainable in terms of the influences of the natural environment. While the men, being given to excess, die early, "on the contrary the women, from being abstemious, reach to a longer period of life and seldom die without having had several husbands" (167). Although the natural environment was as congenial here as anywhere to the attainment of human felicity, the course of societal development reverted into the old tracks of the Old World. There are no new men in *this* part of the New World. "[T]his is the province which has afforded to the first the richest spoils, for nothing can exceed their wealth, their power, and their influence. They have reached the *ne plus ultra* of worldly felicity," he observes with regard to the city dwellers of Charleston, while the country is overspread by "scenes of misery" (167–8). The reflections upon slavery in South Carolina occasion the farmer's exclamation: "Strange order of things! Oh, Nature, where art thou? Are not these blacks thy children as well as we?" (169). The question of interest to the natural historian "Mr. F. B." – "What, then, is the American, this new man?" (69) – thus becomes the question of the anthropologist James: "What, then, is man, this being who boasts so much of the excellence and dignity of his nature among that variety of unscrutable mysteries, of unsolvable problems, with which he is surrounded?" (170). Perhaps men are not "like plants," determined by the natural environment in which they are reared. Rather, their diversity seems to originate beneath the surface of observable phenomena of the natural environment, in their "unscrutable mysteries" and "unsolvable problems."

In "What is an American?" James had informed the natural philosopher Mr. F. B. that if you "recede still farther from the sea," you will arrive "near the great woods." Society there "does not afford a very pleasing spectacle" as it seems to have been thoroughly Americanized by "the unlimited freedom of the woods" (77). Many Europeans who have immigrated to escape oppression live there, "remote from the power of example and check of shame" (75), in "discord, want of unity and friendship, . . . drunkenness or idleness prevail in such remote districts, contention, inactivity, and wretchedness" (72). In short, it was a Hobbesian chaos where a "mongrel breed, half civilized, half savage" (77) lives:

> in a perfect state of war; that of man against man, sometimes decided by blows, sometimes by means of the law; that of man against every wild inhabitant of these venerable woods, of which they are come to dispossess them. There men appear to be no better than carnivorous animals of a superior rank, living on the flesh of wild animals when they can catch them, and when they are not able, they subsist on grain. (72)

However, in the course of *Letters*, J. Hector St. John increasingly debunks the Enlightenment conception of man as a blank slate and emphasizes the importance of innate differences such as race and culture. Culture, for example, explains not only the differences between slavery in the North and slavery in the South and the relapses into civil discord and fratricide during the Revolution, but also the differences between Euro-American colonials and Native American Indians, both living on the frontier. Especially, in the last letter, "Distresses of a Frontier Man," when geographic boundaries between Indians and American farmers appear to blur, James upholds the bulwark of culture. "As long as we keep ourselves busy in tilling the earth," he asserts, "there is no fear of any of us becoming wild" (223). Despite his "respect [for] the simple, the inoffensive society of these people [the Indians]," Crèvecoeur displays little enthusiasm for Diderot's suggestion that the problems of slavery and bloodshed in the American colonies could have been solved "through consanguinity" between "the foreigners and the natives of the place," which would have "made a single and common family." Only then, Diderot had argued, would America need "no weapons, no soldiers, only large numbers of many young women for the men, and many young men for the women."[75] For, within the taxonomies of Natural History, there was no essential difference between Creolized Europeans, Creolized Africans, or Native Americans. They were all, after all, Americans, "like plants" reared in the American soil and climate. Crèvecoeur, by contrast, expresses the "strongest prejudices [which] would make me abhor any alliance with them in blood, disagreeable, no doubt to Nature's intentions, which have strongly divided us by so many indelible characters" (221). Nature, for Crèvecoeur, does not only reside in the natural environment, on the surfaces of flora and fauna, of the climate and air, but rather in the "indelible" difference of blood distinguishing the human races. Thus, while a difference of nature defines the colonial Creole vis-à-vis the Old World, a difference of race and culture defines the colonial Creole vis-à-vis the New. It is, as Robert Lawson-Peebles has observed, an uneasy balance that defines this "middle landscape" into which Euro-American colonial identity is mapped,[76] and colonials were all too conscious of its ill-defined borders. In the Revolutionary context of disintegrating geographical and social boundaries between the subjects and objects in the making of Natural History, differences in human "habits" were made ascribable to innate categories such as race and culture, which became increasingly detached from considerations of the non-human environment in the modern science of anthropology.[77]

A HERD OF MADMEN

Carrió, like Crèvecoeur in his later letters, also discredits America's promise for the renewal of man. After "more than 20 years in these provinces," Carrió de la Vandera's inspector has learned that the "folly" of mankind is universal and eternal. Like James, Concolorcorvo raises the question of the nature of man: "que de hombres suaves y de apacible trato se conviertan en ásperos y soberbios?" ("What makes docile men of gentle manner become harsh and arrogant?"). The inspector sullenly reflects:

No hay tal mudanza...La mayor parte de los hombres es una tropa de locos. Los unos son furiosos, y se huye de ellos. Los otros son graciosos, y se divierte con ellos; y el resto son disimulados y contienen su furia por cobardes y de recelo de encontrar con mayores fuerzas y perder un par de costillas a garrotazos, y así estos, cuando se ven autorizados, son peores que los locos furiosos, porque a éstos cualquiera los contiene con la fuerza o con el arte, y para aquéllos sólo sirve una determinación criminal o un tolerancia insufrible, porque no siempre se proporciona la fuga. (127)

There is no such change...Most men are a herd of madmen. Some are violent and one flees from them; others are funny and one amuses himself with them. And the rest are cunning and restrain their fury out of cowardice or fear of meeting greater strength and losing a couple of ribs from some blow; this group, when they find themselves in authority, are worse than raging lunatics, because the latter may be restrained either with force or with art, while for the others only a criminal decision or an insufferable tolerance serves, because refuge is not always afforded. (187–8)

The inspector's gloomy view of mankind encapsulates, as Julie Greer Johnson has written, Carrió de la Vandera's Spanish American Creole vision of disillusionment – the voice of people who "had witnessed Spain's ambitious plans and good intentions come to naught in the New World."[78]

   To some degree, Carrió, like Crèvecoeur in his descriptions of South Carolina, accepts the explanatory paradigm of Natural History but turns the axis dividing east from west by ninety degrees so as to divide north from south. He emphasizes, for example, the beneficial influences of the natural environment of Peru by comparing it favorably to Mexico. Whereas the theories of environmentally induced degeneracy probably hold true for Mexico, the traveling inspector surmises, the opposite is true for Peru:

Lo cierto es que hay países en que se conserva más que en otras partes la robustez del celebro, y asi entre Lima y México hay una gran diferencia. En México, la sequedad y sutilidad de los aires y otros influjos, destemplan el celebro y [c]ausan inso[m]nios. Al contrario sucede en Lima, porque sus aires espesos y húmedos fortalecen los celebros, conciliando el sueño, con que dejan las potencias ágiles para continuar las tareas de meditación. (219)

It is a fact that there are countries in which the strength of the brain is preserved longer than in others, and in this matter there is a great difference between Lima and Mexico. In Mexico the lightness and dryness of the air, and other influences, dull the brain and cause insomnia. The opposite is true in Lima, because its heavy and damp air strengthens the brain and induces sleep, thus leaving mental powers nimble for pursuing the tasks of cogitation. (292)

Mariselle Meléndez has shown in detail that the discourses of cultural geography, race, and gender in *Lazarillo* play an important role in Carrió's attempt to define a colonial Spanish American identity. His emphasis on alterity in his descriptions of *indios* and mestizos, of the *gauderios* (or gauchos), of blacks, mulattos, and zambos, as well as of women, aims to establish a "social, cultural, and economic order that would contain the diverse practices of these marginalized groups whose racial diversity and social mobility threaten the weak and obsolete colonial system."[79] One conspicuous aspect of his rhetorical productions of identity and alterity is the distinction he draws between rural and urban colonials. In this regard *Lazarillo* most noticeably differs also from *Letters*, which had proposed the pastoral "middle landscape" between the woods and the city as the ideal space for human cultivation. In *Lazarillo*, by contrast, there is no such middle landscape but only the *pampa* – inhabited by a degenerate lot given over to vice, indolence, and stupidity – and the city – where urban Creoles equal or surpass the cultural refinement of Europeans. Even the European inspector is ready to concede that in Lima there are "tantos sabios a proporción, y cualquiera ciudad de las de España comparable a ésta la igualaba en ingenios, juicio y literatura" (214) ("as many learned men as on the peninsula and that any city in Spain comparable to this one would be matched in creative talent, good judgment and literary production" [284]); and the "mujeres en esta ciudad ... son las más pulidas de todas las americanas españoles, y comparables a las sevillanas" (26) ("ladies of this city ... are the most refined of all the Spanish American women, comparable to those from Seville" [59]). Contrary to the theories of European natural historians such as Raynal, he asserts

que ha cerca de cuarenta años que estoy observando en ambas Américas las particularidades de los ingenios de los criollos y no encuentro diferencia, comparados en general, con los de la península. El cotejo que hasta el presente se hizo de los criollos de Lima con los que se avecindan aquí de España es injusto. (213–14)

that for 40 years I have been observing the peculiarities of the talented Creoles in both Americas [Peru and Mexico], and comparing them in general, I find them no different from the peninsulares. The comparison which has been made up to the present between the Creoles from Lima and those from Spain who take up residence here is unjust. (284)

As far as the countryside is concerned, Carrió had little patience for the Neoclassical literary conventions idealizing the American landscape as a Virgilian pastoral. "Muy poco sabía Virgilio," says Concolorcorvo,

de problemas cuando propuso ... [que] no habrá quebradas honas y estrechas, que son tan comunes en toda la América; pero supongamos que no las hay, o que fuese una sola de que tuvo noticia. ¿Es posible que no había elevadas chimeneas? A fe que si yo fuera su pastorcillo me reiría bastante de su pregunta, aunque le consta a V[m.] muy bien que los indios apenas nos reímos tres veces en la vida. (193–4)

Vergil knew very little about problems when he proposed ... that there were no deep and narrow ravines such as are common in all of America. But let us suppose that there are none, or that there was just one from which he got his information. Is it possible that there are no high chimneys? If I were his little shepherd, I would certainly laugh considerably at his question, although you should know very well that we Indians laugh scarcely three times in our lives. (269)

Indeed, his descriptions of the carnivorous excesses, sloth, and waste characterizing South American frontier life bear little resemblance to Virgil's pastures. The rural settlers, and especially the semi-sedentary *gauderios* (gauchos) roaming the vast territories of the La Plata region outside Buenos Aires live in a Hobbesian world of disorder and chaos.[80] "Muchas veces," he reports,

se juntan de éstos, cuatro o cinco y a veces más, con pretexto de ir al campo a divertirse, no llevando más prevención para su mantenimiento que el lazo, bolas y un cuchillo. Se convienen un día para comer la picana de una vaca o un novillo: le lazan, derriban, y, bien trincado de pies y manos, le sacan cuasi vivo toda la rabadilla con su cuero, y, haciéndole unas picaduras por el lado de la carne, la asan mal, y medio cruda se la comen, sin más aderezo que un poco de sal, si la llevan por contingencia. Otras veces matan sólo una vaca o novillo por comer el matahambre, que es la carne que tiene la res entre las costillas y el pellejo. Otras veces matan solamente por comer una lengua, que asan en el rescoldo. Otras se les antojan carcúes, que son los huesos que tienen tuétano, los descarnan bien, y los ponen punta arriba en el fuego, hasta que den un hervorcillo y se liquide bien el tuétano que revuelven con un palito, y se alimentan de aquella admirable sustancia; pero lo más prodigioso es verlos matar una vaca, sacarle el mondongo y todo el sebo, que juntan en el vientre, y con una sola brasa de fuego o un trozo de estiércol seco de las vacas prenden fuego a aquel sebo y, luego que empieza a arder y comunicarse a la carne gorda y huesos, forma una extraordinaria iluminación, y así vuelven a unir el vientre de la vaca, dejando que respire el fuego por la boca y orificio. (22–3)

Frequently four or five, and sometimes more, of these men get together under pretext of going to the country to amuse themselves, taking no provisions for their sustenance other than a lasso, bolas, and a knife. One day they will agree to eat the rump of a cow or a calf; they lasso it, throw it down, and with its four feet securely tied, they pull from it, almost alive, the entire rear quarter with its hide, and making a few punctures in the side of the meat, they roast it badly and devour it half raw without any condiment except a little salt, if by chance they are carrying some. Other times they kill a cow or a calf merely to eat the *matambre*, the meat between the ribs and the skin. Sometimes they kill only to eat the tongue which they roast in embers. Another time they may take a fancy to the *caracuces*, the bones containing the marrow... which they turn over and over with a small stick, and they feast upon that delightful substance; but the greatest monstrosity is to see them kill a cow, extract the tripe and all the fat which they pile together in the belly, and with merely a live coal or a piece of dry cow dung they set fire to that fat; as soon as it begins to burn and the fire spreads to the fat meat and bones, it produces an extraordinary illumination, and then they close up their belly again, allowing the animal to breathe fire through its mouth and nostrils. (55–7)

Thus, both (post-)colonial writers define a "positive space" for the inscription of colonial Creole identity by re-drawing the conceptual frontier separating the semiotic spaces between "Europe" and "America" in terms of its binary dualisms. However, while for Crèvecoeur this ideal landscape is the American farm, for Carrió it is located only in the (white) colonial city. The hinterland, by contrast, is inhabited by a degenerate and shiftless lot of Indians and mestizos. Like Crèvecoeur, Carrió thus frequently debunks the geocultural taxonomies of Natural History in his explanations of the origins of human diversity in a pseudo-scientific satire that renders the entire scientific discourse about environmental influence upon humans preposterous. For example, he redeems the American environment by his report of seeing a "viejo" ("old man") in the country who "parecía de sesenta años y gozaba de vida 104" (91) ("appeared to be 60 years old, but in reality enjoyed 104" [143]) in order to disprove European theories that Creoles age quicker into senility. On the contrary, "con solo ir a tomar sus aires" ("by merely breathing the air [of Peru]"), the people he encounters assure him, "sanan y convalecen hombres y mujeres, en poco tiempo, de todo tipo de enfermedades" ("men and women regain their health and recover in a short time from all sorts of illness"):

Nos aseguró un español muy robusto, de ochenta años, que había conocido a don Simón de Herrera, de 145 años y a doña Tomasa Aballón, de 137, aunque Herrera la acusaba de cercenarse a lo menos ocho años, y que apostaban a quién corría más. (140)

A very robust Spaniard of 80 years assured us that he had known Don Simón de Herrera, who was 145 years old, and Doña Tomasa Aballón, of 137 years, although Herrera accused her of trimming her age by at least 8 years; and they used to bet about which one could run the fastest. (200)

If Americans do appear to age faster than Europeans, he argues, it is a laudable thing because

los americanos saben tanto a la edad de cincuenta años como los europeos a la de sesenta, y fueron tan útiles por su doctrina y escritos, deben ser más aplaudidos, así como aquel operario que con igual perfección hace una estatua en un día, como otro en dos. (219)

Americans know as much at the age of 50 as Europeans do at 70, and are as useful because of their teaching and writing, they should be more applauded, just as that worker who produces in one day a statue of a perfection equal to that of another who executes it in two. (292)

Having discredited explanations of colonial difference in terms of nature, Carrió, like Crèvecoeur, emphasizes as an explanatory paradigm race and culture. He therefore frowns upon the realities of *mestizaje* in colonial society – upon "éstos, que por tales [españoles] se tienen, aunque con más mezclas que el chocolate" (114) ("these settlers, who consider themselves Spaniards, although they have a mixture greater than chocolate" [172]). Because American mestizos such as Concolorcorvo were nursed by Indian mothers or nannies "salieron los mesticillos hablando el idioma de ellas" ("they grew up speaking their language") and have imbibed the Indian dispositions to the effect that, despite all the good instruction they have received, they fail to speak and write proper Spanish. "[C]omo a Vm.," the inspector scolds Concolorcorvo, "a quien no pude sacar de los cascos el que deje de pronunciar y escribir *llovia* y *lluver*, con otros infinitos" ("this is the case with you into whose skull I have not been able to drive the idea that you should stop pronouncing and writing *llovía* and *lluver*, and an infinite number of other errors"). "No es mucho esto," Concolorcorvo protests, "porque yo soy indio neto" ("This is nothing, because I am a pure Indian") – implying that this pronunciation is due to his "natural" innocence. However, the scornful inspector counters:

Vm. tuvo la misma crianza fuera de casa que el resto de los españoles comunes serranos, y siempre sirvío a europeos y no lee otros libros que los que están escritos en castellano, y aunque ve con sus ojos escritos *lluvia* y *llover* siempre lo dice al contrario. (167)

you had the same upbringing outside the home as the rest of the common Spanish highlanders, and you always served Europe and read only books written in Castilian; yet even though with your eyes you see it written *lluvía* and *llover*, you always say just the opposite. (237)

All matters of education and instruction being equal between the "Spanish highlanders" and the mestizo, the difference in "effect" cannot be ascribed to exterior circumstances, Carrió implies, but must be found in Concolorcorvo's innate predisposition deriving from his racial mixture.

Because of the Americanisms in Concolorcorvo's Spanish, some critics have read Carrió's *Lazarillo* as a precursor of "a kind of manifesto of the nineteenth-century nation state" and even as an early example of the romanticist gaucho novel.[81] Similarly, North American critics have read Crèvecoeur's *Letters* as a precursor of the nineteenth-century Romantic investment in the frontier, culminating in Frederick Jackson's Frontier Thesis. However, while many of the topoi are surely present in both texts, they are evaluated with profound ambivalence. In Spanish America, especially, the frontier character would remain an ambivalent figure despite the belated arrival of Romanticism in, for example, Domingo Faustino Sarmiento's *Civilización y barbarie: Vida de Juan Facundo Quiroga* (1845), in which the *caudillo* Quiroga is driven by the forces of barbarism and the wildness of the frontier. More important than the role that these texts played as "precursors" for nationalism and Romanticism, however, is the cultural work that they themselves performed in the opening of a socio-spatial interstice that we might call "culture" in its modern anthropological sense, an interstice that would dominate nineteenth-century scientific discourse in texts such as Alexander von Humboldt's *Essay on New Spain*. While the collapse of the Baconian division miner/speculator was not fully accomplished until the emergence of modern anthropological discourse and its bourgeois hero the professional "scientist" (as opposed to the aristocratic "Man of Science") traveling in "invaded" colonies such as Africa and "Latin" America,[82] both *Letters* and *Lazarillo* deconstruct Enlightenment poetics of Natural History and the institutionalized division of intellectual labor underlying its cultural authority during the eighteenth century. Moreover, both authors engage in a "breakup" of the geocultural taxonomies of Natural History, which had explained observable difference in terms of the influence of the natural environment, and instead emphasize innate differences of race and culture as explanatory paradigms at the same time as they subvert the socio-spatial distance between European metropolitan historians "of the higher order" such as Raynal and Buffon and colonial "feebler birds" like themselves.

In their breakup of the mercantilist epistemic economies, Crèvecoeur and Carrió resemble many other Creole (post-)colonial writers who adopted and adapted the generic conventions governing the Euro-centric production of knowledge about America but manipulated them to fit their own aims. Perhaps the most famous example here is Thomas Jefferson's manipulation of the generic conventions of the "Note," exemplified by Antonio de Ullóa's *Noticias americanas* (Madrid, 1772), which Jefferson himself cites in his *Notes on the State of Virginia*.[83] His own text had originally been conceived as an official report in which he agreed to provide the secretary of the French legation, François de Marbois, with information about Virginia – presumably to aid the latter in his design to write a Natural History – under the familiar set of prescribed natural historical headers – rivers, climate, animals, aborigines, (colonial) towns, manners, and so on. Jefferson later decided to have his collection of data published but called it, significantly, not "The Natural History of Virginia" but rather *Notes on the State of Virginia*. If we wonder how Jefferson conceived of this generic designation, we may perhaps read his discourse on "Manufactures" (Query XIX) as his poetological statement. "[S]uch is our attachment to agriculture," he writes there, "and such our preference for foreign manufactures, that be it wise or unwise, our people will certainly return as soon as they can, to the raising [of] raw materials . . . Carpenters, masons, smiths, are wanting in husbandry: but, for the general operations of manufacture, let our workshops remain in Europe."[84] When his *Notes* were published, however, they undermined not only this very division of intellectual labor, as well as the effacement of the Creole "informant" in the production of natural-historical knowledge, but also the scientific paradigm of "nature" that had rationalized that division of labor. Thus he refutes, point by point, the arguments of Buffon that the influence of the natural environment in the Americas had resulted in a "degeneration" of transplanted species: the difference in human faculties is not explainable in terms of the natural environment, he argues, but rather in terms of race. Whereas Euro-America, despite its historical youth, had already produced a Franklin and a Washington, the achievements of Afro-America, such as the poetry of Phillis Wheatley or the letters of Ignatius

Sancho, inevitably remain "below the dignity of criticism."[85] In other words, if African Americans are inferior, Jefferson suggests, it is not because of the degenerative influences of the American environment but because the African slaves already brought their inferiority along with them from Africa (an argument which Afro-British writers such as Olaudah Equiano would make a point of refuting).[86] Thus, as Dana Nelson has shown, the colonial representation of race played an important role in the construction of early Euro-American colonial and national identities.[87] The emergence of the distinct discourses of "race" and "culture" in these colonial Creole texts must, however, be seen in the larger imperial context of a trans-atlantic debate rationalizing "difference" in Natural History since the sixteenth century. The discourse of race and culture was a rhetorical substitution, in other words, for the discourse of "nature" in order to rationalize a global bourgeois alliance of whites on the one hand and the neo-feudal relation in the (ex-)colonial world between European and African Creoles that upholds that bourgeois order, on the other. In this regard, the "racism" of (post-)colonial writers such as Jefferson, Crèvecoeur, or Carrió is intimately linked to their defensive Creole patriotism, bearing testimony to what Edmund Morgan has called the American "paradox" in which the ideology of "equality" among whites came to be founded as the counterpart of an ideology of Black inferiority and on the material base of Black slavery.[88]

Finally, the differences between Carrió's and Crèvecoeur's eighteenth-century critiques of Baconian science on the one hand and the twentieth-century attack on the authority of the "participant-observer" in ethnography on the other illustrate also important differences between the discursive breakup of what Foucault has called the "classical episteme" of Natural History during the early nineteenth century and the breakup of the "modern episteme" of the human sciences during the late twentieth century. Whereas the paradigm of Natural History had rationalized imperial power during the epoch of settler colonialism in the Americas, the modern human sciences such as ethnography and cultural anthropology rationalized it in the epoch of the so-called "invaded colony" in Asia and Africa. Whereas the former had ordered observable phenomena of human "difference" in terms of environmental determinism ("nature"), the latter ordered them in terms of the essentialisms of race and culture. It is significant to note, however, that in neither case was this "post-colonial" dismantling of scientific authority determined by the racial, ethnic, or national affiliations of these epistemic debunkers but rather was produced by a diverse array of people that crossed binary lines such as colonizer/colonized or White/Black – groups of people, then, who were *bound together by the boundaries* drawn in the colonial process. Thus, neither Crèvecoeur nor Carrió were American-born in America but rather "New Creoles," Europeans who came to the Americas as immigrants, spent significant portions of their lives there, and, in the case of Crèvecoeur, even returned to Europe. By the same token, some of the most influential post-colonial critiques of ethnographic authority during the twentieth century have come not only from individuals who were born in, or descended from, the so-called "Third World," but also from people who were born and raised in the neo-imperial centers of the United States and Europe. Both epochs, however, saw a radical alteration, as Clifford Geertz has observed, of "the nature of the social relationship between those who ask and look and those who are asked and looked at."[89]

Notes

1 PROSPERO'S PROGENY

1. William Shakespeare, *The Tempest*, ed. Stephen Orgel (Oxford: Clarendon Press, 1987), v.i.
2. On the idea of progress in the debates between the Ancients and the Moderns in Renaissance Spain, see José Antonio Maravall, *Antiguos y modernos. La idea de progreso en el desarrollo inicial de una sociedad* (Madrid: Sociedad de Estudios y Publicaciones, 1966); and in Enlightenment England, see Joseph Levine, *The Battle of the Books: History and Literature in the Augustan Age* (Ithaca: Cornell University Press, 1991). For a discussion more specifically focused on the role of the Americas in Western historical thought, see Edmundo O'Gorman, *The Invention of America* (Westport: Greenwood Press, 1972), and Leopoldo Zea, *The Role of the Americas in History*, ed. Amy Oliver, trans. Sonja Karsen (Savage, MD: Rowman and Littlefield, 1992).
3. See, for example, Herbert Butterfield, *The Origins of Modern Science* (New York: The Macmillan Company, 1957); also Ian Hacking, *The Emergence of Probability: A Philosophical Study of Early Ideas about Probability, Induction and Statistical Inference* (Cambridge: Cambridge University Press, 1975).
4. Anthony Grafton, *New Worlds, Ancient Texts. The Power of Tradition and the Shock of Discovery* (Cambridge, MA: Harvard University Press, 1992), 58; Ann Blair, *The Theater of Nature: Jean Bodin and Renaissance Science* (Princeton: Princeton University Press, 1997), 5; see also Nancy Struever, *The Language of History in the Renaissance* (Princeton: Princeton University Press, 1970); Grafton, *Defenders of the Text: The Traditions of Scholarship in an Age of Science 1450–1800* (Cambridge, MA: Harvard University Press, 1991). On the role that Humanism played in the making of modern science, see Pamela Long, "Humanism and Science," in *Renaissance Humanism. Foundations, Forms, and Legacy*, ed. Albert Rabil (Philadelphia: University of Pennsylvania Press, 1988), 486–514, 486–91.
5. See, for example, Barbara Shapiro, *Probability and Certainty in Seventeenth-century England: A Study of the Relationships Between Natural Science, Religion, History, Law, and Literature* (Princeton: Princeton University Press, 1983); Peter Dear, "Introduction," in *The Scientific Enterprise in Early Modern Europe*, ed. Peter Dear (Chicago: University of Chicago Press, 1997); Anthony Grafton and

Nancy Siraisi, "Introduction," in *Natural Particulars: Nature and the Disciplines in Renaissance Europe*, ed. Grafton and Siraisi (Cambridge, MA: MIT Press, 1999); Nicholas Jardine, J. A. Secord, and Emma Spary, eds., *Cultures of Natural History* (Cambridge: Cambridge University Press, 1996); Mario Biagioli, *Galileo, Courtier: The Practice of Science in the Culture of Absolutism* (Chicago: University of Chicago Press, 1993); Stephen Shapin, *A Social History of Truth. Civility and Science in Seventeenth-century England* (Chicago: University of Chicago Press, 1994).

6. See John H. Elliott, *The Old World and the New, 1492–1650* (Cambridge: Cambridge University Press, 1970), 5.

7. For the best study of this New World subtext in *The Tempest*, see Peter Hulme, *Colonial Encounters: Europe and the Native Caribbean* (New York: Methuen, 1986).

8. See Jack Greene and J. R. Pole, eds., *Colonial British America. Essays in the New History of the Early Modern Period* (Baltimore: The Johns Hopkins University Press, 1984); also Jack Greene, *Peripheries and Center. Constitutional Development in the Extended Polities of the British Empire and the United States, 1607–1788* (Athens: University of Georgia Press, 1986); and John McCusker and Russel Menard, *The Economy of British America, 1607–1789* (Chapel Hill: Published for the Institute of Early American History and Culture by the University of North Carolina Press, 1985). For the Spanish American case, see Anthony Pagden, *European Encounters with the New World. From Renaissance to Romanticism* (New Haven: Yale University Press, 1993), and *Spanish Imperialism and the Political Imagination: Studies in European and Spanish American Social and Political Theory, 1513–1830* (New Haven: Yale University Press, 1990).

9. For a seminal "hemispheric" approach to American history, see Herbert Eugene Bolton, *Wider Horizons of American History* (New York: D. Appleton, 1939). For some critical responses to the Bolton thesis, see the essays by Edmundo O'Gorman, Enrique de Gandía, Arthur Whitaker, Germán Arciniegas, and William Binkley in Lewis Hanke, *Do the Americas have a Common History? A Critique of the Bolton Theory* (New York: Knopf, 1964). For some subsequent attempts at understanding the Americas comparatively, see Silvio Zavala, *The Colonial Period in the History of the New World* (Mexico, DF: Instituto Panamericano de Geografía e Historia, 1962); Max Savelle, *From Empires to Nations. Expansion in America, 1713–1824* (Minneapolis: University of Minnesota Press, 1974); Claudio Véliz, *The New World of the Gothic Fox. Culture and Economy in English and Spanish America* (Berkeley: University of California Press, 1994); Patricia Seed, *Ceremonies of Possession in Europe's Conquest of the New World, 1492–1640* (Cambridge: Cambridge University Press, 1995); and Lester Langley, *The Americas in the Age of Revolution, 1750–1850* (New Haven: Yale University Press, 1997).

10. For "Americanist" interpretations of *The Tempest*, see Leo Marx, *The Machine in the Garden: Technology and the Pastoral Ideal in America* (New York: Oxford University Press, 1964), 34–72; and Eric Cheyfitz, *The Poetics of Imperialism. Translation and Colonization from* The Tempest *to* Tarzan (New York:

Oxford University Press, 1991). For Latin Americanist interpretations of the play, see Roberto Fernández Retamar, *Caliban and Other Essays* (Minneapolis: University of Minnesota Press, 1989); and José Enrique Rodó, *Ariel* ([1900] Barcelona: Editorial Cervantes, 1926). On the marginalization of Latin America, see Enrique Düssel, *The Invention of the Americas: Eclipse of "the Other" and the Myth of Modernity*, trans. Michael D. Barber (New York: Continuum, 1995).

11. The notion of a "second conquest" is borrowed from Benedict Anderson's account of the rise of nationalism in the Americas at the turn of the eighteenth century; see *Imagined Communities: Reflections of the Origin and Spread of Nationalism* (London: Verso, 1983). Anderson's account is heavily indebted to John Lynch's *The Spanish American Revolutions, 1808–1826* (New York: Norton, 1973).

12. See Immanuel Wallerstein, *The Modern World System: Capitalist Agriculture and the Origins of the European-World Economy in the Sixteenth Century* (New York: Knopf, 1974); and *Geopolitics and Geoculture: Essays on the Changing World* (Cambridge: Cambridge University Press, 1991).

13. Amérigo Vespucci, *Letters from a New World*, trans. Frederick Pohl (New York: Doubleday, 1944), 57, 8.

14. Shapin, *Social History*, 15, 245.

15. For just a few influential examples, see Talal Asad, ed., *Anthropology and the Colonial Encounter* (London: Ithaca Press, 1973); George Marcus and Michael Fischer, *Anthropology as Cultural Critique: An Experimental Moment in the Human Sciences* (Chicago: University of Chicago Press, 1986); James Clifford and George Marcus, eds., *Writing Culture. The Poetics and Politics of Ethnography* (Berkeley: University of California Press, 1986); James Clifford, "On Ethnographic Authority," *Representations* 1, 2 (1983): 118–46.

16. See Jean François Lyotard, *The Postmodern Condition: A Report on Knowledge*, trans. Geoff Bennington and Brian Massumi (Minneapolis: University of Minnesota Press, 1984); and Michael Hardt and Antonio Negri, *Empire* (Cambridge, MA: Harvard University Press, 2000).

17. Anthony Pagden, *Lords of all the World: Ideologies of Empire in Spain, Britain, and France, 1500–1800* (New Haven: Yale University Press, 1995), 6.

18. On the "ambiguous" coloniality of the Creole, see José Antonio Mazzotti, "Introducción," in *Agencias criollas. La ambigüedad "colonial" en las letras hispanoamericanas*, ed. José Antonio Mazzotti (Pittsburgh, PA: Instituto Internacional de Literatura Iberoamericana, 2000), 7–36, 11; Rolena Adorno, "Reescribiendo las crónicas: culturas criollas y postcolonialidad," in Mazzotti, ed., *Agencias*, 177–90; also Antony Higgins, *Constructing the Criollo Archive: Subjects of Knowledge in the Bibliotheca mexicana and the Rusticatio mexicana* (West Lafayette: Purdue University Press, 2000). On post-colonial theorizations of the "subaltern," see Ranajit Guha, ed., *A Subaltern Studies Reader, 1986–1995* (Minneapolis: University of Minnesota Press, 1997). On post-colonial theory more generally, see Bill Ashcroft, Gareth Griffiths, and Helen Tiffin, eds., *The Empire Writes Back. Theory and Practice in Post-Colonial Literatures* (London,

New York: Routledge, 1989); Ian Adam and Helen Tiffin, eds., *Past the Last Post: Theorizing Post-colonialism and Post-modernism* (Hemel Hempstead: Harvester Wheatsheaf, 1991); Nicholas Thomas, *Colonialism's Culture. Anthropology, Travel, and Government* (Oxford: Polity Press, 1994).

19. On the Hermes-like qualities of Eshu-Elegbara, see Robert Farris Thompson, *Flash of the Spirit: African and Afro-American Art and Philosophy* (New York: Vintage, 1983), 18–22, 79–80; on his New World transmutations, see also Edward Kamau Brathwaite, "The African Presence in Caribbean Literature," in *Africa in Latin America: Essays on History, Culture, and Socialization*, ed. Manuel Moreno Fraginals, trans. Leonor Blum (New York: Holmes and Meier, 1984), 103–44.

20. Aimé Césaire, *A Tempest*, trans. Richard Miller (New York: UBVU Repertory Theater Publications, 1986), 42, 9.

21. For only a few examples of this proto-nationalist paradigm in the Anglo American case, see Perry Miller, *The New England Mind: From Colony to Province* (Cambridge, MA: Harvard University Press, 1953), and *Errand into the Wilderness* (Cambridge, MA: Harvard University Press, 1956); also Sacvan Bercovitch, *The American Jeremiad* (Madison: University of Wisconsin Press, 1978), and *The Puritan Origins of the American Self* (New Haven: Yale University Press, 1975).

22. William Spengeman, *A New World of Words. Redefining Early American Literature* (New Haven: Yale University Press, 1994), and *A Mirror for Americanists: Reflections on the Idea of American Literature* (Hanover: University Press of New England, 1989); also Nancy Armstrong and Leonard Tennenhouse, *The Imaginary Puritan: Literature, Intellectual Labor, and the Origins of Personal Life* (Berkeley: University of California Press, 1992); David Shields, *Oracles of Empire: Poetry, Politics, and Commerce in British America, 1690–1750* (Chicago: University of Chicago Press, 1990); and Philip Gura, "The Study of Colonial American Literature, 1986–1987: A Vade Mecum," *William and Mary Quarterly* 3rd. ser. 45 (1988): 305–42. In Latin American literary scholarship, a "Spanish American" understanding of colonial letters is nothing new, reaching back to Marcelino Menéndez y Pelayo's foundational *Antología de poetas hispano-americanos* (1893–5) and *Historia de la poesía hispano-americana* (1911–13); see Roberto González Echevarría and Enrique Pupo-Walker, eds., *The Cambridge History of Latin American Literature* (Cambridge: Cambridge University Press, 1996), 2 vols., 1: 18–25.

23. Spengeman, *New World*, 49–50, 209.

24. For some previous considerations of early American literature from a comparative perspective, see Gordon Sayre, *Les Sauvages américains: Representations of Native Americans in French and English Colonial Literature* (Chapel Hill and London: North Carolina University Press, 1997), and Alfred Owen Aldridge, *Early American Literature: A Comparatist Approach* (Princeton, NJ: Princeton University Press, 1982).

25. Spengeman, *New World*, 34. On the role of "polyglossia" in early modern generic formations, see Mikhail Bakhtin, "From the Prehistory of Novelistic

Discourse," in *The Dialogic Imagination. Four Essays*, ed. Michael Holquist, trans. Caryl Emerson and Michael Holquist (Austin: University of Texas Press, 1981), 41–83.

26. See Margarita Zamora, *Reading Columbus* (Berkeley: University of California Press, 1993); also Hulme, *Colonial*, on the origins of the new word "cannibal."

27. See Luce López-Baralt, *Islam in Spanish Culture, from the Middle Ages to the Present*, trans. Andrew Hurley (New York: Brill, 1992). For an excellent account of the literary record of these hybridities, see Barbara Fuchs, *Mimesis and Empire: The New World, Islam, and European Identities* (Cambridge: Cambridge University Press, 2001), 35–117.

28. For only a few examples of scholarship illustrating these multicultural complexities of the early Americas, see Vincent Bakpetu Thompson, *The Making of the African Diaspora in the Americas, 1441–1900* (New York: Longman, 1987); Inga Clendinnen, *Ambivalent Conquests. Maya and Spaniards in Yucatan* (Cambridge: Cambridge University Press, 1987); Karen Spalding, *Huarochirí. An Andean Society under Inca and Spanish Rule* (Stanford: Stanford University Press, 1984).

29. See Germán Arciniegas, *Germans in the Conquest of America. A Sixteenth-Century Venture* (New York: The Macmillan Company, 1943).

30. Similarly, King James I of England, who was also James VI of Scotland, claimed that he had learned to speak Latin before he could speak his native Scots and was fluent also in Greek, French, English, Italian, and Spanish; see the *Oxford Dictionary of Quotations*, 3rd. edn. (Oxford, New York: Oxford University Press, 1979).

31. Juan Rodríguez Freile, *Historia de la conquista y del descubrimiento de la Nueva Granada (El Carnero)*, ed. Jaime Delgado (Madrid: Historia, 1986); trans. as *The Conquest of New Granada*, by William Atkinson (London: The Folio Society, 1961), 175.

32. Roland Greene, *Unrequited Conquests: Love and Empire in the Colonial Americas* (Chicago: University of Chicago Press, 1999), 226.

33. For New Critical dismissals of colonial American literatures, see Spengeman, *New World*, 209, 1; also Alfred Coester, *The Literary History of Spanish America*, 2nd. edn. (New York: The Macmillan Company, 1928), vii; Enrique Anderson Imbert, *Spanish American Literature. A History*, 2nd. edn., rev. and updated by Elaine Malley (Detroit: Wayne State University Press, 1969), 1; and Afranio Coutinho, *An Introduction to Literature in Brazil*, trans. Gregory Rabassa (New York: Columbia University Press, 1969), 67.

34. Raymond Williams, "Literature," in *Keywords: A Vocabulary of Culture and Society*, rev. edn. (New York: Oxford University Press, 1983), 184, 186.

35. Fredric Jameson, *The Political Unconscious: Narrative as a Socially Symbolic Act* (Ithaca: Cornell University Press, 1981), 20, 9, 76, see also 87–8.

36. See Michael McKeon, *The Origins of the English Novel* (Baltimore: The Johns Hopkins University Press, 1987), 19; also Roland Greene and Elizabeth Fowler, eds., *The Project of Prose in Early Modern Europe and the World* (Cambridge: Cambridge University Press, 1997); and Paul Hunter, *Before Novels:*

The Cultural Contexts of Eighteenth-Century English Fiction (New York: W. W. Norton, 1990).

37. See Stephen Greenblatt, *Marvelous Possessions: The Wonder of the New World* (Chicago: University of Chicago Press, 1991); Cheyfitz, *The Poetics of Imperialism*; Hulme, *Colonial*; Gesa Mackenthun, *Metaphors of Dispossession. American Beginnings and the Translation of Empire, 1492–1637* (Norman: University of Oklahoma Press, 1997).

38. José Lezama Lima, *La expresión americana* (Santiago de Chile: Editorial Universitaria, 1969), 40 (my translation).

39. See Armstrong and Tennenhouse, *Imaginary*; and Firdous Azim, *The Colonial Rise of the Novel* (London, New York: Routledge, 1993); also Percy Adams, *Travel Literature and the Evolution of the Novel* (Lexington: University Press of Kentucky, 1983).

40. Hayden White, *Tropics of Discourse: Essays in Cultural Criticism* (Baltimore: The Johns Hopkins University Press, 1978), 5.

41. See Kenneth Burke, *A Grammar of Motives and A Rhetoric of Motives* (Cleveland, New York: The World Publishing Company, 1962), 503–17.

42. McKeon, *Origins*, 19, 1–65.

43. Burke, *Grammar*, 507.

44. For the case of Spanish American narrative, Beatriz Pastor has characterized this process as being one of "mythification," "demythification," and "remythification"; see *Discursos narrativos de la conquista: mitificación y emergencia* (Hanover, NH: Ediciones del Norte, 1983).

45. See David Scofield Wilson, *In the Presence of Nature* (Amherst: University of Massachusetts Press, 1978), 8–45.

46. See McKeon, *Origins*, 273–409.

47. Edward Soja, *Postmodern Geographies. The Reassertion of Space in Critical Social Theory* (New York, London: Verso, 1989), 15, 11, 12; see also Henri Lefebvre, *The Production of Space*, trans. Donald Nicholson-Smith (Oxford: Blackwell, 1991); Georges Benko and Ulf Strohmayer, *Space and Social Theory. Interpreting Modernity and Postmodernity* (Oxford: Blackwell, 1997); and Marcus Doel, *Poststructuralist Geographies: The Diabolic Art of Spatial Science* (New York: Rowman & Littlefield, 1999). On world-systems theory, see Wallerstein, *The Modern World System*.

48. Soja, *Postmodern*, 16.

49. Michel Foucault, *The Order of Things. An Archaeology of the Human Sciences* (New York: Vintage Books, 1994), 129, 144; see also his *The Archaeology of Knowledge*, trans. Sheridan Smith (New York: Pantheon Books, 1972).

50. See Michel Foucault, *The Birth of the Clinic; An Archaeology of Medical Perception*, trans. Sheridan Smith (New York: Pantheon Books, 1973), and *Discipline and Punish: The Birth of the Prison* trans. Alan Sheridan (New York: Pantheon, 1977).

51. For only a few examples, see Hans Blumenberg, *The Legitimacy of the Modern Age*, trans. Robert M. Wallace (Cambridge, MA: Harvard University Press,

1983); Timothy Reiss, *The Discourse of Modernism* (Ithaca: Cornell University Press, 1982), and *The Meaning of Literature* (Ithaca: Cornell University Press, 1992); Pamela Long, *Science and Technology in Medieval Society* (New York: New York Academy of Sciences, 1985), and "Humanism and Science."

52. See Michel Foucault, "Of Other Spaces," *Diacritics* (Spring 1986): 23–7.

53. Edward Said, *The World, the Text, and the Critic* (London: Faber, 1984), 222; see also his *Orientalism* (New York: Pantheon, 1978) and *Culture and Imperialism* (New York: Knopf, distributed by Random House, 1993).

54. See Charles Whitney, *Francis Bacon and Modernity* (New Haven: Yale University Press, 1986).

55. Francis Bacon, *The Advancement of Learning* (Alburgh: Archival Facsimiles Limited, 1987), 2, 14, 16.

56. Francis Bacon, *The Works of Francis Bacon*, ed. James Spedding, Robert Leslie Ellis, and Douglas Denon Heath (London: Longman and Co., 1858; rpt. Stuttgart – Bad Cannstatt: Friedrich Fromman Verlag Günther Holzboog, 1963), 14 vols., IV: 254.

57. Quoted in Richard Foster Jones, *Ancients and Moderns. A Study of the Rise of the Scientific Movement in Seventeenth-Century England* (Berkeley: University of California Press, 1965), 118.

58. Thomas Sprat, *History of the Royal Society*, ed. Jackson I. Cope and Harold Whitmore Jones, Washington University ser. 3, no. 7 ([1667] Saint Louis: Washington University Press, 1958), 113.

59. Jones, *Ancients*, 143.

60. See Brian Vickers, *Francis Bacon and Renaissance Prose* (Cambridge: Cambridge University Press, 1968), 141, also 141–201, 211–31.

61. Bacon, *Works*, IV: 431–2.

62. *Ibid.*, 343, 361, 254.

63. Emile Durkheim, *The Division of Labor in Society*, trans. W. D. Halls (New York: Free Press, 1984), 202; see also Karl Mannheim, *Essays on the Sociology of Knowledge*, ed. Paul Kecskemeti (London: Routledge & Paul, 1964).

64. See Max Horkheimer and Theodor Adorno, *Dialectic of Enlightenment*, trans. John Cumming (New York: Herder and Herder, 1972), esp. 242–4.

65. Julian Martin, *Francis Bacon, the State, and the Reform of Natural Philosophy* (Cambridge: Cambridge University Press, 1992), 2–5.

66. Julie Solomon, *Objectivity in the Making. Francis Bacon and the Politics of Inquiry* (Baltimore: The Johns Hopkins University Press, 1998), 10, 23; see also " 'To Know, to Fly, to Conjure': Situating Baconian Science at the Juncture of Early Modern Modes of Reading," *Renaissance Quarterly* 44 (Autumn 1991): 513–58; Lorain Daston, "Objectivity and the Escape from Perspective," *Social Studies of Science* 22 (1992): 597–618; Lorain Daston and Peter Galison, "The Image of Objectivity," *Representations* 40 (Fall 1992): 81–128; and Denise Albenese, *New Science, New World* (Durham: Duke University Press, 1996).

67. See J. P. Sommerville, *Politics and Ideology in England, 1603–1640* (London, New York: Longman, 1986); also Glenn Burgess, *Absolute Monarchy and the Stuart Constitution* (New Haven: Yale University Press, 1996), and *The*

Politics of the Ancient Constitution. An Introduction to English Political Thought, 1603–1642 (University Park: The Pennsylvania State University Press, 1993), esp. 109–78.

68. See Christopher Hill, *Intellectual Origins of the English Revolution* (Oxford: Clarendon Press, 1965).

69. Bacon, *Works*, XI: 118.

70. *Ibid.*, VI: 467, XI: 118; see also XI: 121, VI: 459.

71. *Ibid.*, VI: 457.

72. Wallerstein, *Geopolitics*, 11.

73. Bacon, *Works*, XI: 123.

74. See Friedrich Nietzsche, *On the Genealogy of Morality. A Polemic*, trans. Maudemarie Clark and Alan J. Swensen (Indianapolis, London: Hackett Publishing Company, 1998).

75. For a discussion of this political conflict in *The Tempest*, see David Norbrook, " 'What cares these roarers for the name of King?' Language and Utopia in *The Tempest*," in *The Politics of Tragicomedy. Shakespeare and After*, ed. Gordon McMullan and Jonathan Hope (London: Routledge, 1992), 21–54.

76. For an example of common Anglophone dismissals of Spanish science, see Raymond Phineas Stearns' otherwise encyclopedic *Science in the British Colonies of America* (Urbana: University of Illinois Press, 1970), 42.

77. See Juan Pimentel, "The Iberian Vision: Science and Empire in the Framework of a Universal Monarchy, 1500–1800," *Osiris* 15, 1 (2000): 17–21. (Thanks to Jorge Cañizares-Esguerra, who has brought my attention to this article.)

78. Bacon, *Works*, XIV: 499–500.

79. Perry Anderson, *Lineages of the Absolutist State* (London: Humanities Press, 1974), 61.

80. Salvardo de Madriaga, *The Rise of the Spanish American Empire* (New York: The Free Press, 1947), 11; see also Lyle N. McAlister, *Spain and Portugal in the New World, 1492–1700* (Minneapolis: University of Minnesota Press, 1984), 13–72; and John H. Elliott, *Imperial Spain, 1469–1716* (New York: The New American Library, 1963), 24–74.

81. Anderson, *Lineages*, 70–1.

82. For a more detailed discussion of Charles V's fiscal problems, see Elliott, *Imperial*, 196–208.

83. Quoted in Anderson, *Lineages*, 72–5.

84. Lars Magnusson, *Mercantilism. The Shaping of an Economic Language* (London, New York: Routledge, 1994), 10, 11–12.

85. Elliott, *Imperial*, 179.

86. Angel Rama, *The Lettered City*, ed. and trans. John Charles Chasteen (Durham: Duke University Press, 1996), 24, 9–10.

87. Elliott, *Imperial*, 213.

88. José Antonio Maravall, *Culture of the Baroque. Analysis of a Historical Structure*, trans. Terry Cochran (Minneapolis: University of Minnesota Press, 1986), 71–7.

89. See Simon Varey, Rafael Chabrán, and Dora B. Weiner, eds., *Searching for the Secrets of Nature: The Life and Works of Dr. Francisco Hernández* (Stanford:

Stanford University Press, 2000); Carlos Noreña, *Studies in Spanish Renaissance Thought* (The Hague: Martinus Nijhoff, 1975), *Juan Luis Vives and the Emotions* (Carbondale: Southern Illinois University Press, 1989), and *Juan Luis Vives* (The Hague: Nijhoff, 1970).

90. Luis García Vega, *Juan Huarte de San Juan, patron de la psicología española* (Madrid: Ediciones Académicas, 1991), 2–6.

91. Juan Huarte, *The Examination of Mens Wits* (Gainesville: Scholars' Facsimiles and Reprints, 1959), 17–18.

92. *Ibid.*, 21–2.

93. "To the Maiestie," in *ibid.*, n. p.

94. Huarte, *Examination*, 63.

95. See Antonello Gerbi, *The Dispute of the New World. The History of a Polemic, 1750–1900*, trans. Jeremy Moyle (Pittsburgh: University of Pittsburgh Press, 1973), and *Nature in the New World: From Christopher Columbus to Gonzalo Fernández de Oviedo*, trans. Jeremy Moyle (Pittsburgh: University of Pittsburgh Press, 1985); also Jorge Cañizares-Esguerra, *How to Write the History of the New World: Histories, Epistemologies, and Identities in the Eighteenth-century Atlantic World* (Stanford: Stanford University Press, 2001).

96. Karen Ordahl Kupperman, "Introduction: The Changing Definition of America," in *America in European Consciousness, 1493–1750*, ed. Kupperman (Chapel Hill: University of North Carolina Press, 1995), 1–32, 20.

97. On Spanish America, see Cañizares-Esguerra, *How to Write*, and "New Worlds, New Stars: Patriotic Astrology and the Invention of Indian and Creole Bodies in Colonial Spanish America, 1600–1650," *American Historical Review* 104, 1 (February 1999): 33–68; on British America, see Jared Gardner, *Master Plots: Race and the Founding of an American Literature, 1787–1845* (Baltimore: The Johns Hopkins University Press, 1998), 18–21; also Michael Zuckerman, "Identity in British America: Unease in Eden," in *Colonial Identity in the Atlantic World, 1500–1800*, ed. Nicholas Canny and Anthony Pagden (Princeton: Princeton University Press, 1987), 115–57; and Zuckerman, "The Fabrication of Identity in Early America," *William and Mary Quarterly*, 3rd. ser. 34 (1977): 183–214. On the "lost paradigm of natural history," see Pamela Regis, *Describing Early America: Bartram, Jefferson, Crèvecoeur, and the Rhetoric of Natural History* (DeKalb: Northern Illinois University Press, 1992), 4.

98. Roberto González Echevarría, *Myth and Archive. A Theory of Latin American Narrative* (Cambridge: Cambridge University Press, 1990), 30–2.

99. On the "liberalism" of the British empire, see David Armitage, *The Ideological Origins of the British Empire* (Cambridge: Cambridge University Press, 2000); on the Protestant ideology of a "Republic [rather than a "city"] of Letters," see Jürgen Habermas, *The Structural Transformation of the Public Sphere. An Inquiry into a Category of Bourgeois Society*, trans. Thomas Burger (Cambridge, MA: MIT Press, 1996); also Michael Warner, *The Letters of the Republic: Publication and the Public Sphere in Eighteenth-century America* (Cambridge, MA: Harvard University Press, 1990).

100. For only a few examples of scholarship on early African American subjects, see Vincent Carretta and Philip Gould, eds., *Genius in Bondage: Literature of the Early Black Atlantic* (Lexington: University Press of Kentucky, 2000); and Rolena Adorno, "Estévanico's Legacy," paper read at the First Early Ibero/Anglo Americanist Summit (Tucson, AZ, May 2002). On Native American literatures, see Rolena Adorno, *Guaman Poma: Writing and Resistance in Colonial Peru* (Austin: University of Texas Press, 1986); Raquel Chang-Rodríguez, *La apropiación del signo: tres cronistas indígenas del Perú* (Tempe: Center for Latin American Studies, Arizona State University, 1988); Regina Harrison, *"True" Confessions: Quechua and Spanish Cultural Encounters in the Viceroyalty of Peru* (College Park, MD: Latin American Studies Center, University of Maryland, 1992); Helen Jaskoski, *Early Native American Writing: New Critical Essays* (Cambridge: Cambridge University Press, 1996); Hilary Wyss, *Writing Indians: Literacy, Christianity, and Native Community in Early America* (Amherst: University of Massachusetts Press, 2000). I try to bring some of these critical discourses into dialogue with one another in Bauer, "'EnCountering' colonial Latin American Indian chronicles: Guamán Poma de Ayala," *American Indian Quarterly* 25, 2 (Spring 2001): 274–312.

2 MYTHOS AND EPOS: CABEZA DE VACA'S EMPIRE OF PEACE

1. Virgil, *The Aeneid*, trans. Robert Fitzgerald (New York: Vintage Classics, 1990), Book v, lines 626–7; Miguel de Cervantes, *Don Quixote*, ed. E. C. Riley, trans. Charles Jarvis (New York: Oxford University Press, 1992), 461; Derek Walcott, *Omeros* (New York: Noonday, 1990), 291.
2. "The 1542 *Relación* (Account) of Álvar Núñez Cabeza de Vaca," in Rolena Adorno and Patrick Charles Pautz, *Álvar Núñez Cabeza de Vaca: His Account, His Life, and the Expedition of Pánfilo de Narváez* (Lincoln: University of Nebraska Press, 1999), 3 vols., I: 1–291, 18–19. Unless indicated otherwise, I cite from this work whenever referring to the 1542 edition of Zamora (hereafter 1542: Adorno/Pautz). For the Spanish text of the 1555 edition of Valladolid, I cite from Álvar Núñez Cabeza de Vaca, *La relación o naufragios de Álvar Núñez Cabeza de Vaca*, ed. Martin A. Favata and José Fernández (Potomac, MD: Scripta Humanistica, 1986) (hereafter referred to as 1555: Favata/Fernández); and for an English translation of the 1555 edition, I cite from Álvar Núñez Cabeza de Vaca, *Castaways*, ed. Enrique Pupo-Walker, trans. Frances López Morillas (Berkeley: University of California Press, 1993) (hereafter 1555: López Morillas).
3. T. N. Campbell and T. J. Campbell, *Historical Indian Groups of the Choke Canyon Reservoir and Surrounding Area, Southern Texas* (San Antonio: Center for Archeological Research, University of Texas at San Antonio, 1981); see also Cleve Hallenbeck, *Álvar Núñez Cabeza de Vaca. The Journey and Route of the First European to Cross the Continent of North America, 1534–1536* (Port Washington, NY: Kennikat Press, 1970). For a full account of the works of reception, see 1542: Adorno/Pautz, III: 119–73.

4. Lee H. Dowling, "Story vs. Discourse in the Chronicle of the Indies: Álvar Núñez Cabeza de Vaca's *Relación*," *Hispanic Journal* 5, 2 (1984): 89–99; Antonio Carreño, "*Naufragios* de Álvar Núñez Cabeza de Vaca: Una retórica de la crónica colonial," *Revista Iberoamericana* 53 (1987): 499–516, 512; Soren Triff, "La relación de Álvar Núñez: Historia y persuasión," *Confuencia* 5, 2 (1990): 61–7; and David Lagmanovich, "Los Naufragios de Álvar Núñez como construcción narrativa," *Kentucky Romance Quarterly* 25 (1978): 22–37. See also Juan Francisco Maura, "Truth versus Fiction in the Autobiographical Accounts by the Chroniclers of Exploration," *Monographic Review / Revista Monografica* 9 (1993): 28–35, 29; Robert Lewis, "Los Naufragios de Álvar Núñez: Historia y ficción," *Revista Iberoamericana* 48 (1982): 681–94, 682; and Edgardo Rivera Martínez, "Singularidad y caracter de los naufragios de Álvar Núñez Cabeza de Vaca," *Revista de Crítica Literaria Latinoamericana* 19 (1993): 301–15, 301.

5. Silvia Molloy, "Alteridad y reconocimiento en los *Naufragios* de Álvar Núñez Cabeza de Vaca," *Nueva Revista de Filología Hispánica* 35, 2 (1987): 425–49, 425; see also her "Formulación y lugar del 'yo' en los naufragios de Álvar Núñez Cabeza de Vaca," *Actas del Séptimo Congreso de la Asociación Internacional de Hispanistas* 2 (1980): 7661–6.

6. Beatriz Pastor, *Discursos narrativos de la conquista: mitificación y emergencia* (Hanover, NH: Ediciones del Norte, 1983), 136–45.

7. Peggy Samuels, "Imagining Distance: Spanish Explorers in America," *Early American Literature* 25, 2 (1990): 229–32, 241; David Howard, *Conquistador in Chains. Cabeza de Vaca and the Indians of the Americas* (Tuscaloosa: University of Alabama Press, 1997), 3, 7, 9, 23.

8. Jacqueline Nanfito, "Cabeza de Vaca's *Naufragios y Comentarios*: The Journey Motif in the Chronicle of the Indies," *Revista de Estudios Hispánicos* 21 (1994): 179–87, 180 (my italics).

9. Lidia Díaz, "*Naufragios*, de Álvar Núñez Cabeza de Vaca: ¿Un discurso que revierte al fracaso?" *Lucero* 3 (1992): 11–18, 12. For Latin American protonationalist readings of *Relación*, see Raquel Chang-Rodríguez, *Prosa hispanoamericana virreinal* (Barcelona: Hispam, 1978), 50; David Bost, "Historiography and the Contemporary Narrative," *Latin American Literary Review* 16 (1988): 34–44; and Lagmanovich, "Naufragios," 22–3. For "Chicano" readings, see Juan Bruce-Novoa, "Naufragios en los mares de la significación: De *La Relación* de Cabeza de Vaca a la literatura chicana," *Plural* (February 1990): 12–21; and Rolando Romero, "Materialismo, feminismo y postestructuralismo en la teoría chicana: Caliban, La Malinche, y Cabeza de Vaca," in *Actas Irvine 92*, ed. Juan Villegas (Irvine: University of California Press, 1994) 214–22; and for a "US" reading, Peter Wild, *Álvar Núñez Cabeza de Vaca* (Boise: Boise State University Press, 1991).

10. Enrique Pupo-Walker, "Introduction," in 1555: López Morillas, xxvi. See also his "Pesquisas para una nueva lectura de los naufragios, de Álvar Núñez Cabeza de Vaca," *Revista Iberoamericana* 53 (1987): 517–39, 518.

11. Kun Jong Lee, "Pauline Typology in Cabeza de Vaca's *Naufragios*," *Early American Literature* 34 (1999): 241–62, 241; also Roseanna Mueller, "Two Unofficial Captive Narratives: Gonzalo Guerrero's memorias and Cabeza

de Vaca's *Naufragios*," in *Latin America and Its Literature. Whitestone*, ed. Maria Elena de Valdés (New York: Council on National Literatures, 1995), 20–35.

12. 1542: Adorno/Pautz, I: xix.

13. See Rolena Adorno, "Peaceful Conquest and Law in the *Relación* (*Account*) of Álvar Núñez Cabeza de Vaca," in *Coded Encounters. Writing, Gender, and Ethnicity in Colonial Latin America*, ed. Francisco Javier Cevallos-Canau, Jeffrey A. Cole, Nina M. Scott, and Nicomedes Suárez-Araúz (Amherst: University of Massachusetts Press, 1994), 75–86; also 1542: Adorno/Pautz, I: 402–7.

14. José Rabasa, *Writing Violence on the Northern Frontier: The Historiography of Sixteenth-century New Mexico and Florida and the Legacy of Conquest* (Durham: Duke University Press, 2000), 37, 39, 46.

15. Despite Rabasa's provocative insights into the hegemonic aspects of the discourse of pacification, his own analysis ultimately relapses into the very sort of "ethnographic" reading that would privilege story over discourse when reading Cabeza de Vaca's account as a "narrative of a first encounter" and his empathetic descriptions as a result of his "experience of magical phenomena" and the "historiographic difficulties [he] encountered in telling the story of his experience" (*ibid.*, 50, 49). For other readings in a similarly binary vein, see Maureen Ahern, "The Cross and the Gourd: The Appropriation of Ritual Signs in the Relaciones of Álvar Núñez Cabeza de Vaca and Fray Marcos de Niza," in *Early Images of the Americas. Transfer and Invention*, ed. Jerry M. Williams and Robert E. Lewis (Tucson: University of Arizona Press, 1993), 215–44, 219; Juan Gil, "Álvar Núñez, el chamán blanco," *Boletín de la Real Academia Española* 73 (1993): 69–72; Luisa Pranzetti, "Il naufragio como metáfora (a proposito delle relazioni di Cabeza de Vaca)," *Letterature d'America*, I (1980); Silivia Spitta, "Chamanismo y cristianidad: Una lectura de la lógica intercultural de los *Naufragios* de Cabeza de Vaca," *Revista de Crítica Literaria Latinoamericana* 19 (1993): 317–30; and Nancy Hickerson, "Rituals of Confrontation: Cabeza de Vaca and the Texas Indians," *Intertexts* I, 2 (1997): 169–76.

16. See 1542: Adorno/Pautz, III: 8–83; summarized, III: 83–4.

17. *Ibid.*, 8, 12–15.

18. *Ibid.*, 18–45.

19. *Ibid.*, 12–102, 115–18.

20. Álvar Núñez Cabeza de Vaca, "Naufragios de Álvar Núñez Cabeza de Vaca, y Relación de la jornada que hizo a la Florida con el adelantado Pánfilo de Narváez," in *Historiadores primitivos de las Indias Occidentales*, ed. André González Barcia (Madrid: Barcia Carballido y Zúñiga, 1749).

21. 1542: Adorno/Pautz, III: 90. The 1542 edition was entitled *La relación que dio Álvar núñez cabeça de vaca de lo acaescido en las Indias en la armada donde yua por gouernador Pamphilo de narbaez desde el año de veynte y siete hasta el año de treynta y seis que boluio a Seuilla con tres de su compañia.* The 1555 edition was entitled *La relación y comentarios del gouernador Álvar núñez cabeca de vaca de lo acaescido en las dos jornadas que hizo a las Indias.*

22. See Roberto González Echevarría, "Humanismo, retórica y las Crónicas de la conquista," in *Isla a su vuelo fugitiva. Ensayos criticos sobre literatura hispanoamericana* (Madrid: José Porrúa Turanzas, SA, 1983), 9–26; also *Myth and Archive. A Theory of Latin American Narrative* (Cambridge: Cambridge University Press, 1990); and *The Narrative of America* (Cambridge: Cambridge University Press, 1990).

23. Walter Mignolo, "El métatexto historiográfico y la historiografía indiana," *MLN* 96, 2 (1981): 358–402, 389; see also his "Cartas, crónicas y relaciones del descubrimiento y la conquista," in *Historia de la literatura hispanoamericana; época colonial*, ed. Luis Iñigo Madrigal (Madrid: Ediciones Cátedra, 1982), 57–116.

24. On Philip's choice of Madrid as his permanent capital, see Andrew Wheatcroft, *The Habsburgs: Embodying Empire* (London, New York: Viking, 1995), 143.

25. Roberto González Echevarría, "The Life and Adventures of Cipion: Cervantes and the Picaresque," *Diacritics* 9–10 (1980): 15–26, 20–1.

26. Murdo MacLeod, "The Relaciones de Méritos y Servicios and their Historical and Political Interpretation," in *The Book in the Americas*, ed. Julie Greer Johnson (Providence, RI: John Carter Brown Library, 1987), 1.

27. 1542: Adorno/Pautz, III: 5.

28. The appointment as governor was contingent on verification of the fact that Governor Ayolas was indeed dead. See *ibid.*, I: 378–81.

29. For a version of the La Plata events from the point of view of the settlers, see the account written by the German Ulrich Schmiedel in Luis L. Domínguez, *The Conquest of the River Plate, 1535–1555* (London: The Hakluyt Society, 1907).

30. See 1542: Adorno/Pautz, I: 379–402; also Morris Bishop, *The Odyssey of Cabeza de Vaca* (New York, London: The Century Co., 1933), 270–91; and Samuel Eliot Morison, *The European Discovery of America* (New York: Oxford University Press, 1974), 2 vols., II: 569–80.

31. For a study of the *Comentarios*, see Pedro Lastra, "Espacios de Álvar Núñez: Las transformaciones de una escritura," *Cuadernos Americanos* 254, 3 (1984): 150–64, 159.

32. 1542: Adorno/Pautz, I: 374.

33. Quoted in *ibid.*

34. *Ibid.*, III: 91, 100–1; I: 372–4.

35. See *ibid.*, III: 68–72.

36. See *ibid.*

37. This was, as Adrian Johns has shown, by no means self-evident. The authority of printed books had rather to be created in the course of the fifteenth and sixteenth centuries; see Adrian Johns, *The Nature of the Book. Print and Knowledge in the Making* (Chicago: University of Chicago Press, 1998).

38. F. J. Norton, *Printing in Spain, 1501–1520* (Cambridge: Cambridge University Press, 1966), 119.

39. *Ibid.*, 121.

40. See Mariano Alcocer y Martínez, *Catálogo razonado de obras impresas en Valladolid, 1481–1800* (Valladolid: Imprenta de la Casa Social Católica, 1926), 14, 63, 116–17, 314.

41. On this aspect of Cabeza de Vaca's biography, see 1542: Adorno/Pautz, I: 398–407.

42. Adorno and Pautz's translation of "privilegio" as "authorization" (*ibid.*, I: 282, III: 87) is a bit confusing here because it seems to conflate the Crown's older, promotional involvement in book publishing by granting "privilegios" with the newer, repressive policy coming into being with the royal edict of 1554 – which made the Council of Castile the licensing body for the printing of all books – as well as with the new 1556 law, which required a royal license to print for all books dealing with the Spanish Indies (see *ibid.*, III: 87–8). While it is true that the 1555 edition was *also* published with an explicit "license and authorization," the practice of granting an author a royal "privilege" – the exclusive right to print and sell at a fixed price for a fixed period – was independent of these new repressive measures and had been practiced as part of the Crown's "pro-active" involvement in the publishing business for decades; see Norton, *Printing in Spain*, 121.

43. See 1542: Adorno/Pautz, I: 282–3.

44. *Ibid.*

45. Quoted in *ibid.*, III: 88.

46. See Alcocer y Martínez, *Catálogo*, 76–117.

47. Jürgen Habermas, *The Structural Transformation of the Public Sphere. An Inquiry into a Category of Bourgeois Society*, trans. Thomas Burger (Cambridge, MA: MIT Press, 1996), 18.

48. Clarence Henry Haring, *The Spanish Empire in America* (New York: Oxford University Press, 1947), 75.

49. Quentin Skinner, *The Foundations of Modern Political Thought* (Cambridge: Cambridge University Press, 1978), 2 vols., II: 129; see also Luis Weckmann, *The Medieval Heritage of Mexico*, trans. Frances M. López-Morillas (New York: Fordham University Press, 1992), 72–84.

50. Haring, *The Spanish Empire in America*, 76.

51. Mark Burkholder and Lyman Johnson, *Colonial Latin America*, 2nd. edn. (New York: Oxford University Press, 1994), 73–5.

52. Lyle N. McAlister, *Spain and Portugal in the New World, 1492–1700* (Minneapolis: University of Minnesota Press, 1984), 188–91.

53. See Lewis Hanke, *Aristotle and the American Indians* (Bloomington: Indiana University Press, 1970), 56.

54. David Brading, *The First America: The Spanish Monarchy, Creole Patriots, and the Liberal State, 1492–1867* (Cambridge: Cambridge University Press, 1991), 68.

55. Brading, *First*, 68; Weckmann, *The Medieval*, 76; see also McAlister, *Spain*, 191–4; and Lawrence Stone, *The Crisis of the Aristocracy, 1558–1641* (London, New York: Oxford University Press, 1967).

56. Brading, *First*, 72.

57. See Lewis Hanke, *The Spanish Struggle for Justice in the Conquest of America* (Philadelphia: University of Pennsylvania Press, 1965), 117; also Burkholder and Johnson, *Colonial*, 62; and Brading, *First*, 70–1.

58. Spain, "Ordenanzas de Su Magestad...," in *Colección de documentos inéditos relativos al descubrimiento, conquista y organización de las Antiguas Posesiones españoles de América y oceanía* (Madrid: Imprenta del Hospicio, 1871) vol. XVI: 142–87, 152, 181.

59. Tzvetan Todorov, *The Conquest of America: The Question of the Other* (New York: Harper and Row, 1984), 174–5.

60. Las Casas quoted in Francisco Morales Padrón, *Fisonomía de la conquista indiana*, Publicaciones de la Escuela de Estudios Hispano-Americanos, 93 (Seville: Universidad de Sevilla, 1955), 43.

61. See Eric Cheyfitz, *The Poetics of Imperialism. Translation and Colonization from The Tempest to Tarzan* (New York: Oxford University Press, 1991).

62. See Hernán Cortés, *Letters from Mexico*, ed. and trans. Anthony Pagden (New Haven: Yale University Press, 1986), 26–8.

63. Rolena Adorno, "Literary Production and Suppression: Reading and Writing about Amerindians in Colonial Spanish America," *Dispositio XI*, 28–9 (1986): 1–25.

64. See Rómulo D. Carbía, *La Crónica oficial de las Indias occidentales* (Buenos Aires: Ediciones Buenos Aires, 1940).

65. See Marcel Bataillon, "Hernán Cortés, autor prohibido," in *Libro Jubilar de Alfonso Reyes* (Mexico, DF: Universidad Nacional Autónoma de México, 1956), 77–82, 95; also Anthony Pagden, "Introduction," in Cortés, *Letters*, lviii.

66. On the role that the re-conquest of Spain played in the conquest of America, see Antonio Garido Aranda, *Moriscos e indios. Precedentes hispánicos de la evangelización en México* (Mexico, DF: Universidad Nacional Autónoma de México, 1980); also C. Boxer, *The Church Militant and Iberian Expansion 1440–1770* (Baltimore: The Johns Hopkins University Press, 1978); and Barbara Fuchs, *Mimesis and Empire. The New World, Islam, and European Identities* (Cambridge: Cambridge University Press, 2001), 18–20.

67. See Irving Leonard, *Books of the Brave. Being an Account of Books and of Men in the Spanish Conquest and Settlement of the Sixteenth-Century New World*, ed. Rolena Adorno (Berkeley: University of California Press, 1992), 75–90.

68. See 1542: Adorno/Pautz, III: 87–8.

69. See Adorno, "Peaceful Conquest"; also Mary Gaylord, "Spain's Renaissance Conquests and the Retroping of Identity," *Journal of Hispanic Philology* 16 (1992): 125–36, 133.

70. See 1542: Adorno/Pautz, III: 87, 89; see also 1: 374.

71. 1555: Favata/Fernández, 14; I prefer "deserted us" here to López Morillas' translation – "were lost to us" (1555: López Morillas, 5) – since it is closer to the original ("nos faltaron") and illustrates my point here better.

72. Alejandro González Acosta, "Álvar Núñez Cabeza de Vaca: Náufrago y huérfano," *Cuadernos Americanos* n.s. 49–51 (1995): 165–99, 170.

73. Marie Tanner, *The Last Descendant of Aeneas. The Hapsburgs and the Mythic Image of the Emperor* (New Haven, London: Yale University Press, 1993), 9.
74. Pier Luigi Crovetto, "El naufragio en el Nuevo Mundo: De la escritura formulizada a la prefiguración de lo novelesco," *Palinure* (1985–6): 30–41, 40.
75. For a list of the differences between the 1542 and 1555 version, see the appendix of 1555: Favata/Fernández, 149–61. For a discussion of these differences, including also Oviedo's text, see 1542: Adorno/Pautz, I: 14–279 and III: 86–97; also Doñatella Ferro, "Oviedo / Cabeza de Vaca: Débito testuale e 'tarea de acumulación y corrección,'" in *Studi de lett. iberiche e ibero-americane offerti a Giuseppe Bellini*, ed. Giovanni Battista de Cesare and Silvana Serafín, El Girador I–II (Rome: Bulzoni, 1993), 425–35.
76. 1555: Favata/Fernández, 8; 1555: López Morillas, 8. This passage corresponds to 1542: Adorno/Pautz, 24–5.
77. See 1542: Adorno/Pautz, III: 38.
78. *Ibid.*, 60.
79. See Gonzalo Fernández de Oviedo y Valdés, *Historia general y natural de las Indias*, ed. Juan Pérez de Tudela Bueso (Madrid: Real Academia, 1959), 5 vols., IV: 291.
80. See John Phelan, *The Millennial Kingdom of the Franciscans in the New World* (Berkeley, Los Angeles: University of California Press, 1956), 54; Robert Ricard, *The Spiritual Conquest of Mexico* (Berkeley: University of California Press, 1966), 239–63; Brading, *First*, 114–15; José Toribio Medina, *Historia del Tribunal del Santo Oficio de la Inquisición en México* (Mexico: Consejo Nacional para la Cultura y las Artes, 1991), 41–55; Fernando Cervantes, *The Devil in the New World. The Impact of Diabolism in New Spain* (New Haven: Yale University Press, 1994), 16.
81. Quoted in Gaylord, "Spain's Renaissance," 133.
82. 1542: Adorno/Pautz, III: 62.
83. *Ibid.*, I: 401.
84. On the role of this trope in Baroque culture, see José Antonio Maravall, *Culture of the Baroque. Analysis of a Historical Structure*, trans. Terry Cochran (Minneapolis: University of Minnesota Press, 1986), 149–72.
85. See Jacque Lafaye, "Los milagros de Álvar Núñez Cabeza de Vaca (1527–1536)," in *Mesías, cruzadas, utopías: El judeo-cristianismo en las sociedades ibéricas*, trans. Juan José Utrilla (Mexico City: Fondo de Cultura Económica, 1984), 65–84, 67; also Clara Vitorino, "Histoire et littérature: la réception de los Naufragios de Alvar Núñez Cabeza de Vaca," *Dedalus* 3–4 (Lisbon, 1993–4): 139–47.
86. Rabasa, *Writing*, 49–50.
87. Nothing could therefore be further from the mark than to speak of a "*real maravilloso* (magic realism) in the Naufragios," as Rabasa does (ibid., 51); for "magic realism" depends on a recognition on the part of the author of an epistemological "antinomy" shared or accepted by his or her audience, which is being "resolved" by the magico-realist text. On magic realism, see Amaryll Beatrice Chanady, *Magic Realism and the Fantastic. Resolved Versus Unresolved Antinomy* (New York: Garland, 1985).

88. William Christian, *Local Religion in Sixteenth-Century Spain* (Princeton: Princeton University Press, 1982); Cervantes, *Devil*, 58.
89. Cervantes, *Devil*, 58.
90. For more on this, see Leonard, *Books*, 250.
91. Columbus quoted in Inga Clendinnen, *Ambivalent Conquests. Maya and Spaniard in Yucatán, 1517–1570* (New York, Cambridge: Cambridge University Press, 1987), 13; see also 3–37.
92. Cervantes, *Devil*, 60.
93. *Ibid.*
94. See *ibid.*, 31–9.
95. See *ibid.*, 19.
96. Keith Thomas, *Religion and the Decline of Magic* (Oxford: Oxford University Press, 1971; rpt. 1997), 657.
97. *Ibid.*, 473.
98. *Ibid.*, 470, 478.
99. See 1542: Adorno/Pautz, II: 274–85, III: 61.
100. For a discussion of this, see Cervantes, *Devil*, 25–31.
101. See Thomas, *Religion*, 177–211.
102. See here also Rolena Adorno, "The Negotiation of Fear in Cabeza de Vaca's *Naufragios*," *Representations* 33 (1991): 163–99, 183, 197–8.
103. See 1542: Adorno/Pautz, III: 95.
104. For a detailed discussion of this, see *ibid.*, III: 135–63.
105. Lee, "Pauline," 245.
106. See Bishop, *Odyssey*; also Lucía Invernizzi Santa Cruz, "Naufragios e Infortunios: Discursos que transforma fracasos en triunfos," *Revista Chilena de Literatura* 29 (1987): 7–22, 16.
107. Pastor, *Discursos*, 286–8; also González Acosta, "Álvar Núñez," 167, 182–3.
108. 1542: Adorno/Pautz, I: 129, marginal note e. I am here obliged to Rolena Adorno, who, when commenting on an early draft of this chapter, brought my attention to the problem in Frances López Morillas' translation (used in Pupo-Walker's edition).
109. See 1542: Adorno/Pautz, III: 67–8, 91.
110. See Oviedo, *Historia*, IV: 287. All further references to this edition are given parenthetically in the text.
111. 1542: Adorno/Pautz, III: 42, 43.
112. Gonzalo Fernández de Oviedo y Valdés, *The Journey of the Vaca Party: The Account of the Narváez Expedition, 1528–1536*, trans. Basil C. Hedrick and Carroll L. Riley (Carbondale: University Museum, Southern Illinois University, 1974), 1–2. All further English translations of this text refer to this edition unless otherwise indicated.
113. Max Horkheimer and Theodor Adorno, *Dialectic of Enlightenment*, trans. John Cumming (New York: Herder and Herder, 1972), 66.
114. *Ibid.*, 64.
115. *Ibid.*, 54.

116. See *The Odyssey of Homer*, trans. Robert Fitzgerald (New York: Vintage Classics, 1990), 105 (Book VI: 238–46).

117. See Thomas Bleicher, *Homer in der deutschen Literatur (1450–1740). Zur Rezeption der Antike und zur Poetologie der Neuzeit* (Stuttgart: Metzlersche Verlagsbuchhandlungen, 1972), 4–10. Although the sixteenth-century acquisition of the Byzantine manuscripts by Frencesco Filfelfo had resulted in the first early modern edition of the *Odyssey* in Florence (1488) by Demetrios Chalkondyles, this was only published in ancient Greek.

118. David Quint, *Epic and Empire. Politics and Generic Form from Virgil to Milton* (Princeton: Princeton University Press, 1993), 91, 95.

119. Quoted in P. A. Blunt, "Laus imperii," in *Imperialism in the Ancient World*, ed. P. A. Garnsey and C. R. Whittaker (Cambridge: Cambridge University Press, 1978), 159–91, 168.

120. See Pupo-Walker, "Pesquisas"; also his "Notas para la caracterización de un texto seminal: Los *Naufragios* de Álvar Núñez Cabeza de Vaca," *Nueva Revista de Filología Hispánica* 38, 1 (1990): 163–96; "Sobre el legado retórico en los Naufragios de Álvar Núñez Cabeza de Vaca," *Revista de Estudios Hispanicos* 9 (1992): 179–88; and "Los *Naufragios* de Álvar Núñez Cabeza de Vaca y la narrativa de viajes: ecos de la codificación literaria," in *Los hallazgos de la lectura: Estudio dedicado a Miguel Enguídanos*, ed. John Crispin (Madrid: Porrúa Turanzas, 1989), 63–83.

121. Pupo-Walker, "Pesquisas," 535.

122. Dante Alighieri, *Inferno*, trans. Allen Mandelbaum (New York: Bantam Books, 1982), 12–13 (Canto I: 10, 22–7). "Selva oscura" has most commonly been read in its political connotations, as "the wood of political darkness, of Florence, of Italy, of papal corruption, of the absence of imperial authority"; see Mandelbaum's note no. 2, in Dante, *Inferno*, 344.

123. Richard H. Lansing, "Two Similes in Dante's *Commedia*: The Shipwrecked Swimmer and Elijah's Ascent," *Romance Philology* 28, 2 (1974): 161–77, 162 n. 1, 168.

124. Teodolinda Barolini, "Dante's Ulysses: Narrative and Transgression," in *Dante: Contemporary Perspectives*, ed. Amilcare Iannucci (Toronto: University of Toronto Press, 1997), 116; see also John Freccero, *Dante: The Poetics of Conversion*, ed. Rachel Jacoff (Cambridge, MA: Harvard University Press, 1986); David Thompson, *Dante's Epic Journey* (Baltimore: The Johns Hopkins University Press, 1974); also Giuseppe Mazzotta, *Dante, Poet of the Desert: History and Allegory in the* Divine Comedy (Princeton: Princeton University Press, 1979), and *Dante's Vision and the Circle of Knowledge* (Princeton: Princeton University Press, 1993).

125. Dante, *Inferno*, 242–3 (Canto XXVI: 90–8).

126. Thompson, *Dante's*, 53.

127. Mazzotta, *Dante*, 83, 69; see also his *Dante's Vision*.

128. For Oviedo's use of these figures, see *Historia*, VI: 299.

129. See here José Rabasa, "De la allegoresis etnográfica en los *Naufragios* de Álvar Núñez Cabeza de Vaca," *Revista Iberoamericana* 61 (1995): 175–85, especially 176–9.
130. Quint, *Epic*, 10.
131. *Ibid.*, 84.
132. Bronislaw Malinowski, *Argonauts of the Western Pacific: An Account of Native Enterprise and Adventure in the Archipelagos of Melanesian New Guinea* (New York: Dutton, 1960).
133. Horkheimer and Adorno, *Dialectic*, 68.
134. See 1542: Adorno/Pautz, III: 37, 65.
135. Hans Blumenberg, *Shipwreck with Spectator. Paradigm of a Metaphor for Existence* (Cambridge, MA: The MIT Press, 1997), 21.
136. For some appreciations of the "picaresque," "novelistic," and "modern" aspects of the representation of reality in *Naufragios*, see Carreño, "Naufragios," 512; Lagmanovich, "Naufragios," 35; Juan Francisco Maura, "Álvar Núñez: Mesias del nuevo mundo," *Mundi* 4, 8 (1990): 97–116; Crovetto, "El naufragio"; and Rivera Martínez, "Singularidad," 308.
137. Michel Foucault, *The Order of Things. An Archaeology of the Human Sciences* (New York: Vintage Books, 1994), 48.
138. Luiz Costa Lima, *Control of the Imaginary: Reason and Imagination in Modern Times*, trans. Ronald W. Sousa (Minneapolis: University of Minnesota Press, 1988), 32.

3 THE GEOGRAPHY OF HISTORY: SAMUEL PURCHAS AND "HIS" PILGRIMS

1. Michel Foucault, *Power/knowledge*, ed. C. Gordon (New York: Pantheon Books, 1980), 133. Samuel Purchas, *Purchas his Pilgrimage; or Relations of the World. And the Religions observed in all Ages and Places. Discovered, from the Creation unto this Present. Contayning a Theological and Geographical Historie of Asia, Africa, and America* (London: printed by William Stansby, 1613), 643.
2. Richard Hakluyt, *Virginia Richly Valued by the Description of the maine land of Florida her next neighbor*, by the Gentleman of Elvas [1609]; rpt. as *The Worthye and Famous History of the Travails, Discovery, and Conquest of that Great Continent of Terra Florida*, ed. William B. Rye (London: The Hakluyt Society, 1851), "Dedicatory Epistle," 1.
3. Rolena Adorno and Patrick Pautz surmise that Hakluyt had direct access to Cabeza de Vaca's *Relación*. See Rolena Adorno and Patrick Charles Pautz, *Álvar Núñez Cabeza de Vaca: His Account, His Life, and the Expedition of Pánfilo de Narváez* (Lincoln: University of Nebraska Press, 1999), 3 vols., III: 159 (cited hereafter as 1542: Adorno/Pautz).
4. See David B. Quinn, "North America," in *The Purchas Handbook. Studies in the Life, Times, and Writings of Samuel Purchas, 1577–1626*, ed. L. E. Pennington (London: The Hakluyt Society, 1997), 2 vols., I: 312–28, 316.

5. *Hakluytus posthumus, or Purchas his Pilgrimes* (London: For Henry Fetherston, 1625) 4 vols., IV: 1499–530. Unless otherwise noted, all further citations appear in parentheses and refer to the 1906 edition by the Hakluyt Society (Glasgow: James MacLehose & Sons, 1905–7), 20 vols. There Cabeza de Vaca's narrative can be found in XVII: 437–525.

6. Purchas claims that he had "translated out of Ramusio, and abbreviated" (XVII: 437). The Italian translation in question is to be found in Gian Battista Ramusio, *Navigationi et viaggi* (Venice: Nella stamperia de Giunti, 1550–9), 3 vols., III (1556): fols. 310–30. A comparison of Purchas', Ramusio's, and Cabeza de Vaca's own version of 1542, which was Ramusio's source (1542: Adorno/Pautz, III: 140–1), shows that these changes originated with Purchas, not Ramusio.

7. Purchas, *Pilgrimage* (1613), 643.

8. Djelal Kadir, *Columbus and the Ends of the Earth. Europe's Prophetic Rhetoric as Conquering Ideology* (Berkeley: University of California Press, 1992), 126. On the "Black Legend," see Charles Gibson, *The Black Legend. Anti-Spanish Attitudes in the Old World and the New* (New York: Knopf, 1971); also Carolyn Prager, "Early English Transfer and Invention of the Black in New Spain," in *Early Images of the Americas. Transfer and Invention*, ed. Jerry M. Williams and Robert E. Lewis (Tucson: University of Arizona Press, 1993), 93–110; Bernadette Bucher, *La Sauvage aux seins pendants* (Paris: Herman, 1977); Stelio Cro, *The Noble Savage. Allegory of Freedom* (Waterloo, Ontario: Wilffrid Laurier University Press, 1990); and Enrique Düssel, *The Invention of the Americas: Eclipse of "the Other" and the Myth of Modernity*, trans. Michael D. Barber (New York: Continuum, 1995).

9. Richard Dunn, "Seventeenth-century English Historians of America," in *Seventeenth-century America: Essays in Colonial History*, ed. James Morton Smith (Chapel Hill: University of North Carolina Press and the Institute of Early American History and Culture, 1959), 195–225, 207; Jack Beeching, ed., *Voyages and Discoveries* (New York: Penguin Books, 1972), 25; and Quinn, "North America," 312–28, 315, 318. For other commentaries of this sort see Philip Barbour, "Samuel Purchas: The Indefatigable Encyclopedist who lacked Good Judgment," in *Essays in Early Virginia Literature honoring Richard Beale Davis*, ed. Leo Lemay (New York: Burt Franklin, 1977), 35–52; P. Barbour, "The Honorable George Percy: Premier Chronicler of the First Virginia Voyage," *Early American Literature* 6 (1971): 7–17; and Howard Mumford Jones, *The Literature of Virginia in the Seventeenth Century* (Charlottesville: University Press of Virginia, 1968), 13–15.

10. See L. E. Pennington, "Samuel Purchas: His Reputation and the Uses of his Worlds," in Pennington, ed., *The Purchas Handbook*, I: 3–120, 4–12.

11. D. B. Quinn, "Introduction," in *The Hakluyt Handbook*, ed. Quinn, 2nd. ser., 144 (London: The Hakluyt Society, 1974), 2 vols., I: 1–73, 43.

12. On changes in early modern geography, see Peter Dear, "Totius in verba: Rhetoric and Authority in the Early Royal Society," in *The Scientific Enterprise in Early Modern Europe*, ed. Peter Dear (Chicago: University of Chicago Press,

1997), 255–72. On John Dee, see William H. Sherman, *John Dee: The Politics of Reading and Writing in the English Renaissance* (Amherst: University of Massachusetts Press, 1995); and Nicholas H. Clulee, *John Dee's Natural Philosophy. Between Science and Religion* (London and New York: Routledge, 1988). On the genre of "chorography" in Elizabethan England, see Richard Helgerson, *Forms of Nationhood. The Elizabethan Writing of England* (Chicago: University of Chicago Press, 1992), 178–89.

13. See Colin Steele, "From Hakluyt to Purchas," in Quinn, ed., *The Hakluyt Handbook*, 1: 74–96.

14. Jorge Cañizares-Esguerra, *How to Write the History of the New World: Histories, Epistemologies, and Identities in the Eighteenth-century Atlantic World* (Stanford: Stanford University Press, 2001), 1.

15. Jerome Turler, *The Traveiler* ([1575] Gainesville, FL: Scholars' Facsimiles & Reprints, 1951), 50.

16. Thomas Palmer, *An Essay of the Meanes hovv to make our Travailes, into forraine Countries, the more profitable and honorable* (London: imprinted by H. L. for Mathew Lownes, 1606), "Epistle," n. p.; "To the Reader," 35, 81–126.

17. Palmer, *Essay*, 38, 44.

18. See Anthony Grafton and Nancy Siraisi, "Introduction," in *Natural Particulars: Nature and the Disciplines in Renaissance Europe*, ed. Anthony Grafton and Nancy Siraisi (Cambridge, MA: MIT Press, 1999); Barbara Shapiro, *Probability and Certainty in Seventeenth-century England: A Study of the Relationships Between Natural Science, Religion, History, Law, and Literature* (Princeton: Princeton University Press, 1983).

19. Robert Boyle, "General Heads for a Natural History of a Countrey, Great or small, imparted likewise by Mr. Boyle," *Philosophical Transactions of the Royal Society of London*, 1, 11 (1665): 186–91, 186, 188.

20. Pennington, "Samuel Purchas," 42.

21. For an excellent discussion of Herodotus' historiographic method, see François Hartog, *The Mirror of Herodotus. The Representation of the Other in the Writing of History* (Berkeley: University of California Press, 1988); see also Michel de Certeau, *The Writing of History*, trans. Tom Conley (New York: Columbia University Press, 1988).

22. Peter Novick, *That Noble Dream: The "Objectivity Question" and the American Historical Profession* (Cambridge: Cambridge University Press, 1988), 4.

23. See Hayden White, *The Content of the Form: Narrative Discourse and Historical Representation* (Baltimore: The Johns Hopkins University Press, 1987), especially 115–19.

24. For a discussion of these seventeenth-century changes in historiography in particular, see D. R. Woolf, *The Idea of History in Early Stuart England: Erudition, Ideology, and "The Light of Truth" from the Accession of James I to the Civil War* (Toronto: University of Toronto Press, 1990); for a cultural history of these changes in Natural Philosophy, see Stephen Shapin, *A Social History of Truth. Civility and Science in Seventeenth-century England* (Chicago: University of Chicago Press, 1994); also Lorraine Daston, *Classical Probability in*

the Enlightenment (Princeton: Princeton University Press, 1988); L. Daston, "Objectivity and the Escape from Perspective," *Social Studies of Science* 22 (1992): 597–618; Lorraine Daston and Peter Galison, "The Image of Objectivity," *Representations* 40 (Fall 1992): 81–128; Julie Solomon, *Objectivity in the Making. Francis Bacon and the Politics of Inquiry* (Baltimore: The Johns Hopkins University Press, 1998).

25. Purchas, *Pilgrimage* (1613), 737.

26. Mary Louise Pratt, *Imperial Eyes. Travel Writing and Transculturation* (New York: Routledge, 1992), 15–37.

27. Loren Pennington, "*Hakluytus posthumus*: Samuel Purchas and the Promotion of English Overseas Expansion," *Emporia State Research Studies* 14, 3 (1966), 32.

28. Woolf, *The Idea of History*, 239, 220, 242.

29. Francis Jennings, *The Invasion of America: Indians, Colonialism, and the Cant of Conquest* (Chapel Hill: University of North Carolina Press, 1975), 77–82.

30. James Boon, *Other Tribes, Other Scribes. Symbolic Anthropology in the Comparative Study of Cultures, Histories, Religions, and Texts* (Cambridge: Cambridge University Press, 1982), 17.

31. Purchas, *Pilgrimage* (1613), 606; see also the fourth edition (London: printed by William Stansby, 1626), 795.

32. This argument is made most explicitly, though not in reference to Purchas, by Cañizares-Esguerra in his *How to Write*; but see also Düssel, *Invention*; Claudio Sánchez-Albornoz, *Espana, un enigma historico* (Buenos Aires: Editorial Sudamericana, 1956), 2 vols.; and Leopoldo Zea, *The Role of the Americas in History*, ed. Amy Oliver, trans. Sonja Karsen (Savage, MD: Rowman and Littlefield, 1992).

33. Pennington, "Samuel Purchas," 14–15.

34. For a discussion of these differences, see Nicholas Canny, "The Permissive Frontier: Social Control in English Settlements in Ireland and Virginia, 1550–1650," in *The Westward Enterprise*, ed. K. Andrews, N. Canny, and P. Hair (Detroit: Wayne State University Press, 1979), 17–44, 18; and H. J. Parry, "Introduction: The English in the New World," in Andrews *et al.*, eds., *The Westward Enterprise*, 1–16.

35. Walter Ralegh, *The Discoverie of the Large, Rich, and Bewtiful Empyre of Guiana*, transcribed, annotated and introduced by Neil. L. Whitehead (Norman: University of Oklahoma Press, 1997), 136–7.

36. Jeffrey Knapp, *An Empire Nowhere: England, America, and Literature from Utopia to The Tempest* (Berkeley: University of California Press, 1992); see here especially his discussion of Spenser's uses of Ralegh's "disgrace" (186, 175–219).

37. For a comprehensive discussion of this shift in British economic philosophy from an emphasis on precious metals to an emphasis on balance of trade, see George Louis Beer, *The Old Colonial System, 1660–1754* (New York: Peter Smith, 1933), 2 vols., II: 132–54. The best discussion of the theological and philosophical ramifications of this change still remains Max Weber's *The Protestant Ethic and the Spirit of Capitalism*, trans. Talcott Parsons (New York: Scribner,

1958); but see also Perry Miller, *Errand into the Wilderness* (Cambridge, MA: Harvard University Press, 1956), especially 117–21; and Sacvan Bercovitch, *The Puritan Origins of the American Self* (New Haven: Yale University Press, 1975).

38. William Strachey, *The Historie of Travell into Virginia Britania*, ed. Louis B. Wright ([1612] London: printed for the Hakluyt Society, 1953), 21.

39. David Armitage, *The Ideological Origins of the British Empire* (Cambridge: Cambridge University Press, 2000), 67, 80, 77, 81, 66, 91; see also 24–60.

40. See Knapp, *An Empire Nowhere*, 1–54.

41. A report of royal commissioners sent to investigate the New England colonies (1661), quoted in Jack Greene, *Peripheries and Center. Constitutional Development in the Extended Polities of the British Empire and the United States, 1607–1788* (Athens: University of Georgia Press, 1986), 12, 13.

42. *Ibid.*, 13.

43. For a comprehensive discussion of these differences, see Patricia Seed, *Ceremonies of Possession in Europe's Conquest of the New World, 1492–1640* (Cambridge: Cambridge University Press, 1995). On the medieval origins of the English concept of landed property, see Alan Macfarlane, *The Origins of English Individualism: The Family, Property, and Social Transition* (Oxford: Blackwell, 1978).

44. John Rolfe, *A true relation of the State of Virginia lefte by Sir Thomas Dale, knight, in May last 1616* ([1616] Charlottesville: published for the Association for the Preservation of Virginia Antiquities by the University Press of Virginia, 1971), 10.

45. John Smith, *The Complete Works of Captain John Smith, 1580–1631*, ed. Philip Barbour (Chapel Hill and Williamsburg: University of North Carolina Press and the Institute for Early American History and Culture, 1986), 3 vols., 1: 203. The sources of all further quotations from this edition will appear as parenthetical references in the text.

46. William Crashaw, *A sermon preached in London before the right honorable the Lord Lawarre, Lord Governour and Captaine Generall of Virginia* (London, 1610), A 3r.

47. Joseph Hall, *Quo vadis? A jvst censvre of Travell as it is commony undertaken by the Gentelmen of our Nation* (London: printed by Edward Griffin for Henry Fetherstone, 1617), 11, 24.

48. In Peter Force, ed., *Tracts and Other Papers relating principally to the Origin, Settlement, and Progress of the Colonies in North America, from the Discovery of the Country to the year 1776* (Gloucester, MA: Peter Smith, 1963), 4 vols., III: 5–6.

49. Robert Williams, *The American Indian in Western Legal Thought: The Discourse of Conquest* (New York: Oxford University Press, 1990), 201–21, 201; see also Gary B. Nash, *Red, White, and Black. The Peoples of Early America*, 2nd. edn. (Englewood Cliffs, NJ: Prentice Hall, 1982), 60–6; Karen Ordahl Kupperman, *Settling with the Indians: The Meeting of English and Indian Cultures in America, 1580–1640* (Totowa, NJ: Rowan and Littlefield, 1980), 176–81; and Jennings, *Invasion*.

50. Edward Waterhouse, *A Declaration of the State of the Colonie and Affaires in Virginia* (London, 1622), 22, 24.

51. John Donne, *The Works of John Donne. With a Memoir of his Life*, ed. Henry Alford (London: J. W. Parker, 1839), 6 vols., VI: 231–2. For a discussion of the role played by the Anglican clergy in these affairs, see Louis B. Wright, *Religion and Empire: The Alliance between Piety and Commerce in English Expansion 1558–1625* (Chapel Hill: University of North Carolina Press, 1943).

52. See John Juricek, "English Territorial Claims in North America under Elizabeth and the Early Stuarts," *Terrae Incognitae* 7 (1976): 7–22, 21.

53. Quoted in Wesley Craven, *The Dissolution of the Virginia Company; The Failure of a Colonial Experiment* (Gloucester, MA: P. Smith, 1964), 203.

54. For a discussion of the questions that overseas imperialism would raise in politico-philosophical discourses about the "common good" during the eighteenth century, see Peter Miller, *Defining the Common Good: Empire, Religion, and Philosophy in Eighteenth-century Britain* (Cambridge: Cambridge University Press, 1994), especially 150–213; for a discussion of the politics surrounding the dissolution of the Virginia Company, see Craven, *Dissolution*, 318; also Perry Miller, *Errand*, 128; and Brown, *English Politics in Early Virginia History* (New York: Russel & Russel, 1968), 252–9.

55. In Force, ed., *Tracts*, I: vi, 8.

56. Purchas, *Pilgrimage* (1613), 632.

57. In Susan Kingsbury, *The Records of the Virginia Company of London* (Washington, DC: Government Printing Office, 1906–33), 4 vols., II: 362.

58. David Beers Quinn argued that the reason for their estrangement was Hakluyt's frustration with Purchas' habit of not returning the materials he borrowed, which prevented him from making it clear that Purchas should inherit his collection (Quinn, "North America," 316 n. 1).

59. Helgerson, *Forms*, 187, 188, 173, 178–9, 181, 185, 188, 187–9. In fairness to Helgerson, it should be pointed out that he was interested more in Hakluyt than in Purchas, who figured into his account more as an afterthought to Hakluyt.

60. Adam Smith, *An Inquiry into the Nature and Causes of the Wealth of Nations* (New York: A. M. Kelley, 1966), 2 vols., I: 65.

61. Dunn, "Seventeenth-century," 206.

62. Perry Anderson, *Lineages of the Absolutist State* (London: Humanities Press, 1974), 60–84. On the rise of middle-class culture, see Louis B. Wright, *Middle-Class Culture in Elizabethan England* (Ithaca: Cornell University Press, 1958).

63. John Hagthorpe, *England's Exchequer* (London: printed for Nathaniel Butter and Nicholas Bourne, 1625), 19, 13.

64. Quoted in S. G. Culliford, *William Strachey, 1572–1621* (Charlottesville: University of Virginia Press, 1965), 61.

65. *Ibid.*, 92.

66. *Ibid.*, 151–4.

67. See Stephen Orgel, "Introduction," in William Shakespeare, *The Tempest*, ed. Orgel (Oxford: Clarendon Press, 1987), 1–92, 42.

68. Quinn, "North America," 320.

69. *Ibid.*, 320 n. 3.
70. Culliford, *William Strachey*, 162.
71. *Ibid.*, 163.
72. If I here, for the sake of convenience, refer to "Strachey" as the author of "A True reportory," I thereby mean to say "Strachey as mediated by Purchas."
73. Canny, "Permissive," 34.
74. Noel Malcolm speculates that Hobbes may have known Purchas through attendance at the Virginia Company courts, and that he was probably familiar with Purchas' writings; see "Hobbes, Sandys, and the Virginia Company," *Historical Journal* 24 (1981): 297–321.
75. Barbour, in a note to this passage, points out that Smith was mistaken here. The borrowed passage was actually not from *Purchas His Pilgrimage* but rather from *Purchas His Pilgrimes*, where it is also "borrowed" from Edward Brerewood's *Enquiries touching the Diversity of Languages* (London, 1614). See J. Smith, *Works*, III: 95 n. 2.
76. Thomas Jefferson, *The Portable Thomas Jefferson*, ed. Merrill Peterson (New York: Viking, 1975), 230.
77. Bradford Smith, *Captain John Smith. His Life and Legend* (Philadelphia: J. B. Lippincott, 1953), 266–7.
78. Philip Barbour, *The Three Worlds of Captain John Smith* (Boston: Houghton Mifflin Company, 1964) 368, 261.
79. B. Smith, *Captain John Smith*, 263.
80. On this rhetorical tradition in Western literature, Erich Auerbach, *Mimesis. The Representation of Reality in Western Literature*, trans. Willard Trask (Princeton: Princeton University Press, 1953); for a discussion of mimesis in the context of the European conquest of the New World, see Barbara Fuchs, *Mimesis and Empire. The New World, Islam, and European Identities* (Cambridge: Cambridge University Press, 2001).
81. B. Smith, *Captain John Smith*, 260.
82. *Ibid.*, 262.
83. Barbour, *Three Worlds*, x.
84. Garcilaso de la Vega, el Inca, *Obras completas del Inca Garcilaso de la Vega*, ed. P. Carmelo Saenz de Santa Maria (Madrid: Real Academia Española, 1960), 3 vols., II: 31–2.

4 "TRUE HISTORIES": THE CAPTIVITIES OF FRANCISCO NÚÑEZ DE PINEDA Y BASCUÑÁN AND MARY WHITE ROWLANDSON

1. Fisher Ames, *The Works of Fisher Ames*, ed. E. B. Allen (Indianapolis: Liberty Classics, 1983), 22.
2. Benedict Anderson, *Imagined Communities: Reflections of the Origin and Spread of Nationalism* (London: Verso, 1983), 57.
3. See Mary Rowlandson, *The Soveraignty and Goodness of God*, in *So dreadfull a judgment: Puritan Responses to King Philip's War, 1676–1677*, ed. Richard Slotkin

and James K. Folsom (Middletown, CT: Wesleyan University Press, 1978); all page references to this edition will appear parenthetically in the text.

4. Hernán Díaz Arrieta, *Historia personal de la literatura chilena* (Santiago de Chile: Zig-Zag, 1954), 86. Francisco Núñez de Pineda y Bascuñán, *Cautiverio feliz, y razón de las guerras dilatadas de Chile*, ed. Diego Barros Arana (Santiago de Chile: Imprenta del Ferrocarril, 1863). All citations from the Spanish text refer to this edition and page references are given parenthetically. I also cite, whenever possible and adequate, the abridged translation by William Atkinson, *The Happy Captive* (London: Folio Society, 1977). Otherwise, translations from the Spanish are mine.

5. See Roy Harvey Pearce, "The Significances of the Captivity Narrative," *American Literature* 19 (1948): 1–20; Nancy Armstrong and Leonard Tennenhouse, *The Imaginary Puritan: Literature, Intellectual Labor, and the Origins of Personal Life* (Berkeley: University of California Press, 1992); James Hartman, *Providence Tales and the Birth of American Literature* (Baltimore: The Johns Hopkins University Press, 1999), 10. On the proto-novelesque potential of the Rowlandson narrative, see also Philip Carleton, "The Indian Captivity Narrative," *American Literature* 15 (1943): 169–80; and Christopher Castiglia, *Bound and Determined: Captivity, Culture-Crossing, and White Womanhood from Mary Rowlandson to Patty Hearst* (Chicago: University of Chicago Press, 1996). On *Cautiverio feliz* in this vein, see Ramón Soriano, "*El cautiverio feliz* de Francisco Núñez de Pineda y Bascuñán: Cuadro de costumbres, ficción novelesca, y crítica de la guerra de Arauco y de los funcionarios del Reino de Chile," *Anuario de Estudios Americanos* 44 (1987): 3–21; and Fresia Castillo Sánchez, "El *Cautiverio feliz* de Francisco Núñez de Pineda. ¿Primera novela chilena?" in *Actas del X Congreso de la Asociación de Hispanistas*, ed. Antonio Vilanova (Barcelona: Promociones y Publicaciones Universitarias, 1994), III: 529–35.

6. See Roberto Castillo Sandoval, " '¿Una misma cosa con la vuestra?': Ercilla, Pedro de Oña y la apropiación post-colonial de la patria araucana," *Revista Iberoamericana* 61, 170–1 (January–June 1995): 231–47. On the role that Ercilla's epic played in the making of a Creole "post-colonial" literary history, see R. Bauer "Colonial Discourse and Early American Literary History: Ercilla, the Inca Garcilaso, and Joel Barlow's Conception of a New World Epic," *Early American Literature* 30, 3 (1995): 203–32.

7. Vicente Aguirre, *El cautiverio feliz de Bascuñán* (Santiago de Chile: La Estrella de Chile, 1873), 597.

8. Mariano Picón-Salas, *De la conquista a la independencia* (Mexico, DF: Fondo de Cultura Económica, 1944), 83.

9. Domingo Amunátegui y Solar, *Bosquejo histórico de la literatura chilena. Período colonial* (Santiago de Chile: Imprenta Universitaria, 1918), 14.

10. Alejandro Vicuña, *Bascuñán, el cautivo* (Santiago de Chile: Nascimiento, 1948), 9.

11. Angel Custodio González, ed., *El cautiverio feliz de Pineda y Bascuñán* (Santiago de Chile: Zig-Zag, 1948), 38.

12. Sergio Corréa Bello, *El "Cautiverio feliz" en la vida política chilena del siglo XVII* (Santiago de Chile: Editorial Andrés Bello, 1965), 26.

13. José Anadón, *Pineda y Bascuñán. Defensor del Araucano. Vida y escritos de un criollo chileno del siglo XVII* (Santiago de Chile: Editorial Universitaria, 1977), 66.

14. José Anadón, *Historiografía literaria de América hispánica* (Santiago de Chile: Ediciones Universidad Católica de Chile, 1988), 145–72.

15. On the literary sources of Pineda's ethnographic descriptions, see David Bost, "From Conflict to Mediation: Humanization of the Indian in *Cautiverio feliz*," *SECOLAS Annals Southeastern Conference on Latin American Literature* 29, 2/3 (1985): 8–15; also Gaspar Garrote Bernal, "El cautiverio feliz de Núñez de Pineda y Bascuñán, entre la crónica de Indias y la doctrina politico-moral. Analecta Malacitana," *Revista de la Sección de Filología de la Facultad de Filosofía y Letras* 13, 1 (Malaga, 1990): 49–68.

16. Raquel Chang-Rodríguez, "El propósito del *Cautiverio feliz* y la crítica," *Cuadernos Hispánoamericanos* 297 (1975): 657–63, 660–1. Some critics have begun to answer Chang's call for a discursive reading in a historical context; see for example Lucía S. C. Invernizzi, "Recursos de la argumentación judicial-deliberativa en el *Cautiverio feliz* de Pineda y Bascuñán," *Revista Chilena de Literatura* 43 (1993): 5–30; Dennis Pollard, "The King's Justice in Pineda y Bascuñán's *Cautiverio feliz*," *Dispositio* 11, 28–9 (1986): 113–35; and Fresia Castillo Sánchez, "El discurso en *El cautiverio feliz*," in *Actas Irvine-92*, ed. Juan Villegas (Irvine: University of California Press, 1994), 5: 227–34.

17. Jean Franco, *An Introduction to Spanish American Literature* (Cambridge: Cambridge University Press, 1994), 204.

18. See Firdous Azim, *The Colonial Rise of the Novel* (London: Routledge, 1993).

19. See Michael McKeon, *The Origins of the English Novel* (Baltimore: The Johns Hopkins University Press, 1987), 19, 65–89, 120; also Percy Adams, *Travelers and Travel Liars, 1660–1800* (Berkeley: University of California Press, 1962) and *Travel Literature and the Evolution of the Novel* (Lexington: University Press of Kentucky, 1983). On the rise of the "philosophical" traveler and historian, see Jorge Cañizares-Esguerra, *How to Write the History of the New World: Histories, Epistemologies, and Identities in the Eighteenth-Century Atlantic World* (Stanford: Stanford University Press, 2001), 1–50.

20. On the (post-)colonial poetics of "writing back," see Bill Ashcroft, Gareth Griffiths, and Helen Tiffin, eds., *The Empire Writes Back. Theory and Practice in Post-Colonial Literatures* (London and New York: Routledge, 1989).

21. For a historical reconstruction of the drama, which has not been preserved, as well as for the circumstances of its performance, see Guillermo Lohmann Villena, *El arte dramático en Lima durante el virreinato* (Madrid: Estades, artes gráficas, 1945), 213–16. For the role that the Araucanian wars (and the Araucanian "Noble Savage" warriors) played on the Baroque stage of the *siglo de oro* in Peninsular Spain, see Monica Lucia Lee, "De la crónica a la escena: Arauco en el teatro del Siglo de oro" (Ph.D. dissertation, Vancouver: University of British Columbia, 1993).

22. See John Robert Fisher, *The Economic Aspects of Spanish Imperialism* (Liverpool: Liverpool University Press, 1997), 84, 65–9.

23. See Eugene Korth, *Spanish Policy in Colonial Chile. The Struggle for Social Justice, 1535–1700* (Stanford: Stanford University Press, 1968), 183; also Corréa Bello, *El "Cautiverio feliz"*, 89–98; and Sergio Villalobos, *La vida fronteriza en Chile* (Madrid: Editorial MAPFRE, 1992), 255–64.

24. The most important texts contained in this literary history are three epics, Ercilla's *La Araucana*, Pedro de Oña's *Arauco Domado*, and Alvarez de Toledo's *Purén indómito*, as well as prose texts such as Pedro de Valdivia's *Cartas*, Alonso de Góngora Marmolejo's *Historia de Chile*, Pedro Marino de Lobera's *Crónica del Reino de Chile*, Cristóbal Suárez de Figueroa's *Hechos de Don García Hurtado de Mendoza*, and Alonso de Ovalle's *Histórica relación del reino de Chile*.

25. Pedro de Valdivia, *Cartas de Don Pedro de Valdivia*, ed. Miguel Rojas Mix (Madrid: Quinto Centenario; Santiago: Editorial Andrés Bello; Barcelona: Editorial Lumen, 1991), 92. Diego de Rosales, while repeating the story surrounding Valdivia's death, also notes that it was probably apocryphal; see *Historia General del reino de Chile, Flandes Indiano*, 2nd. edn. by Mario Góngora ([1677] Santiago de Chile: Editorial Andrés Bello, 1989), 2 vols., I: 437.

26. Qtd. in Bernard Lavallé, *Las promesas ambiguas. Ensayos sobre el criollismo colonial en los Andes* (Lima: Pontificia Universidad Católica del Peru, 1993), 16.

27. Garcilaso de la Vega, el Inca, *Obras completas del Inca Garcilaso de la Vega*, ed. P. Carmelo Saenz de Santa Maria (Madrid: Real Academia Española, 1960), 3 vols., I: 281.

28. Lavallé, *Las promesas*, 18. On Creole identity in Spanish America, see also Anthony Pagden, "Identity Formation in Spanish America," in *Colonial Identity in the Atlantic World, 1500–1800*, ed. Nicholas Canny and Anthony Pagden (Princeton: Princeton University Press, 1987), 115–57; Solange Alberro, *Del Gachupín al Criollo: o de como los españoles de México dejaron de serlo* (Mexico, DF: Colegio de México, 1992); and José Antonio Mazzotti, ed., *Agencias criollas. La ambigüedad "colonial" en las letras hispanoamericanas* (Pittsburgh, PA: Instituto Internacional de Literatura Iberoamericana, 2000).

29. See Antonello Gerbi, *The Dispute of the New World. The History of a Polemic, 1750–1900*, trans. Jeremy Moyle (Pittsburgh: University of Pittsburgh Press, 1973), 36–41, 60–79; also *Nature in the New World: From Christopher Columbus to Gonzalo Fernandez de Oviedo*, trans. Jeremy Moyle (Pittsburgh, PA: University of Pittsburgh Press, 1985).

30. Bernardino de Sahagún, *Historia General de las Cosas de Nueva España* ([compl. 1590] Mexico, DF: Editorial Pedro Robredo, 1938), 3 vols., III: 82.

31. José Juan Arrom, *Certidumbre de América. Estudios de letras, folklore y cultura*, 2nd. edn. (Madrid: Editorial Gredos, 1971), 54.

32. Juan López de Velasco, *Geografía y descripción universal de las Indias recopiladas por el cosmógrafo-cronista Juan López de Velasco desde el año de 1571 al de 1574* (Madrid: Establ. tip. de Fortanet, 1894), 37–8.

33. Qtd. in B. Anderson, "Exodus," *Critical Inquiry* 21 (Winter 1994): 314–27, 315.

34. A. Pagden, "Identity," 57, 81.

35. For studies of Spanish imperial historiography, see Francisco Esteve Barba, *Historiografía indiana* (Madrid: Editorial Gredos, 1964); Rómulo D. Carbía, *La crónica oficial de las Indias occidentales* (Buenos Aires: Ediciones Buenos Aires, 1940); David Brading, *The First America: The Spanish Monarchy, Creole Patriots, and the Liberal State, 1492–1867* (Cambridge: Cambridge University Press, 1991), 203–27; Cañizares-Esguerra, *How to Write*; and José Rabasa, *Inventing America: Spanish Historiography and the Formation of Eurocentrism* (Norman: University of Oklahoma Press, 1993).

36. For a listing of the sources, see Antonio de Herrera y Tordesillas, *Historia general de los hechos de los castellanos en las islas y tierrafirme del mar oceano o "Decadas"*, ed. Mariano Cuesta Domingo ([1601–15] Madrid: Universidad Complutense, 1991), 5 vols., I: 59–80.

37. *Ibid.*, IV: 215, 415–43; III: 783–4; VI: 676.

38. Stelio Cro, *The Noble Savage. Allegory of Freedom* (Waterloo, Ontario: Wilfrid Laurier University Press, 1990), 81.

39. J. Anadón, *Pineda*, 66.

40. Cotton Mather, *Magnalia Christi Americana; or, the Ecclesiastical History of New England* (Hartford: published by Silas Andrus, 1855) 2 vols., II: 573.

41. See John McCusker and Russel Menard, *The Economy of British America, 1607–1789* (Chapel Hill, London: published for the Institute of Early American History and Culture by the University of North Carolina Press, 1985), 91–117.

42. Qtd. in McCusker and Menard, *Economy*, III; George Louis Beer, *The Old Colonial System, 1660–1754* (New York: Peter Smith, 1933), 2 vols., I: 233.

43. The classic accounts on this are still by Perry Miller, *Errand into the Wilderness* (Cambridge, MA: Harvard University Press, 1956), 1–15, and *The New England Mind. The Seventeenth Century* (Cambridge, MA: Harvard University Press, 1954); see also Theodore Dwight Bozeman, *To Live Ancient Lives: The Primitivist Dimension in Puritanism* (Chapel Hill: University of North Carolina Press, 1988).

44. See John Demos, *Little Commonwealth* (New York: Oxford University Press, 1970); Kenneth Lockridge, *New England Town* (New York: Norton, 1970); and Philip Greven, *Four Generations* (Ithaca: Cornell University Press, 1970). For an opposing view, see John Martin, *Profits in the Wilderness* (Chapel Hill: University of North Carolina Press, 1991).

45. See here, for example, the famous "Eliot Tracts," republished as "Tracts Relating to the Attempts to Convert To Christianity the Indians of New England Society," *Collections of the Massachusetts Historical Society*, 3rd. ser., 4 (Cambridge, MA: 1834).

46. Jack Greene, *Peripheries and Center. Constitutional Development in the Extended Polities of the British Empire and the United States, 1607–1788* (Athens: University of Georgia Press, 1986), 13.

47. Stephen Saunders Webb, *1676: The End of American Independence* (New York: Knopf, 1984), 169–244.

48. Greene, *Peripheries*, 18.

49. Reprinted in Mather, *Magnalia*, II: 557.

50. William Castell, *A Short Discovery of the Coasts and Continent of America* (London, 1644), 20–30, 41.

51. Peter Heylyn, *Cosmography in Four Books* (London, 1652), 109.

52. George Gardyner, *A Description of the New world or America, Islands and Continent as they were all in the Year 1649* (London, 1651), 92. See also Eric Hinderaker, "The 'Four Indian Kings' and the Imaginative Construction of the First British Empire," *William and Mary Quarterly* 53 (1996): 487–526, 489.

53. John Ogilby, *America* (London: printed by the Author, 1671; microfilm, Ann Arbor, MI: University Microfilms, 1976), 142.

54. Samuel Groom, *A Glass for the People of New England in which they may see themselves* (London, 1676), 16.

55. Joseph Mede, *Works. Corrected and Enlarged according to the Author's Manuscript* (London: Flesher for R. Royston, 1663–4), 800.

56. Morgan Godwin, *The Negro's and Indians Advocate, Suing for their Admission into the Church* (London, 1680), Preface, n. p.

57. In Michael Warner and Myra Jehlen, *The English Literatures of America, 1500–1800* (New York: Routledge, 1997), 302, 400.

58. Gary Ebersole, *Captured by Texts. Puritan to Post-Modern Images of Indian Captivity* (Charlottesville: University Press of Virginia, 1995), 16–17.

59. See Kathryn Zabelle Derounian-Stodola, "The Publication, Promotion, and Distribution of Mary Rowlandson's Indian Captivity Narrative in the Seventeenth Century," *Early American Literature* 23 (1988): 239–61, 246.

60. Increase Mather, *An Essay for the Recording of Illustrious Providences*, ed. James Levernier (Delmar, NY: Scholars' Facsimiles and Reprints, 1977), A3. For the role that New England divines, such as Mather as well as John Winthrop, Jr., played in the Royal Society, see Frederick Brasch and Raymond Phineas Stearns, *Science in the British Colonies of America* (Urbana: University of Illinois Press, 1970); also Frederick Brasch, "The Royal Society of London and its Influence upon Scientific Thought in the American Colonies," *Scientific Monthly* 33 (October, November, 1931): 336–55, 448–69.

61. Walter Woodward, " 'Matters of Present Utility': John Winthrop, Jr., the Royal Society, and the Politics of Intelligence in Restoration New England," a paper delivered at "From Bacon to Bartram: Early American Inquiries into the Natural World," a conference sponsored by the Omohundro Institute of Early American History and Culture, 22–24 March 2002, at the American Museum of Natural History, New York.

62. Jim Egan, *Authorizing Experience: Refigurations of the Body Politic in Seventeenth-Century New England Writing* (Princeton: Princeton University Press, 1999), 11.

63. J. Hartman, *Providence Tales*, 25.

64. Denise Albenese, *New Science, New World* (Durham: Duke University Press, 1996), 68; see also Carolyn Merchant, *The Death of Nature: Women, Ecology, and the Scientific Revolution* (San Francisco: Harper and Row, 1980).

65. Stephen Shapin, *A Social History of Truth. Civility and Science in Seventeenth-Century England* (Chicago: University of Chicago Press, 1994), 223.

66. Gonzalo Fernández de Oviedo y Valdes, *Historia general y natural de las Indias*, ed. Juan Pérez de Tudela Bueso (Madrid: Real Academia, 1959), 5 vols., 1: 55.
67. Kathryn Zabelle Derounian-Stodola and James Arthur Levernier, *The Indian Captivity Narrative, 1550–1900* (New York: Twayne Publishers, 1993), 107.
68. For such an argument, Richard Slotkin, *Regeneration through Violence: The Mythology of the American Frontier, 1600–1860* (Middletown, CT: Wesleyan Press, 1974), 110–15.
69. Anthony Pagden, *European Encounters with the New World. From Renaissance to Romanticism* (New Haven: Yale University Press, 1993), 52; also Cañizares-Esguerra, *How to Write*.
70. Pagden, *European*, 53.
71. Mitchell Breitwieser, *American Puritanism and the Defense of Mourning. Religion, Grief, and Ethnology in Mary White Rowlandson's Captivity Narrative* (Madison: University of Wisconsin Press, 1990), 74; Derounian-Stodola and Levernier, *The Indian Captivity Narrative*, 101.
72. Pagden, *European*, 67.
73. Michel de Certeau, *The Writing of History*, trans. Tom Conley (New York: Columbia University Press, 1988), 223–4; see also *Heterologies: Discourse on the Other*, trans. Brian Massumi (Minneapolis: University of Minnesota Press, 1986).
74. Michel de Montaigne, *Essays* (Garden City: Doubleday, 1947), 162–3.
75. Michelle Burnham, *Captivity and Sentiment: Cultural Exchange in Early America, 1682–1861* (Dartmouth: University Press of New England, 1997), 33–40.
76. On Baroque aesthetics, see Octavio Paz, *Sor Juana, or the Traps of Faith* (Cambridge, MA: Harvard University Press, 1988); on the comparison with the aesthetics of the "Gothic," see also Claudio Véliz, *The New World of the Gothic Fox. Culture and Economy in English and Spanish America* (Berkeley: University of California Press, 1994).
77. Kenneth Burke, *Attitudes toward History* (New York: The New Republic, 1937), 2 vols., 1: 176.
78. Hayden White, "The Forms of Wildness: Archaeology of an Idea," in *The Wild Man Within: An Image in Western Thought from the Renaissance to Romanticism*, ed. Edward Dudley and Maximillian Novak (Pittsburgh: University of Pittsburgh Press, 1973), 3–38, 20–1; see also Roger Barta, *Wild Men in the Looking Glass. The Mythic Origins of European Otherness* (Ann Arbor: The University of Michigan Press, 1994).
79. Hans Staden, *Wahrhaftige Historia und Beschreibung einer Landschaft der wilden, nacketen, grimmigen Menschenfresser Leute in der neuen Welt Amerika gelegen*, ed. Robert Lehmann Nitsche (Buenos Aires, 1921), 242 (my translation).
80. Álvar Núñez Cabeza de Vaca, *La Relación o Naufragios de Álvar Núñez Cabeza de Vaca*, ed. Martin A. Favata y José Fernández (Potomac, MD: Scripta Humanistica, 1986), 127; *Castaways*, ed. E. Pupo-Walker, trans. Frances López Morillas (Berkeley: University of California Press, 1993), 112.

81. Garcilaso de la Vega, el Inca, *Obras*, I: 281; *The Florida of the Inca*, ed. and trans. John Grier Varner and Jeannette Johnson Varner (Austin: University of Texas Press, 1951), 78.

82. See, for example, Samuel Purchas, *Hakluytus posthumus, or Purchas his Pilgrimes* (Glasgow: James MacLehose & Sons, 1905–7), 20 vols., XVII: 525–50.

83. Bernal Díaz del Castillo, *Historia verdadera de la conquista de la Nueva España*, ed. Miguel León-Portilla (Madrid: Historia 16) 2 vols., I: 135.

84. Garcilaso de la Vaga, el Inca, *Obras*, II: 17, 18, 29; and *The Royal Commentaries*, trans. Sir Paul Rycault (London: printed by M. Flesher for C. Wilkinson, 1688), 29. In Peru, the word "Serrano" is to this day virtually synonymous with "Indian." The story of Serrano was also translated into English by Samuel Purchas; see *Hakluytus Posthumus*, XVII: 311–412.

85. Abdul JanMohamed, "The Economy of Manichean Allegory: The Function of Racial Difference in Colonialist Literature," *Critical Inquiry* 12, 1 (Autumn 1985): 2–25, 19.

86. De Certeau, *Writing*, 221.

87. See Breitwieser, *American Puritanism*, 70–4.

88. See John Seelye, *Prophetic Waters. The River in Early American Life and Literature* (New York: Oxford University Press, 1977).

89. Walter Mignolo, "Afterword: Human Understanding and (Latin) American Interests – The Politics and Sensibilities of Geocultural Locations," *Poetics Today* 16, 1 (1995): 171–214, 174, 188.

90. See Michael Zuckerman, "Identity in British America: Unease in Eden," in Canny and Pagden, eds., *Colonial Identity in the Atlantic World*, 183–214. On "Red Puritans," see James Axtell, *The European and the Indian: Essays in the Ethnohistory of Colonial North America* (New York: Oxford University Press, 1981), 39–86, 272–316.

91. José Promís, *The Identity of Hispanoamerica. An Interpretation of Colonial Literature*, trans. Alita Kelley and Alec E. Kelley (Tucson: University of Arizona Press, 1991), 118.

92. Andrew Wiget, "Reading against the Grain: Origin Stories and American Literary History," *American Literary History* 3 (1991): 210–31, 220.

93. See here also Tara Fitzpatrick, "The Figure of Captivity: The Cultural Work of the Puritan Captivity Narrative," *American Literary History* 3 (1991): 1–20.

94. See also Lisa Logan, "Mary Rowlandson's Captivity and the 'Place' of the Woman Subject," *Early American Literature* 28 (1993): 255–77.

95. See Patricia Seed, *Ceremonies of Possession in Europe's Conquest of the New World, 1492–1640* (Cambridge: Cambridge University Press, 1996).

96. Alistair Hennessy, *The Frontier in Latin American History* (Albuquerque: University of New Mexico Press, 1978), 19; also David Weber, *The Spanish Frontier in North America* (New Haven: Yale University Press 1992), 12; see also Paula H. Covington, ed., *Latin American Frontiers, Borders and Hinterlands* (Albuquerque: University of New Mexico Press, 1990); and Jane M. Rausch and David Weber, eds., *Where Cultures Meet: Frontiers in Latin American History* (Wilmington: University of Delaware Press, 1994).

5 "FRIENDS AND COMPATRIOTS": CARLOS DE SIGÜENZA Y GÓNGORA AND THE PIRACY OF KNOWLEDGE

1. On wonders, popular science, and religion in New England, see David Hall, *Worlds of Wonder, Days of Judgment: Popular Religious Belief in Early New England* (New York: Knopf, distributed by Random House, 1989), esp. 77–8 on this incident.

2. See Elías Trabulse, *Ciencia y religión en el siglo XVII* (Mexico City: El Colegio de México, 1974), 25–30. On the intellectual debt of Sigüenza y Góngora's scientific thought to Pierre Gassendi, see Ruth Hill, *Sceptres and Sciences in the Spains: Four Humanists and the New Philosophy (ca. 1680–1740)* (Liverpool: Liverpool University Press, 2000).

3. Increase Mather, *An Essay for the Recording of Illustrious Providences*, ed. James Levernier (Delmar, NY: Scholars' Facsimiles and Reprints, 1977), 45.

4. See Carlos de Sigüenza y Góngora, *Primavera indiana, poema sacro-histórico, idea de María Santísima de Guadalupe copiada de flores* (Mexico City: Vargas Rea, 1945); and *Glorias de Querétaro en la nueva congregación eclesiástica de María Santísima de Guadalupe* (Querétaro: Ediciones Cimatario, 1945). For the best account of Sigüenza's role in the evolution of this cult, see Jacques Lafaye, *Quetzalcóatl and Guadalupe. The Formation of Mexican National Consciousness*, trans. Benjamin Keen (Chicago: University of Chicago Press, 1987), 60–7.

5. Carlos Sigüenza y Góngora, *Seis obras*, ed. William G. Bryant (Caracas: Biblioteca Ayacucho, 1984), 250.

6. See J. S. Cummins, "The Philippines Glimpsed in the First Latin American Novel," *Philippine Studies* 26 (1978): 91–101, 98.

7. Carlos Sigüenza y Góngora, *Obras históricas* (Mexico: Editorial Porrua, 1944), 12. All further citations in the Spanish are from this edition. Wherever possible, I also cite from the only English translation *The Misadventures of Alonso Ramírez*, trans. Edwin H. Peasants (Mexico: Imprenta Mexicana, 1962); otherwise translations are mine.

8. See Kimberly López, "Identity and Alterity in the Emergence of a Creole Discourse: Sigüenza y Góngora's *Los infortunios de Alonso Ramírez*," *Colonial Latin American Review* 5, 2 (1996): 253–76.

9. Angel Rama, *The Lettered City*, ed. and trans. John Charles Chasteen (Durham: Duke University Press, 1996).

10. Enrique Anderson Imbert, *Spanish-American Literature; A History*, 2nd. edn., rev. and updated by Elaine Malley (Detroit: Wayne State University Press, 1969), 95; Jean Franco, *An Introduction to Spanish American Literature* (Cambridge: Cambridge University Press, 1994), 31; José Arrom, *Esquema generacional de las letras hispanoamericanas* (Bogotá: Caro y Cuervo, 1963), 80; Antonio Castro Leal, *La novela del México colonial* (Mexico: Aguilar, 1964), 44; Ester González, "Mapas y textos," *MLN* 95 (1980): 388–9; Willebaldo Bazarte, "La primera novela mexicana," *Sin Nombre* 5, 2 (1974): 89–107; María Casas de Faunce, *La novela picaresca latinoamericana* (Madrid: Cupsa Editorial, 1977).

11. Estelle Irizarry, "One Writer, Two Authors: Resolving the Polemic of Latin America's First Published Novel," *Literary and Linguistic Computing: Journal of the Association for Literary and Linguistic Computing* 6, 3 (1991): 175–9; see also Julio López Arias, "El género en *Los infortunios de Alonso Ramírez*," *Hispanic Journal* 15, 1 (1994 Spring): 185–201; Beatriz González, "Narrativa de la 'estabilización' colonial: *Peregrinación de Bartolomé Lorenzo* (1586) de José de Acosta, *Infortunios de Alonso Ramirez* (1690) de Carlos Sigüenza y Góngora," *Ideologies and Literature: Journal of Hispanic and Lusophone Discourse Analysis* 2, 1 (1987 Spring): 7–52; Mabel Moraña, "Máscara autobiográfica y conciencia criolla en *Infortunios de Alonso Ramírez*," *Dispositio/n: American Journal of Cultural Histories and Theories* 15, 40 (1990): 107–17; Julio López Arias, "El género en *Los infortunios de Alonso Ramírez*," *Hispanic Journal* 15, 1 (1994 Spring): 185–201; Romero Sacido, "La ambigüedad genérica de los *Infortunios de Alonso Ramírez* como producto de la dialéctica entre discurso oral y discurso escrito," *Bulletin Hispanique* 94, 1 (1992 January–June): 119–39; J. S. Cummins, "*Infortunios de Alonso Ramírez*: 'A Just History of Fact?' " *Bulletin of Hispanic Studies* 61, 3 (1984 July): 295–303; Aníbal González-Pérez, "Los *Infortunios de Alonso Ramírez*: Picaresca y historia," *Hispanic Review* 2 (1983): 189–204.

12. Irving Leonard, *Don Carlos de Sigüenza y Góngora. A Mexican Savant from the Seventeenth Century* (Berkeley: University of California Press, 1929), 202.

13. Kathleen Ross, *The Baroque Narrative of Carlos de Sigüenza y Góngora* (Cambridge: Cambridge University Press, 1993), 17–39.

14. Ross, *Baroque*, 52–3; also "Cuestiones de género en *Infortunios de Alonso Ramírez*," *Revista Iberoamericana* 61 (1995): 591–603, 595–600.

15. Hernán Vidal, "Literatura hispanoamericana de la estabilización colonial," *Casa de las Américas* 122 (1980); also B. González, "Narrativa."

16. Mariano Picón Salas, *De la conquista a la independencia* (Mexico, DF: Fondo de Cultura Económica, 1944), 123.

17. See John Horace Parry, *The Spanish Seaborne Empire* (New York: Knopf, 1966), 350–5.

18. Jonathan Israel, *Race, Class, and Politics in Colonial Mexico, 1610–1670* (New York: Oxford University Press, 1975), 88.

19. Andrés Cavo quoted in Irving Leonard, *Don Carlos de Sigüenza y Góngora. A Mexican Savant from the Seventeenth Century* (Berkeley: University of California Press, 1929), 128.

20. Sigüenza y Góngora, *Seis obras*, 113. For discussions of this and other narratives about this event, see Kathleen Ross, "*Alboroto y motín de México*: Una noche triste criolla," *Hispanic Review* 56 (Spring 1988): 181–90; Rossana Nofal, "La letra y el poder en la colonia: Alboroto y motín de los indios en México," *Cuadernos Americanos* 1, 49 (January–February 1995): 231–5; Sam Cogdell, "Criollos, gachupines y 'plebe tan en extremo plebe': Retórica e ideología criollas en *Alboroto y motín de México* de Sigüenza y Góngora," in *Relecturas del barroco de indias*, ed. Mabel Moraña (Hanover, NH: Ediciones del Norte, 1994); and Mabel Moraña, "El 'tumulto de indios' de 1692 en los pliegues de la

fiesta barroca. Historiografía, subversión popular y agencia criolla en el México colonial," in José Antonio Mazzotti, ed., *Agencias criollas. La ambigüedad "colonial" en las letras hispanoamericanas*, ed. José Antonio Mazzotti (Pittsburgh, PA: Biblioteca de América, 2000), 161–76.

21. Lafaye, *Quetzalcóatl*, 67. On Creole appropriations of the indigenous past during the eighteenth century, see also Antony Higgins, *Constructing the Criollo Archive: Subjects of Knowledge in the Biblioteca mexicana and the Rusticatio mexicana* (West Lafayette: Purdue University Press, 2000).

22. Antonio de Solís y Rivadeneyra, *Historia de la conquista de Méjico* (Buenos Aires: Emecé Editores, 1944), 2 vols., I: 15, 25–6, 27. For a comprehensive discussion of Solís, see Luis Arocena, *Antonio de Solís, cronista indiano: Estudio sobre las formas historiográficas del barroco* (Buenos Aires: Editorial Universitaria de Buenos Aires, 1963); also see Peter Burke, "America and the Rewriting of World History," in *America in European Consciousness, 1493–1750*, ed. Karen Ordahl Kupperman (Chapel Hill: University of North Carolina Press, 1995), 33–51.

23. See Irving Leonard, *Books of the Brave. Being an Account of Books and of Men in the Spanish Conquest and Settlement of the Sixteenth-Century New World*, ed. Rolena Adorno (Berkeley: University of California Press, 1992), 198–9.

24. For a general discussion of the "patrimonialist" production of knowledge in the absolutist state, see Max Weber, "Bureaucracy," in *From Max Weber*, ed. and trans. H. H. Gerth and C. Wright Mills (New York: Oxford University Press, 1946), 196–244.

25. Quoted in Leonard, *Don Carlos*, 46.

26. *Ibid.*, 45.

27. Kino quoted in Sigüenza y Góngora, *Seis obras*, 250. For a more detailed account of this dispute, see Trabulse, *Ciencia*, 25–30.

28. Sigüenza y Góngora, *Seis obras*, 250.

29. *Ibid.*, 312–13.

30. Samuel Purchas, *Hakluytus posthumus, or Purchas his Pilgrimes* (Glasgow: James MacLehose & Sons, 1905–7), 20 vols., XV: 412, 414.

31. Sigüenza y Góngora, *Seis obras*, 181.

32. *Ibid.*, 181–2.

33. See Angel González Palencia, "Prólogo," in Juan de Castellanos, *Discurso de el Capitán Francisco Draque que compuso Joan de Castellanos* (Madrid: Instituto de Valencia de D. Juan, 1921), vii–cxviii, viii–xiv.

34. Castellanos, *Discurso*, 42.

35. *Ibid.*, 32.

36. Nina Gerassi-Navarro, *Pirate Novels: Fictions of Nation Building in Spanish America* (Durham, NC: Duke University Press, 1999), 39–55.

37. Walter Ralegh, *The Works of Sir Walter Raleigh* (Oxford: Oxford University Press, 1829), 8 vols., IV: 684. Ironically, Gamboa's own description of the South American coast line, *Viages al Estreche de Magellanes*, was not published in Madrid until the eighteenth century and translated into English by The Hakluyt Society in 1895; Castellanos' censored elegy on Drake would be found a

few years later – at a rare-book auction in London (see González Palencia, "Prólogo").

38. In Carlos de Sigüenza y Góngora, *Obras históricas* (Mexico: Editorial Porrua, 1944), 117–299.

39. José de Acosta, *Obras*, ed. P. Francisco Mateos (Madrid: Ediciones Atlas, 1954), 305.

40. See Angel Delgado-Gomez, *Spanish Historical Writing about the New World, 1493–1700*, with a bibliographical supplement by Susan Newbury (Providence: The John Carter Brown Library, 1992), 56, 119.

41. See Roberto González Echevarría, *Myth and Archive. A Theory of Latin American Narrative* (Cambridge: Cambridge University Press, 1990), 30.

42. On Sigüenza's role in the history of journalism, see Irving Leonard, "Introduction," in Carlos de Sigüenza y Góngora, *Mercurio volante* (Los Angeles: The Quivira Society, 1932), 13–48; on the inter-relationship between these two generic histories, see Aníbal González, *Journalism and the Development of Spanish American Narrative* (Cambridge: Cambridge University Press, 1993).

43. On the history of journalism in colonial Latin America, see Leonard, "Introduction"; on the history of printing in Mexico, see José Toribio Medina, *La imprenta en México, 1539–1821* (Amsterdam: N. Israel, 1965); on the connections between print and modernity in Protestant Europe, see Jürgen Habermas, *The Structural Transformation of the Public Sphere. An Inquiry into a Category of Bourgeois Society*, trans. Thomas Burger (Cambridge, MA: MIT Press, 1996); in North America, Michael Warner, *The Letters of the Republic: Publication and the Public Sphere in Eighteenth-century America* (Cambridge, MA: Harvard University Press, 1990); on the connection between print and nationalism, Benedict Anderson, *Imagined Communities: Reflections of the Origin and Spread of Nationalism* (London: Verso, 1983).

6 *"HUSQUENAWING"*: WILLIAM BYRD'S "CREOLEAN HUMOURS"

1. William Byrd II, "Letter to Charles Boyle III, Earl of Orrery," in *The Correspondence of the Three William Byrds of Westover, Virginia*, ed. Marion Tinlin (Charlottesville: University of Virginia Press, 1977), 2 vols., 1: 326.

2. See Michael McKeon, *The Origins of the English Novel* (Baltimore: The Johns Hopkins University Press, 1987), 105–17.

3. Isaac Newton, *The Principia. Mathematical Principles of Natural Philosophy*, trans. Bernard Cohen and Anne Whitman (Berkeley: University of California Press, 1999) 2 vols., 1: 397.

4. Mary Louise Pratt, *Imperial Eyes. Travel Writing and Transculturation* (New York: Routledge, 1992), 1–37; on the politics of the Newton/Descartes controversy over kinetics, see Bernard Cohen, "Introduction," in Newton, *Principia*, 1: 43–9. On the significance of Newton's Natural Philosophy for Enlightenment thought more generally, see Peter Gay, *The Enlightenment: An Interpretation*, vol. II: *Science of Freedom* (New York: Norton, 1966), 128–40, 174–87; also

Simon Schaffer, "Natural Philosophy," in G. S. Rousseau and Roy Porter, eds., *The Ferment of Knowledge: Studies in the Historiography of Eighteenth-century Science* (Cambridge: Cambridge University Press, 1980), 55–91.

5. Newton to Hooke, 5 February 1676, in *The Correspondence of Isaac Newton*, ed. H. W. Turnbull, J. F. Scott, and A. R. Hall (Cambridge: Cambridge University Press, 1959–77), 7 vols., 1: 416; see also Robert K. Merton, *On the Shoulders of Giants: A Shandean Postscript*, foreword by Umberto Eco, afterword by Denis Donoghue (Chicago: University of Chicago Press, 1993), 1–38.

6. Carole Shammas, "English-Born and Creole Elites in Turn-of-the-Century Virginia," in *The Chesapeake in the Seventeenth Century. Essays on Anglo-American Society*, ed. Thad Tate and David Ammerman (Chapel Hill: University of North Carolina Press, 1979), 274–96, 274; see also Michael Zuckerman, "Identity in British America: Unease in Eden," in *Colonial Identity in the Atlantic World, 1500–1800*, ed. Nicholas Canny and Anthony Pagden (Princeton: Princeton University Press, 1987), 115–57.

7. See Philip Curtin, *The Rise and Fall of the Plantation Complex. Essays in Atlantic History* (Cambridge: Cambridge University Press, 1990). On the notion of a "circum-Atlantic" (rather than trans-atlantic) system, see Sidney Mintz, *The Birth of African American Culture. An Anthropological Approach* (Boston: Beacon Press, 1992); and Joseph Roach, *Cities of the Dead: Circum-Atlantic Performance* (New York: Columbia University Press, 1996), 4.

8. See V. Y. Mudimbe, *The Invention of Africa: Gnosis, Philosophy, and the Order of Knowledge* (Bloomington: University of Indiana Press, 1988); and Homi Bhabha, *The Location of Culture* (London, New York: Routledge, 1994), 5.

9. On the former upheaval, see Edmund Morgan, *American Slavery, American Freedom. The Ordeal of Colonial Virginia* (New York: Norton, 1975); on the latter transformation, see Rhys Isaac, *The Transformation of Virginia, 1740–1790* (Chapel Hill: University of North Carolina Press, 1982).

10. Byrd, *Correspondence*, 1: 355.

11. Lewis Simpson, "William Byrd and the South," *Early American Literature* 7, 2 (Fall 1972): 187–95, 190.

12. John McCusker and Russel Menard, *The Economy of British America, 1607–1789* (Chapel Hill: University of North Carolina Press, 1985), 117–43; also David Galenson, *White Servitude in Colonial America: An Economic Analysis* (New York: Cambridge University Press, 1982).

13. Morgan, *American Slavery*, 215–70.

14. See Kenneth Lockridge, *The Diary, and Life, of William Byrd II of Virginia, 1674–1744* (Chapel Hill: University of North Carolina Press, 1987), 144, 149; on Byrd's life, see also Pierre Marambaud, *William Byrd of Westover, 1674–1744* (Charlottesville: University of North Carolina Press, 1971); Percy Adams and William Boyd, "Introduction," in William Byrd, *William Byrd's Histories of the Dividing Line betwixt Virginia and North Carolina* (New York: Dover, 1967); and Kevin Berland, Jan Kirsten Gilliam, and Kenneth Lockridge, *The Commonplace Book of William Byrd II of Westover* (Chapel Hill: University of North Carolina Press, 2001), 1–115.

15. Timothy Breen, *Tobacco Culture. The Mentality of the Great Tidewater Planters on the Eve of Revolution* (Princeton: Princeton University Press, 1985), 86; see also Allan Kulikoff, *Tobacco and Slaves: The Development of Southern Cultures in the Chesapeake, 1680–1800* (Chapel Hill: University of North Carolina Press, 1986), 118–61, 288–90; and James Horn, *Adapting to a New World: English Society in the Seventeenth-century Chesapeake* (Chapel Hill: University of North Carolina Press, 1994), 24–38.

16. Stephen Saunders Webb, *1676: The End of American Independence* (New York: Knopf, 1984), 201, 205.

17. Shammas, "English-Born," 277.

18. *Ibid.*, 284.

19. Gov. Edmund Andros to William Blathwayt, 3 March 1692/3, quoted in *ibid.*, 286.

20. See Marambaud, *William Byrd*, 30; also Berland, Gilliam, and Lockridge, *Commonplace*, 9–10.

21. Lockridge, *Diary*, 79.

22. *Ibid.*, 31.

23. *Ibid.*, 29, 34.

24. William Byrd, *The Secret Diary of William Byrd of Westover, 1709–1712*, ed. Louis B. Wright and Marion Tinlin (Richmond: Dietz Press, 1941), 80, 90–1, 146, 159, 197, 210–11, 488, 492, 499.

25. Berland, Gilliam, and Lockridge, *Commonplace*, 48.

26. See *ibid.*, 48–57; also Frederick Brasch, "The Royal Society of London and its Influence upon Scientific Thought in the American Colonies," *Scientific Monthly* 33 (October, November, 1931): 337–55.

27. *Philosophical Transactions of the Royal Society of London* 19, 235 (December 1697): 781–2, 781.

28. Byrd, *Correspondence*, I: 261.

29. Louis B. Wright, *The First Gentlemen of Virginia. Intellectual Qualities of the Early Colonial Ruling Class* (Charlottesville: University of Virginia Press, 1964), 332–3.

30. Sloane to Byrd, 7 December 1709, in Maude Woodfin, "William Byrd and the Royal Society," *Virginia Magazine of History and Biography* 40, 2 (April 1932): 111–23, 123.

31. Byrd, *Correspondence*, II: 586.

32. See Marambaud, *William Byrd*, 36, 30, 47.

33. David Smith, "William Byrd Surveys America," *Early American Literature* 11, 3 (Winter 1976/7): 296–310, 300–1.

34. Byrd, *Correspondence*, II: 494.

35. Robert Arner, "Westover and the Wilderness: William Byrd's Images of Virginia," *Southern Literary Journal* 7, 2 (Spring 1975): 105–23, 120–1.

36. See also Donald Siebert, "William Byrd's Histories of the Line: The Fashioning of a Hero," *American Literature* 47, 4 (January 1976): 535–51, 545.

37. Jeffrey Folks, "Crowd Types in William Byrd's Histories," *Southern Literary Journal*, 26, 2 (Spring 1994): 3–10, 8.

38. Susan Manning and James Wohlpart have each seen Byrd's quest for order as the central preoccupation behind his writing and revising his accounts of the border survey; see Susan Manning, "Industry and Idleness in Colonial Virginia: A New Approach to William Byrd II," *Journal of American Studies* 28, 2 (August 1994): 169–90; James Wohlpart, "The Creation of the Ordered State: William Byrd's (Re)Vision in the History of the Dividing Line," *Southern Literary Journal* 25 (1992): 3–18.

39. Douglas Anderson, "Plotting William Byrd," *William and Mary Quarterly* 56 (1999): 701–22, 702, 709.

40. Byrd, *Histories*, 92. All further references to this edition will be given parenthetically in the text.

41. While Byrd also would have known John Ogilby's *Africa* (London, 1670), Ogilby had only been concerned with northern, not sub-Saharan, Africa.

42. On Byrd's relationship with Catesby, see Amy R. W. Meyers and Margaret Beck Pritchard, "Introduction: Toward an Understanding of Catesby," in *Empire's Nature: Mark Catesby's New World Vision*, ed. Meyers and Pritchard (Chapel Hill: University of North Carolina Press, 1998), 1–33, 3–4; Peter Martin, *The Pleasure Gardens of Virginia: From Jamestown to Jefferson* (Princeton: Princeton University Press, 2001), 59–66, 201–2.

43. Percival quoted in Kevin Hayes, *The Library of William Byrd of Westover* (Madison: Madison House, 1997), 136.

44. See Hayes, *Library*, 136.

45. Quoted in *ibid*.

46. See Joseph Ewan and Nesta Ewan, *John Banister and His Natural History of Virginia, 1678–1692* (Urbana: University of Illinois Press, 1970), 4.

47. Peter Kolb, *The Present State of the Cape of Good Hope*, ed. Peter Carstens (New York: Johnson Reprint Corp., 1968), 56. As Mary Louise Pratt has pointed out, Kolb's *Present State* predates the "modern racist categories," which emerged only later in the century in the context of developing European colonialism in Africa; see Pratt, *Imperial*, 49.

48. Kolb, *Present State*, 5–6.

49. Guido Medley, "Preface," in *ibid.*, xviii, xvii. Further references to this edition of the volume will appear parenthetically in the text.

50. Lockridge, *Diary*, 100.

51. Marambaud, *William Byrd*, 132.

52. See also Norman Grabo, "Going Steddy: William Byrd's Literary Masquerade," *Yearbook of English Studies* 13 (1983): 84–96.

53. Marambaud, *William Byrd*, 132.

54. See William Byrd, *The London Diary (1717–1721) and other Writings*, ed. Louis B. Wright and Marion Tinling (New York: Oxford University Press, 1958), 601–32.

55. Ebenezer Cook, *The Sot-Weed Factor: A Voyage to Maryland*, in *The Heath Anthology of American Literature*, 3rd. edn., ed. Paul Lauter *et al.* (Boston: Houghton Mifflin, 1979), 2 vols., II: 641–58, lines 18–26.

56. *Ibid.*, lines 66–70.

57. Leo Lemay, *Men of Letters in Colonial Maryland* (Knoxville: University of Tennessee Press, 1972), 56–8.
58. Quoted in Bhabha, *Location of Culture*, 5.
59. Martin Heidegger, *Being and Time*, trans. Joan Stambaugh (Albany: State University of New York Press, 1996), 333–5.

7 DISMEMBERING THE EMPIRE: ALONSO CARRIÓ DE LA VANDERA AND J. HECTOR ST. JOHN DE CRÈVECOEUR

1. Vincent Crapanzano, "Hermes' Dilemma: The Masking of Subversion in Ethnographic Description," in *Writing Culture. The Poetics and Politics of Ethnography*, ed. James Clifford and George Marcus (Berkeley: University of California Press, 1986), 53; John Bartram, *The Correspondence of John Bartram, 1734–1777*, ed. Edmund Berkeley and Dorothy Smith Berkeley (Gainesville: University of Florida Press, 1992), 534; Derek Walcott, *Omeros* (New York: The Noonday Press, 1990), 208.
2. Samuel Ayscough, *Remarks on the Letters from an American farmer; or a detection of the errors of Mr. J. Hector St. John; pointing out the pernicious tendancy of these letters to Great Britain* (London: printed for John Fielding, 1783), 7–8, 17.
3. Grantland Rice, *The Transformation of Authorship in America* (Chicago: University of Chicago Press, 1997), 120; see also Jürgen Habermas, *The Structural Transformation of the Public Sphere. An Inquiry into a Category of Bourgeois Society*, trans. Thomas Burger (Cambridge, MA: MIT Press, 1996); and Michael Warner, *The Letters of the Republic: Publication and the Public Sphere in Eighteenth-century America* (Cambridge, MA: Harvard University Press, 1990).
4. On the creation of the cultural authority of the eighteenth-century "Man of Science," see Brame Fortune Brandon and Deborah J. Warner, *Franklin and his Friends. Portraying the Man of Science in Eighteenth-Century America* (Philadelphia: University of Pennsylvania Press, 1999).
5. Pamela Regis, *Describing Early America: Bartram, Jefferson, Crèvecoeur, and the Rhetoric of Natural History* (DeKalb: Northern Illinois University Press, 1992), x; see also David Scofield Wilson, *In the Presence of Nature* (Amherst: University of Massachusetts Press, 1978), 51.
6. See Jorge Cañizares-Esguerra, "New Worlds, New Stars: Patriotic Astrology and the Invention of Indian and Creole Bodies in Colonial Spanish America, 1600–1650," *American Historical Review* 104, 1 (February 1999): 33–68.
7. See Marie Louise Pratt, "Fieldwork in Common Places," in *Writing Culture. The Poetics and Politics of Ethnography*, ed. James Clifford and George Marcus (Berkeley: University of California Press, 1986) 27–50, 28–35; also Talal Asad, ed., *Anthropology and the Colonial Encounter* (London: Ithaca Press, 1973).
8. See James Clifford, "On Ethnographic Authority," *Representations* 1, 2 (1983): 118–46. While this "de-colonization" marked the end of British "imperialism" based on "invaded" colonies, it did not mark the end of "empire"; for more on

this, see Michael Hardt and Antonio Negri, *Empire* (Cambridge, MA: Harvard University Press, 2000).

9. For biographical accounts on Crèvecoeur, see Gay Wilson Allen and Roger Asselineau, *St. John de Crèvecoeur* (New York: Viking, 1987); Albert Stone, "Introduction," in J. Hector St. John de Crèvecoeur, *Letters from an American Farmer and Sketches of Eighteenth-Century America*, ed. Stone (London: Penguin Books, 1981); and Thomas Philbrick, *St. John de Crèvecoeur* (New York: Twayne Publishers, 1970).

10. Henri Bourdin, Ralph Gabriel, and Stanley Williams, *Sketches of Eighteenth-century America* (New Haven: Yale University Press, 1925); and Dennis Moore's recent edition of Crèvecoeur, *More Letters from the American Farmer* (Athens: University of Georgia Press, 1995), which includes all letters that remained unpublished in 1782.

11. On the political background of this decision, see Magnus Mörner, "Introduction," in *The Expulsion of the Jesuits from Latin America*, ed. Mörner (New York: Knopf, 1965), 3–32.

12. Benedict Anderson, *Imagined Communities: Reflections of the Origin and Spread of Nationalism* (London: Verso, 1983), 57.

13. For accounts of Carrió's life, see Emilio Carilla, *El libro de los "misterios"* (Madrid: Gredos, 1976); Evaristo Penha de Souza, *La función ideológica de la ironía en "El lazarillo de ciegos caminantes"* (Ann Arbor: University Microfilms, 1986); and Walter Bose, *El lazarillo de ciegos caminantes y su problema histórico* (La Plata: Publicación de la Universidad Nacional de La Plata, 1941).

14. Lester Langley, *The Americas in the Age of Revolution, 1750–1850* (New Haven: Yale University Press, 1997), 153.

15. On the impact of the British imperial war against the French on the colonial relationship to the metropolis, see Langley, *The Americas*, 13–14; Peggy Liss, *Atlantic Empires: The Network of Trade and Revolution, 1713–1826* (Baltimore: The Johns Hopkins University Press, 1982), 25–33.

16. Stephen Saunders Webb, *The Governors-General: The English Army and the Definition of the Empire, 1569–1681* (Chapel Hill: published for the Institute of Early American History and Culture, Williamsburg, VA, by the University of North Carolina Press, 1979), 465.

17. On the breakdown of the idea of the "common good" in the American Revolution, see Peter Miller, *Defining the Common Good: Empire, Religion, and Philosophy in Eighteenth-century Britain* (Cambridge: Cambridge University Press, 1994), 349–98; on British economic policy toward the colonies during the late eighteenth century, see Michael Kammen, *Empire and Interest: The American Colonies and the Politics of Mercantilism* (Philadelphia: Lippincott, 1970); also Alison Olson, *Making the Empire Work: London and American Interest Groups, 1690–1790* (Cambridge, MA: Harvard University Press, 1992); on the significance of the trans-atlantic economic crisis, see John McCusker and Russel Menard, *The Economy of British America, 1607–1789* (Chapel Hill: published for the Institute of Early American History and Culture, Williamsburg, VA, by the University of North Carolina Press, 1985), 352.

18. Jack Greene, *Peripheries and Center. Constitutional Development in the Extended Polities of the British Empire and the United States, 1607–1788* (Athens: University of Georgia Press, 1986), 79.

19. See John Lynch, *The Spanish American Revolutions, 1808–1826* (New York: Norton, 1973), 1–36.

20. Richard Morse, "Political Foundations" in *Man, State and Society in Latin American History*, ed. Sheldon B. Liss and Peggy K. Liss (New York: Praeger Publishers, 1972), 72–98, 97; see also Mark Burkholder and S. Chandler, *From Impotence to Authority: The Spanish Crown and the American audiencias, 1687–1808* (Columbia: University of Missouri Press, 1977), 89–98, 115–19.

21. John Robert Fisher, *The Economic Aspects of Spanish Imperialism* (Liverpool: Liverpool University Press, 1997), 129.

22. Qtd. in Langley, *The Americas*, 162.

23. Lynch, *Spanish*, 287.

24. David Brading, *The First America: The Spanish Monarchy, Creole Patriots, and the Liberal State, 1492–1867* (Cambridge: Cambridge University Press, 1991), 468–91, 468; see also Brading, *Miners and Merchants in Bourbon Mexico, 1763–1810* (Cambridge: Cambridge University Press, 1971); Barbara Stein and Stanley Stein, *The Colonial Heritage of Latin America. Essays in Economic Dependence in Perspective* (New York: Oxford University Press, 1970), 101–2; and Jorge Domínguez, *Insurrection or Loyalty. The Breakdown of the Spanish American Empire* (Cambridge, MA: Harvard University Press, 1980), 46–58.

25. Pedro de Peralta Barnuevo, "Diálogos de los muertos: la causa académica," in Jerry Williams, *Censorship and Art in Pre-Enlightenment Lima* (Potomac, MD: Scripta Humanista, 1994), 169.

26. Langley, *The Americas*, 151; see also D. K. Fieldhouse, *The Colonial Empires: A Comparative Survey from the Eighteenth Century* (New York: The Macmillan Company, 1991).

27. See Rubén Vargas Ugarte, "¿Quién fue el autor del *Lazarillo de ciegos caminantes?*" *Mercurio Peruano* 20 (Lima, 1929): 137–8, 105; also Carilla, *Libro*, 27.

28. Julie Greer Johnson, *Satire in Colonial Spanish America. Turning the New World Upside Down* (Austin: University of Texas Press, 1993), 111; see also Bose, *El lazarillo*, 219–40.

29. Philbrick, *St. John de Crèvecoeur*, 74, 88; see also Allen and Asselineau, *St. John de Crèvecoeur*, 74. On *Lazarillo* in this vein, see Richard Mazzara, "Some Picaresque Elements in Concolorcorvo's *El lazarillo de ciegos caminantes*," *Hispania* 40, 2 (1957): 323–7; and Carilla, *El libro*, 54–5.

30. On Crèvecoeur, see Stephen C. Arch, "The 'Progressive Steps' of the Narrator in Crèvecoeur's 'Letters from an American Farmer,'" *Studies in American Fiction* 18, 2 (1990): 145–59, 154; Rice, *Transformation*, 120; also Robert P. Winston, "'Strange order of things': The Journey to Chaos in Letters from an American Farmer," *Early American Literature* 19 (Winter 1984–5): 249–67.

31. Leo Marx, *The Machine in the Garden; Technology and the Pastoral Ideal in America* (New York: Oxford University Press, 1964), 109.

32. See Marcel Bataillon, "Introducción a Concolorcorvo y a su intinerario de Buenos Aires a Lima," *Cuadernos Americanos* 19 (1960): 192–216.
33. Christian Wentzlaff-Eggerbert, "Alonso Carrió de la Vandera: *El lazarillo de ciegos caminantes*," in *Der Hispanoamerikanische Roman*, vol. 1: *Von den Anfängen bis Carpendier*, ed. Volker Rolof and Harald Wentzlaff-Eggerbert (Darmstadt: Wissenschaftliche Buchgesellschaft, 1992), 375–94, 17.
34. See Enrique Pupo-Walker, *La vocación literaria de pensamiento histórico en América: desarollo de la prosa de ficción, siglos XVI, XVII, XVIII y XIX* (Madrid: Editorial Gredos, 1982), 171; Johnson, *Satire*, 114; and Karen Stolley, *"El lazarillo de ciegos caminantes": Un itinerario crítico* (Hanover: Ediciones del Norte, 1992), 21.
35. Regis, *Describing*, 108.
36. Carilla, *El libro*, 45; see also Penha, *La función*, 22.
37. François Charlevoix, *Histoire et description générale de la Nouvelle France microform* (Paris: Nyon fils, 1744), 9.
38. Stone, ed., *Letters*, 90. All further references to this edition will appear parenthetically in the text.
39. Alonso Carrió de la Vandera, *El lazarillo de ciegos caminantes*, Introduction by Antonio Lorente Medina (Caracas: Biblioteca Ayacucho, 1985), 5; *El lazarillo. A Guide for Inexperienced Travelers between Buenos Aires and Lima. 1773*, trans. Walter D. Kline (Bloomington: Indiana University Press, 1965), 27. All further references to these editions will appear parenthetically in the text.
40. For an excellent discussion of these discursive practices in eighteenth-century culture, see Dena Goodman, *The Republic of Letters: A Cultural History of the French Enlightenment* (Ithaca and New York: Cornell University Press, 1994), 90–182.
41. Pupo-Walker, *Vocación*, 178.
42. See Annette Kolodny, *The Lay of the Land: Metaphor as Experience and History in American Life and Letters* (Chapel Hill: University of North Carolina Press, 1975), 57; Mary Rucker, "Crèvecoeur's *Letters* and Enlightenment Doctrine," *Early American Literature* 13 (1978): 193–212, 198; Nathaniel Philbrick, "The Nantucket Sequence in Crèvecoeur's *Letters from an American Farmer*," *New England Quarterly* 64, 3 (1991): 414–33, 415; Elayne Rapping, "Theory and Experience in Crèvecoeur's America," *American Quarterly* 19 (1967), 713; and Arch, " 'Progressive,' " 154.
43. Bernard Chevignard, "St. John de Crèvecoeur in the Looking Glass: *Letters from an American Farmer* and the Making of the Man of Letters," *Early American Literature* 19 (1984): 173–90, 184. Jean Beranger notes that Mr. F. B. resembles Dr. Fothergill, the European patron of John Bartram; see "The Desire for Communication: Narrator and Narratee in *Letters from an American Farmer*," *Early American Literature* 12 (1977): 73–85, 74.
44. Barbara Stafford, *Voyage into Substance. Art, Science, and the Illustrated Travel Account, 1760–1840* (Cambridge, MA: MIT Press, 1984), 148.
45. D. H. Lawrence, *Studies in Classic American Literature* (New York: Penguin Books, 1961), 38.

46. Stone, "Introduction," 18–19.

47. Rucker, "Crèvecoeur's *Letters*," 194; on the "noble Savage" and European utopias, see Stelio Cro, *The Noble Savage. Allegory of Freedom* (Waterloo, Ontario: Wilffrid Laurier University Press, 1990).

48. On the role of *Letters* in an "American tradition of book as Anthology and authorship as editing" of an authentic American voice, see Norman Grabo, "Crèvecoeur's American: Beginning the World Anew," *William and Mary Quarterly* 48, 2 (1991): 159–73, 167.

49. Robert Lawson-Peebles, *Landscape and Written Expression in Revolutionary America* (Cambridge: Cambridge University Press, 1988), 103. On Crèvecoeur's "masking," see also Chevignard, "St. John de Crèvecoeur"; A. W. Plumstead, "Hector St. John de Crèvecoeur," in *American Literature 1764–1789: The Revolutionary Year*, ed. Everett Emerson (Madison: University of Wisconsin Press, 1977), 220; and Marcus Cunliffe, "Introduction to Hector St. John de Crèvecoeur," in *The Divided Loyalist: Crèvecoeur's America*, ed. Cunliffe (London: The Folio Society, 1978), 7–18.

50. See Arch, " 'Progressive,' " 145–59.

51. See Regis, *Describing*, 114.

52. See Antonello Gerbi, *The Dispute of the New World. The History of a Polemic, 1750–1900*, trans. Jeremy Moyle (Pittsburgh: University of Pittsburgh Press, 1973), 35–51.

53. Rice, *Transformation*, 97.

54. Francis Bacon, *The Works of Francis Bacon*, ed. James Spedding, Robert Leslie Ellis, and Douglas Denon Heath (London: Longman and Co., 1858; rpt. Stuttgart - Bad Cannstatt: Friedrich Fromman Verlag Günther Holzboog, 1963), 14 vols., III: 254.

55. See Mazzara, "Some Picaresque"; however, see also Segismundo Woyski, "El léxico americano en 'El lazarillo de ciegos caminantes' de Concolorcorvo," in *La Picaresca. Orígenes, textos y estructuras*, ed. Manuel Criado de Val (Madrid: Fundación Universitaria Española, 1979), 1013–30.

56. On the picaresque, see Claudio Guillén, *Literature as System. Essays toward the Theory of Literary History* (Princeton: Princeton University Press, 1971), 137–44.

57. Stolley, *Lazarillo*, 1–34.

58. Mariselle Meléndez, "Entre historia y creación: El viaje como creación de espacios discursivos en *El lazarillo de ciegos caminantes*," *SECOLASA* (24 March 1993): 69–76, 69; see also her *Raza, género e hibridez en* El lazarillo de ciegos caminantes (Chapel Hill: University of North Carolina Press, 1999); and "The Reevaluation of the Image of the Mestizo in *El lazarillo de ciegos caminantes*," *Indiana Journal of Hispanic Literatures* 2, 2 (Spring 1994): 171–84.

59. Chris Tiffin and Alan Lawson, "Introduction," in *De-scribing Empire: Postcolonialism and Textuality*, ed. Tiffin and Lawson (London: Routledge, 1994), 3.

60. Guillaume Thomas François Raynal, *A Philosophical and Political History of the Settlements and Trade of the Europeans in the East and West Indies*, trans. J. Justamond (London: printed for T. Cadell, 1776), 6 vols., I: 3.

61. On the Menippean tradition in *Lazarillo*, see Johnson, *Satire*, 120.
62. See Walter Mignolo, *The Darker Side of the Renaissance. Literacy, Territoriality, and Colonization* (Ann Arbor: University of Michigan Press, 1995); also Jorge Cañizares-Esguerra, *How to Write the History of the New World. Histories, Epistemologies, and Identities in the Eighteenth-century Atlantic World* (Stanford: Stanford University Press, 2001).
63. See Garcilaso de la Vega, el Inca, *Obras completas del Inca Garcilaso de la Vega*, ed. P. Carmelo Saenz de Santa Maria (Madrid: Real Academia Española, 1960), 4 vols., II: 11.
64. Johnson, *Satire*, 119.
65. See Roberto Ventura, "Lectures de Raynal en Amérique latine aux XVIIIe et XIXe siècle," *Studies on Voltaire and the Eighteenth Century* 286 (1991): 34–59.
66. Penha, *La función*, 18.
67. Ivette Malverde Disselkoen, "La palabra mestiza en *El lazarillo de ciegos caminantes*," *Acta Literaria* 17 (1992): 127–35, 127–8.
68. Bataillon, "Introducción," 211.
69. For an excellent, historically informed, political reading of *Lazarillo*, see Penha, *La función*, 146.
70. Stephen Slemon, "Unsettling the Empire: Resistance Theory for the Second World," *World Literature in English* 30, 2 (1990): 3–28; rpt. in *The Postcolonial Studies Reader*, ed. Bill Ashcroft, Gareth Griffiths, and Helen Tiffin (London: Routledge, 1995), 104–10, 110.
71. Jorge Klor de Alva, "The Postcolonization of the (Latin) American Experience: A Reconsideration of 'Colonialism,' 'Postcolonialism,' and 'Mestizaje,'" in *‸ ⸜onialism. Imperial Histories and Postcolonial Displacement*, ed. Gyan · Princeton University Press, 1995), 241–78.

‸ ⸜ic conflict played in the "breakdown
⸜ Domínguez, *Insurrection*, 28–45.
⸜rences to this edition will be given

⸜roduction," in *Race: The Origins of an
⸜: Thoemmes Press, 1996), ix–xxxiii, xiii;
⸜merica: Origins and Evolution of a World-
⸜s, 1993), 168–9; on Spanish America, see
⸜"

⸜2 and 132–65.
⸜nployed by Carrió in his descriptions of the
⸜that these descriptions perform in the forma-
⸜ity, see *ibid.*, 93–131.
⸜s Literary Presentation in *El Lazarillo de ciegos
⸜ungen* 91 (1979): 92–5, 93.

82. See Mary Louise Pratt, *Imperial Eyes. Travel Writing and Transculturation* (New York: Routledge, 1992); also Nicholas Thomas, *Colonialism's Culture. Anthropology, Travel, and Government* (Oxford: Polity Press, 1994).
83. Thomas Jefferson, *Notes on the State of Virginia*, in *The Portable Thomas Jefferson*, ed. Merrill Peterson (New York: Viking, 1975), 55.
84. *Ibid.*, 216–17.
85. *Ibid.*, 179.
86. See Olaudah Equiano, *The Interesting Narrative and Other Writings*, ed. Vincent Carretta (New York: Penguin, 1995), 45.
87. See Dana Nelson, *The Word in Black and White. Reading "Race" in American Literature, 1638–1867* (New York: Oxford University Press, 1992).
88. See Edmund Morgan, *American Slavery, American Freedom. The Ordeal of Colonial Virginia* (New York: Norton, 1975); also Jared Gardner, *Master Plots: Race and the Founding of an American Literature, 1787–1845* (Baltimore: The Johns Hopkins University Press, 1998), 18–21; and Cañizares-Esguerra, "New Worlds."
89. Clifford Geertz, *Works and Lives. The Anthropologist as Author* (Stanford: Stanford University Press, 1988), 131.

Index